Introduction to
the Theory of Logic

Introduction to the Theory of Logic

José L. Zalabardo

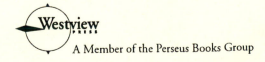

Westview
PRESS
A Member of the Perseus Books Group

Copyright © 2000 by Westview Press, A Member of the Perseus Books Group

Published in 2000 in the United States of America by Westview Press, 5500 Central Avenue, Boulder, Colorado 80301-2877, and in the United Kingdom by Westview Press, 12 Hid's Copse Road, Cumnor Hill, Oxford OX2 9JJ

Find us on the World Wide Web at www.westviewpress.com

Library of Congress Cataloging-in-Publication Data
Zalabardo, José L.
    Introduction to the theory of logic / José L. Zalabardo.
        p.   cm.
    Includes index.
    ISBN 0-8133-9061-3 (hc.)—ISBN 0-8133-6602-X (pbk.)
    1. Logic.   I. Title.

BC108. Z35   1999
160—dc21   99-045588

The paper use in this publication meets the requirements of the American National Standards for Permanence of Paper for Printed Library Materials Z39.48-1984.

10   9   8   7   6   5   4

PERSEUS
POD
ON DEMAND

For Inma

Contents

Chapter 8:
Decidability

Preface

Formal logic courses are widely taught in philosophy departments, often as compulsory components of undergraduate and graduate programs. This is as it should be, since the issues that formal logic deals with are among the central concerns of philosophy. Nevertheless, as students soon realize, sometimes to their dismay, formal logic is in many respects closer to mathematics than to other areas of philosophy.

The historical roots of this phenomenon lie in the second half of the nineteenth century, when logic underwent a revolution based to a large extent on the application of mathematical methods to the study of deductive reasoning. The formal languages and deductive systems studied in our introductory formal logic courses are the main achievements of the first stage of this revolution. Their basic features were presented by Gottlob Frege in his *Begriffsschrift* of 1879.

In the second decade of the twentieth century, contemporary logic entered a second phase, in which these formal systems ceased to be a mere tool for the study of deductive reasoning, and their scope and limits became the subject matter of logical research. This field is often known as *metalogic*. The main results in metalogic are of the greatest philosophical importance, and they are covered in more advanced courses in formal logic taught in many philosophy departments. Unfortunately, many of the best available textbooks at this level are written by mathematicians to be used in logic courses in mathematics departments, and presuppose a degree of familiarity with mathematical concepts and techniques that philosophy students often lack.

The main goal of this book is to present some of the central ideas and results in metalogic without presupposing a substantial mathematical background. It doesn't attempt to provide a mathematics-free presentation of the subject, since some mathematical concepts and techniques are indispensable tools in contemporary logic. But it aims to make the subject accessible to the nonmathematician—by providing a self-contained introduction to these mathematical tools.

The book is primarily intended for use as a textbook in logic courses for students who want to deepen their understanding of the subject after having mastered the contents of a standard introductory course in formal logic. Mastery of this material is not indispensable, since Chapters 2 to 4 provide a self-contained presentation of the syntax, semantics and deductive systems for propositional and first-order logic. But it is certainly desirable, as the discussion in those chapters will be much more accessible for someone who is already familiar with the subject at a more informal level.

If no mathematical background is presupposed, the book provides enough material for a two-semester sequence, covering Chapters 1 to 5 in the first semester and Chapters 6 to 8 in the second. With mathematically sophisticated students, the whole book could be covered in one semester, especially if enough set theory can be taken for granted to go over Chapters 1 and 6 fairly quickly. The discussion is sufficiently rigorous for logic courses in mathematics departments.

I have tried to present the material in such a way as to render its philosophical significance as perspicuous as possible, but specifically philosophical issues are discussed only occasionally. The choice of topics in the last three chapters is conditioned by my goal of presupposing no mathematical background. This, in addition to the intrinsic interest of the subject, explains the extensive coverage of cardinality in Chapter 6, since the notion plays a central role in much of the discussion in Chapter 7. It also explains why Gödel's Incompleteness Theorems are not covered in any depth. An adequate presentation of this area of logic in which no mathematical ideas are taken for granted would probably require a whole separate book.

Numerous exercises are provided throughout the book. They are integrated in the text, and they are meant to promote the kind of active engagement that the study of this material calls for—by leaving to the reader either a part of a proof or a complete proof which is similar to one provided in the text.

I have made extensive use of other textbooks in this area. My approach has been most heavily influenced by H. Enderton's *A Mathematical Introduction to Logic* (San Diego, 1972), in Chapters 7 and 8; H. Ebbinghaus, J. Flum and W. Thomas's *Mathematical Logic* (New York, 1984), in Chapter 4; and H. Enderton's *Elements of Set Theory* (San Diego, 1977), A. Fraenkel's *Abstract Set Theory* (Amsterdam, 4th ed., 1976) and P. Halmos's *Naïve Set Theory* (Princeton, 1960), all for Chapter 6.

I have used the first five chapters in my logic courses in Birmingham. I am grateful to the students of these courses for their comments and suggestions. An earlier draft was read by Richard Kaye, Concha Martínez, Stephen Read and Bernhard Weiss. Their comments have improved the book in many important ways. I am very grateful for their generosity.

José L. Zalabardo
Birmingham

Chapter 1

The Elements

1. Introduction

Many people wish that Elvis were alive, and some actually believe that he is. These desires and beliefs involve a way for things to be, i.e. Elvis being alive, which may or may not coincide with the way things are. These ways for things to be that figure in beliefs, desires and related phenomena are known as *propositions*. Those which coincide with how things are are true propositions, and those which don't coincide with how things are are false propositions. Thus the desire that Elvis were alive, and the belief that he is, involve the proposition that Elvis is alive, which is true if he is alive, and false if he isn't.

Many propositions can be characterized in terms of which individuals instantiate certain properties and relations. Thus, e.g., the proposition that Mars is a planet is the proposition that the individual Mars instantiates the property of being a planet, and the proposition that Mars has no satellites is the proposition that no individual bears to Mars the relation *...is a satellite of....* We shall refer to propositions that can be characterized in these terms as *first-order propositions*. Properties, relations and individuals figure in first-order propositions according to recognizable patterns. Thus, e.g., the way in which the individual Mars and the property of being a planet figure in the proposition that Mars is a planet is the way in which the individual Madonna and the property of being rich figure in the proposition that Madonna is rich. And the way in which the individual Mars and the relation *...is a satellite of...* figure in the proposition that Mars has no satellites is the way in which the individual Madonna and the relation *...is a son of...* figure in the proposition that Madonna has no sons. These patterns can be used to provide uniform characterizations of how the propositions in which they are present acquire their truth values—of what the world has to be like in order for these ways for the world to be to coincide or fail to coincide with how things are. Thus a proposition which exhibits the first of the two patterns we have just considered will be true if a certain individual exemplifies a certain property, and false otherwise, and a proposition which exhibits the second pattern will be true if no individual bears a certain relation to a certain individual, and false otherwise.

We can also detect patterns in the way in which properties, relations and individuals figure in collections of first-order propositions. Thus take, on the one hand, the propositions that Mars has no satellites, that Mars is not an asteroid, and that some asteroids have satellites, and, on the other, the propositions that Madonna has no sons, that Madonna is not rich and that some rich people have sons. We can say that the way in which the property of being an asteroid, the relation *...is a satellite of...* and the individual Mars figure in the first three propositions is the way in which the property of being rich, the relation *...is a son of...* and the individual Madonna figure in the last three propositions.

The pattern according to which properties, relations and individuals figure in a collection of first-order propositions sometimes generates links between their truth values. Thus, e.g., the pattern according to which a property, a relation and an individual figure in each of the collections of propositions in the preceding paragraph makes it impossible for all of the propositions in each of the collections to be false. If any two propositions in one of the collections are false, the remaining proposition has to be true.

One of the links between the truth values of propositions generated in this way is of special interest, since it underlies a good deal of what is known as deductive reasoning. Sometimes properties, relations and individuals figure in a collection of propositions in such a way that one of them has to be true if the others are all true. Take, e.g., the propositions that no asteroid has satellites, that Mars has a satellite and that Mars is not an asteroid. The property of being an asteroid, the relation *...is a satellite of...* and the individual Mars figure in these propositions in such a way that if the first and the second were true, the third would also have to be true. And the same situation obtains whenever a property, a relation and an individual figure in a proposition according to this pattern. Many other patterns of this kind generate the same situation: If all the propositions in a collection are true, another proposition also has to be true. When a proposition is related to a collection of propositions in this way, we say that the proposition *follows* from, or is a *logical consequence* of, the collection.

The study of these phenomena is known as *first-order logic*. Logic has been concerned with these issues since its inception. Thus, Aristotle's theory of the syllogism can be seen as the study of certain patterns according to which three properties figure in three propositions making one of them a logical consequence of the other two. For the next twenty-two centuries, logic developed largely within the paradigm established by Aristotle's work, but in the second half of the nineteenth century it underwent a revolution that resulted in a much more general and illuminating account of these phenomena. Our goal in this book is to present the central ideas of this account.

2. Extensionality

One of the most prominent features of contemporary logic is the way in which it construes the involvement of properties and relations in first-order propositions. Properties and relations have the power to single out certain individuals—those that instantiate them. Thus the property of being a planet singles out those individuals which are planets, and the relation ...*is a satellite of*... singles out those pairs of individuals whose first member is a satellite of the second. It is by virtue of this power that properties and relations contribute to the truth value of the first-order propositions in which they figure. Thus, e.g., the proposition that Mars is a planet is true if Mars is among the individuals singled out by the property of being a planet, and false otherwise. And the proposition that Mars has no satellites is true if the pairs of individuals singled out by the relation ...*is a satellite of*... include no pairs with Mars as its second member. Nevertheless, there is more to a property or a relation than its power to single out certain individuals or pairs of individuals. Let's focus on properties first. The identity of a property is not uniquely determined by which individuals it singles out, as witnessed by the fact different properties can in principle be exemplified by exactly the same individuals. To adapt an example from W.V.O. Quine, the property of being a marine mammal alive in 1940 might be regarded as different from the property of being a whale or a porpoise alive in 1940, but both properties are exemplified by exactly the same individuals. Those other respects in which properties may differ from each other do not affect the truth value of the first-order propositions in which they figure. Hence, to study the patterns according to which first-order propositions obtain their truth values it would be useful to leave them out of consideration. Contemporary logic achieves this with the notion of *set*. Sets, like properties, have the power to single out certain individuals, known as their *elements* or *members*. But, unlike properties, sets are uniquely identified by the individuals they single out. This feature of sets is known as *extensionality*, and is expressed by the following principle:

Principle of Extensionality: If two sets are different, then there is at least one object which is an element of one but not of the other.

When an object a is an element of a set B we shall also say that a is *contained* in B, and write $a \in B$. If a is not an element of B (a is not contained in B) we shall write $a \notin B$.

Sets differ from many properties in another important respect. Some people are clearly rich, and other people are clearly not rich, but there are lots of people of which we would want to say neither that the property of being rich is definitely present in them nor that it is definitely absent from them. Also, we may want to say that the question whether an individual exemplifies a property doesn't always make sense. Thus, e.g., we may think that it doesn't make sense to say that the property of being rich is either present in, or absent from, a stone. Whatever we want to say about properties, sets have neither of these features. The question whether an object is an element of a set will always be meaningful and have a determinate answer. This is expressed by the following principle:

Principle of Determinacy: For every object a and every set S, either a is an element of S or a is not an element of S.

Thus sets are used in contemporary logic as extensional (and determinate) surrogates of properties. First-order propositions which can be characterized as involving properties are characterized instead as involving sets. And the way in which they obtain their truth values is explained, not in terms of which individuals exemplify certain properties, but in terms of which individuals are elements of certain sets. Thus, e.g., the proposition that Mars is a planet is characterized as involving the individual Mars and the set of planets, combined in such a way that the proposition is true if Mars is an element of the set of planets, and false otherwise.

3. Sets

Sets are the subject matter of a branch of mathematics known as *set theory*. Its basic concepts and techniques are indispensable tools in contemporary logic. We shall not undertake here a systematic presentation of set theory, but in the rest of this chapter, and in Chapter 6, we shall introduce the main set-theoretic ideas that contemporary logic employs.

The Principle of Extensionality tells us that a set has been fully identified when we have specified which objects are its elements. Notice, however, that this doesn't settle the question of when a collection of objects is such that there is a set having precisely these objects as its elements, i.e. the question of which sets there are. This question raises issues of great technical complexity and philosophical depth, and we shall not try to provide a satisfactory answer here. Nevertheless we need to adopt some sort of policy for deciding when we are entitled to say of a collection of objects that there is a set having precisely those objects as its elements. The policy that we shall adopt is expressed by the following principle:

> *Principle of Specification*: Whenever we can specify a determinate totality of objects, we shall say that there is a set whose elements are precisely the objects that we have specified.

We should emphasize that the Principle of Specification is *not* a satisfactory answer to the question of which sets there are. The main reason is that, as we shall see in Chapter 6, §10, some instances of the principle generate contradictions. It is possible to restrict the Principle of Specification in such a way as to avoid this difficulty. An account of how this can be done lies outside the scope of this book. Nevertheless, we shall implement the principle with some confidence, relying on the fact that the contexts in which we will want to apply it are not of the problematic kind, and that our applications would still be allowed by a restricted version of the principle which avoids this difficulty. An additional reason for not treating the Principle of Specification as an answer to the question of which sets there are is that, as we shall see in Chapter 6, §11, we may want to assert the existence of some sets whose elements we cannot specify. But for our immediate purposes, this issue can be safely left aside.

According to the Principle of Specification, we can assert the existence of a set once we have specified which objects we are going to count as its members. We can think of the process of specifying the objects that we are going to count as the members of a set as a *definition* of the set. We are going to employ three methods for defining sets. We shall introduce the first two in this section, and the third in Chapter 2.

First, we can define a set by *enumeration*, i.e. simply by listing the objects that we are going to count as its elements. We can use this procedure, e.g., to define the set containing Mars, Madonna and the Atlantic Ocean. We shall represent the sets that we define in this way by enclosing their elements in curly brackets, separated by commas. Thus the set defined above can be represented as {Mars, Madonna, the Atlantic Ocean}.

Notice that it follows from the Principle of Extensionality that when we define a set by enumeration the order in which we list its elements doesn't make a difference. Thus, e.g., if a and b are arbitrary objects, we have that the set $\{a, b\}$ and the set $\{b, a\}$ have the same elements, and hence that they are one and the same set, i.e. $\{a, b\} = \{b, a\}$ (we shall write $X = Y$ to express that X and Y are the same object, and $X \neq Y$ to express that they are different objects). Similarly, if we list an element more than once we don't get a different set, as we are not ascribing to the set a new element. Thus, e.g., we have that $\{a, b, b\} = \{a, b\}$.

The second procedure that we are going to use to define sets is known as the method of *abstraction*. We define a set by abstraction when we specify its elements as the instances of a property, pretending in each case that they form a determinate totality. We can use the method of abstraction, e.g., to define the set of planets. To represent the sets that we define in this way we shall write $\{x \mid x$ is $P\}$ where P is the property that we are using in the definition. Thus, e.g., the set of planets will be represented as $\{x \mid x$ is a planet$\}$, which can be read as the set of objects x such that x is a planet. We may want to treat enumerative definitions as a special case of definition by abstraction. For the set {Mars, Madonna, the Atlantic Ocean} can also be represented as $\{x \mid x =$ Mars, $x =$ Madonna or $x =$ the Atlantic Ocean$\}$.

Notice that it follows from the principle of extensionality that different definitions may result in the same set, so long as the same objects are singled out in each case. Thus, going back to the example used above, we have that $\{x \mid x$ is a marine mammal alive in 1940$\} = \{x \mid x$ is a whale or a porpoise alive in 1940$\}$. Similarly, we have that $\{11, 13, 17, 19\} = \{x \mid x$ is a prime number between 10 and 20$\}$.

Notice also that it is possible for a definition by abstraction to single out no objects. Take, e.g. $\{x \mid x$ is a German city in the Southern hemisphere$\}$. This set is a peculiar one, as it has no elements. There is only one such set. For, according to the Principle of Extensionality, two sets can only be different if there is an object which is an element of one and not of the other, and sets with no elements cannot be so related. Thus, e.g., we have that $\{x \mid x$ is a German city in the Southern hemisphere$\}$ = $\{x \mid x$ is a prime number between 10 and 20 divisible by 2$\}$. The set with no elements is known as the *empty set*, and represented by the symbol Ø.

Two different sets cannot share all their elements, but they may or may not have some elements in common. When two sets have no element in common, we say that they are *disjoint*. We will often be interested in whether every element of a set A is an element of a set B.

DEFINITION: A set A is a *subset* of, or is *included* in, a set B, written $A \subseteq B$, just in case every element of A is an element of B. (When A is not a subset of B, we write $A \nsubseteq B$.)

Examples: $\{x \mid x$ is a dog$\} \subseteq \{x \mid x$ is a mammal$\}$, and $\{$Mars, Madonna$\} \nsubseteq \{x \mid x$ is a planet$\}$.

Occasionally, when A is a subset of B, we shall say that B is a *superset* of A.

From the definition of the subset relation it follows that the empty set is a subset of every set, as for every set A, Ø has no elements which are not elements of A. It also follows that every set is a subset of itself, since for any set A, we have that every element of A is an element of A. It will be useful to define a relation that a set bears to all its subsets except itself. We say that a set A is a *proper subset* of a set B, written $A \subset B$, when $A \subseteq B$ and $A \neq B$. (When A is not a proper subset of B we write $A \not\subset B$.)

Among the objects that we can single out as elements of a set are sets themselves. Thus let a, b and c be three different objects, none of which is a set. We can define the set $\{a, b\}$. This set is eligible as an element of a set. Thus, e.g., we can define the set $\{\{a, b\}, c\}$. Notice that this set is not the same as $\{a, b, c\}$. For $\{a, b, c\}$ has three elements, a, b and c, whereas $\{\{a, b\}, c\}$ has only two, the set $\{a, b\}$ and c. In particular, neither a nor b is an element of $\{\{a, b\}, c\}$. A set might have nothing but sets as elements, as, e.g., the set $\{\{a, b\}, \{b, c\}\}$, whose elements are the sets $\{a, b\}$ and $\{b, c\}$, or the set $\{\{a\}\}$, whose only element is the set $\{a\}$.

EXERCISE 1. 1: Let a, b and c be three different objects none of which is a set. Say which of the following pairs of sets are identical. Explain why:

(1) $\{a, b, c\}$ $\{a, b, \{c\}\}$
(2) $\{a, b, \{c\}\}$ $\{a, \{b\}, c\}$
(3) $\{a, b, c\}$ $\{\{a, b, c\}\}$
(4) $\{a, b, b\}$ $\{a, b, \{b\}\}$
(5) $\{a\}$ $\{a, \{a\}\}$

(6) {{a}}   {{a}, {a, a}}
(7) {a}   {a, Ø}
(8) Ø   {Ø}

It is important to bear in mind that the question whether a set A is a subset of, or is included in, a set B is different from the question whether A is an element of, or is contained in, B. In some cases both questions will have the same answer. Thus, e.g., if a and b are different objects, neither of which is a set, we have that both $\{a\} \subseteq \{a, \{a\}\}$ and $\{a\} \in \{a, \{a\}\}$, and that $\{a\} \not\subseteq \{b, \{a, \{a\}\}\}$ and $\{a\} \notin \{b, \{a, \{a\}\}\}$. But in many cases each question will have to be answered differently. Thus, e.g., we have that $\{a\} \subseteq \{a, b\}$ but $\{a\} \notin \{a, b\}$, and that $\{a\} \in \{\{a\}, b\}$ but $\{a\} \not\subseteq \{\{a\}, b\}$.

EXERCISE 1. 2: List the elements and the subsets of each set in Exercise 1. 1.

EXERCISE 1. 3: Let a, b and c be different objects none of which is a set. For each of the following pairs of sets, indicate whether the first set is an element and/or a subset of the second. Explain why:

(1) Ø   {Ø, a}
(2) Ø   {a, b}
(3) {b}   {a, b}
(4) {b, a}   {a, b}
(5) {c}   {a, b}
(6) {a}   {{a}}
(7) {a}   {{{a}}}
(8) {{a}}   {{{a}}}
(9) {{a}, b}   {{a}, {{a}, b}, b}

DEFINITION: The *power set* of a set A, written $\wp A$, is the set whose elements are the subsets of A.

Example: The power set of the set $\{a, b, c\}$ is the set $\{\{a, b, c\}, \{a, b\}, \{a, c\}, \{b, c\}, \{a\}, \{b\}, \{c\}, Ø\}$.

DEFINITION: The *union* of sets A and B, written $A \cup B$, is the set whose elements are all the elements of A and all the elements of B.

DEFINITION: The *intersection* of sets A and B, written $A \cap B$, is the set whose elements are all the objects which are contained both in A and in B.

DEFINITION: The *difference* of sets A and B, written $A - B$, is the set whose elements are the elements of A which are not elements of B.

Examples: The union of sets {*a*, *b*, *c*, *d*} and {*c*, *d*, *e*} is the set {*a*, *b*, *c*, *d*, *e*}; their intersection is the set {*c*, *d*}, and their difference is the set {*a*, *b*}.

Notice that these four definitions can be formulated using the notation we have introduced for definitions by abstraction. Thus, the power set of a set *A* is the set {*x* | *x* ⊆ *A*}. Similarly, if *A* and *B* are sets, their union is the set {*x* | *x* ∈ *A* or *x* ∈ *B*}, their intersection {*x* | *x* ∈ *A* and *x* ∈ *B*}, and their difference {*x* | *x* ∈ *A* and *x* ∉ *B*}. The union, intersection and difference of two sets *A*, *B*, are represented by the shaded areas in the diagrams of Figure 1, in which *A* and *B* are represented by the areas enclosed by circles.

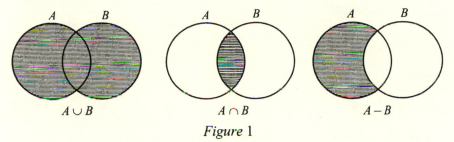

$$A \cup B \qquad A \cap B \qquad A - B$$

Figure 1

4. Mathematical Proof

As we indicated above, contemporary logic relies heavily on the basic concepts of set theory that we have started to introduce in the preceding section. But the involvement of contemporary logic with mathematics goes beyond the employment of mathematical concepts. Contemporary logic has also adopted the main ingredients of the mathematical method: precise definitions of concepts and rigorous proofs of claims formulated in terms of them. It has also borrowed the procedures employed by mathematicians for constructing proofs, and familiarity with these procedures is essential for understanding contemporary logic in any depth. This may seem to reverse the natural order of things, since one of the main goals of logic is to develop a theory of the principles of deductive reasoning underlying proof procedures in mathematics and other disciplines. But since these procedures are an indispensable tool in the development of the theory, we have to master the procedures in order to understand what logic has to say about them.

One of the goals of the present book is to introduce the reader with no background in mathematics to the mathematical methods of proof employed in contemporary logic. We shall not undertake a systematic presentation of these methods. We shall present them instead in the context of the proofs in which we apply them. We shall start by establishing a few relatively simple consequences of the definitions of the preceding section. The reader may feel that a moment's reflection or a small piece of informal reasoning would suffice to convince anyone that these claims follow from the relevant definitions, and that the methods that we are going to employ to establish them are unnecessarily elaborate. But our goal is to introduce proof strategies that will enable us to deal with more involved claims later on. The exercises will offer opportunities to practice these strategies. We start with the following result (relatively unimportant claims will be labeled as *lemmas*, and more important claims will be called *theorems*).

LEMMA 1. 4: If a set X is a subset of a set Y, and Y is a subset of a set Z, then X is a subset of Z; i.e. if $X \subseteq Y$ and $Y \subseteq Z$, then $X \subseteq Z$.

Proof: The first step towards constructing a proof of a claim is to consider the *form* of the claim, as this will determine how the proof has to proceed. This lemma is of the following form: Any objects which satisfy a condition (being three sets such that the first is a subset of the second and the second is a subset of the third) satisfy another condition (being such that the first is a subset of the third). Let's refer to claims of this form as *universal implications*. Many of the claims that we shall establish throughout the book are universal implications, and the method of proof that we are going to use for the present lemma can be applied to many of them.

To prove a universal implication we focus our attention on an arbitrary combination of objects of which we assume that they satisfy the first condition, and try to prove that it follows from this assumption that these objects also satisfy the second condition. In this case, we focus our attention on three sets of which we assume that the first is a subset of the second and the second is a subset of the third, and try to prove that it follows from this assumption that the first is a subset of the third. It is often convenient to assign names to the arbitrary objects on which we focus our attention. To express this "baptism," we say: let A, B and C be sets such that $A \subseteq B$ and $B \subseteq C$. In so doing, we specify what we are entitled to assume about A, B and C—namely that $A \subseteq B$ and $B \subseteq C$. From this assumption alone, plus the relevant definitions, we have to prove that $A \subseteq C$. On the face of it, we would only be proving that three particular sets satisfy the second condition of the universal implication, but if we could establish this result without assuming anything about these sets other than that they satisfy the first condition, this would be tantamount to proving the universal implication—that *any* objects which satisfy the first condition also satisfy the second. Hence it is of the greatest importance that we don't invoke surreptitiously additional assumptions about A, B and C. Thus, e.g., we cannot assume that they are different sets or that they are not empty.

Thus our goal is to prove that $A \subseteq C$, and we have to do this invoking only (i) the assumption that $A \subseteq B$ and $B \subseteq C$, (ii) the definitions of the concepts with which the result is formulated—in this case the definition of $\subseteq$, and (iii) valid principles of deductive reasoning. By the definition of $\subseteq$, the claim that $A \subseteq C$ is equivalent to the claim that, for every object x, if $x \in A$, then $x \in C$. Hence the proof will be complete once we have established the latter claim. Notice that since this claim is itself a universal implication, we could apply once again the procedure outlined above. Thus let $a \in A$. Our goal now is to prove that $a \in C$. To achieve this, we can invoke (i) our assumption that $a \in A$, (ii) our earlier assumption that $A \subseteq B$ and $B \subseteq C$, (iii) the definitions of the concepts with which the claim is formulated, and (iv) valid principles of deductive reasoning. (Notice that in saying "let $a \in A$" we are not introducing the illicit assumption that A is not empty. We introduce a as a device for showing that any elements that A might have would also be elements of B.)

We argue as follows. Since $a \in A$, by the definition of $\subseteq$ and our assumption that $A \subseteq B$, we have that $a \in B$. And again by the definition of $\subseteq$ and the assumption that $B \subseteq C$, it follows from this that $a \in C$, as desired.

Notice that the argument in the preceding paragraph can be seen as a string of implications, starting with the assumption $a \in A$ and ending with the claim that we want to establish, $a \in C$. Hence we can present the argument as a succession of claims about a, each connected with the next by the symbol $\Downarrow$, indicating that the claim above the arrow entails the claim below the arrow, adding when necessary an explanation of why this is so. Thus presented, the argument looks like this:

$a \in A$

$\quad \Downarrow$ (by the definition of $\subseteq$ and our assumption that $A \subseteq B$)

$a \in B$

$\quad \Downarrow$ (by the definition of $\subseteq$ and our assumption that $B \subseteq C$)

$a \in C$

This argument contains the core of the proof. What goes before can be considered mere stage-setting, which can be greatly abbreviated once the structure of this kind of proof is firmly in place. Nevertheless it is important to understand, at each stage in a proof, first, what we are supposed to prove, and second, what we are entitled to assume, and making the structure of the proof explicit may help to promote this understanding.

LEMMA 1. 5: If a set X is a subset of a set Y, then the intersection of X and a set Z is a subset of the intersection of Y and Z; i.e. if $X \subseteq Y$, then $X \cap Z \subseteq Y \cap Z$.

Proof: This claim is another universal implication, and we proceed as in the proof of Lemma 1. 4. Let A, B, C be sets such that $A \subseteq B$. We want to prove that $A \cap C \subseteq B \cap C$, i.e. that for every object x, if $x \in A \cap C$, then $x \in B \cap C$. Let $a \in A \cap C$. We need to prove that $a \in B \cap C$. We argue as follows:

$a \in A \cap C$

$\Downarrow$ (by the definition of $\cap$)

$a \in A$ and $a \in C$

$\Downarrow$ (from the assumption that $A \subseteq B$ and the definition of $\subseteq$)

$a \in B$ and $a \in C$

$\Downarrow$ (by the definition of $\cap$)

$a \in B \cap C$

This completes the proof. We shall mark the end of a proof with the symbol ∎.

EXERCISE 1. 6: Prove that for all sets X, Y, Z, if X is a subset of Y, then the union of X and Z is a subset of the union of Y and Z; i.e. if $X \subseteq Y$, then $X \cup Z \subseteq Y \cup Z$.

Hint: Proceed as with Lemma 1. 4 and Lemma 1. 5.

EXERCISE 1. 7: Prove that if a set X is a subset of a set Y, then the difference of a set Z and Y is a subset of the difference of Z and X; i.e. if $X \subseteq Y$, then $Z - Y \subseteq Z - X$.

EXERCISE 1. 8: Prove that for all sets X, Y, if $X \subseteq Y$ and $Y \subseteq X$, then $X = Y$.

Notice that by virtue of this result, to show that two sets are identical it will suffice to show that each of them is a subset of the other. We shall use this fact in many proofs later on.

LEMMA 1. 9: It is not the case for all sets X, Y, Z that if $X \in Y$ and $Y \in Z$ then $X \in Z$.

Proof: This result has the form of the negation of a universal implication, i.e. it asserts the existence of at least one *counterexample* to the universal implication—a case in which the first condition is satisfied but the second isn't. The most direct way of proving that such a case exists is to exhibit one. In this case, we need to find three sets such that the first is an element of the second, and the second is an element of the third, but the first is not an element of the third. Let a be an arbitrary object which isn't a set. Consider the sets $\{a\}$, $\{\{a\}\}$ and $\{\{\{a\}\}\}$. We have that $\{a\} \in \{\{a\}\}$ and $\{\{a\}\} \in \{\{\{a\}\}\}$, but $\{a\} \notin \{\{\{a\}\}\}$, since $\{\{a\}\}$ is the only element of $\{\{\{a\}\}\}$, and $\{\{a\}\} \neq \{a\}$. ∎

EXERCISE 1. 10: Show that it is not the case for all sets X, Y, Z that if $X \in Y$ and $Y \not\subseteq Z$ then $X \notin Z$.

Hint: Proceed as with Lemma 1. 9.

LEMMA 1. 11: Sets X and Y are subsets of a set Z if and only if the union of X and Y is a subset of Z; i.e. $X \subseteq Z$ and $Y \subseteq Z$ if and only if $X \cup Y \subseteq Z$.

Proof: This lemma is of the form: all objects are such that they satisfy one condition (being three sets such that the first two are subsets of the third) if and only if they satisfy another condition (being such that the union of the first two is a subset of the third). We shall refer to claims of this form as *universal equivalences*. A universal equivalence can be seen as the conjunction of two universal implications. Thus the present lemma can be reformulated as the double claim that (i) if sets X and Y are subsets of a set Z then the union of X and Y is a subset of Z *and* (ii) if the union of sets X and Y is a subset of set Z, then both X and Y are subsets of Z. Hence we will have proved the lemma once we have established universal implications (i) and (ii).

For (i), let A, B and C be sets such that $A \subseteq C$ and $B \subseteq C$. We want to prove that $A \cup B \subseteq C$, i.e. that, for every object x, if $x \in A \cup B$, then $x \in C$. Let $a \in A \cup B$. We want to prove that $a \in C$. We argue as follows:

$a \in A \cup B$

⇓ (by the definition of $\cup$)

$a \in A$ or $a \in B$

⇓ (from the assumption that $A \subseteq C$ and $B \subseteq C$ and the definition of $\subseteq$)

$a \in C$

For (ii), let A, B and C be sets such that $A \cup B \subseteq C$. We want to prove (1) that $A \subseteq C$ and (2) that $B \subseteq C$. For (1) we will have to show that for every object x, if $x \in A$, then $x \in C$. Let $a \in A$. We want to prove that a $\in C$. We argue as follows:

$a \in A$

$\Downarrow$ (by the definition of $\cup$)

$a \in A \cup B$

$\Downarrow$ (from the assumption that $A \cup B \subseteq C$)

$a \in C$

We can deal with (2) in exactly the same way.   ∎

EXERCISE 1. 12: Prove that a set Z is a subset of sets X and Y if and only if Z is a subset of the intersection of X and Y; i.e. $Z \subseteq X$ and $Z \subseteq Y$ if and only if $Z \subseteq X \cap Y$.

Hint: Proceed as with Lemma 1. 11. It is a common mistake to present a proof of one of the universal implications into which a universal equivalence can be analyzed as a complete proof of the universal equivalence.

By combining the operations of union, intersection and difference, we can define sets in terms of other sets. Thus, e.g., from the sets $\{a\}$, $\{b, c\}$, $\{a, b\}$, we can define the set $(\{a, b\} - \{a\}) \cup \{b, c\}$. We know that different definitions can in principle result in the same set, and we can establish general claims to the effect that different ways of combining the operations of union, intersection and difference always result in the same sets. The following result is a claim of this kind.

LEMMA 1. 13: For all sets X, Y, $X \cup (Y - X) = X \cup Y$.

Proof: Let A, B be sets. We need to prove that $A \cup (B - A) = A \cup B$. Notice that it follows from Exercise 1. 8 that the claim that two sets are identical is equivalent to the claim that each of them is a subset of the other. Hence to establish that $A \cup (B - A) = A \cup B$, it will suffice to show (i) that $A \cup (B - A) \subseteq A \cup B$ and (ii) that $A \cup B \subseteq A \cup (B - A)$.

For (i) we will have to show that for every object x, if $x \in A \cup (B - A)$ then $x \in A \cup B$. Let $a \in A \cup (B - A)$. We want to prove that $a \in A \cup B$. By the definition of $\cup$, we have that either $a \in A$ or $a \in B - A$. By the definition of $-$, it follows from this that either $a \in A$, or $a \in B$ and $a \notin A$. From this, it follows that either $a \in A$, or $a \in B$, which, by the definition of $\cup$, yields $a \in A \cup B$, as desired.

For (ii), we will have to show that for every object x, if $x \in A \cup B$ then $x \in A \cup (B - A)$. Let $a \in A \cup B$. We want to prove that $a \in A \cup (B - A)$. By the definition of $\cup$, we have that either $a \in A$ or $a \in B$ (or both).

It follows from this that either $a \in A$, or $a \in B$ and $a \notin A$. To see this, notice that, contrary to what may seem, the possibility that a is an element of both A and B is not ruled out by the claim that either $a \in A$, or $a \in B$ and $a \notin A$. For in that case we have, in particular, that a is an element of A, which is allowed by this claim. Now, by the definition of $-$, from the claim that either $a \in A$, or $a \in B$ and $a \notin A$, it follows that either $a \in A$ or $a \in B - A$, which, by the definition of $\cup$, gives us $a \in A \cup (B - A)$, as desired.

Notice that the arguments that we have provided for (i) and (ii) can be represented as two sequences of claims about an arbitrary object, and that what we assume about this object in each of these sequences is what we attempt to show about it in the other. Furthermore, the sequence that we have used for (ii) can be obtained by reversing the sequence that we have used for (i). This circumstance enables us to merge the two arguments by proving, for an arbitrary object a, about which nothing is assumed, that $a \in A \cup B$ if and only if $a \in A \cup (B - A)$. The argument can be presented as a succession of claims about a, starting with $a \in A \cup B$ and ending with $a \in A \cup (B - A)$, or vice versa, with each claim connected to the next by the symbol $\Updownarrow$, indicating that the claims above and below the double arrow entail each other, adding an explanation of why this is so. Thus organized the argument looks like this:

$a \in A \cup (B - A)$

$\quad \Updownarrow \quad$ (by the definition of $\cup$)

either $a \in A$ or $a \in B - A$

$\quad \Updownarrow \quad$ (by the definition of $-$)

either $a \in A$, or $a \in B$ and $a \notin A$

$\quad \Updownarrow \quad$ (by the reasoning provided above)

either $a \in A$ or $a \in B$

$\quad \Updownarrow \quad$ (by the definition of $\cup$)

$a \in A \cup B$ ∎

LEMMA 1. 14: For all sets X, Y, $(X \cup Y) - (X \cap Y) = (X - Y) \cup (Y - X)$.

Proof: Let A, B be sets. We need to prove that $(A \cup B) - (A \cap B) = (A - B) \cup (B - A)$. Let a be an object (about which nothing is assumed). By the reasoning provided in the proof of Lemma 1. 13, it will suffice to show that $a \in (A \cup B) - (A \cap B)$ if and only if $a \in (A - B) \cup (B - A)$. We argue as follows:

$a \in (A \cup B) - (A \cap B)$

   ⇕   (by the definition of –)

$a \in (A \cup B)$ and $a \notin (A \cap B)$

   ⇕   (by the definitions of $\cup$ and $\cap$)

$a \in A$ or $a \in B$, and it is not the case that both $a \in A$ and $a \in B$

   ⇕

Either $a \in A$ and $a \notin B$, or $a \in B$ and $a \notin A$

   ⇕   (by the definition of –)

Either $a \in A - B$ or $a \in B - A$

   ⇕   (by the definition of $\cup$)

$a \in (A - B) \cup (B - A)$ ■

EXERCISE 1. 15: Show that the following claims hold for all sets X, Y, Z:
   (1) $X \cup Y = Y \cup X$
   (2) $X \cap Y = Y \cap X$
   (3) $X \cup (Y \cup Z) = (X \cup Y) \cup Z$
   (4) $X \cap (Y \cap Z) = (X \cap Y) \cap Z$
   (5) $X \cap (Y \cup Z) = (X \cap Y) \cup (X \cap Z)$
   (6) $X \cup (Y \cap Z) = (X \cup Y) \cap (X \cup Z)$
   (7) $Z - (X \cup Y) = (Z - X) \cap (Z - Y)$
   (8) $Z - (X \cap Y) = (Z - X) \cup (Z - Y)$

(The fact that (1) and (2) hold for all sets is expressed by saying that $\cup$ and $\cap$ are *commutative*. The fact that (3) and (4) hold for all sets is expressed by saying that $\cup$ and $\cap$ are *associative*. (5) and (6) are known as the *distributive laws*, and (7) and (8) as the *de Morgan laws*.)

Hint: Proceed in each case as with the proofs of Lemma 1. 13 and Lemma 1. 14.

LEMMA 1. 16: For all sets X, Y, $X \cap (Y - X) = \emptyset$.

Proof: Let A, B be sets. We need to prove that $A \cap (B - A) = \emptyset$. To show this, we will have to establish that, for every object x, $x \in A \cap (B - A)$ if and only if $x \in \emptyset$. Since $\emptyset$ has no elements, this amounts to showing that, for every object x, $x \notin A \cap (B - A)$. To show this, we use a strategy known as *reductio (ad absurdum)*, which consists in establishing a claim by showing that its negation generates a contradiction. To achieve this, we assume the negation of the claim that we want to establish, and show that a contradiction follows from this assumption. Thus we assume, towards a contradiction, that $A \cap (B - A)$ has at least one element, and try to derive a contradiction from this assumption. To derive a conclusion from an assumption to the effect that there is at least one object satisfying a certain condition, we focus our attention on an arbitrary object, about which we assume that it satisfies the condition. Then any conclusion that we can derive from this assumption will also be a consequence of the existential assumption itself. Following this procedure, we argue as follows. Let $a \in A \cap (B - A)$.

$a \in A \cap (B - A)$

$\Downarrow$ (by the definition of $\cap$)

$a \in A$ and $a \in B - A$

$\Downarrow$ (by the definition of $-$)

$a \in A$ and $a \in B$ but $a \notin A$

But this last claim is contradictory, since it asserts that a both is and is not an element of A, as desired. ∎

EXERCISE 1. 17: Show that the following claims hold for all sets X, Y:
  (1) $X \cup \emptyset = X$
  (2) $X \cap \emptyset = \emptyset$
  (3) $X - \emptyset = X$
  (4) $\emptyset - X = \emptyset$
  (5) $(X \cap Y) \cup (X - Y) = X$

When all the elements of a set are themselves sets, we say that it is a *collection*.

DEFINITION: The *union* of a collection A, written $\bigcup A$, is the set containing all the elements of each set in A; i.e. $\bigcup A = \{x \mid$ for at least one set B, $B \in A$ and $x \in B\}$.

DEFINITION: The *intersection* of a nonempty collection A, written $\bigcap A$, is the set containing the objects which are elements of every set in A; i.e. $\bigcap A = \{x \mid$ for every set B such that $B \in A, x \in B\}$.

Example: The union of the collection $\{\{a, b\}, \{b, c\}, \{b, d\}\}$ is the set $\{a, b, c, d\}$, and its intersection the set $\{b\}$.

EXERCISE 1. 18: Show that for all sets X, Y, $\bigcup\{X, Y\} = X \cup Y$.

EXERCISE 1. 19: Show that for all sets X, Y, $\bigcap\{X, Y\} = X \cap Y$.

EXERCISE 1. 20: Show that every element of a collection is a subset of its union.

EXERCISE 1. 21: Show that different collections can have the same union.

Hint: To prove that this is a possibility, you just need to find an instance of this situation, i.e. two collections with the same union.

EXERCISE 1. 22: Show that, for every set X, $\bigcup\{X\} = X$.

EXERCISE 1. 23: Show that $\bigcup\emptyset = \emptyset$.

Hint: See the proof of Lemma 1. 16.

EXERCISE 1. 24: Show that, for every collection X, $\bigcup \wp X = X$.

EXERCISE 1. 25: Show that, for every collection X, $X \subseteq \wp\bigcup X$.

EXERCISE 1. 26: Show that it is not the case for every collection X that $\wp\bigcup X = X$.

Hint: See the proof of Lemma 1. 9.

5. Relations

Contemporary logic accords to relations the same extensional treatment as to properties. Just as properties are replaced by sets in the characterization of the first-order propositions in which they figure, relations are replaced by sets of pairs. Notice that the order in which two objects figure in a pair may make a difference to whether it is singled out by a relation. Thus, the relation ...*is a satellite of*... singles out the pair in which the Moon figures first and the Earth second, but not the pair in which these objects appear in reverse order. To accommodate this feature of relations, we introduce the notion of *ordered pair*. An ordered pair will single out two individuals, one as its first member and one as its second member. The identity of an ordered pair will be uniquely determined by which individuals it singles out as its first and second member. Hence different ordered pairs will have either different first members or different second members (or both). We shall represent an ordered pair by enclosing its members in angle brackets, listed in the right order and separated by a comma. Thus, e.g., ⟨the Moon, the Earth⟩ is the ordered pair with the Moon as its first member and the Earth as its second member. It is different from ⟨the Moon, Mars⟩, ⟨Mars, the Earth⟩ and ⟨the Earth, the Moon⟩. Notice that an ordered pair can have the same individual as its first and second member, as, e.g., the pair ⟨the Moon, the Moon⟩.

Contemporary logic uses sets of ordered pairs as extensional surrogates of relations. Thus, first-order propositions which can be characterized as involving a relation are characterized instead as involving the set of ordered pairs that it singles out. And the way in which they obtain their truth values is explained, not in terms of which ordered pairs exemplify certain relations, but in terms of which ordered pairs are elements of certain sets of ordered pairs. Thus, e.g., the proposition that Mars has no satellites is characterized as involving the individual Mars and the set of ordered pairs whose first members are satellites of their second members, combined in such a way that the proposition is true if this set contains no pairs with Mars as the second member, and false otherwise.

We can refer to relations like *...is a satellite of...*, whose instances involve two individuals, as *binary* or *two-place relations*. Other relations involve more individuals, like, e.g., the relation connecting three planets when the orbit of the first is between the orbits of the other two. Other relations involve even more individuals. For every positive integer *n* greater than 1, we shall refer to a relation whose instances involve *n* individuals as an *n-place relation* (the positive integers are 1, 2, 3,.... See §8, below). We shall treat all relations along the same lines as binary relations. For this purpose we need to extend the notion of an ordered pair by introducing, for every positive integer *n* greater than 1, the notion of an *n-tuple*, which singles out *n* individuals, one for each of its *n* positions, and whose identity is uniquely determined by which individual it singles out for each of its positions. Ordered pairs are two-member tuples. We shall refer to three-member tuples as *triples*. We can represent an *n*-tuple like an ordered pair, by enclosing its members in angle brackets, listed in the right order and separated by commas. It will be convenient in some contexts to have at our disposal the notion of a 1-*tuple*. If *a* is an object, we shall say that the 1-tuple whose first and only member is *a*, written ⟨*a*⟩, is identical with *a* itself.

In our characterization of first-order propositions, sets of *n*-tuples will replace *n*-place relations. Nevertheless, in order to distinguish sets of *n*-tuples from other sets, we shall refer to them as *n-place relations* (in the extensional sense), bearing in mind that, since they are sets, the Principle of Extensionality holds for them. Similarly, we shall refer to sets of pairs as *binary relations* (in the extensional sense). For the sake of uniformity, we may want to regard the sets that we use as surrogates of properties as one-place relations, and their elements as 1-tuples. Then all the sets that replace properties and relations in our characterization of first-order propositions will be treated as relations (in the extensional sense).

6. Some Binary Relations

Most of the relations that we shall study will be binary relations. If R is a binary relation and a and b are two objects such that $\langle a, b \rangle \in R$, we shall sometimes say that a bears R to b or that a is R-related to b, and write aRb. If A and B are sets, we say that a binary relation R is a *relation from A to B* if, for every $\langle x, y \rangle \in R$, $x \in A$ and $y \in B$. Thus, e.g., the relation *...is a citizen of...* is a relation from the set of people to the set of countries. If R is a binary relation, the set whose elements bear R to something ($\{x \mid \langle x, y \rangle \in R$ for at least one $y\}$) is the *domain* of R. The set to whose elements something bears R ($\{x \mid \langle y, x \rangle \in R$ for at least one $y\}$) is the *range* of R. R is a relation from A to B if and only if the domain of R is a subset of A and the range of R is a subset of B.

DEFINITION: The *Cartesian product* of sets A and B, written $A \times B$, is the relation which pairs every element of A with every element of B; i.e. $A \times B = \{\langle x, y \rangle \mid x \in A$ and $y \in B\}$.

Notice that every relation from A to B is a subset of the Cartesian product of A and B. As a special case, we have that $A \times A$ is the set of all the ordered pairs of elements of A.

EXERCISE 1. 27: Show that, for all sets X, Y, Z,
   (1) $X \times (Y \cup Z) = (X \times Y) \cup (X \times Z)$
   (2) $X \times (Y \cap Z) = (X \times Y) \cap (X \times Z)$
   (3) $X \times (Y - Z) = (X \times Y) - (X \times Z)$
   (4) $X \times \emptyset = \emptyset \times X = \emptyset$

Hint: For (1)–(3), proceed as with the proofs of Lemma 1. 13 and Lemma 1. 14. For (4) see the proof of Lemma 1. 16.

We can generalize the notion of the Cartesian product of two sets to any finite number of sets. For every positive integer n, the Cartesian product of a sequence of n sets is the set of all n-tuples whose m-th member, for each positive integer m less than or equal to n, is an element of the m-th set of the sequence.

If all the objects paired by a binary relation R are elements of a set A, we say that R is a *relation in A*. Thus, e.g., the relation *...is married to...* is a relation in the set of married people, as well as a relation in the set of all people. Sometimes, when a binary relation R pairs objects outside a set A, it is convenient to "shrink" R to fit A, i.e. to define the relation that we would get if we deleted from R every pair with at least one member outside A. This relation can be defined by abstraction as the set $\{\langle x, y \rangle \mid \langle x, y \rangle \in R, x \in A$ and $y \in A\}$. We shall sometimes refer to this as the relation R *defined on A*. Thus, e.g., the relation *...is married to...* defined on the set of U.S. citizens is the set of pairs both of whose members are U.S. citizens who are married to each other. We consider next two kinds of binary relation which are of particular interest.

i. Equivalence Relations

DEFINITION: A binary relation R is *reflexive* in a set A just in case every element of A bears R to itself.

DEFINITION: A binary relation R is *symmetric* just in case whenever an object x bears R to an object y, y also bears R to x.

DEFINITION: A binary relation R is *transitive* just in case whenever an object x bears R to an object y and y bears R to an object z, x also bears R to z.

Example: Consider the relation *...trusts...* defined on the set of U.S. senators. If every senator trusts him/herself, the relation is reflexive (in this set). If every senator trusts every senator by whom he or she is trusted, the relation is symmetric. And if every senator trusts every senator who is trusted by a senator he or she trusts, the relation is transitive.

EXERCISE 1. 28: Let R be a binary relation in a set A, and let every element of A bear R to at least one element of A. Show that if R is symmetric and transitive, it is also reflexive in A.

EXERCISE 1. 29: Let R be a symmetric, transitive relation. Show that whenever an object x bears R to two objects y, z, y and z bear R to each other.

DEFINITION: A binary relation R in a set A is an *equivalence relation* in A just in case R is reflexive in A, symmetric and transitive.

Examples: The relation *...weighs the same as...* defined on a set of people is an equivalence relation in that set, and the relation *...is parallel to...* defined on the set of lines in the (Euclidean) plane is an equivalence relation in that set.

Equivalence relations have some properties that will make them useful for us later on. Let R be a binary relation in a set A. If a is an element of A, we can define the set of objects to which a is R-related, i.e. $\{x \mid aRx\}$. This notion is particularly useful in the case of equivalence relations.

DEFINITION: If R is an equivalence relation in a set A, and a is an element of A, the *equivalence class* generated (with R) by a, written $[a]_R$, is the set of objects to which a bears R.

LEMMA 1. 30: Let R be an equivalence relation in a set A. If two elements of A are R-related, then they generate the same equivalence class, i.e. for all $x, y \in A$, if xRy, then $[x]_R = [y]_R$.

Proof: By Exercise 1. 8, it will suffice to show (i) that for all $x, y \in A$, if xRy, then $[y]_R \subseteq [x]_R$, and (ii) that for all $x, y \in A$, if xRy, then $[x]_R \subseteq [y]_R$. (We shall write "for every $x \in A$" to abbreviate "for every x such that $x \in A$," and "$x, y \in A$" to abbreviate "$x \in A$ and $y \in A$.")

For (i), let $a, b \in A$, and let aRb. We want to show that $[b]_R \subseteq [a]_R$, i.e. that for every $z \in [b]_R$, $z \in [a]_R$. Let $c \in [b]_R$. We need to show that $c \in [a]_R$. We argue as follows:

$c \in [b]_R$

$\Downarrow$ (by the definition of equivalence class)

bRc

$\Downarrow$ (from the assumption that aRb and the transitivity of R)

aRc

$\Downarrow$ (by the definition of equivalence class)

$c \in [a]_R$

For (ii), let $a, b \in A$, and let aRb. We need to show that $[a]_R \subseteq [b]_R$. Since a bears R to b, by the symmetry of R we have that b also bears R to a. Now we can invoke (i) to conclude from this that $[a]_R \subseteq [b]_R$, as desired.   ■

EXERCISE 1. 31: Let R be an equivalence relation in a set A. Show that every element of A is an element of the equivalence class that it generates, i.e. for every $x \in A$, $x \in [x]_R$.

Hint: Invoke the reflexivity of R.

EXERCISE 1. 32: Let R be an equivalence relation in a set A. Show that if two elements of A generate the same equivalence class, then they are R-related, i. e. for all $x, y \in A$, if $[x]_R = [y]_R$, then xRy.

The most interesting feature of equivalence relations is that if R is an equivalence relation in a set A, every element of A is in exactly one of the equivalence classes generated (with R) by the elements of A. This fact is expressed by saying that R *partitions* A. That every element of A is in at least one of them is a direct consequence of Exercise 1. 31, which tells us that every element of A is in the equivalence class that it generates. To show that every element of A is in at most one of the equivalence classes generated by the elements of A, it will suffice to establish that the equivalence classes generated (with R) by two elements of A do not share any elements unless they are identical. This result is expressed by the following lemma.

LEMMA 1. 33: Let R be an equivalence relation in a set A. For all x, y, z $\in A$, if $x \in [y]_R$ and $x \in [z]_R$, then $[y]_R = [z]_R$.

Proof: Let a, b, $c \in A$, and let $a \in [b]_R$, $a \in [c]_R$. We need to show that $[b]_R = [c]_R$. We reason as follows:

$a \in [b]_R$ and $a \in [c]_R$

⇓   (by the definition of equivalence class)

bRa and cRa

⇓   (by Lemma 1. 30)

$[b]_R = [a]_R$ and $[c]_R = [a]_R$

⇓   (since two objects which are identical to a third are identical to each other)

$[b]_R = [c]_R$ ∎

ii.   Orderings

DEFINITION: A binary relation R is *antisymmetric* just in case, whenever an object x bears R to a *different* object y, y doesn't bear R to x.

Notice that it follows from the definition that to prove that a relation R is antisymmetric it will suffice to establish that if x and y bear R to each other, x and y have to be the same object. Antisymmetry can be used to define another important category of binary relations.

DEFINITION: A binary relation R in a set A is a *partial ordering* of A just in case R is reflexive in A, antisymmetric and transitive.

Examples: If m and n are positive integers, we say that m is a *power* of n just in case m results from raising n to the power of some positive integer, i.e. just in case there is a positive integer p such that $n^p = m$. Thus, e.g., 8 is a power of 2, since $8 = 2^3$. The relation pairing each positive integer with its powers is a partial ordering of the set of positive integers. It is reflexive in this set, since raising a positive integer to the power of 1 (itself a positive integer) always yields that same number. It is also anti-symmetric, since for any two different positive integers one is greater than the other, and the smaller number never results from raising the greater to the power of a positive integer. And it is transitive, since a power of a power of a positive integer n is also a power of n. Also, the relation $\subseteq$ defined on any collection of sets is a partial ordering of the collection. $\subseteq$ is reflexive in any collection, since every set is a subset of itself. Lemma 1. 4 tells us that $\subseteq$ is transitive, and it follows from Exercise 1. 8 that $\subseteq$ is also antisymmetric.

Notice that a relation can be a partial ordering of a set even if some of its elements are not related to each other. Thus, e.g., 8 isn't a power of 10 and 10 isn't a power of 8, and a collection can contain two sets neither of which is a subset of the other.

DEFINITION: A partial ordering R of a set A is *linear* just in case, for any two elements of A, one of them bears R to the other.

Example: The relation ...*is less than or equal to*... (written $\leq$) is a linear ordering of the set of positive integers.

As the term indicates, if R is a linear ordering of A, all the elements of A can be arranged in a single line, without loops or bifurcations, so that every element of A bears R to every object that appears later in the line (as well as to itself), and doesn't bear R to any object that appears earlier.

DEFINITION: If R is a partial ordering of a set A, an element of A is *maximal* (with respect to R) just in case it doesn't bear R to any other element of A. And an element of A is *minimal* (with respect to R) just in case no other element of A bears R to it.

Examples: The relation pairing each positive integer with its powers has one maximal element, 1, since 1 has no powers other than itself, but every other positive integer does. And it has infinitely many minimal elements—the positive integers which are not powers of other positive integers. The relation $\leq$ defined on the positive integers doesn't have any maximal elements, but it has one minimal element—namely 1.

EXERCISE 1. 34: Show that a linear ordering has at most one minimal element and at most one maximal element.

Hint: Prove by *reductio*, assuming, towards a contradiction, that a linear ordering has more than one minimal or maximal element. See the proof of Lemma 1. 16.

EXERCISE 1. 35: Let *A* be a set with at least two elements. Show that the relation $\subseteq$ defined on the power set of *A* is not a linear ordering, and that it has a minimal and a maximal element.

DEFINITION: If *R* is a partial ordering of a set *A*, and *B* is a subset of *A*, *B* is a *chain* in *A* (with respect to *R*) just in case *R* (defined on *B*) is a linear ordering of *B*.

Example: The set {4, 16, 4096} is a chain in the set of positive integers with respect to the relation pairing each positive integer with its powers.

Notice that for any partial ordering *R* of a set *A*, Ø is a chain in *A*, since *R* (defined on Ø) is vacuously reflexive in Ø, antisymmetric and transitive. The same goes for any one-element subset *B* of *A*, since *R* (defined on *B*) is reflexive in *B*, and any relation defined on a one-element set is (vacuously) antisymmetric and transitive.

DEFINITION: A binary relation *R* is *irreflexive* just in case no object bears *R* to itself.

Using this notion, we can define another important type of ordering.

DEFINITION: A binary relation *R* in a set *A* is a *strict ordering* of *A* just in case *R* is irreflexive and transitive.

Examples: $\subset$ is a strict ordering of any collection. The relation *...is less than...* (written <) is a strict ordering of the set of positive integers.

The notions of *strict linear ordering* and of a *maximal* and *minimal* elements of a set with respect to a strict ordering can be defined in the same way as the corresponding notions for partial orderings.

DEFINITION: A binary relation *R* is *asymmetric* just in case, whenever an object *x* bears *R* to an object *y*, *y* doesn't bear *R* to *x*.

Notice that, unlike antisymmetry, asymmetry rules out the possibility that an object bears *R* to itself. For if *R* is an asymmetric relation, *xRx* would entail that it is not the case that *xRx*.

EXERCISE 1. 36: Show that if *R* is a strict ordering of a set *A*, *R* is asymmetric.

Remember that we have defined $\subset$ in terms of $\subseteq$ as follows: $x \subset y$ if and only if $x \subseteq y$ and $x \neq y$. If we had defined $\subset$ independently, we could then have defined $\subseteq$ in terms of $\subset$ as follows: $x \subseteq y$ if and only if $x \subset y$ or $x = y$. We could use these procedures to define < in terms of ≤ or ≤ in terms of <, defined on the set of positive integers. The same procedures would enable us to define a strict ordering in terms of any given partial ordering, and a partial ordering in terms of any given strict ordering. This general claim is expressed by the following two results.

LEMMA 1. 37: Let R be a partial ordering of a set A, and let R' be the relation in A defined as follows: for all $x, y \in A$, $xR'y$ if and only if xRy and $x \neq y$. R' is a strict ordering.

Proof: We need to show that R' is (i) irreflexive and (ii) transitive.

For (i), we need to prove that nothing bears R' to itself. We prove this by *reductio*. We assume, towards a contradiction, that there is an element of A which bears R' to itself. By the definition of R', it follows that any such object is not identical with itself, which is a contradiction.

For (ii), we need to establish that for any three objects x, y, z, if x bears R' to y and y bears R' to z, then x bears R' to z. Let a bear R' to b and let b bear R' to c. We argue as follows:

$aR'b$ and $bR'c$

⇓   (by the definition of R')

aRb, $a \neq b$, and bRc

⇓   (since, by the transitivity of R, aRb and bRc entail aRc, and by the antisymmetry of R, aRb, $a \neq b$, and bRc entail $a \neq c$)

aRc and $a \neq c$

⇓   (by the definition of R')

$aR'c$ ∎

EXERCISE 1. 38: Let R be a strict ordering of a set A, and let R' be the relation in A defined as follows: for all $x, y \in A$, $xR'y$ if and only if xRy or $x = y$. Show that R' is a partial ordering.

Hint: Proceed as in the proof of Lemma 1. 37.

7. Functions

Sometimes the role of a relation in a proposition is to single out an individual. This is the role, e.g., that the relation pairing planets with their satellites plays in the proposition that the satellite of the Earth is not inhabited. The truth value of this proposition is determined by whether the individual to which the Earth bears this relation instantiates the property of being inhabited. The relation pairing planets with their satellites succeeds in singling out an individual in this proposition because the Earth bears this relation to exactly one individual. Sometimes a relation has this feature with respect to every element of a set. These relations are known as *functions*.

DEFINITION: A binary relation R from a set A to a set B is a *function* from A to B just in case every element of A bears R to exactly one element of B.

Example: The relation pairing the athletes who competed in the 1996 Olympics with the countries they represented is a function from the set of athletes who competed in the 1996 Olympics to the set of countries which were represented, as well as to the set of all countries and to any other set whose elements include all the countries represented in the 1996 Olympics.

Notice that a binary relation R from a set A to a set B will only fail to be a function from A to B if either some element of A doesn't bear R to any element of B or some element of A bears R to more than one element of B. Hence, to show that R is a function, it will suffice to rule out these possibilities.

If f is a function from A to B, and a is an element of A, a will be paired by f with a unique element of B (f, g and h, in lower case, are the letters most commonly used to represent functions). This element of B is known as the *image* of a under f, written $f(a)$. Thus the U.S. is the image of Carl Lewis under the function that we have been considering.

Since functions are binary relations, to define a function we need to specify the pairs that we are going to treat as its elements. We can do this using any of the standard methods for defining a set. Thus let f be the function pairing the athletes who competed in the 1996 Olympics with the countries they represented. We can define f by abstraction, as follows: $f = \{\langle x, y \rangle \mid x$ is an athlete, y is a country and x represented y in the 1996 Olympics$\}$. But we shall often formulate the definition of a function in a different way, by specifying, for every element of the intended domain, the object that we are going to count as its image under the function. Thus, if we take this approach, the definition of the function f pairing the athletes who competed in the 1996 Olympics with the countries they represented will look like this: for every athlete x who competed in the 1996 Olympics, $f(x)$ = the country that x represented. Notice that if we proceed in this way, we shall only succeed in defining a function if the expression on the right-hand side of the identity sign satisfies two requirements: (i) it has to single out *at least* one object for each element x of the intended domain and (ii) it has to single out *at most* one object for each element x of the intended domain. If we say that for every athlete x who competed in the 1996 Olympics, $g(x)$ = the spouse of *x*, we will fail to define a function (with the intended domain) because some of the athletes who competed in the 1996 Olympics were single. And if we say that for every athlete *x* who competed in the 1996 Olympics, $h(x)$ = the event in which *x* competed, we will fail to define a function because some athletes competed in more than one event.

Let *f* be a function, and let *A* be the domain of *f*. If the range of *f* is a subset of *A*, we say that *f* is a *function in A*. Thus, e.g., the function pairing each person sitting around a table with his or her neighbor to the left is a function in the set of people sitting around the table, and the function pairing each positive integer with the result of multiplying it by itself is a function in the set of positive integers.

Consider the relation pairing each U.S. senator and each U.S. state with the number of days the senator spent in the state in 1998. We can represent this relation as a function from the Cartesian product of the set of U.S. senators and the set of U.S. states to the set of natural numbers, since it assigns one and only one number to every pair with a U.S. senator as its first member and a U.S. state as its second member (the natural numbers are 0, 1, 2, 3,.... See §8, below). Functions like this one whose domain is the Cartesian product of two sets are known as *two-place functions*. To represent the image under a two-place function *f* of a pair $\langle a, b \rangle$ in its domain, we write $f(a, b)$. We can also use this notation to define two-place functions. Thus, e.g., if we refer to the function pairing each U.S. senator and each U.S. state with the number of days the senator spent in the state in 1998 as *f*, we can formulate its definition as follows: for every U.S. senator *x* and every U.S. state *y*, $f(x, y)$ = the number of days *x* spent in *y* in 1998. When the domain of a two-place function is the Cartesian product of a set *A* with itself, and its range is a subset of *A*, we say that it is a two-place function in *A*. Thus, e.g., the function pairing two natural numbers with the result of raising the first to the power of the second is a two-place function in the set of natural numbers.

We can speak in the same way of *n*-place functions for every positive integer *n*. Thus, e.g., the function pairing each U.S. senator, each U.S. state and each day of the week with the number of times the senator was in the state that day of the week in 1998 is a three-place function. And so is the function *f* defined as follows: for all natural numbers *x*, *y*, *z*, $f(x, y, z) = x + (y \cdot z)$. If *f* is an *n*-place function, we shall say that it has *n* *argument-places*. When the domain of a function is the set of *n*-tuples of elements of a set *A*, and its range is a subset of *A*, we shall say that it is an *n*-place function in *A*.

Consider the function pairing each person with his or her (biological) mother, and the function pairing each person with his or her (biological) father. We can combine these two functions to define a third function, pairing each person with the mother of his or her father (i.e. with his or her paternal grandmother). We can define this operation along the following lines:

DEFINITION: If *f* and *g* are functions such that the range of *f* is a subset of the domain of *g*, the *composition* of *g* and *f*, written *g* ∘ *f*, is the function which pairs each element of the domain of *f* with the image under *g* of its image under *f*; i.e., for every element *x* of the domain of *f*, *g* ∘ *f*(*x*) = *g*(*f*(*x*)).

Notice that the order of composition may make a difference. The function pairing each person with his or her father's mother is different from the function pairing each person with his or her mother's father. Notice that a function can also be composed with itself, provided that its range is a subset of its domain. Thus, the composition with itself of the function pairing each person with his or her father will pair each person with his or her paternal grandfather.

DEFINITION: If *f* is a function, and *A* is a subset of the domain of *f*, the *restriction* of *f* to *A*, written *f*⎾ *A*, is the function pairing each element of *A* with its image under *f*.

Example: The function pairing the long-distance runners who competed in the 1996 Olympics with the countries they represented is the restriction to the set of long-distance runners who competed in the 1996 Olympics of the function pairing the athletes who competed in the 1996 Olympics with the countries they represented.

As some of our examples illustrate, the definition of function doesn't rule out the possibility that two objects have the same image under a function. Thus, e.g., Carl Lewis and Gwen Torrence have the same image under the function pairing the athletes who competed in the 1996 Olympics with the countries they represented.

DEFINITION: A function is *one-to-one* just in case it never assigns the same image to more than one object.

Example: The function pairing each ambassador in Washington with the country he or she represents is one-to-one.

EXERCISE 1. 39: Show that if *f* and *g* are one-to-one functions, and the range of *f* is a subset of the domain of *g*, then *g* ∘ *f* is a one-to-one function.

An interesting feature of one-to-one functions is that the result of reversing the pairs in a one-to-one function is also function.

DEFINITION: If f is a one-to-one function, the *inverse* of f, written f^{-1}, is the function pairing each element x of the range of f with the unique element of the domain of f having x as its image.

Thus, e.g., the inverse of the function pairing each ambassador in Washington with the country he or she represents is the function pairing each country which has an ambassador in Washington with the person holding that office. Notice that this function is also one-to-one. The next lemma expresses the result that the inverse of every one-to-one function is itself a one-to-one function.

LEMMA 1. 40: If f is a one-to-one function with domain A and range B, then the inverse of f is a one-to-one function with domain B and range A.

Proof: Let f be a one-to-one function with domain A and range B. We need to prove (i) that f^{-1} never pairs an element of its domain with two different objects, (ii) that f^{-1} never pairs two elements of its domain with the same object, (iii) that its domain is B and (iv) that its range is A. We'll deal with (i), and leave (ii), (iii) and (iv) as an exercise.

We prove (i) by *reductio*. Thus we assume towards a contradiction that there is an object a which f^{-1} pairs with two different objects b and c. Then, by the definition of f^{-1}, f pairs both b and c with a, which contradicts the hypothesis that f is one-to-one.   ■

EXERCISE 1. 41: Establish (ii), (iii) and (iv) in the proof of Lemma 1. 40.

Hint: You can use *reductio* in each case.

EXERCISE 1. 42: Show that every one-to-one function is identical with the inverse of its inverse, i.e., for every one-to-one function f, $f = (f^{-1})^{-1}$.

EXERCISE 1. 43: Show that, for every one-to-one function f, $f^{-1} \circ f$ is the function pairing each element of the domain of f with itself, and $f \circ f^{-1}$ is the function pairing each element of the range of f with itself.

DEFINITION: A *one-to-one correspondence* between a set A and a set B is a one-to-one function from A to B whose range is (the whole of) B.

Notice that if f is a one-to-one correspondence between A and B, and C is a set with B as a proper subset, f will be a one-to-one function from A to C, but not a one-to-one correspondence between A and C. A consequence of Lemma 1. 40 is that if f is a one-to-one correspondence between A and B, then f^{-1} is a one-to-one correspondence between B and A, and hence that there is a one-to-one correspondence between A and B if and only if there is a one-to-one correspondence between B and A.

Since functions are sets, we can apply to them the standard set-theoretic operations of union, intersection and difference, although the result may not be a function.

EXERCISE 1. 44: Show that the intersection of two functions is a function.

EXERCISE 1. 45: Show that the union of two functions is a function if and only if both assign the same image to each element of the intersection of their domains.

EXERCISE 1. 46: Show that the union of two one-to-one correspondences with disjoint domains and disjoint ranges is a one-to-one correspondence between the union of their domains and the union of their ranges.

The set of all functions from a set A to a set B is represented as $^A B$.

EXERCISE 1. 47: Show that for all sets $X, Y, {}^X Y \subseteq \wp(X \times Y)$.

EXERCISE 1. 48: Use the $\{x \mid Px\}$ notation to define the set of functions from a set A to a set B.

Hint: You may find it convenient to invoke the notion of the Cartesian product of A and B.

Definitions of set-theoretic notions often have surprising consequences for the empty set. The reason is that every claim to the effect that all the elements of a set have a certain property is true of $\emptyset$, since a set can only make such a claim false by having an element which doesn't have the property in question. This is the reason why $\emptyset$ is a subset of every set, as well as a chain in every partially ordered set. The next three results express similar claims about the empty set which follow from the definitions in this section.

LEMMA 1. 49: $\emptyset$ is a one-to-one correspondence between $\emptyset$ and $\emptyset$.

Proof: A set A can only fail to be a one-to-one correspondence between sets B and C on the following counts: (i) If some of the elements of A are not ordered pairs whose first member is an element of B and whose second member is an element of C. (ii) If A contains two ordered pairs with the same first member but different second members or with the same second member but different first members. (iii) If some element of B is not the first member of any pair in A or some element of C is not the second member of any pair in A. Each of these features requires A, B or C to have at least one element. Hence $\emptyset$ cannot fail to be a one-to-one correspondence between $\emptyset$ and $\emptyset$. ∎

LEMMA 1. 50: For every set Y, $^\emptyset Y = \{\emptyset\}$.

Proof: Let A be a set. We need to show (i) that $\{\emptyset\} \subseteq {}^\emptyset A$ and (ii) that $^\emptyset A \subseteq \{\emptyset\}$. For (i), we need to show that $\emptyset$ is a function from $\emptyset$ to A. This follows from Lemma 1. 49, since if $\emptyset$ is a one-to-one correspondence between $\emptyset$ and $\emptyset$, it is a function from $\emptyset$ to any set. For (ii) we need to show that $\emptyset$ is the only function from $\emptyset$ to A. Let f be a nonempty function. We need to show that f is not a function from $\emptyset$ to A. For this it will suffice to show that $\emptyset$ is not the domain of f. Since f is not empty, it has at least one pair. Let $\langle a, b \rangle \in f$. Then, a is an element of the domain of f. But $a \notin \emptyset$. Hence the domain of f is not $\emptyset$, as desired. ∎

EXERCISE 1. 51: Show that, for every nonempty set X, $^X\emptyset = \emptyset$.

8. Numbers

Although numbers won't play a major role in our discussion, we shall invoke a few basic facts about them. The goal of this section is to present these facts, informally and without proof. The only numbers that will play any role before Chapter 6 are the *natural numbers*. The natural numbers are 0, 1, 2, 3,.... They are linearly ordered by $\leq$ in a sequence with 0 as its only minimal element and no maximal elements. We shall refer to the set of all natural numbers as ω.

For many practical purposes we will want to use the natural numbers other than 0, which are known as *positive integers*. One of the ways in which we shall use positive integers is as *indices* to designate the elements of a set or the members of a tuple. If we are discussing an n-element set A, we can refer to its elements, say, as $a_1, a_2,..., a_{n-1}, a_n$. And if we are discussing an n-tuple T, we can refer to its members, say, as $t_1, t_2,..., t_{n-1}, t_n$. Notice that the indices of the elements of a set and the indices of the members of a tuple carry different information. When we index the elements of A, the order in which we take them is arbitrary. No significance is attached to which particular index an element of A receives. All that matters is that every element of A is paired with one and only one positive integer less than or equal to n, and every positive integer less than or equal to n is paired with one and only one element of A. Hence, in particular, if i and j are different positive integers less than or equal to n, then $a_i \neq a_j$. When we index the members of a tuple, by contrast, order is all that matters. The index that an object receives indicates the position it occupies in the tuple. For every positive integer i less than or equal to n, t_i is the object occupying the i-th position in T.

But since a single object can occupy more than one position in a tuple, we can have two positive integers j, k less than or equal to n such that $t_j = t_k$.

Starting in Chapter 6, three other kinds of number will figure in our discussion—the integers, the rational numbers and the real numbers. The *integers* are the positive integers, 1, 2, 3, 4..., the *negative integers*, -1, -2, -3,..., and 0. They are linearly ordered by $\leq$ in the sequence ...-2, -1, 0, 1, 2,..., with no minimal or maximal element. We shall refer to the set of integers as **Z**, to the set of positive integers as $\mathbf{Z}^+$, and to the set of negative integers as $\mathbf{Z}^-$.

The *rational numbers* are those which can be represented by a fraction, e.g., 2/3, $-237/133$, 0/3, $-25/5$. We shall refer to the set of rational numbers as **Q**. Different fractions can represent the same rational number. Thus, e.g., $2/3 = 4/6 = 66/99$. Notice that all the integers are rational numbers, since every integer a is represented by the fraction $a/1$ (among others). Like the integers, the rational numbers are linearly ordered by $\leq$ in a chain with no minimal or maximal elements. But the ordering of the rationals differs from the ordering of the integers in that between any two rational numbers there is a third rational number, i.e., if a and b are different rational numbers such that $a \leq b$, then there is a rational number c different from a and b such that $a \leq c \leq b$. Orderings with this property are known as *dense*.

A rational number can also be represented in decimal form, i.e. with an integer possibly followed by (a decimal point and) a sequence of decimals. Thus, e.g., $3/4 = 0.75$, $-7/3 = -2.3333...$ and $25/5 = 5$. This way of representing a rational number is known as its *decimal expansion*. The decimal expansion of an integer has no decimals. The decimal expansion of every other rational number has at least one decimal. The sequence of decimals of a decimal expansion can be finite, as in 0.75, or infinite, as in 2.333.... When it is infinite, it consists, after a certain decimal place, of the infinite repetition of a finite sequence of digits. Thus, e.g., the sequence of decimals of the decimal expansion of $-7/3$ consists, from the first decimal place, of an infinite string of 3's, and the sequence of decimals of the decimal expansion of 3/14 consists, from the second decimal place, of the infinite repetition of the sequence 142857.

It will be convenient for our purposes later on to make the sequence of decimals of every decimal expansion infinite, by appending a decimal point and an infinite sequence of 0's to every integer, and adding an infinite sequence of 0's to the right of the last digit of each decimal expansion with a finite sequence of decimals. Thus the decimal expansion of 3/4 becomes 0.75000..., and the decimal expansion of 5/1 becomes

5.000.... We shall refer to decimal expansions which have nothing but 0's to the right of a certain decimal place as *terminating*.

A fact about decimal expansions which may come as a surprise to those who are not familiar with them is that every rational number (other than 0) with a terminating decimal expansion also has a nonterminating decimal expansion. Thus, e.g., we have that $1/1 = 1.000...$, but also $1/1 = 0.999...$ (and hence $1.000... = 0.999...!$). To see this, notice that $1/1 = 3/3 = 1/3 \cdot 3 = 0.333... \cdot 3 = 0.999...$ Similarly we have that $5/8 = 0.625$ and $5/8 = 0.624999...$ It will simplify our discussion in Chapter 6 to proceed as if every rational number had a unique decimal expansion. Hence we stipulate that when a rational number a has a terminating and a nonterminating decimal expansion, by "the decimal expansion of a" we shall refer to its terminating decimal expansion.

Many familiar numbers are not represented by a fraction. They include π, $\sqrt{2}$ and the square root of every other natural number whose square root is not a natural number, e.g. $\sqrt{3}$, $\sqrt{5}$, etc. All these numbers are included in a wider category known as the *real numbers*, which can be characterized as the numbers which are represented by a decimal expansion. We shall refer to the set of the real numbers as $\Re$. Real numbers which are not rational are known as *irrational*. As we have seen, the decimal expansion of a rational number ends with an infinite string of 0's or with the infinite repetition of another sequence of digits. The decimal expansions of irrational numbers lack this uniformity.

Like the rational numbers, the real numbers are linearly ordered by $\leq$ in a dense chain with no minimal or maximal elements, but the ordering of the reals has an interesting feature which is absent from the ordering of the rationals. We can divide a linearly ordered set A into two nonempty subsets in such a way that every element of A is in exactly one of the subsets and every element of one (the *lower subset*) is less than every element of the other (the *higher subset*). Let's refer to any such division of a linearly ordered set as a *cut*. Notice that if we arrange the elements of A in a line representing their ordering, a cut will split the line into two segments.

Cuts can be classified in three categories, known as jumps, gaps and continuous cuts. *Jumps* are cuts in which the lower subset has a last element and the higher subset has a first element. *Gaps* are cuts in which the lower subset has no last element and the higher subset has no first element. And *continuous cuts* are those in which either the lower subset has a last element but the higher subset doesn't have a first element or the higher subset has a first element but the lower subset doesn't have a last element.

No cut in a dense ordering can be a jump. For if the lower subset had a last element l, and the higher subset had a first element f, there wouldn't be any elements between l and f. Hence neither the ordering of the rationals nor the ordering of the reals has jumps. Both orderings have continuous cuts. Thus, e.g., we obtain a continuous cut in either ordering if we let the lower subset be the set of all rational/real numbers up to and including 0. Then the higher subset would have no first element, since for every positive rational/real number, there is a smaller positive rational/real number.

What brings the ordering of the rationals and the ordering of the reals apart is that the former has gaps, but the latter doesn't. We get a gap in the ordering of the rationals if we let the lower subset be the set of all rational numbers smaller than $\sqrt{2}$ (in the ordering of the reals). Then the lower subset would have no last element and the higher subset would have no first element, since for every rational number a there is another rational number which is closer to $\sqrt{2}$ than a. In the ordering of the reals, by contrast, this is not a possibility. Every cut in the ordering of the reals is a continuous cut. This is expressed by saying that $\leq$ is a *continuous ordering* of the set of real numbers. For this reason, the ordering of the reals is sometimes known as *the continuum*.

One of the main assets of set theory is the possibility of constructing these number systems as collections of sets, i.e. to find, for each of them, a collection of sets which exhibits the same structure, and to derive its properties from set-theoretic principles (see Chapter 6, §6). These constructions are presented in most introductions to set theory. Here we shall ignore this possibility, treating numbers as independently given objects.

Chapter 2

Propositional Logic

1. Introduction

Many propositions can be characterized as built from other propositions in such a way that the truth value of the compound is uniquely determined by the truth values of the components. We find this kind of structure, e.g., in the proposition that Mars is a planet which has no satellites, which can be characterized as built from the propositions that Mars is a planet and that Mars has satellites in such a way that the compound is true if the first component is true and the second false, and false otherwise. When a proposition can be characterized along these lines, we shall say that it is a *truth-functional compound*.

This phenomenon is of logical interest because the patterns according to which truth-functional compounds are built from their components can generate links between the truth values of propositions. In particular, they are responsible for many instances of logical consequence. Take, e.g., the propositions (1) that either there are secret exits or the fugitive is in the building, (2) that the fugitive is not in the building and (3) that there are secret exits. The propositions that there are secret exits and that the fugitive is in the building figure in (1), (2) and (3) in such a way that if (1) and (2) are true, (3) must also be true. The area of logic dealing with these issues is known as *propositional logic*. Our goal in this chapter will be to present some of the main ideas of propositional logic. Both these ideas and the techniques we shall use to deal with them will play an important role in our discussion of first-order logic in subsequent chapters.

Truth functional compounds seem to be generated by a few *composition devices*. Negation is one of them. By negating the proposition that Mars has satellites, we form the proposition that Mars has no satellites, which is true if the proposition that Mars has satellites is false, and false otherwise. Conjunction is another device of this kind. The conjunction of the propositions that Mars is a planet and that Mars has satellites is the proposition that Mars is a planet which has satellites, which is true if the propositions from which it is formed are both true, and false otherwise. These and other composition devices can be combined to generate further truth-functional compounds. Thus, e.g., the conjunction of the proposition that Mars is a planet and the negation of the proposition that Mars has satellites is the proposition that Mars is a planet which has no satellites.

We are going to study the way in which composition devices of this kind can be used to generate truth-functional compounds. We are going to focus on four composition devices: *negation, conjunction, (inclusive) disjunction* and *material implication*. We shall see later on that our decision to concentrate on these particular composition devices is to some extent arbitrary, since many other collections of devices would do exactly the same job. It will be useful to introduce some terminology to speak about truth-functional compounds. We shall say that the negation of a proposition A is a *negative* proposition and A the proposition it negates. We shall say that the conjunction of two propositions A and B is a *conjunctive* proposition and that A and B are its *conjuncts*. Similarly, we shall say that the (inclusive) disjunction of two propositions A and B is a *disjunctive* proposition and that A and B are its *disjuncts*. Finally we shall refer to a proposition built with material implication as a *material conditional*, to its first component as its *antecedent*, and to its second component as its *consequent*.

The features of composition devices that we are interested in can be usefully divided into *syntactic* and *semantic* features. Syntactically characterized, negation is a device for forming a proposition with any other proposition as its component. Conjunction, disjunction and material implication are devices for forming a proposition with any two propositions as its components. The semantic features of composition devices that we want to study consist in the way in which they make the truth values of compounds depend on the truth values of their components. We have already characterized negation and conjunction in these terms. A negative proposition is true if the proposition that it negates is false, and false otherwise, and a conjunctive proposition is true if both its conjuncts are true, and false otherwise. Disjunction and material implication can be characterized along the same lines. A disjunctive proposition is false if both its disjuncts are false, and true otherwise, and a material conditional is false if its antecedent is true and its consequent false, and true otherwise.

We are going to treat these characterizations of composition devices as stipulations. Nevertheless, they provide a fairly accurate representation of the behavior of the propositions that we normally describe as negative and conjunctive, and of many of those that we describe as disjunctive. Thus, e.g., the propositions that the fugitive is not in the building is true if the proposition that the fugitive is in the building is false, and false otherwise. The proposition that there are secret exits and the fugitive is in the building is true if the propositions that there are secret exits and that the fugitive is in the building are both true, and false otherwise. The proposition that either there are secret exits or the fugitive is in the building is false if the propositions that there are secret exits and that the fugitive is in the building are both false, and true otherwise.

Conditionals are a different matter. The proposition that if there are no secret exits, then the fugitive is in the building is certainly false if the proposition that there are no secret exits is true and the proposition that the fugitive is in the building is false. But the other combinations of truth values for antecedent and consequent don't seem to single out a unique truth value for the conditional. In those cases, the truth value of the conditional seems to depend on additional factors. Suppose, e.g., that antecedent and consequent are both true, i.e. that there are no secret exits and the fugitive is in the building. We may want to say that in this case the truth value of the conditional depends on whether there are other ways, beside secret exits, in which the fugitive could have left the building. As this example suggests, many conditional propositions do not seem to behave like material conditionals, not because they behave like a different kind of truth-functional compound, but because they don't behave like truth-functional compounds at all. Nevertheless, since it is truth-functional compounds that we are interested in, material conditionals are the only kind of conditionals we shall discuss.

Our main goal is going to be to study the syntactic and semantic features of negation, conjunction, disjunction and material implication. For this purpose, we are going to focus on the following scenario. Suppose that we start with a collection of propositions which we shall call *basic propositions*, to mark the fact that we are going to treat them as potential components of truth-functional compounds without taking any notice of the structure that they themselves may exhibit. We shall assume that each basic proposition is either true or false. We can use our composition devices to form truth-functional compounds whose components are basic propositions. These compounds can in turn figure as components in further compounds, etc. To study the syntactic features of composition devices, we are going to consider how they can generate truth functional compounds from basic propositions. To study the semantic features of composition devices, we are going to consider how the truth values of the compounds generated in this way are determined by the truth values of their components.

We are going to study these phenomena with the help of a formal language. The way in which truth-functional compounds are built from their components is mirrored to some extent by the English sentences which express them. Thus, e.g., a conjunctive proposition can often be expressed by a sentence of the form "*A* and *B*," where "*A*" and "*B*" are sentences which express its conjuncts. A similar correlation obtains between negation and sentences of the form "it is not the case that *A*," between disjunction and sentences of the form "either *A* or *B*," and between material implication and sentences of the form "if *A* then *B*." Using this correlation, we could study the syntactic and semantic features of composition devices by looking at the English constructions corresponding to them. But this way of proceeding would be marred by the complexity of the correlation between composition devices and English constructions. A composition pattern can be represented by several grammatical structures, and a grammatical structure can represent several composition patterns.

The idea of using a language to study the behavior of composition devices would be much more appealing if we had at our disposal a language with just the right structure—whose sentences are built from basic components according to principles that can be neatly correlated with the ways in which composition devices generate truth-functional compounds from basic propositions. No one speaks such a language, but to study the structure of truth-functional compounds we don't need to use a language which is actually used by a community as a means of communication. We can simply define a language to suit our needs.

We can see what would be involved in the task of defining a language if we reflect that an English sentence is a string of English words put together according to the rules of English grammar. Thus, if we call the set of English words W, an English sentence can be seen as a tuple whose members are elements of W. But not all tuples of elements of W are English sentences. The six-tuple ⟨"the", "cat", "is", "on", "the", "mat"⟩ is one, but the triple ⟨"is", "cat", "the"⟩ isn't. For the former respects the rules of English grammar, but the latter doesn't. If we pretend that English grammar is fully determinate, we can say that its rules define the set of tuples of elements of W which are English sentences.

From this point of view, in order to define a language we have to start by designating a set V as its *vocabulary*. We shall refer to the elements of the vocabulary of a formal language as the *symbols* of the language. A language with V as its vocabulary will be a set of (finite) tuples of elements of V. Then we have to specify which tuples of elements of V are going to count as *sentences* of the language, i.e. to define the set of sentences of the language. We will sometimes identify the language with this set. Languages which are explicitly defined in this way are known as *formal languages*.

Formal languages constitute a very powerful tool for the study of the structure of propositions. Starting in Chapter 3, we shall use formal languages to study the way in which first-order propositions are built from properties, relations and individuals. In this chapter we are going to introduce the technique by applying it to the study of the syntactic and semantic features of composition devices.

2. Induction and Formal Languages

Using the relation ...*is an ancestor of*..., defined on the set of people, we can easily define the set Q containing Queen Victoria and all her ancestors as the set $\{x \mid x$ is Queen Victoria or x is an ancestor of Queen Victoria$\}$. Suppose however that we wanted to define Q, not in terms of the relation ...*is an ancestor of*..., but in terms of the functions pairing each person with his or her mother and with his or her father. We could, perhaps, try something like $\{x \mid x$ is Queen Victoria, or x is Queen Victoria's mother, or x is Queen Victoria's father, or x is Queen Victoria's mother's mother, or...$\}$, but this approach would only enable us to define the set containing Queen Victoria and her ancestors *up to a certain generation*. A more promising idea would be to define Q as the set satisfying the following three conditions:

(1) Queen Victoria is an element of Q.

(2) The mother and father of each element of Q are also elements of Q.

(3) Q contains no other elements beside those which are required to satisfy (1) and (2); i.e. no proper subset of Q satisfies (1) and (2).

Intuitively, (1) and (2) ensure that Q contains Queen Victoria and all her ancestors, since, by (1), Q contains Queen Victoria, and, by (2), Q contains her mother and father, and, again by (2), Q contains the mother and father of each of these, etc. And (3) guarantees that Q contains nothing else, for the set containing nothing but Queen Victoria and her ancestors satisfies (1) and (2), and any other set which satisfies (1) and (2) will have it as a proper subset.

This definition of Q exemplifies a procedure for defining sets known as *inductive definition* (or *definition by induction*). We can simplify matters by presenting it as a method for defining a subset B of a given set A—in the case of Q, for example, as a subset of the set of all people. Every inductive definition proceeds in three stages. At the first stage, known as the *base*, we stipulate that certain elements of A will be elements of B. Thus the base of our definition of Q is (1), in which we stipulate that Queen Victoria will be an element of Q. The second stage is a (finite or infinite) series of *inductive clauses*. Each inductive clause uses a function f in A, of any number of argument-places, and stipulates that B contains the image under f of every element (or tuple of elements) of B; i.e. if f is an n-place function in A, an inductive clause of the definition of B using f would stipulate that, for all $a_1, ..., a_n \in B, f(a_1, ..., a_n) \in B$. Thus, our inductive definition of Q contains two inductive clauses (expressed by (2)), using the functions pairing each person with his or her mother and with his or her father. Each of them stipulates that, for every person x, if x is an element of Q, then the image of x under the relevant function (i.e. x's mother or x's father) is also an element of Q. The final stage of an inductive definition is a *closure clause* ((3) in our definition of Q), stipulating that no proper subset of B satisfies the base and the inductive clauses of the definition.

Intuitively, we can see an inductively defined set as "growing" from its base by successive applications of the inductive clauses. Thus we can see Q as starting with Queen Victoria as its only element, and then spreading to encompass her mother and father, and then the mother and father of each of these, etc. An inductively defined set may be infinite, but each of its elements "enters" the set after a finite sequence of applications of the inductive clauses to the objects in the base.

We are going to treat inductive definition as a valid method for defining sets, and we will make heavy use of it throughout the book. In so doing, we are assuming that for every inductive definition there is exactly one set satisfying it. Using the set-theoretic notions introduced in Chapter 1, we can prove that this is so. In fact, we can provide in each case a definition by abstraction of the unique set satisfying a given inductive definition. The idea is that, for every inductive definition of a subset of A, the intersection of all the subsets of A which satisfy the base and the inductive clauses of the definition will satisfy the base, the inductive clauses and the closure clause, and no other set will.

We shall prove here that this result holds for our inductive definition of Q. The general result can be proved in the same way, although notational complexities make the proof more cumbersome. Consider the collection C of the sets of people which contain Queen Victoria and the mother and father of each of their elements, i.e. $C = \{X \mid X$ is a subset of the set of persons, Queen Victoria is an element of X, and, for every person y, if y is an element of X, then y's mother and father are also elements of $X\}$. The following lemma expresses the result that the intersection of C is the unique set of persons satisfying the base, inductive clauses and closure clause of our definition of Q.

LEMMA 2. 1: $\bigcap C$ satisfies (1), (2) and (3), and no other set does.

Proof: That $\bigcap C$ satisfies (1) follows from the fact Queen Victoria is an element of every set in C and the definition of $\bigcap$. To see that $\bigcap C$ satisfies (2), assume towards a contradiction that there is a person a such that a is in $\bigcap C$ but a's father (or a's mother) is not in $\bigcap C$. Then, by the definition of $\bigcap$, a is an element of every set in C, but there is at least one set in C which doesn't contain a's father (or a's mother), which contradicts the hypothesis that every set in C contains the mother and father of each of its elements. To see that $\bigcap C$ satisfies (3), assume towards a contradiction that there is a set A such that Queen Victoria is an element of A, A contains the mother and father of each of its elements, and A is a proper subset of $\bigcap C$. Then, by the definition of $\bigcap$, $A \notin C$, which contradicts the hypothesis that C contains all the sets of persons containing Queen Victoria and the mother and father of each of their elements.

To see that $\bigcap C$ is the only set of persons satisfying (1), (2) and (3), assume, towards a contradiction, that there is a set B of persons different from $\bigcap C$ which satisfies (1), (2) and (3). Since B satisfies (1) and (2), it will have to be one of the sets in C. Then, by the definition of $\bigcap$, $\bigcap C \subseteq B$, and, since $\bigcap C \neq B$, $\bigcap C \subset B$. But this contradicts the hypothesis that B satisfies (3), since $\bigcap C$ is a proper subset of B which satisfies (1) and (2).∎

Inductive definitions are widely used in mathematics. We can use the method, e.g., to define the set $\mathbf{Z}^+$ of the positive integers as a subset of the set $\mathbf{Q}$ of the rationals. The definition would go as follows:

1. *Base*: $1 \in \mathbf{Z}^+$.

2. *Inductive Clause*: For every $x \in \mathbf{Z}^+, x + 1 \in \mathbf{Z}^+$.

3. Nothing else is in $\mathbf{Z}^+$.

EXERCISE 2. 2: Define by induction the set $\mathbf{Z}$ of the integers (as a subset of $\mathbf{Q}$).

Hint: Use two inductive clauses, using the functions $f(x) = x + 1$ and $g(x) = x - 1$.

EXERCISE 2. 3: Define by induction the set of odd positive integers (as a subset of $\mathbf{Z}^+$).

EXERCISE 2. 4: Define by induction the subset of $\mathbf{Z}^+$ containing the powers of 6, i.e. 6, 6^2, 6^3 ....

Inductive definitions are also one of the fundamental tools of contemporary logic. They are particularly useful for defining formal languages. As we saw in §1, a formal language is a set of tuples whose members are drawn from the elements of a given set—the vocabulary or set of symbols of the language. We can use the inductive method to define the set of tuples of elements of a given vocabulary that we are going to treat as sentences of a formal language.

The base and closure clause of an inductive definition of a formal language work as in any other inductive definition. The base stipulates that certain tuples are sentences of the language, and the closure clause stipulates that the language only contains those tuples which are required to satisfy the base and the inductive clauses of the definition.

Each inductive clause of a definition of a formal language uses a function in the set of tuples of elements of the vocabulary. The functions that are normally used for this task are known as *concatenation functions*. The *concatenation* of two tuples t and u (written tu) is the tuple whose members are the members of t, in the order in which they appear in t, followed by the members of u, in the order in which they appear in u. Thus, e.g., the concatenation of $\langle a, b, c \rangle$ and $\langle c, a \rangle$ is the tuple $\langle a, b, c, c, a \rangle$. Concatenation functions are based on this notion. Let A be the set $\{a, b, c, d\}$, and let T be the set of tuples (including one-tuples) of elements of A. An n-place concatenation function in T will single out as the image of n elements of T the tuple that results from concatenating them in a certain order, possibly with other fixed elements of T. Thus, e.g., we can define a one-place concatenation function in T as follows: for every $t \in T, f(t) = \langle a \rangle t$. Then the image of $\langle b, c, b \rangle$ under f will be the concatenation of $\langle a \rangle$ and $\langle b, c, b \rangle$, i.e. the tuple $\langle a, b, c, b \rangle$, and the image of this tuple under f will be the tuple $\langle a, a, b, c, b \rangle$. As an example of a two-place concatenation function in T consider the function defined as follows: for all $t, u \in T, g(t, u) = t\langle b, b \rangle u\langle d \rangle$. Thus, e.g., the image of $\langle a, a, d \rangle$ and $\langle c \rangle$ under g is the tuple $\langle a, a, d, b, b, c, d \rangle$.

EXERCISE 2. 5: Choose five tuples in T and indicate their images under f and the images under f of their images under f.

EXERCISE 2. 6: Choose five pairs of tuples in *T* and for each of the chosen pairs indicate $g(x, y)$, $g(x, f(y))$ and $g(g(x, y), f(g(y, x)))$, where *x* and *y* are the two chosen tuples.

EXERCISE 2. 7: Define two three-place concatenation functions in *T*. Give some examples of the image that each of these functions assigns to three tuples in *T*.

We can see these ideas at work in the following example. Let *a*, *b* and * be three different objects, let *A* be the set {*a*, *b*, *}* and let *T* be the set of (finite) tuples (including 1-tuples) of elements of *A*. We can define by induction a language *L* with *A* as its vocabulary as follows (we shall adopt the convention of using lower case letters of the Greek alphabet to stand for arbitrary tuples).

1. *Base*: $\langle a, *, b \rangle \in L$ and $\langle b, *, a \rangle \in L$.

2. *Inductive Clause*: For all $\phi, \psi \in L$, $\phi\langle*\rangle\psi \in L$.

3. Nothing else is in *L*.

Notice that the inductive clause of the definition of *L* uses the concatenation function defined as follows: for all $\phi, \psi \in T$, $f(\phi, \psi) = \phi\langle*\rangle\psi$. It stipulates that for any two elements of *L*, *L* contains their image under *f*. To improve the appearance of the sentences of formal languages, from now on we shall represent tuples of elements of the vocabulary of a language by writing the members of the tuple in the right order, without angle brackets or commas. Now our definition of *L* will look like this:

1. *Base*: $a*b \in L$ and $b*a \in L$.

2. *Inductive Clause*: For all $\phi, \psi \in L$, $\phi*\psi \in L$.

3. Nothing else is in *L*.

Each sentence of an inductively defined formal language can be generated by successive applications of the inductive clauses to the sentences in the base. Thus, in the case of *L*, we have, e.g., that, by the base, $a*b \in L$. By the inductive clause, it follows from this that $a*b*a*b \in L$, and by the base and the inductive clause again, it follows from this that $a*b*a*b*b*a \in L$.

EXERCISE 2. 8: Find three *L*-sentences each generated by five applications of the inductive clause, and three tuples in *T* which are not *L*-sentences.

One of the main advantages of defining a set by induction is that it enables us to use a very powerful method of proof, known as *proof by in-*

duction, to establish a claim about every element of the set. To prove by induction that every element of an inductively defined set A has a property P, we proceed in two stages. First we prove that every object in the base of the definition of A has property P. Then we prove that the function used in each inductive clause of the definition "preserves P" in A, i.e., in the case of a one-place function, that if an element of A has P, then its image under the function also has P, and in general, for an n-place function, that if n elements of A have P, then their image under the function also has P. This stage of the proof is known as *inductive step*. These two stages complete a proof by induction of the claim that every element of A has P.

To see that this is a valid procedure for establishing that every element of A has P, notice that a proof with this structure will show that P is present in every object in the base and in every object that results from successive applications of the inductive clauses to the objects in the base. And this is all we need, since, as we have seen, these objects are the only elements of A. Alternatively, we can reason that an inductive proof establishes that the set of objects with property P satisfies the base and the inductive clauses of the definition of A, but we know that A is a subset of every set with these features. Hence an inductive proof establishes that every element of A has P by showing that A is a subset of the set of objects in which P is present.

We are going to use the method of proof by induction repeatedly to establish claims about every sentence of an inductively defined formal language, and it is important to understand how inductive proofs work. The proof of the following lemma provides the first application of the method.

LEMMA 2. 9: For every L-sentence ϕ, the first three symbols of ϕ are either $a*b$ or $b*a$, and the last three symbols of ϕ are either $a*b$ or $b*a$.

Proof: We prove the lemma by induction.

Base: First we have to prove that every L-sentence in the base has the relevant property, i.e. that in $a*b$ and in $b*a$ the first three symbols are either $a*b$ or $b*a$ and the last three symbols are either $a*b$ or $b*a$. It is obvious that this holds.

Inductive step: Then we need to show that the inductive clause preserves this property in L, i.e. that for all ϕ, $\psi \in L$, if ϕ and ψ have the property so does $\phi*\psi$. This claim is a universal implication, and we can prove it using the method presented in Chapter 1. Thus let α, $\beta \in L$, and assume that in both α and β the first three symbols are either $a*b$ or $b*a$ and the last three symbols are either $a*b$ or $b*a$. (The assumption that plays this role in an inductive proof is known as *inductive hypothesis*, abbreviated IH.) We need to prove from this assumption that in α*β the first three symbols are either *a*b* or *b*a* and the last three symbols are either *a*b* or *b*a*. But this follows directly, since the first three symbols of α*β are the first three symbols of α, and the last three symbols of α*β are the last three symbols of β.   ∎

EXERCISE 2. 10: Show that for every *L*-sentence φ, the strings *a*a*a* and *b*b*b* do not appear in φ.

Hint: Prove by induction. Lemma 2. 9 will be useful for the inductive step.

3. Syntax

We want to use the techniques developed in the preceding section to study the syntactic and semantic features of composition devices—how they generate truth-functional compounds and how the truth values of the compounds that they generate are determined by the truth values of their components. To study the syntactic features of composition devices, we are going to use the inductive method to define a formal language which models the way in which they generate truth-functional compounds from a given range of basic propositions. The sentences in the base will play the role of basic propositions, and the inductive clauses will play the role of composition devices. The sentences which are generated by successive applications of the inductive clauses to the sentences in the base will play the role of truth-functional compounds. Then, to study the semantic features of composition devices, we shall use this formal language to model the way in which the truth values of the compounds that they generate are determined by the truth values of their components.

   We shall refer to the formal language that we are going to define for this purpose as *PL*. The vocabulary of *PL* will have three categories of symbols. First, it will contain a range of symbols playing the role of basic propositions. We shall refer to these symbols as *atoms*. The vocabulary of *PL* will contain infinitely many different atoms. Second, the vocabulary of *PL* will contain symbols corresponding to our chosen composition devices: the *negation symbol*, represented as ¬, the *conjunction symbol*, represented as ∧, the *disjunction symbol*, represented as ∨, and the *conditional symbol*, represented as →. We shall refer to these symbols as *connectives*. Third, the vocabulary of *PL* will contain two auxiliary symbols: the *left-hand bracket*, represented as (and the *right-hand bracket*, represented as). We shall assume that ¬, ∧, ∨, →, (and) are different from each other and from each of the atoms. We shall also assume that no element of the vocabulary is identical with an n-tuple of elements of the vocabulary, for any n greater than 1. We won't make any other assumptions about the identity of the elements of the vocabulary of *PL*.

Thus, if we let A be the set of atoms, the vocabulary of *PL* will be the set $A \cup \{\neg, \wedge, \vee, \rightarrow, (,)\}$. The sentences of *PL*, also known as *PL*-sentences, will be tuples of elements of this set. Notice that, since every object is identical with the 1-tuple having it as its only member, each symbol of *PL* is also a 1-tuple of symbols of *PL*. Hence a symbol of *PL* can also be a *PL*-sentence. We define the set of *PL*-sentences by induction as follows.

1. *Base*: Every atom is in *PL*.

2. *Inductive Clauses*:
   i. For every $\phi \in PL$, $\neg\phi \in PL$.
   ii. For all $\phi, \psi \in PL$, $(\phi \wedge \psi) \in PL$.
   iii. For all $\phi, \psi \in PL$, $(\phi \vee \psi) \in PL$.
   iv. For all $\phi, \psi \in PL$, $(\phi \rightarrow \psi) \in PL$.

3. Nothing else is in *PL*.

As with other inductive definitions, the inductive clauses of the definition of *PL* can be applied repeatedly to objects in the base to generate new elements of *PL*. Thus, e.g., if a, b and c are atoms, we have, by the base, that $a, b, c \in PL$. Then, by Inductive Clause ii, $(a \wedge b) \in PL$, and by Inductive Clause i, $\neg c \in PL$. Hence, by Inductive Clause iv, $((a \wedge b) \rightarrow \neg c) \in PL$, and by another application of Inductive Clause i, we have that $\neg((a \wedge b) \rightarrow \neg c) \in PL$. Showing in this way how we can get $\neg((a \wedge b) \rightarrow \neg c)$ by applying the inductive clauses of the definition to the objects in the base amounts to proving that $\neg((a \wedge b) \rightarrow \neg c)$ is a *PL*-sentence. Notice that the inductive clauses for $\wedge$, $\vee$ and $\rightarrow$ generate a *PL*-sentence from two *PL*-sentences. We shall refer to connectives with this feature as *binary*.

EXERCISE 2. 11: Find three *PL*-sentences, each requiring six applications of the inductive clauses.

EXERCISE 2. 12: Let a, b and c be atoms. Show that each of the following tuples of symbols is a *PL*-sentence by showing how it can be generated by applying the inductive clauses of the definition to the objects in the base:
   (1) $(a \rightarrow (\neg b \vee \neg\neg a))$
   (2) $(b \wedge \neg(a \rightarrow (a \vee (c \wedge \neg b))))$
   (3) $(((c \rightarrow b) \wedge \neg a) \rightarrow \neg(c \vee b))$

We can also invoke the definition of *PL* to show that a tuple of symbols of the vocabulary of *PL* is *not* a *PL*-sentence. Take, e.g., the tuple $(a \neg\rightarrow b)$, where a and b are atoms. By the closure clause of the definition, we know that a tuple can only be a *PL*-sentence if it is an atom, a tuple of the form $\neg\alpha$, where α is a *PL*-sentence (i.e. the concatenation of $\neg$ and a *PL*-sentence), or a tuple of the form $(\alpha \wedge \beta)$, $(\alpha \vee \beta)$ or $(\alpha \rightarrow \beta)$, where α and β are *PL*-sentences (i.e. the concatenation of (, a *PL*-sentence, a binary connective, a *PL*-sentence and)). $(a \neg\rightarrow b)$ is not an atom, since we have assumed that no symbol is identical with a six-tuple of symbols. It is not of the form $\neg\alpha$ either, since its first symbol is not $\neg$. It is not of the forms $(\alpha \wedge \beta)$ or $(\alpha \vee \beta)$ either, since neither $\wedge$ nor $\vee$ occurs in it. Hence it can only be of the form $(\alpha \rightarrow \beta)$, where $a\neg$ is α and c is β. But α and β have to be *PL*-sentences, and $a\neg$ isn't one, as we could see if we went, once again, down the list of possibilities.

EXERCISE 2. 13: Let a, b and c be atoms. Show that the following tuples of symbols are not *PL*-sentences.
  (1) $(a \wedge (\neg b\, c))$
  (2) $(b \rightarrow\rightarrow a)$
  (3) $(\neg a) \vee b)$

As we saw in the preceding section, defining a set by induction enables us to use the method of proof by induction to establish that all the elements of the set have a certain property. This applies, in particular, to *PL*. We can prove by induction that all the *PL*-sentences have a certain property. The proof of the next result illustrates the application to *PL* of the inductive method of proof.

BRACKET PARITY LEMMA: For every *PL*-sentence ϕ, the number of left-hand brackets in ϕ equals the number of right-hand brackets in ϕ.

Proof: We prove this lemma by induction on *PL*.

Base: We need to prove that every atom has an equal number of left and right brackets. This is trivially true, as atoms contain no brackets of either kind.

Inductive Step: Now we need to prove that bracket parity is preserved in *PL* by the function used in each of the inductive clauses—i.e. that for every $\phi \in PL$, if ϕ has the same number of brackets of each kind, then the same goes for $\neg\phi$, and that for all ϕ, $\psi \in PL$ if each of ϕ and ψ has the same number of brackets of each kind, then the same goes for $(\phi \vee \psi)$, $(\phi \wedge \psi)$, and $(\phi \rightarrow \psi)$.

For the $\neg$-clause, let α be a *PL*-sentence with the same number of brackets of each kind. We need to prove that it follows from this that $\neg\alpha$

has the same number of brackets of each kind. This follows directly, since ¬α has the same brackets as α.

For the other inductive clauses, let α, β be *PL*-sentences each of which has the same number of brackets of each kind. We need to prove that it follows from this that the same is true of (α ∨ β), (α ∧ β) and (α → β). But this again follows directly. Since each of α and β has the same number of left and right brackets, it follows that α and β, taken together, have the same number of brackets of each kind. And it follows from this that (α ∨ β), (α ∧ β) and (α → β) also have the same number of brackets of each kind, since each of them has the same number of brackets of each kind as α and β plus one. ∎

EXERCISE 2. 14: If φ is a tuple, we say that ψ is an *initial tuple* of φ just in case, for some tuple γ, φ is the concatenation of ψ and γ; i.e. an initial tuple of φ is a tuple that results from removing some but not all the members of φ starting from the right. Show that for every *PL*-sentence α, every initial tuple of α containing at least one bracket has more left than right brackets.

Hint: Prove by induction on *PL*. Feel free to invoke the Bracket Parity Lemma.

EXERCISE 2. 15: Show that, for every *PL*-sentence φ, every initial tuple of φ containing any symbols other than ¬ contains at least one bracket.

4. Semantics

The definition of *PL* ensures that the connectives model the syntactic features of the composition devices they represent. If we think of the atoms as representing basic propositions, non-atomic *PL*-sentences will represent truth-functional compounds that the composition devices generate from them. Our next goal is to make the connectives model the semantic features of the composition devices that they represent—the way in which the truth values of the compounds they generate is determined by the truth values of their components.

We can characterize the semantic features of composition devices in the following terms: Let *P* be the set containing all the basic propositions and all the compounds that the composition devices generate from them. Consider all the possible ways of ascribing a unique truth value to each proposition in *P*. The semantic features of composition devices will rule out many of these possibilities as inadmissible. They will rule out, for example, ascriptions which yield the same truth value for a proposition and for its negation, or ascriptions which yield the value true for a conjunctive proposition and the value false for one of its conjuncts. Thus, the semantic features of composition devices can be characterized in terms of which ways of ascribing truth values to the propositions in *P* they rule out, or, equivalently, of which ways of ascribing truth values they allow.

We are going to use this idea to make the connectives model the semantic features of the composition devices that we want them to represent. Let's say that a *truth assignment on PL* (a *PL-assignment*) is a function from *PL* to the set $\{T, F\}$. We are going to think of *T* and *F* as the truth values true and false, but for our purposes all we need to assume about the identity of these objects is that they are different from each other. To model in *PL* the way in which the semantic features of composition devices classify ascriptions of truth values to the propositions in *P* as admissible or inadmissible, we define the notion of an admissible *PL-*assignment.

DEFINITION: A *PL*-assignment *v* is *admissible* just in case it satisfies the following conditions:

(i) For every *PL*-sentence of the form $\neg\alpha$,

$$v(\neg\alpha) = \begin{cases} T \text{ if } v(\alpha) = F, \\ F \text{ otherwise.} \end{cases}$$

(ii) For every *PL*-sentence of the form $(\alpha \wedge \beta)$,

$$v((\alpha \wedge \beta)) = \begin{cases} T \text{ if } v(\alpha) = v(\beta) = T, \\ F \text{ otherwise.} \end{cases}$$

(iii) For every *PL*-sentence of the form $(\alpha \vee \beta)$,

$$v((\alpha \vee \beta)) = \begin{cases} F \text{ if } v(\alpha) = v(\beta) = F, \\ T \text{ otherwise.} \end{cases}$$

(iv) For every *PL*-sentence of the form $(\alpha \rightarrow \beta)$,

$$v((\alpha \rightarrow \beta)) = \begin{cases} F \text{ if } v(\alpha) = T \text{ and } v(\beta) = F, \\ T \text{ otherwise.} \end{cases}$$

These conditions are also expressed by the tables of Figure 2. We can see how this definition makes the connectives model the semantic features of the composition devices we want them to represent. Thus, e.g., just as the semantic features of negation rule out the possibility that a negative proposition has the same truth value as the proposition it negates, it follows from the definition of admissibility that if v is an admissible *PL*-assignment, then for every *PL*-sentence ϕ, $v(\neg\phi) \neq v(\phi)$. Similarly, just as the semantic features of conjunction make it impossible that a conjunctive proposition is true if one of its conjuncts is false, it follows from the definition of admissibility that for every admissible *PL*-assignment v and all *PL*-sentences ϕ, ψ, if $v(\phi) = F$, then $v(\phi \wedge \psi) = v(\psi \wedge \phi) = F$.

α	$\neg\alpha$
T	F
F	T

α	β	$(\alpha \wedge \beta)$	$(\alpha \vee \beta)$	$(\alpha \rightarrow \beta)$
T	T	T	T	T
T	F	F	T	F
F	T	F	T	T
F	F	F	F	T

Figure 2

We said in §1 that the patterns according to which truth-functional compounds are built from their components are responsible for many instances of logical consequence. We can now use the notion of admissible *PL*-assignment to model in *PL* the relation of logical consequence that these patterns generate, as well as other related notions.

DEFINITION: A *PL*-sentence ϕ is a *logical consequence* of a set Γ of *PL*-sentences, written $\Gamma \vDash \phi$, just in case for every admissible *PL*-assignment v, if $v(\gamma) = T$ for every $\gamma \in \Gamma$, then $v(\phi) = T$. (When ϕ is not a logical consequence of Γ, we write $\Gamma \nvDash \phi$.)

Notice that, according to the definition, the only way in which ϕ can fail to be a logical consequence of Γ is if there is an admissible *PL*-assignment v such that (i) $v(\gamma) = T$ for every $\gamma \in \Gamma$, but (ii) $v(\phi) = F$. If no such truth assignment exists, then $\Gamma \vDash \phi$. Hence to prove that ϕ is a logical consequence of Γ, we need to establish that no admissible *PL*-assignment has these two features.

We present the procedure for establishing logical consequence claims with an example. Let α, β, γ be three *PL*-sentences. To prove that $(\alpha \rightarrow \gamma)$ is a logical consequence of $\{(\alpha \rightarrow \beta), (\beta \rightarrow \gamma)\}$, we will have to show that, for every admissible *PL*-assignment v, if $v((\alpha \rightarrow \beta)) = v((\beta \rightarrow \gamma)) = T$, then $v((\alpha \rightarrow \gamma)) = T$. This claim has the form of a universal implication. We prove it using the standard procedure described in Chapter 1. Let v be an admissible *PL*-assignment such that $v((\alpha \rightarrow \beta)) = v((\beta \rightarrow \gamma)) = T$. We want to show that it follows from this that $v((\alpha \rightarrow \gamma)) = T$. We reason as follows:

$v((\alpha \to \beta)) = v((\beta \to \gamma)) = T$

$\Downarrow$ (by the definition of admissibility)

(i) It is not the case that $v(\alpha) = T$ and $v(\beta) = F$, and (ii) it is not the case that $v(\beta) = T$ and $v(\gamma) = F$

$\Downarrow$ (since, if $v(\alpha) = T$, then, by (i), $v(\beta) = T$, and then, by (ii), $v(\gamma) = T$)

It is not the case that $v(\alpha) = T$ and $v(\gamma) = F$

$\Downarrow$ (by the definition of admissibility)

$v((\alpha \to \gamma)) = T$

EXERCISE 2. 16: Show that for all *PL*-sentences α, β, γ, the following claims hold:
  (1) $\{\alpha, \beta\} \vDash (\alpha \wedge \beta)$
  (2) $\{(\alpha \wedge \beta)\} \vDash \alpha$ and $\{(\alpha \wedge \beta)\} \vDash \beta$
  (3) $\{\alpha\} \vDash (\alpha \vee \beta)$ and $\{\beta\} \vDash (\alpha \vee \beta)$
  (4) $\{(\alpha \vee \beta), (\alpha \to \gamma), (\beta \to \gamma)\} \vDash \gamma$
  (5) $\{(\alpha \to \beta), \alpha\} \vDash \beta$
  (6) $\{\alpha, \neg\alpha\} \vDash \beta$

Hint: For (1)–(5), proceed as with $\{(\alpha \to \beta), (\beta \to \gamma)\} \vDash (\alpha \to \gamma)$, above. Prove (6) by *reductio*, assuming, towards a contradiction, that there is an admissible *PL*-assignment v such that $v(\alpha) = v(\neg\alpha) = T$ and $v(\beta) = F$.

EXERCISE 2. 17: Show that for all *PL*-sentences α, β, γ, δ, the following claims hold:
  (1) $\{\neg(\beta \to \alpha)\} \vDash (\alpha \to \beta)$
  (2) $\{(\alpha \to \beta), (\alpha \wedge \gamma)\} \vDash (\beta \wedge \gamma)$
  (3) $\{(\alpha \vee \beta), \neg\beta\} \vDash \alpha$
  (4) $\{\alpha, \neg\beta\} \vDash (\alpha \to \beta) \to \gamma$
  (5) $\{(\alpha \to \neg\beta), (\gamma \to \beta)\} \vDash \neg(\alpha \wedge \gamma)$
  (6) $\{(\alpha \to \gamma), (\beta \to \delta)\} \vDash ((\alpha \wedge \beta) \to (\gamma \wedge \delta))$
  (7) $\{(\alpha \to \gamma), \neg(\beta \to \gamma)\} \vDash \neg(\beta \to \alpha)$

EXERCISE 2. 18: Show that for all *PL*-sentences ϕ, ψ, α, and all sets of *PL*-sentences Γ, Δ, Σ, the following claims hold:
  (1) If $\phi \in \Gamma$, then $\Gamma \vDash \phi$
  (2) If $\Gamma \vDash \phi$ and $\Delta \vDash \psi$, then $\Gamma \cup \Delta \vDash (\phi \wedge \psi)$
  (3) If $\Gamma \vDash (\phi \wedge \psi)$, then $\Gamma \vDash \phi$ and $\Gamma \vDash \psi$
  (4) If $\Gamma \vDash \phi$ or $\Gamma \vDash \psi$, then $\Gamma \vDash (\phi \vee \psi)$

(5) If $\Gamma \vDash (\phi \vee \psi)$, $\Delta \cup \{\phi\} \vDash \alpha$ and $\Sigma \cup \{\psi\} \vDash \alpha$,
 then $\Gamma \cup \Delta \cup \Sigma \vDash \alpha$

(6) If $\Gamma \cup \{\phi\} \vDash \psi$, then $\Gamma \vDash (\phi \to \psi)$

(7) If $\Gamma \vDash \phi$ and $\Delta \vDash (\phi \to \psi)$, then $\Gamma \cup \Delta \vDash \psi$

(8) If $\Gamma \cup \{\phi\} \vDash \psi$, and $\Delta \cup \{\phi\} \vDash \neg\psi$, then $\Gamma \cup \Delta \vDash \neg\phi$

(9) If $\Gamma \vDash \neg\neg\phi$, then $\Gamma \vDash \phi$

Hint: Assume the antecedent and, proceeding as with $\{(\alpha \to \beta), (\beta \to \gamma)\} \vDash (\alpha \to \gamma)$, try to show that the consequent follows.

EXERCISE 2. 19: Show that for all *PL*-sentences ϕ, ψ, and all sets of *PL*-sentences Γ, Δ, the following claims hold:

(1) If $\Gamma \vDash \phi$ and $\Gamma \subseteq \Delta$, then $\Delta \vDash \phi$

(2) If $\Delta \vDash \phi$, and $\Gamma \vDash \delta$ for every $\delta \in \Delta$, then $\Gamma \vDash \phi$

(3) If $\Gamma \vDash \phi$ and $\Delta \cup \{\phi\} \vDash \psi$, then $\Gamma \cup \Delta \vDash \psi$

(4) If $\Gamma \vDash \phi$, then $\Gamma \vDash \neg\neg\phi$

(5) If $\Gamma \vDash \phi$, then $\Gamma \vDash \neg(\neg\phi \wedge \neg\psi)$

(6) If $\Gamma \vDash \psi$ and $\Delta \vDash \neg\psi$, then $\Gamma \cup \Delta \vDash \phi$

(7) If $\Gamma \cup \{\phi\} \vDash \psi$, then $\Gamma \cup \{\neg\psi\} \vDash \neg\phi$

(8) If $\Gamma \cup \{\neg\psi\} \vDash \phi$, then $\Gamma \vDash (\phi \vee \psi)$

EXERCISE 2. 20: Let a, b, c be atoms. Establish the following claims:

(1) $\{(a \vee b), a\} \nvDash \neg b$

(2) $\{(a \to b), b\} \nvDash a$

(3) $\{(a \to (b \to c)), (a \vee b)\} \nvDash c$

Hint: To prove that a *PL*-sentence ϕ is not a logical consequence of a set Γ of *PL*-sentences, you just need to show that we can assign the value T to every element of Γ and the value F to ϕ without violating the conditions of the definition of admissibility.

We can now define in terms of the notion of admissible *PL*-assignment a few related concepts.

DEFINITION: Two *PL*-sentences ϕ, ψ are *logically equivalent*, written $\phi \rightleftharpoons \psi$, just in case, for every admissible *PL*-assignment v, $v(\phi) = v(\psi)$.

DEFINITION: A set Γ of *PL*-sentences is *satisfiable* just in case there is at least one admissible *PL*-assignment v such that, for every $\gamma \in \Gamma$, $v(\gamma) = T$. Otherwise Γ is *unsatisfiable*.

DEFINITION: A *PL*-sentence ϕ is *logically true*, written $\vDash \phi$, just in case, for every admissible *PL*-assignment v, $v(\phi) = T$.

EXERCISE 2. 21: Show that for all *PL*-sentences α, β, the following claims hold:

(1) $\vDash (\alpha \rightarrow (\beta \rightarrow \alpha))$
(2) $\vDash (\alpha \vee \neg\alpha)$
(3) $\vDash \neg(\alpha \wedge \neg\alpha)$
(4) $\vDash (\alpha \rightarrow (\neg\alpha \rightarrow \beta))$
(5) $\vDash ((\alpha \rightarrow \neg\alpha) \rightarrow \neg\alpha)$
(6) $\vDash (((\alpha \rightarrow \beta) \rightarrow \alpha) \rightarrow \alpha)$

EXERCISE 2. 22: Show that for all *PL*-sentences α, β, γ, the following claims hold:

(1) $(\alpha \vee \beta) \doteq (\beta \vee \alpha)$
(2) $(\alpha \wedge \beta) \doteq (\beta \wedge \alpha)$
(3) $((\alpha \vee \beta) \vee \gamma) \doteq (\alpha \vee (\beta \vee \gamma))$
(4) $((\alpha \wedge \beta) \wedge \gamma) \doteq (\alpha \wedge (\beta \wedge \gamma))$
(5) $(\alpha \wedge (\beta \vee \gamma)) \doteq ((\alpha \wedge \beta) \vee (\alpha \wedge \gamma))$
(6) $(\alpha \vee (\beta \wedge \gamma)) \doteq ((\alpha \vee \beta) \wedge (\alpha \vee \gamma))$
(7) $\neg(\alpha \vee \beta) \doteq (\neg\alpha \wedge \neg\beta)$
(8) $\neg(\alpha \wedge \beta) \doteq (\neg\alpha \vee \neg\beta)$

(The fact that (1) and (2) hold is expressed by saying that $\vee$ and $\wedge$ are *commutative*. The fact that (3) and (4) hold is expressed by saying that $\vee$ and $\wedge$ are *associative*. (5) and (6) are known as the *distributive laws*, and (7) and (8) as the *de Morgan laws*. Compare with Exercise 1. 15)

Hint: By the definition of $\doteq$, the claim that $\phi \doteq \psi$ is the claim that, for every admissible *PL*-assignment v, $v(\phi) = T$ if and only if $v(\psi) = T$. This claim has the form of a universal equivalence. See Chapter 1 for the standard strategy for dealing with claims of this form.

EXERCISE 2. 23: Show that for all *PL*-sentences α, β, γ, the following claims hold:

(1) $(\alpha \wedge \beta) \doteq \neg(\neg\alpha \vee \neg\beta)$
(2) $(\alpha \wedge \beta) \doteq \neg(\alpha \rightarrow \neg\beta)$
(3) $(\alpha \vee \beta) \doteq \neg(\neg\alpha \wedge \neg\beta)$
(4) $(\alpha \vee \beta) \doteq (\neg\alpha \rightarrow \beta)$
(5) $(\alpha \rightarrow \beta) \doteq \neg(\alpha \wedge \neg\beta)$
(6) $(\alpha \rightarrow \beta) \doteq (\neg\alpha \vee \beta)$

(Notice that it follows from this exercise that each binary connective can be "defined" in terms of each of the other two and $\neg$. See §8, below, for the consequences of this fact)

EXERCISE 2. 24: Show that for all *PL*-sentences α, β, γ, the following claims hold:

(1) $(\alpha \rightarrow \beta) \doteq (\neg\beta \rightarrow \neg\alpha)$
(2) $(\alpha \rightarrow (\beta \rightarrow \gamma)) \doteq ((\alpha \wedge \beta) \rightarrow \gamma)$

    (3) $(\alpha \wedge (\alpha \vee \beta)) \rightleftharpoons \alpha$
    (4) $(\alpha \vee (\alpha \wedge \beta)) \rightleftharpoons \alpha$
    (5) $\alpha \rightleftharpoons \neg\neg\alpha$

EXERCISE 2. 25: Let ϕ be a logically true *PL*-sentence. Prove that, for every set Γ of *PL*-sentences, $\Gamma \vDash \phi$.

EXERCISE 2. 26: Let Γ be an unsatisfiable set of *PL*-sentences. Prove that, for every *PL*-sentence ϕ, $\Gamma \vDash \phi$.

EXERCISE 2. 27: Prove that for all *PL*-sentences ϕ, ψ, $\phi \rightleftharpoons \psi$ if and only if $\{\phi\} \vDash \psi$ and $\{\psi\} \vDash \phi$.

EXERCISE 2. 28: Prove that a *PL*-sentence ϕ is logically true ($\vDash \phi$) if and only if it is a logical consequence of the empty set ($\varnothing \vDash \phi$).

EXERCISE 2. 29: Prove that $\Gamma \vDash \phi$ if and only if $\Gamma \cup \{\neg\phi\}$ is unsatisfiable.

EXERCISE 2. 30: Define satisfiability in terms of logical consequence. Prove that your definition is correct (i.e. equivalent to the one given above).

5. Unique Readability

Intuitively, the semantic features of composition devices make the truth values of the compounds they generate "flow upwards" from the truth values of their components, and ultimately from the truth values of the basic propositions which figure in them. Thus, e.g., if A, B and C are basic propositions, the truth values of A and B yield a unique truth value for the conjunction of A and B, the truth value of C yields a unique truth value for the negation of C, and the truth values of the conjunction of A and B and of the negation of C yield a unique truth value for the material conditional with the former as antecedent and the latter as consequent. We can ask whether this situation holds in general—whether, for every way of ascribing truth values to all the basic propositions, there is one and only one way of ascribing a truth value to each compound which is compatible with the truth values that we have ascribed to the basic propositions and with the semantic features of the composition devices.

    Invoking the way in which the semantic features of composition devices are modeled by the connectives, we can raise an analogous question for *PL*. Let's say that an *atomic truth assignment* is a function yielding a unique truth value for each atom, i.e. a function from the set of atoms to the set $\{T, F\}$. And let's say that a *PL*-assignment f *extends* an atomic truth assignment g just in case g is the restriction of f to the set of atoms. If g is an atomic truth assignment and f is an admissible *PL*-assignment which extends g, we shall say that f is an *admissible extension* of g to *PL*. Then the analogue for *PL* of the question we have raised in the preceding paragraph is the question whether every atomic truth assignment has exactly one admissible extension to *PL*.

This question can be usefully subdivided into the question of *uniqueness*—whether each atomic truth assignment has *at most one* admissible extension to *PL*— and the question of *existence*—whether each atomic truth assignment has *at least one* admissible extension to *PL*. The question of uniqueness is answered in the affirmative by the following lemma.

LEMMA 2. 31: For every atomic truth assignment v, if v_1 and v_2 are admissible extensions of v to *PL*, then for every *PL*-sentence ϕ, $v_1(\phi) = v_2(\phi)$.

Proof: Let v be an atomic truth assignment, and let v_1 and v_2 be admissible extensions of v to *PL*. We show by induction on *PL* that, for every *PL*-sentence ϕ, $v_1(\phi) = v_2(\phi)$.

Base: We need to show that for every atom α, $v_1(\alpha) = v_2(\alpha)$. This follows directly from the fact that v_1 and v_2 extend v, since this means that, for every atom α, $v_1(\alpha) = v_2(\alpha) = v(\alpha)$.

Inductive Step: We shall deal with the ¬-clause, leaving the rest as an exercise. We need to show that, for every *PL*-sentence ϕ, if $v_1(\phi) = v_2(\phi)$, then $v_1(\neg\phi) = v_2(\neg\phi)$. Let α be a *PL*-sentence, and assume (IH) that $v_1(\alpha) = v_2(\alpha)$. We have to show that it follows from this that $v_1(\neg\alpha) = v_2(\neg\alpha)$. Since v_1 and v_2 are both admissible, we have that if $v_1(\alpha) = v_2(\alpha) = T$, then $v_1(\neg\alpha) = v_2(\neg\alpha) = F$, and if $v_1(\alpha) = v_2(\alpha) = F$, then $v_1(\neg\alpha) = v_2(\neg\alpha) = T$, as desired. ∎

EXERCISE 2. 32: Complete the proof of Lemma 2. 31 by dealing with the remaining inductive clauses.

Lemma 2. 31 tells us that if an atomic truth assignment has an admissible extension to *PL*, this extension will be unique. We turn now to the question of whether every atomic truth assignment has an admissible extension to *PL*. This question also has to be answered in the affirmative, although we shall not provide a formal proof of this result. Instead, we shall discuss informally the features of *PL* from which the result follows. The best way to see which features of *PL* guarantee that every atomic truth assignment has an admissible extension to *PL* is to compare *PL* with a similar language for which the result does not hold. For this pur-

pose, we define by induction a formal language *PL** with the same vocabulary as *PL*:

1. *Base*: Every atom is in *PL**.

2. *Inductive Clauses*:
   i. For every $\phi \in PL^*$, $\neg\phi \in PL^*$.
   ii. For all $\phi, \psi \in PL^*$, $\phi \wedge \psi \in PL^*$.
   iii. For all $\phi, \psi \in PL^*$, $\phi \vee \psi \in PL^*$.
   iv. For all $\phi, \psi \in PL^*$, $\phi \rightarrow \psi \in PL^*$.

3. Nothing else is in *PL**.

We can see that the nonatomic sentences of *PL** are generated from the
atoms in the same way as the nonatomic sentences of *PL*, except that in
PL*-sentences no brackets are used. The notion of admissible truth assignment on *PL** can be defined in the same way as for *PL*. But no *PL**-
assignment satisfies the definition—every *PL**-assignment is inadmissible. Hence no atomic truth assignment has an admissible extension to
PL*. Two features of *PL**-sentences are responsible for this outcome.

To illustrate the first problem, let *a* and *b* be atoms, and let *v* be an
atomic truth assignment such that $v(b) = F$. To show that *v* has no admissible extension to *PL**, we assume, towards a contradiction, that it
has one. Let *v'* be an admissible extension of *v* to *PL**. Consider the
PL*-sentence $\neg a \wedge b$. We have that $\neg a$ and *b* are *PL**-sentences. Hence
$\neg a \wedge b$ is a *PL**-sentence of the form $\phi \wedge \psi$, where ϕ is $\neg a$ and ψ is *b*.
Since *v'* extends *v*, we have that $v'(b) = F$. And since *v'* is admissible, it
follows that $v'(\neg a \wedge b) = F$. But we also have that $a \wedge b$ is a *PL**-
sentence. Hence $\neg a \wedge b$ is a *PL**-sentence of the form $\neg\gamma$, where γ is $a \wedge$
b. Since *v'* extends *v*, we have that $v'(b) = F$. And since *v'* is admissible,
we have that $v'(a \wedge b) = F$ and $v'(\neg a \wedge b) = T$. Hence we have that $v'(\neg a$
$\wedge b) = F$ and $v'(\neg a \wedge b) = T$, which is a contradiction.

We can diagnose the problem as arising from the fact that $\neg a \wedge b$ is
both of the form $\neg\gamma$, for a *PL**-sentence γ, and of the form $\phi \wedge \psi$, for
PL*-sentences ϕ, ψ. In other words, (the restrictions to *PL** of) the functions used in the inductive clauses of the definition of *PL** do not have
disjoint ranges. $\neg a \wedge b$ is both the image of $\neg a$ and *b* under the function
used in the $\wedge$-clause, and the image of $a \wedge b$ under the function used in
the $\neg$-clause.

Notice that a similar difficulty would arise if an atom could also be of
the form $\neg\phi$, for some *PL**-sentence ϕ, or of the form $\phi \wedge \psi$, $\phi \vee \psi$ or ϕ
$\rightarrow \psi$, for *PL**-sentences ϕ, ψ—if the set of atoms were not disjoint with
the ranges of (the restrictions to *PL** of) the functions used in the inductive clauses. Thus, e.g., if *a* and *b* are atoms and *a* is $\neg b$, then any atomic

truth assignment which ascribes the same truth value to a and b will have no admissible extension.

To illustrate a second kind of problem, let a, b, and c be atoms, and let v be an atomic truth assignment such that $v(a) = v(c) = F$. To show that v has no admissible extension to PL^*, we assume, towards a contradiction, that it has one. Let v' be an admissible extension of v to PL^*. Consider now the PL^*-sentence $a \rightarrow b \rightarrow c$. We have, on the one hand, that $a \rightarrow b$ and c are PL^*-sentences. Hence $a \rightarrow b \rightarrow c$ is a PL^*-sentence of the form $\phi \rightarrow \psi$, where ϕ is $a \rightarrow b$ and ψ is c. Since v' extends v, we have that $v'(a) = v'(c) = F$. Hence, since v' is admissible, $v'(a \rightarrow b) = T$ and $v'(a \rightarrow b \rightarrow c) = F$. But, on the other hand, we have that a and $b \rightarrow c$ are PL^*-sentences. Hence $a \rightarrow b \rightarrow c$ is a PL^*-sentence of the form $\gamma \rightarrow \delta$, where γ is a and δ is $b \rightarrow c$. We know that that $v'(a) = F$. Hence, since v' is admissible, we have that $v'(a \rightarrow b \rightarrow c) = T$. Therefore, we have that $v'(a \rightarrow b \rightarrow c) = F$ and $v'(a \rightarrow b \rightarrow c) = T$, which is a contradiction.

In this case the problem can be diagnosed as arising from the fact that $a \rightarrow b \rightarrow c$ is of the form $\phi \rightarrow \psi$ for PL^*-sentences ϕ and ψ and of the form $\gamma \rightarrow \delta$ for PL^*-sentences γ and δ, where $\phi \neq \gamma$ and $\psi \neq \delta$. In other words, the problem is that (the restrictions to PL^* of) the functions used in the inductive clauses of the definition of PL^* are not one-to-one. Thus, e.g., $a \rightarrow b \rightarrow c$ is the image under the function used in the $\rightarrow$-clause both of $a \rightarrow b$ and c and of a and $b \rightarrow c$.

To sum up, a PL^*-sentence can be of the following forms: (1) an atom, (2) $\neg\phi$, where ϕ is a PL^*-sentence, (3) $\phi \wedge \psi$, where ϕ and ψ are PL^*-sentences, (4) $\phi \vee \psi$, where ϕ and ψ are PL^*-sentences, and (5) $\phi \rightarrow \psi$, where ϕ and ψ are PL^*-sentences. We have identified two reasons why atomic truth assignments have no admissible extensions to PL^*. First, some PL^*-sentences are of more than one of these forms. Second, some PL^*-sentences are of one of the forms (3)–(5) for more than one pair of PL^*-sentences ϕ, ψ. It can be shown, although we won't do it here, that if neither of these situations arises in PL, then every atomic truth assignment will have an admissible extension to PL. Hence, to show that this is so, it will suffice to establish that the definition of PL rules out the problematic situations. This result is expressed by the following theorem.

UNIQUE READABILITY THEOREM: For every PL-sentence ϕ, at most one of the following holds:

(1) ϕ is an atom.
(2) ϕ is of the form $\neg\alpha$ for some PL-sentence α.
(3) ϕ is of the form $(\alpha \wedge \beta)$ for some PL-sentences α, β.
(4) ϕ is of the form $(\alpha \vee \beta)$ for some PL-sentences α, β.

(5) φ is of the form (α → β) for some *PL*-sentences α, β.
Also, each of (3)–(5) holds for at most one pair of *PL*-sentences α, β, and (2) holds for at most one *PL*-sentence α.

Proof: We need to show, for each of (1)–(5), that if it holds of a *PL*-sentence, then none of the others does, and that whenever one of (2)–(5) holds of a *PL*-sentence, the uniqueness condition is satisfied.

Suppose, first, that (1) holds of φ, i.e. that φ is an atom. Recall that we have assumed that none of the atoms is a tuple of symbols of *PL* more than one symbol long. But every *PL*-sentence of which one of (2)–(5) holds has more than one symbol. Hence none of (2)–(5) holds of φ.

Suppose now that (2) holds of φ, i.e. that φ is of the form ¬α for some *PL*-sentence α. We have seen that it follows from this that (1) doesn't hold of φ. It also follows that none of (3)–(5) holds of φ, since the first symbol of ¬α is ¬, and the first symbol of every *PL*-sentence of which one of (3)–(5) holds is (, and we have assumed that ¬ and (are not the same symbol. The uniqueness condition is trivial in this case. There is only one tuple with which ¬ can be concatenated to form ¬α—namely α.

Suppose now that at least one of (3)–(5) holds of φ. We know already that it follows from this that neither (1) nor (2) holds of φ. We now need to show that at most one of (3)–(5) holds of φ and that, for the one which holds, the uniqueness condition is satisfied. Notice that, in order to show this, it will suffice to rule out that φ is of the form

where α, β, γ and δ are *PL*-sentences such that α ≠ γ and β ≠ δ, and * and # are binary connectives. For if more than one of (3)–(5) held of φ, φ would be of this form, with * ≠ #, and if φ didn't satisfy the uniqueness condition for one of (3)–(5) which holds of it, φ would be of this form with * = #.

We assume, towards a contradiction, that φ is of this form. Then we have that α and γ are *PL*-sentences, and α is an initial tuple of γ. Hence, since γ is a *PL*-sentence, by Exercise 2. 14 we have that either α has more left than right brackets or α has no brackets. If α has more left than right brackets, then, by the Bracket Parity Lemma, it follows that α is not a *PL*-sentence. And if α has no brackets it follows, by Exercise 2. 15, that α is a string of ¬'s, and hence obviously not a *PL*-sentence. Either way, we generate a contradiction with the assumption that α is a *PL-sentence*.   ∎

The comparison between *PL* and *PL** may give the impression that brackets are indispensable for securing the unique readability of a language which can be used to model the behavior of composition devices. However, it is possible to define uniquely readable languages which can be used for this purpose whose sentences contain no symbols other than the atoms and the connectives. One way of achieving this, known as *Polish notation*, consists in placing the binary connectives before, instead of between, the sentences they connect. This is the approach taken in the language *PL'*, defined by induction as follows.

1. *Base*: Every atom is in *PL'*.

2. *Inductive Clauses*:
   i. For every $\phi \in PL'$, $\neg\phi \in PL'$.
   ii. For all $\phi, \psi \in PL'$, $\wedge \phi \psi \in PL'$.
   iii. For all $\phi, \psi \in PL'$, $\vee \phi \psi \in PL'$.
   iv. For all $\phi, \psi \in PL'$, $\rightarrow \phi \psi \in PL'$.

3. Nothing else is in *PL'*.

EXERCISE 2. 33: Prove that in every *PL'*-sentence the number of occurrences of atoms exceeds by one the number of occurrences of binary connectives.

Hint: Prove by induction on *PL'*.

EXERCISE 2. 34: Prove that every initial tuple of a *PL'*-sentence has at least as many occurrences of binary connectives as of atoms.

Hint: Prove by induction on *PL'*.

EXERCISE 2. 35: Formulate and prove a unique readability theorem for *PL'*.

Hint: Proceed as we did for *PL*. But in this case Exercise 2. 33 and Exercise 2. 34 will be very useful.

6. Recursive Definitions

In the preceding section we have argued that every atomic truth assignment has a unique admissible extension to *PL*. This entails that, for every atomic truth assignment v, the following definition singles out a unique function.

DEFINITION: If v is an atomic truth assignment, the *canonical extension* of v, written v^*, is the *PL*-assignment which satisfies the following conditions:

(1) For every atom α, $v^*(\alpha) = v(\alpha)$.

(2) For every *PL*-sentence of the form $\neg\alpha$,

$$v^*(\neg\alpha) = \begin{cases} T \text{ if } v^*(\alpha) = F, \\ F \text{ otherwise.} \end{cases}$$

(3) For every *PL*-sentence of the form $(\alpha \wedge \beta)$,

$$v^*((\alpha \wedge \beta)) = \begin{cases} T \text{ if } v^*(\alpha) = v^*(\beta) = T, \\ F \text{ otherwise.} \end{cases}$$

(4) For every *PL*-sentence of the form $(\alpha \vee \beta)$,

$$v^*((\alpha \vee \beta)) = \begin{cases} F \text{ if } v^*(\alpha) = v^*(\beta) = F, \\ T \text{ otherwise.} \end{cases}$$

(5) For every *PL*-sentence of the form $(\alpha \rightarrow \beta)$,

$$v^*((\alpha \rightarrow \beta)) = \begin{cases} F \text{ if } v^*(\alpha) = T \text{ and } v^*(\beta) = F, \\ T \text{ otherwise.} \end{cases}$$

The structure of this definition can be characterized in the following terms. We define v^* in two steps. First, we specify (clause (1)) the image under v^* of each object in the base of the definition of *PL* (i.e. of every atom). We use for this purpose a function, v, from the set of objects in the base to the intended range of v^*, i.e. $\{T, F\}$. Then we specify (clauses (2)–(5)) how the image under v^* of the output of each inductive clause of the definition of *PL* is determined by the image under v^* of the input of the inductive clause. For each inductive clause, we achieve this with a function in the intended range of v^*. Thus, e.g., for the $\neg$-clause, we use the function g in $\{T, F\}$ defined as follows: $g(T) = F$ and $g(F) = T$.

A definition with this structure is known as a definition *by recursion on PL*. We can use the recursive method to define functions with *PL* as their domain. We have defined in this way, for each atomic truth assignment, a function from *PL* to the set $\{T, F\}$. But we can also define by recursion functions from *PL* to any other set. Any definition by recursion on *PL* will be guaranteed to single out exactly one function. It will single out at most one function because *PL* contains only atoms and sentences which can be generated from the atoms by the inductive clauses (notice that Lemma 2. 31 can be seen as establishing this for the definition of canonical extension). And it will single out at least one function because *PL* is uniquely readable.

In general, the recursive method can be used to define functions whose domain is any inductively defined, uniquely readable language, and we shall use it extensively for this purpose in subsequent chapters. More generally, the recursive method can be used to define functions whose domain is any inductively defined set *A* with the following features: (i) the restrictions to *A* of the functions used in the inductive clauses of the definition of *A* are one-to-one, and (ii) the ranges of the restrictions to *A* of the functions used in the inductive clauses of the definition of *A* are disjoint from each other and from the set of objects in the base. (When the base and the inductive clauses of an inductive definition of a set *A* have these features, we say that *A* is *freely generated* from the base by the inductive clauses.)

For the moment, we shall restrict the application of the recursive method to functions with *PL* as their domain. Next we define by recursion a function pairing each *PL*-sentence ϕ with a unique positive integer, known as the rank of ϕ (written $r(\phi)$), which can be seen intuitively as measuring the "complexity" of ϕ (if m and n are different positive integers, $Max(m, n)$ is the greater of the two; if they are the same number, $Max(m, n)$ is that number).

DEFINITION: The *rank* of a *PL*-formula is its image under the unique function satisfying the following conditions:

(1) For every atom α, $r(\alpha) = 1$.

(2) For every *PL*-sentence of the form $\neg\phi$, $r(\neg\phi) = r(\phi) + 1$.

(3) For every *PL*-sentence of the form $(\phi \wedge \psi)$, $r((\phi \wedge \psi)) = Max(r(\phi), r(\psi)) + 1$.

(4) For every *PL*-sentence of the form $(\phi \vee \psi)$, $r((\phi \vee \psi)) = Max(r(\phi), r(\psi)) + 1$.

(5) For every *PL*-sentence of the form $(\phi \rightarrow \psi)$, $r((\phi \rightarrow \psi)) = Max(r(\phi), r(\psi)) + 1$.

EXERCISE 2. 36: Determine the rank of $(a \rightarrow \neg(b \vee c))$.

EXERCISE 2. 37: Define by recursion the function pairing each *PL*-sentence with the number of occurrences of symbols it contains and the function pairing each *PL*-sentence with the number of occurrences of connectives it contains.

EXERCISE 2. 38: Let's say that the *sentential components* of a *PL*-sentence φ are the *PL*-sentences which occur in φ (including φ itself). Define by recursion the function pairing each *PL*-sentence φ with the set of sentential components of φ.

EXERCISE 2. 39: Show that, for every *PL*-sentence ψ, if φ, φ* are *PL*-sentences such that φ ≡ φ*, then the *PL*-sentence which results from replacing every occurrence of φ in ψ with an occurrence of φ* is logically equivalent to ψ.

Hint: Prove by induction on *PL*.

Lemma 2. 31 tells us that for every *PL*-sentence φ, if two admissible *PL*-assignments ascribe the same truth value to every atom, then they ascribe the same truth value to φ. Intuitively, it should be possible to refine this result, since the truth values of atoms which do not occur in a *PL*-sentence should not affect its truth value. We should be able to show that for every *PL*-sentence φ, if two admissible *PL*-assignments ascribe the same truth value to every atom which occurs in φ, then they ascribe the same truth value to φ. The following exercise expresses this result.

EXERCISE 2. 40: Show that, for every *PL*-sentence φ and all admissible *PL*-assignments v, v', if for every atom α which occurs in φ, $v(\alpha) = v'(\alpha)$, then $v(\phi) = v'(\phi)$.

7. Expressive Completeness

The truth value of each compound that the composition devices generate from a given range of basic propositions is determined by the truth values of the basic propositions from which it is built. Hence, to each of the compounds that can be formed in this way, there corresponds a way in which the truth value of a proposition can be determined by the truth values of finitely many basic propositions. We can look at this correspondence from the other end, and consider whether for every way in which the truth value of a proposition can be determined by the truth values of finitely many basic propositions, the composition devices generate a compound whose truth value is determined in this way by the truth values of these basic propositions. Once more, we can invoke the way in which *PL* models the behavior of the composition devices to raise a parallel question for *PL*.

DEFINITION: If A is a finite set of atoms, a *truth assignment on* A is a function pairing each element of A with a unique truth value, i.e. a function from A to the set $\{T, F\}$.

DEFINITION: If A is a finite set of atoms, a *truth function on* A is a function pairing each truth assignment on A with a unique truth value, i.e. a function from the set of truth assignments on A to the set $\{T, F\}$.

We shall reserve the label *truth function* for functions of this kind, i.e. those whose domain is the set of truth assignments on a *finite* set of atoms.

The truth assignments and the truth functions on a finite set of atoms can be represented in table form. Thus, e.g., if a and b are atoms, the table on the left-hand side of Figure 3 represents all the truth assignments on $\{a, b\}$, with each truth assignment represented by a row. To represent a truth function on $\{a, b\}$, we just need to add to that table a column representing the image under the function of each truth assignment on $\{a, b\}$, as, e.g., in the table on the right-hand side of Figure 3.

a	b
T	T
T	F
F	T
F	F

a	b	g
T	T	F
T	F	T
F	T	F
F	F	F

Figure 3

We can think of truth functions as corresponding to ways in which the truth values of finitely many basic propositions can determine the truth value of a compound. Thus, e.g., the truth function g, in Figure 3, corresponds to a way in which the truth values of two basic propositions can determine the truth value of a compound. Our next goal is to find a relation between *PL*-sentences and truth functions which models the relation between a compound and the way in which its truth value is determined by the truth values of basic propositions.

We can see in intuitive terms that the *PL*-sentence $(a \wedge \neg b)$ is related in this way to g, since the truth value that $(a \wedge \neg b)$ receives from an admissible *PL*-assignment v will be determined by the truth values that a and b receive from v, i.e. by $v \restriction \{a, b\}$ (see Exercise 2. 40), and will coincide in each case with the image under g of this truth assignment on $\{a, b\}$: for every admissible *PL*-assignment v, $v((a \wedge \neg b)) = g(v \restriction \{a, b\})$. This idea is captured by the following notion:

DEFINITION: A *PL*-sentence ϕ *represents* a truth function f on a finite set A of atoms just in case, for every admissible *PL*-assignment v, $v(\phi) = f(v \upharpoonright A)$.

This is the notion that we are going to use to model in *PL* the relation between a compound and the way in which its truth value is determined by the truth values of basic propositions.

EXERCISE 2. 41: Let a and b be different atoms. For every truth function on $\{a, b\}$, find a *PL*-sentence which represents it. (Wittgenstein's own solution to this exercise can be found in the *Tractatus*, § 5.101)

Which truth functions are represented by a *PL*-sentence will be determined by the truth value it receives from each admissible *PL*-assignment. One consequence of this is that, since logically equivalent *PL*-sentences receive the same truth values from every admissible *PL*-assignment, they will represent the same truth functions. The proof of this result is left as an exercise.

EXERCISE 2. 42: Show that if ϕ and ψ are two *PL*-sentences such that $\phi \rightleftharpoons \psi$, then for every truth function f, ϕ represents f if and only if ψ represents f.

The analogue for *PL* of the question that we raised at the beginning of this section is the question whether every truth function is represented by at least one *PL*-sentence. This question is answered in the affirmative by the following theorem.

EXPRESSIVE COMPLETENESS THEOREM FOR *PL*: Every truth function is represented by at least one *PL*-sentence.

Proof: Let f be a truth function on a finite set of atoms A, and let $a_1,\ldots,$ a_n be the elements of A. Our goal is to find a *PL*-sentence which represents f. f will fall under one of the following categories: (1) f yields the value T for exactly one truth assignment on A, (2) f yields the value T for more than one truth assignment on A, or (3) f yields the value F for every truth assignment on A. We shall consider each of these cases separately.

(1) Let v_0 be the only truth assignment on A whose image under f is T. Our goal is to find a *PL*-sentence which receives the value T from every admissible extension of v_0 to *PL* (i.e. from every admissible *PL*-assignment v such that $v \upharpoonright A = v_0$), and the value F from every other admissible *PL*-assignment. To motivate the strategy that we are going to employ, consider the *PL*-sentence $b_1 \wedge \ldots \wedge b_k \wedge \neg c_1 \wedge \ldots \wedge \neg c_l$, where $b_1,\ldots, b_k, c_1,\ldots, c_l$ are atoms. (This is not, in fact a *PL*-sentence. To turn it into a *PL*-sentence we would need to add one pair of brackets for each

occurrence of $\wedge$. There are many ways of doing this resulting in different *PL*-sentences. But it follows from Exercise 2. 22 (4) that all of them will be logically equivalent, and, by Exercise 2. 42, that they represent the same truth functions. With these facts in mind, we shall write strings of conjunctions (and of disjunctions) without brackets to represent any of the *PL*-sentences that we could get by adding brackets.)

Notice that $b_1 \wedge...\wedge b_k \wedge \neg c_1 \wedge...\wedge \neg c_l$ will receive the value T from every admissible *PL*-assignment in which all of $b_1,..., b_k$ are true and all of $c_1,..., c_l$ are false, since any such assignment will make each of its conjuncts true. Notice also that this *PL*-sentence will receive the value F from every other admissible *PL*-assignment. For an admissible *PL*-assignment will yield the value F for it if it yields the value F for at least one of its conjuncts, and this will happen if it yields the value F for at least one of $b_1,..., b_k$ or the value T for at least one of $c_1,..., c_l$.

We shall use this idea to describe a *PL*-sentence which receives the value T from every admissible extension of v_0 to *PL* and the value F from every other admissible *PL*-assignment. Let ϕ be the *PL*-sentence $\alpha_1 \wedge...\wedge \alpha_n$, where, for every positive integer i less than or equal to n,

$$\alpha_i = \begin{cases} a_i \text{ if } v_0(a_i) = T, \\ \neg a_i \text{ if } v_0(a_i) = F. \end{cases}$$

We need to prove (i) that for every admissible extension v of v_0 to *PL*, $v(\phi) = T$, and (ii) that for every other admissible *PL*-assignment v, $v(\phi) = F$.

For (i), let v be an admissible extension of v_0 to *PL*, i.e. for every $x \in A$, $v(x) = v_0(x)$. We need to show that $v(\alpha_1 \wedge...\wedge \alpha_n) = T$. For this, by the admissibility of v, it will suffice to show that, for every positive integer i less than or equal to n, $v(\alpha_i) = T$. Let p be a positive integer less than or equal to n. We know that α_p is either a_p or $\neg a_p$. Suppose, first, that α_p is a_p. Then, by the definition of α_i, $v_0(a_p) = T$. But then, since v extends v_0, $v(a_p) = T$ and $v(\alpha_p) = T$. Suppose now that α_p is $\neg a_p$. Then, by the definition of α_i, $v_0(a_p) = F$. Hence, since v extends v_0, we have that $v(a_p) = F$, and since v is admissible, $v(\neg a_p) = T$ and $v(\alpha_p) = T$. Either way, $v(\alpha_p) = T$, as desired.

For (ii), let v be an admissible *PL*-assignment which doesn't extend v_0, i.e. for at least one $x \in A$, $v(x) \neq v_0(x)$. We need to show that $v(\alpha_1 \wedge...\wedge \alpha_n) = F$. For this, by the admissibility of v, it will suffice to show that, for at least one positive integer i less than or equal to n, $v(\alpha_i) = F$. Let q be a positive integer less than or equal to n such that $v(a_q) \neq v_0(a_q)$. If, on the one hand, $v_0(a_q) = T$, then $v(a_q) = F$. But by the definition of α_i, α_q is a_q. Hence $v(\alpha_q) = F$. If, on the other hand, $v_0(a_q) = F$, we have that $v(a_q) = T$, and, by the admissibility of v, $v(\neg a_q) = F$. But by the definition of α_i, α_q is $\neg a_q$. Hence $v(\alpha_q) = F$. Either way $v(\alpha_q) = F$, as desired.

(2) Let $v_1, \ldots, v_m$ be the truth assignments on A whose image under f is T. Our goal is to find a *PL*-sentence which receives the value T from every admissible extension to *PL* of one of $v_1, \ldots, v_m$, and the value F from every other admissible *PL*-assignment. We know from part 1 of the proof how to find a *PL*-sentence which receives the value T from an admissible *PL*-assignment just in case it extends a given truth assignment on A. We can build such a sentence for each of $v_1, \ldots, v_m$. The sentence that we are looking for will be the disjunction of these m sentences. For if an admissible *PL*-assignment v extends one of $v_1, \ldots, v_m$, then v will yield the value T for one of its disjuncts, and therefore for the whole disjunction. And if v doesn't extend any of the $v_1, \ldots, v_m$, then v will yield the value F for all the disjuncts, and therefore for the whole disjunction.

We provide now a more formal presentation of the reasoning of the preceding paragraph. For every positive integer j less than or equal to m, let β^j be the *PL*-sentence $\alpha_1^j \wedge \ldots \wedge \alpha_n^j$, where for every positive integer i less than or equal to n,

$$\alpha_i^j = \begin{cases} a_i \text{ if } v_j(a_i) = T, \\ \neg a_i \text{ if } v_j(a_i) = F. \end{cases}$$

Now let ϕ be the *PL*-sentence $\beta^1 \vee \ldots \vee \beta^m$. We need to show (i) that for every admissible extension v to *PL* of one of $v_1, \ldots, v_m$, $v(\phi) = T$, and (ii) that for every other admissible *PL*-assignment v, $v(\phi) = F$.

For (i), let v be an admissible extension of v_p to *PL*, for a positive integer p less than or equal to m. We need to show that $v(\beta^1 \vee \ldots \vee \beta^m) = T$. For this, by the admissibility of v, it will suffice to show that $v(\beta^p) = T$, i.e. that $v(\alpha_1^p \wedge \ldots \wedge \alpha_n^p) = T$. We can show this with exactly the same argument that we used in part 1 of the proof.

For (ii), let v be an admissible *PL*-assignment which doesn't extend any of $v_1, \ldots, v_m$. We need to show that $v(\beta^1 \vee \ldots \vee \beta^m) = F$. For this, by the admissibility of v, it will suffice to show that, for every positive integer j less than or equal to m, $v(\beta^j) = F$, i.e. $v(\alpha_1^j \wedge \ldots \wedge \alpha_n^j) = F$. Let q be a positive integer less than or equal to m. We need to show that $v(\alpha_1^q \wedge \ldots \wedge \alpha_n^q) = F$. Since we know that v is an admissible *PL*-assignment which doesn't extend v_q, we can show this with the same argument that we employed in part 1 of the proof.

(3) Let f be a truth function on A which assigns the value F to every truth assignment on A. f will be represented by any *PL*-sentence which

receives the value F from every admissible PL-assignment, such as, e.g., $a_1 \land \neg a_1$. ■

EXERCISE 2. 43: Let a, b, c, d, e be different atoms, and let v_1, v_2, v_3 be the truth assignments on $\{a, b, c, d, e\}$ defined by the table in Figure 4. Let f be the truth function on $\{a, b, c, d, e\}$ such that $f(v_1) = f(v_2) = f(v_3) = T$, and for every other truth assignment v on $\{a, b, c, d, e\}$, $f(v) = F$. Use the method of the proof of the Expressive Completeness Theorem to find a PL-sentence which represents f.

	a	b	c	d	e
v_1	T	F	T	T	F
v_2	F	F	T	T	T
v_3	F	T	F	F	F

Figure 4

Let's say that a PL-sentence is in *disjunctive normal form* just in case it is a disjunction of conjunctions of atoms or negations of atoms, including "one-disjunct disjunctions" and "one-conjunct conjunctions." Thus, e.g., $(a \land \neg b) \lor (\neg b \land \neg c) \lor (\neg a \land d \land e)$ is in disjunctive normal form, but so are $\neg a \land d \land e$, a one-disjunct disjunction, $(a \land \neg b) \lor e$, whose second disjunct is a one-conjunct conjunction, $c \lor \neg d$, each of whose disjuncts is a one-conjunct conjunction, and b, a one-disjunct disjunction whose only disjunct is a one-conjunct conjunction. A rigorous definition of the set of PL-sentences in disjunctive normal form can be easily provided. This is left as an exercise.

EXERCISE 2. 44: Use the inductive method to define the set of PL-sentences in disjunctive normal form.

Hint: First define by induction the set of PL-sentences which can figure as disjuncts in a PL-sentence in disjunctive normal form.

The following exercise is a direct consequence of the argument in the proof of the Expressive Completeness Theorem.

EXERCISE 2. 45: Show that for every PL-sentence ϕ, there is a PL-sentence ϕ' in disjunctive normal form which is logically equivalent to ϕ, such that every atom which occurs in ϕ' also occurs in ϕ.

8. Expressively Complete Languages

An interesting feature of our proof of the expressive completeness of *PL* is that the *PL*-sentences that we have used to represent truth functions don't contain any occurrences of $\rightarrow$. In light of this fact, we can see the proof as establishing, in effect, the expressive completeness of a different language—a proper subset of *PL*. Suppose that we delete the $\rightarrow$-clause from the definition of *PL*. The resulting inductive definition defines the language which contains all the atoms, all the *PL*-sentences in which $\rightarrow$ doesn't occur, and nothing else. Let's refer to this language as $PL^{(\neg, \wedge, \vee)}$. We can then define the notion of $PL^{(\neg, \wedge, \vee)}$-assignment and of admissible $PL^{(\neg, \wedge, \vee)}$-assignment in the obvious way. And in terms of the notion of admissible $PL^{(\neg, \wedge, \vee)}$-assignment, we can define a relation pairing each $PL^{(\neg, \wedge, \vee)}$-sentence with the truth functions it represents. A $PL^{(\neg, \wedge, \vee)}$-sentence ϕ *represents* a truth function f on a finite set A of atoms just in case, for every admissible $PL^{(\neg, \wedge, \vee)}$-assignment v, $v(\phi) = f(v \upharpoonright A)$. $PL^{(\neg, \wedge, \vee)}$ will be expressively complete if every truth function is related in this way to at least one $PL^{(\neg, \wedge, \vee)}$-sentence.

The argument of the proof of the expressive completeness of *PL* establishes something very close to this. Let f be a truth function on a finite set A of atoms. The argument establishes that there is a $PL^{(\neg, \wedge, \vee)}$-sentence ϕ such that $v(\phi) = f(v \upharpoonright A)$ holds for every admissible truth assignment v *on PL*. To establish the expressive completeness of $PL^{(\neg, \wedge, \vee)}$, we need to show that this holds for every admissible truth assignment v *on* $PL^{(\neg, \wedge, \vee)}$. But we can easily show that what we need follows from what we have. This is left as an exercise.

EXERCISE 2. 46: Let f be a truth function on a finite set A of atoms, and let ϕ be a $PL^{(\neg, \wedge, \vee)}$-sentence. Show that if, for every admissible *PL*-assignment v, $v(\phi) = f(v \upharpoonright A)$, then for every admissible $PL^{(\neg, \wedge, \vee)}$-assignment v', $v'(\phi) = f(v' \upharpoonright A)$.

Hence, the argument of the proof of the expressive completeness of *PL* establishes that $PL^{(\neg, \wedge, \vee)}$ is expressively complete. We can now ask which of the other subsets of *PL* that we can generate in this way would also be expressively complete languages. Let $PL^{(\neg, \wedge)}$ be the language defined by the result of deleting the $\vee$-clause and the $\rightarrow$-clause from the definition of *PL*. We define in the obvious way the notions of $PL^{(\neg, \wedge)}$-assignment, admissible $PL^{(\neg, \wedge)}$-assignment and the truth functions represented by a $PL^{(\neg, \wedge)}$-sentence. Our next goal is to prove that $PL^{(\neg, \wedge)}$ is expressively complete. For this purpose we can take advantage of the fact that we have already established the expressive completeness of $PL^{(\neg,\wedge,\vee)}$. By virtue of Exercise 2. 42, to show that $PL^{(\neg,\wedge)}$ is expressively complete, it will suffice to show that every $PL^{(\neg,\wedge,\vee)}$-sentence is logically equivalent to at least one $PL^{(\neg,\wedge)}$-sentence. This is expressed by the following result.

LEMMA 2. 47 *(Expressive Completeness of $PL^{(\neg,\wedge)}$)*: For every $PL^{(\neg,\wedge,\vee)}$-sentence ϕ, there is a $PL^{(\neg,\wedge)}$-sentence ψ such that $\phi \Rightarrow \psi$.

Proof: We prove this theorem by induction on $PL^{(\neg,\wedge,\vee)}$.

Base: We need to prove first that every atom is logically equivalent to a $PL^{(\neg,\wedge)}$-sentence. This holds trivially, since every atom is also a $PL^{(\neg,\wedge)}$-sentence, and every sentence is logically equivalent to itself.

Inductive Step: We shall deal with the clauses for $\neg$ and $\vee$, leaving the clause for $\wedge$ as an exercise.

($\neg$) We need to show that, for every $PL^{(\neg,\wedge,\vee)}$-sentence ϕ, if there is a $PL^{(\neg,\wedge)}$-sentence which is logically equivalent to ϕ, then there is a $PL^{(\neg,\wedge)}$-sentence which is logically equivalent to $\neg\phi$. Let α be a $PL^{(\neg,\wedge,\vee)}$-sentence, and let α^* be a $PL^{(\neg,\wedge)}$-sentence such that $\alpha \Rightarrow \alpha^*$. We need to show that it follows from this that there is a $PL^{(\neg,\wedge)}$-sentence which is logically equivalent to $\neg\alpha$. From $\alpha \Rightarrow \alpha^*$, it follows by Exercise 2. 39 that $\neg\alpha \Rightarrow \neg\alpha^*$. But since α^* is a $PL^{(\neg,\wedge)}$-sentence, so is $\neg\alpha^*$. Hence $\neg\alpha^*$ is a $PL^{(\neg,\wedge)}$-sentence which is logically equivalent to $\neg\alpha$, as desired.

($\vee$) We need to show that for all $PL^{(\neg,\wedge,\vee)}$-sentences ϕ, ψ, if each of ϕ, ψ is logically equivalent to at least one $PL^{(\neg,\wedge)}$-sentence, then $(\phi \vee \psi)$ is logically equivalent to at least one $PL^{(\neg,\wedge)}$-sentence. Let α, β be $PL^{(\neg,\wedge,\vee)}$-sentences, and let α^*, β^* be $PL^{(\neg,\wedge)}$-sentences such that $\alpha \Rightarrow \alpha^*$, $\beta \Rightarrow \beta^*$. We need to show that it follows from this that $(\alpha \vee \beta)$ is logically equivalent to at least one $PL^{(\neg,\wedge)}$-sentence. From $\alpha \Rightarrow \alpha^*$ and $\beta \Rightarrow \beta^*$, it follows by Exercise 2. 39 that $(\alpha \vee \beta) \Rightarrow (\alpha^* \vee \beta^*)$. From Exercise 2. 23 (3), we get that $(\alpha^* \vee \beta^*) \Rightarrow \neg(\neg\alpha^* \wedge \neg\beta^*)$. But since α^* and β^* are $PL^{(\neg,\wedge)}$-sentences, the same goes for $\neg(\neg\alpha^* \wedge \neg\beta^*)$. Therefore $\neg(\neg\alpha^* \wedge \neg\beta^*)$ is a $PL^{(\neg,\wedge)}$-sentence which is logically equivalent to $(\alpha \vee \beta)$, as desired.   ∎

Notice that, as with $PL^{(\neg,\wedge,\vee)}$, what we have shown, in the first instance, is that for every truth function f on a finite set A of atoms, there is a $PL^{(\neg,\wedge)}$-sentence ϕ such that $v(\phi) = f(v \restriction A)$ holds for every admissible truth assignment v *on PL*. But once again it follows that this holds for every admissible truth assignment *on $PL^{(\neg,\wedge)}$*, as needed (see Exercise 2. 46).

EXERCISE 2. 48: Complete the proof of the preceding lemma by dealing with the remaining inductive clause.

EXERCISE 2. 49: Let $PL^{(\neg,\vee)}$ be the language defined by the result of deleting the $\wedge$-clause and the $\rightarrow$-clause from the definition of PL. Prove that $PL^{(\neg,\vee)}$ is expressively complete.

Hint: Follow the same procedure that we have used for $PL^{(\neg,\wedge)}$.

EXERCISE 2. 50: Let $PL^{(\neg,\rightarrow)}$ be the language defined by the result of deleting the $\wedge$-clause and the $\vee$-clause from the definition of PL. Prove that $PL^{(\neg,\rightarrow)}$ is expressively complete.

We have established that $PL^{(\neg,\wedge)}$, $PL^{(\neg,\vee)}$ and $PL^{(\neg,\rightarrow)}$ are expressively complete languages. If we formulate these results in terms of expressively complete sets of connectives, we have established that any set containing $\neg$ and at least one of $\wedge$, $\vee$ and $\rightarrow$ is expressively complete. It turns out that we can't manage with less than this. Every other subset of $\{\neg, \wedge, \vee, \rightarrow\}$ is not expressively complete. To show this, it will suffice to establish that the languages $PL^{(\neg)}$ and $PL^{(\wedge,\vee,\rightarrow)}$, defined in the obvious way, are not expressively complete.

Consider $PL^{(\neg)}$ first. To establish that $PL^{(\neg)}$ is not expressively complete, we need to show that there are truth functions which are not represented by any $PL^{(\neg)}$-sentence. For any finite set A of atoms, we say that a truth function on A is *constant* if it yields the same value (either T or F) for every truth assignment on A. Let f be a constant truth function on a set A of atoms, and let ϕ be a PL-sentence which represents f, i.e., for every admissible PL-assignment v, $v(\phi) = f(v \restriction A)$. Since f is constant, we have that for all admissible PL-assignments v, v', $f(v \restriction A) = f(v' \restriction A)$. Hence, for all admissible PL-assignments v, v', $v(\phi) = v'(\phi)$. In other words, in order to represent a constant truth function, a PL-sentence would have to receive the same truth value from every admissible PL-assignment. We establish that $PL^{(\neg)}$ is not expressively complete by showing that this is not the case for any $PL^{(\neg)}$-sentence. (In fact, we need to show that no $PL^{(\neg)}$-sentence receives the same truth value from every admissible truth assignment *on* $PL^{(\neg)}$. But this is a direct consequence of the corresponding result about admissible assignments on PL. See Exercise 2. 46)

LEMMA 2. 51 *(Expressive Incompleteness of $PL^{(\neg)}$)*: For every $PL^{(\neg)}$-sentence ϕ, there are two admissible PL-assignments v, v' such that $v(\phi) \neq v'(\phi)$.

Proof: By induction on $PL^{(\neg)}$.

Base: Let α be an atom, and let v, v' be atomic truth assignments such that $v(\alpha) \neq v'(\alpha)$. Then the canonical extensions of v and v' also yield different truth values for α.

Inductive Step: We need to prove that, for every $PL^{(\neg)}$-sentence ϕ, if there are two admissible PL-assignments which yield different values for ϕ, then there are two admissible PL-assignments which yield different values for $\neg\phi$. Let α be a $PL^{(\neg)}$-sentence, and let v, v' be admissible PL-assignments such that $v(\alpha) \neq v'(\alpha)$. Since v and v' are admissible, we have that $v(\alpha) = T$ if and only if $v(\neg\alpha) = F$, and $v'(\alpha) = T$ if and only if $v'(\neg\alpha) = F$. Therefore, $v(\neg\alpha) \neq v'(\neg\alpha)$, as desired. ∎

Let's turn now to $PL^{(\wedge,\vee,\rightarrow)}$. As with $PL^{(\neg)}$, our goal is to show that there are truth functions which are not represented by any $PL^{(\wedge,\vee,\rightarrow)}$-sentence. Let A be a finite set of atoms, and let v_0 be the truth assignment on A which yields the value T for every element of A. A truth function f on A is *contrary* if $f(v_0) = F$. Let f be a contrary truth function on a set A of atoms, and let ϕ be a PL-sentence which represents f, i.e., for every admissible PL-assignment v, $v(\phi) = f(v \restriction A)$. Let v_T be the canonical extension of the atomic truth assignment which yields the value T for every atom. Since f is contrary, we have that $f(v_T \restriction A) = F$. Hence $v_T(\phi) = F$. In other words, to represent a contrary truth function, a PL-sentence has to receive the value F from v_T. We establish that $PL^{(\wedge,\vee,\rightarrow)}$ is not expressively complete by showing that no $PL^{(\wedge,\vee,\rightarrow)}$-sentence has this feature.

EXERCISE 2. 52: Show that, for every $PL^{(\wedge,\vee,\rightarrow)}$-sentence ϕ, $v_T(\phi) = T$.

Hint: Prove by induction on $PL^{(\wedge,\vee,\rightarrow)}$.

One outcome of our discussion of expressively complete subsets of PL is that no one-element subset of $\{\neg, \wedge, \vee, \rightarrow\}$ is a complete set of connectives. We may wonder whether there are other connectives which can do the job by themselves. We close our discussion of expressive completeness by considering the question in the case of binary connectives. Let $PL^{(\blacklozenge)}$ be a language defined like PL except that all the inductive clauses are replaced by the following: For all ϕ, $\psi \in PL^{(\blacklozenge)}$, $(\phi \blacklozenge \psi) \in PL^{(\blacklozenge)}$. The definition of admissible $PL^{(\blacklozenge)}$-assignment would also have only one clause, specifying which value a $PL^{(\blacklozenge)}$-sentence of the form $(\phi \blacklozenge \psi)$ would receive from an admissible $PL^{(\blacklozenge)}$-assignment for each combination of truth values for ϕ and ψ. The columns of the table in Figure 5 represent all the different ways in which we could define admissibility for $PL^{(\blacklozenge)}$.

The question that we want to address is whether any of these possibilities results in an expressively complete language. Notice that columns 3,

5 and 8 represent →, ∨ and ∧, and we know that none of these can be used on its own. We can adapt the reasoning that we employed for $PL^{(\wedge,\vee,\to)}$ to rule out all of the first eight possibilities. Notice that the definition of admissibility represented by each of them entails that for every admissible $PL^{(\blacklozenge)}$-assignment v and all $PL^{(\blacklozenge)}$-sentences ϕ, ψ, if $v(\phi) = v(\psi) = T$, then $v((\phi \blacklozenge \psi)) = T$. We can show that it follows from this that contrary truth functions are not represented by any $PL^{(\blacklozenge)}$-sentence, and hence that $PL^{(\blacklozenge)}$ is not expressively complete. This is left as an exercise.

ϕ	ψ							(ϕ ♦ ψ)								
		1	2	3	4	5	6	7	8	9	10	11	12	13	14	15	16
T	T	T	T	T	T	T	T	T	T	F	F	F	F	F	F	F	F
T	F	T	T	F	F	T	T	F	F	T	T	F	F	F	T	T	F
F	T	T	F	T	F	T	F	T	F	T	F	T	F	T	F	T	F
F	F	T	T	T	T	F	F	F	F	F	F	F	F	T	T	T	T

Figure 5

EXERCISE 2. 53: Assume that for every admissible $PL^{(\blacklozenge)}$-assignment v and all $PL^{(\blacklozenge)}$-sentences ϕ, ψ, if $v(\phi) = v(\psi) = T$, then $v((\phi \blacklozenge \psi)) = T$. Show that it follows from this that contrary truth functions are not represented by any $PL^{(\blacklozenge)}$-sentence.

Hint: Proceed as with $PL^{(\wedge,\vee,\to)}$.

A similar reasoning would rule out possibilities 5-12. This is also left as an exercise.

EXERCISE 2. 54: Assume that for every admissible $PL^{(\blacklozenge)}$-assignment v and all $PL^{(\blacklozenge)}$-sentences ϕ, ψ, if $v(\phi) = v(\psi) = F$, then $v((\phi \blacklozenge \psi)) = F$. Show that it follows from this that $PL^{(\blacklozenge)}$ is not expressively complete.

Hint: Proceed as with the first eight possibilities. Consider the "converse" of a contrary truth function.

Exercise 2. 53 and Exercise 2. 54 leave us with a shortlist containing the last four possibilities. Columns 13 and 14 should also raise suspicion: 13 would make the truth value of (ϕ ♦ ψ) in an admissible $PL^{(\blacklozenge)}$-assignment depend on the truth value that it yields for ϕ alone, in the same way in which the truth value of ¬ϕ depends on the truth value of ϕ; 14 would make the truth value of (ϕ ♦ ψ) depend on the truth value of ψ in the same way. In light of these parallelisms, it should come as no surprise that each of these possibilities would exhibit the same shortcoming as $PL^{(\neg)}$—constant truth functions would not be expressed by any $PL^{(\blacklozenge)}$-

sentence, and hence $PL^{(\bullet)}$ would not be expressively complete. The following exercise expresses this result for column 13. Column 14 can be dealt with in exactly the same way.

EXERCISE 2. 55: Assume that for every admissible $PL^{(\bullet)}$-assignment v and all $PL^{(\bullet)}$-sentences ϕ, ψ, $v((\phi \bullet \psi)) \neq v(\phi)$. Show that it follows from this that $PL^{(\bullet)}$ is not expressively complete.

Hint: Proceed as with $PL^{(\neg)}$.

This leaves us with only two candidates—the definitions of admissibility for $PL^{(\bullet)}$ represented by the last two columns. And both do the job. The connective represented by column 15 is usually written |, and known as the *Sheffer stroke*. It corresponds to the composition device which generates from two propositions A, B the compound *not both A and B*. The connective represented by column 16 is usually written $\downarrow$. It corresponds to the composition device which generates from two propositions A, B the compound *neither A nor B*. Both $PL^{(|)}$ and $PL^{(\downarrow)}$ are expressively complete. We shall establish the expressive completeness of $PL^{(\downarrow)}$, and leave $PL^{(|)}$ as an exercise. The easiest way to show that $PL^{(\downarrow)}$ is expressively complete is to show, for a language already known to be expressively complete, that each of its sentences is logically equivalent to a $PL^{(\downarrow)}$-sentence. We shall use $PL^{(\neg,\wedge)}$ for this purpose. We want to show that, for every $PL^{(\neg,\wedge)}$-sentence ϕ, there is a $PL^{(\downarrow)}$-sentence ψ such that $\phi \rightleftharpoons \psi$. But logical equivalence is defined in terms of admissible truth assignments *on a language*. Hence we can only make sense of the issue, whether a $PL^{(\neg,\wedge)}$-sentence and a $PL^{(\downarrow)}$-sentence are logically equivalent with respect to a language to which both belong. To solve this difficulty we define in the obvious way the language $PL^{(\neg,\wedge,\downarrow)}$, of which both $PL^{(\neg,\wedge)}$ and $PL^{(\downarrow)}$ are subsets. Our goal is to prove that, for every $PL^{(\neg,\wedge)}$-sentence ϕ, there is a $PL^{(\downarrow)}$-sentence ψ which is logically equivalent to ϕ in $PL^{(\neg,\wedge,\downarrow)}$, i.e. that ϕ and ψ receive the same truth value from every admissible $PL^{(\neg,\wedge,\downarrow)}$-assignment. From this, it will follow by the analogue for $PL^{(\neg,\wedge,\downarrow)}$ of Exercise 2. 42 that ϕ and ψ represent the same truth functions in $PL^{(\neg,\wedge,\downarrow)}$. And we could easily derive from this that ϕ represents a truth function f in $PL^{(\neg,\wedge)}$ if and only if ψ represents f in $PL^{(\downarrow)}$, as desired (see Exercise 2. 46).

LEMMA 2. 56: For every $PL^{(\neg,\wedge)}$-sentence ϕ, there is a $PL^{(\downarrow)}$-sentence ψ such that $\phi \rightleftharpoons \psi$.

Proof: By induction on $PL^{(\neg,\wedge)}$. The base is trivial, since every atom is a $PL^{(\downarrow)}$-sentence, and every sentence is logically equivalent to itself.

Inductive Step:

(¬) We need to prove that, for every $PL^{(¬,∧)}$-sentence ϕ, if there is a $PL^{(↓)}$-sentence which is logically equivalent to ϕ, then there is a $PL^{(↓)}$-sentence which is logically equivalent to $¬\phi$. Let α be a $PL^{(¬,∧)}$-sentence, and let α^* be a $PL^{(↓)}$-sentence such that $\alpha = \alpha^*$. Then, by the analogue for $PL^{(¬,∧,↓)}$ of Exercise 2. 39, we would get that $¬\alpha = ¬\alpha^*$. But $¬\alpha^* = (\alpha^* ↓ \alpha^*)$ (a $PL^{(↓)}$-sentence). The proof of this claim is left as an exercise.

(∧) We need to show that, for all $PL^{(¬,∧)}$-sentences ϕ, ψ, if there is a $PL^{(↓)}$-sentence which is logically equivalent to ϕ, and a $PL^{(↓)}$-sentence which is logically equivalent to ψ, then there is a $PL^{(↓)}$-sentence which is logically equivalent to $(\phi ∧ \psi)$. Let α, β be $PL^{(¬,∧)}$-sentences, and let α^*, β^* be $PL^{(↓)}$-sentences such that $\alpha = \alpha^*$ and $\beta = \beta^*$. By the analogue for $PL^{(¬,∧,↓)}$ of Exercise 2. 39, we would get that $(\alpha ∧ \beta) = (\alpha^* ∧ \beta^*)$. But we have that $(\alpha^* ∧ \beta^*) = ((\alpha^* ↓ \alpha^*) ↓ (\beta^* ↓ \beta^*))$. The proof of this is left as an exercise. ∎

EXERCISE 2. 57: Show that for every $PL^{(¬,∧,↓)}$-sentence ϕ, $¬\phi = (\phi ↓ \phi)$, and that for all $PL^{(¬,∧,↓)}$-sentences ϕ, ψ, $(\phi ∧ \psi) = ((\phi ↓ \phi) ↓ (\psi ↓ \psi))$.

EXERCISE 2. 58: Prove that $PL^{(|)}$ is expressively complete.

Hint: Proceed as with $PL^{(↓)}$.

Chapter 3

First-Order Logic:
Syntax and Semantics

1. Introduction

We start in this chapter the study of first-order logic. We are going to adopt the same strategy as in our presentation of propositional logic in Chapter 2—using formal languages to model the structure of first-order propositions. As in propositional logic, we can classify the features of the structure of first-order propositions that we are interested in as syntactic and semantic. The syntactic features concern the patterns according to which properties, relations and individuals figure in first-order propositions. We shall refer to these patterns as the *syntactic patterns* of first-order propositions. The semantic features relate to the way in which the truth value of a first-order proposition is determined by which individuals instantiate the properties and relations which figure in it. We shall refer to this connection between the truth value of a first-order proposition and the instantiation of the properties and relations which figure in it as its *semantic pattern*. To study the syntactic features of first-order propositions, we shall define formal languages whose sentences model their syntactic patterns. To study the semantic features of first-order propositions, we shall model their semantic patterns in the formal languages that we are going to define. The formal languages that we shall use for this purpose are known as *first-order languages*. First-order languages are more complex than the languages used in propositional logic. This section is devoted to an informal presentation of the devices with which first-order languages will model the syntactic patterns of first-order propositions.

i. Properties, Relations and Individuals

Many first-order propositions are built from a property and an individual in such a way that the proposition is true just in case the individual instantiates the property. Other first-order propositions are built from a binary relation and two individuals in such a way that the proposition is true just in case the pair formed by the two individuals (in the right order) instantiates the relation. The propositions that the Earth is a planet and that the Earth is bigger than Venus are examples of these syntactic patterns.

To model the syntactic patterns of these propositions, the vocabulary of a first-order language contains two categories of symbols, known as *individual constants* and *predicates*. Individual constants play the role of individuals, and predicates play the role of properties and relations. Predicates are classified as one-place, two-place, three-place, etc., according to whether they play the role of properties, binary relations, three-place relations, etc. Individual constants are normally represented by lower-case letters from the beginning of the alphabet, and predicates by upper-case letters. In our examples in this section, a and b will be individual constants, P a one-place predicate and R a two-place predicate. The syntactic pattern of a proposition which is true just in case a certain property is instantiated by a certain individual will be modeled in first-order languages by sentences in which a one-place predicate is followed by an individual constant. Thus, e.g., the sentence Pa will model the syntactic pattern of the proposition that the Earth is a planet. The syntactic pattern of a proposition which is true just in case a certain binary relation is instantiated by a certain pair of individuals will be modeled in first-order languages by sentences in which a two-place predicate is followed by two individual constants. Thus, e.g., the sentence Rab will model the syntactic pattern of the proposition that the Earth is bigger than Venus. In general, the syntactic pattern of a proposition which is true just in case a certain n-place relation is instantiated by a certain n-tuple will be modeled by sentences in which an n-place predicate is followed by n individual constants.

ii. Truth-Functional Composition

From the first-order propositions that can be built with properties, relations and individuals, we can generate other first-order propositions with the composition devices that we studied in Chapter 2. Thus, e.g., the negation of the proposition that the Earth is bigger than Venus is the proposition that the Earth is not bigger than Venus, which is true just in case the Earth doesn't bear to Venus the relation ...*is bigger than*.... And the conjunction of the proposition that the Earth is a planet and the negation of the proposition that the Earth is bigger than Venus is the proposition that the Earth is a planet no bigger than Venus, which is true just in case the Earth has the property of being a planet and doesn't bear to Venus the relation ...*is bigger than*....

To model the syntactic patterns of these propositions, the vocabulary of a first-order language will use the connectives of the language *PL* of Chapter 2. Thus, e.g., the sentence ¬*Rab* will model the syntactic pattern of the proposition that the Earth is not bigger than Venus, and the sentence (*Pa* ∧ ¬*Rab*) will model the syntactic pattern of the proposition that the Earth is a planet no bigger than Venus.

iii. Functions

As we saw in Chapter 1, the role of a function in a first-order proposition can be to single out an individual. This is the role, e.g., of the function *the mother of...* in the proposition that Princess Stephanie's mother was American. This proposition is true just in case a certain individual instantiates the property of being American, and this individual is singled out as the image of Princess Stephanie under the function *the mother of*....

To model the syntactic patterns of propositions in which individuals are singled out in this way, a first-order language will contain a category of symbols known as *function symbols*. Function symbols are classified as one-place, two-place, three-place, etc., corresponding to the different kinds of function. In our examples in this section, *f* and *g* will be one-place function symbols, and *h* will be a two-place function symbol. A one-place function symbol can figure in a sentence followed by an individual constant enclosed in brackets. Thus, e.g., *f*(*a*) will figure in a sentence modeling the syntactic patterns of propositions in which an individual is singled out as the image of an individual under a one-place function. We shall refer to tuples of symbols of this form as *functional terms*.

Functional terms figure in sentences in the same way as individual constants, i.e. following predicates. Thus, e.g., the sentence *Pf*(*a*) will model the syntactic pattern of the proposition that Princess Stephanie's mother was American. A function symbol can generate a functional term, not only from an individual constant, but also from a functional term. Thus *g*(*f*(*a*)) will be a functional term which can figure in sentences modeling the syntactic patterns of propositions in which an individual is singled out as the image under a function of the image under another function of a certain individual, as, for example, in the sentence $Pg(f(a))$, which models the syntactic pattern of the proposition that Princess Stephanie's mother's father was American.

Many-place function symbols work in the same way. A two-place function symbol will be followed by two individual constants or functional terms separated by commas and enclosed in brackets. Thus the functional term $h(a, b)$ will figure in sentences modeling the syntactic patterns of propositions in which an individual is singled out as the image of a pair of individuals under a two-place function. The sentence $Ph(a, f(b))$ will model the syntactic pattern, e.g., of the proposition that 1 + 3^2 is an even number (i.e. that the property of being an even number is instantiated by the image under the two-place function *the sum of...and...* of 1 and the image of 3 under the function *the square of...*). In general, an *n*-place function symbol will form a functional term when followed by *n* individual constants or functional terms, separated by commas and enclosed in brackets.

iv. Identity

Consider the proposition that Grace Kelly was Princess Stephanie's mother. This proposition can be characterized as built from two individuals, a function and a binary relation, according to the same pattern as, say, the proposition that Edward VII was taller than Queen Victoria's father. Thus characterized, the syntactic pattern of each of these propositions could be modeled in a first-order language with the resources already at our disposal, e.g., with the sentence $Raf(b)$. But the relation which figures in the former proposition is a very special one—identity, which every individual bears to itself and to nothing else. We want to treat the fact that a proposition is built with the identity relation, as opposed to any other binary relation, as a structural feature of the proposition. For this purpose, a first-order language will contain a special symbol, $\approx$, known as the *identity symbol*, used to model the role of the identity relation in first-order propositions. The identity symbol will occur with an individual constant or a functional term on either side. Thus, e.g., the sentence $a \approx f(b)$ will model the syntactic pattern of the proposition that Grace Kelly was Princess Stephanie's mother. Sentences of this form will figure in truth-functional compounds in the same way as sentences built with standard predicates. Thus, e.g., the sentence $(Pa \wedge a \approx f(b))$ will model the syntactic pattern of the proposition that Grace Kelly was American and she was Princess Stephanie's mother.

v.   Quantification

When an individual figures in a first-order proposition, the proposition can be characterized as being true just in case the individual satisfies a certain condition. Thus, e.g., the proposition that the Earth is a planet no bigger than Venus can be characterized as true just in case the Earth satisfies the condition ...*is a planet no bigger than Venus*. These conditions can be thought of as "proposition matrices." We form a proposition from a proposition matrix by "inserting" an individual. If we insert, say, the individual Jupiter in the matrix ...*is a planet no bigger than Venus*, we form the proposition that Jupiter is a planet no bigger than Venus. The resulting proposition will be true or false according to whether the individual satisfies the matrix.

We have a device for generating from a given proposition matrix a proposition which is true just in case every individual satisfies the matrix. This device is known as *universal quantification*. When applied to the matrix ...*is a planet no bigger than Venus*, it generates the proposition that everything is a planet no bigger than Venus. A similar device known as *existential quantification* enables us to form from a given proposition matrix a proposition which is true just in case at least one individual satisfies the matrix. From the matrix ...*is a planet no bigger than Venus*, it generates the proposition that at least one thing is a planet no bigger than Venus.

It is often useful to think of universal and existential quantification as forming propositions relative to a restricted range of individuals. Then the truth values of the propositions they generate will depend on the chosen range. Thus, e.g., relative to the range of bodies in the solar system, the proposition that everything is a planet no bigger than Venus is false, but the proposition that at least one thing is a planet no bigger than Venus is true. Relative to the range including Mercury, Mars and Pluto, both propositions are true, but relative to the range including the Earth, the Sun and Jupiter, both propositions are false.

First-order languages contain resources to model the syntactic patterns of the propositions generated by applying universal and existential quantification to proposition matrices. They use for this purpose the symbols ∀, known as *universal quantifier*, and ∃, known as *existential quantifier*, and a range of auxiliary symbols known as *variables*, normally represented by lower-case letters from the end of the alphabet. We will use x and y as variables in our examples. Since the sentence $(Pa \land \neg Rab)$ models the syntactic pattern of the proposition that the Earth is a planet no bigger than Venus, the result of removing from this sentence the individual constant playing the role of the Earth, i.e. $(P... \land \neg R...b)$, will model the syntactic pattern of the proposition matrix ...*is a planet no bigger than Venus*. To form a sentence which models the syntactic pattern of the proposition that everything is a planet no bigger than Venus, we fill the gaps in this "sentence matrix" with occurrences of a variable, and prefix the resulting string of symbols with the universal quantifier and another occurrence of the same variable, as, e.g., $\forall x\ (Px \wedge \neg Rxb)$. To model the syntactic pattern of the proposition that at least one thing is a planet no bigger than Venus, we proceed in the same way with the existential quantifier, as, e.g., $\exists x\ (Px \wedge \neg Rxb)$.

We can use this procedure to form a sentence with the universal or existential quantifier from any given sentence matrix. A sentence matrix can contain, not only predicates, individual constants and connectives, but also function symbols and the identity symbol. Thus, e.g., the sentence matrix $a \approx f(...)$ would model the syntactic pattern of the proposition matrix *Grace Kelly is ... 's mother*, from which we can form the sentence $\exists x\ a \approx f(x)$, which models the syntactic pattern of the proposition that there is at least one individual whose mother is Grace Kelly. Sentence matrices can also contain quantifiers. Thus, e.g., the sentence matrix $\exists x\ R...x$ would model the syntactic pattern of the proposition matrix ...*is bigger than at least one thing*. If we apply the universal quantifier to this matrix, we generate the sentence $\forall y \exists x\ Ryx$, which models the syntactic pattern of the proposition that everything is bigger than at least one thing. When more than one quantifier is involved, we use different variables to keep track of which quantifier affects each variable occurrence.

2. Syntax

Our goal in this section is to define the formal languages that we are going to use to model the syntactic and semantic patterns of first-order propositions. In our presentation of propositional logic in Chapter 2, we used a single language, *PL*, to model the syntactic and semantic features of composition devices. Then we considered a few other languages which were either plainly inadequate for the task or basically interchangeable with *PL*. In first-order logic, by contrast, we are going to use a family of languages which will enable us to model the syntactic and semantic patterns of different collections of first-order propositions.

First-order languages will only differ from each other in their vocabularies. We shall classify the symbols of a first-order language as *logical* or *extralogical*. All the first-order languages that we shall consider will have the same logical vocabulary, containing the connectives of *PL*, $\neg$, $\wedge$, $\vee$ and $\rightarrow$, the quantifiers, $\forall$ and $\exists$, the identity symbol, $\approx$, two brackets, (

and), a comma, , , and infinitely many different variables. We shall refer to the connectives, the quantifiers and the identity symbol as *logical operators*. First-order languages will only differ from each other in their extralogical vocabulary. The extralogical vocabulary of a first-order language may contain individual constants, predicates and function symbols, with predicates and function symbols classified as one-place, two-place, etc.

We shall assume that all the symbols of a first-order language are different from each other and from any tuple of more than one symbol of the language. We shall make no further assumptions about their identity. Notice that it follows from this that the only differences between extralogical vocabularies which we shall contemplate concern the number of symbols in each category, i.e. the number of individual constants, one-place predicates, one-place function symbols, two-place predicates, etc. For our purposes, there is only one extralogical vocabulary, say, containing two individual constants, one two-place predicate, two one-place function symbols, and nothing else.

Since first-order languages will only differ from each other in their extralogical vocabularies, for each collection of individual constants, predicates and function symbols, there will be a unique first-order language with these symbols as its extralogical vocabulary. As with any other formal language, the sentences of a first-order language will be tuples whose members are elements of its vocabulary. To define a first-order language, we need to specify which tuples of symbols of the language will count as sentences. We shall use for this purpose the inductive method of definition, but instead of providing a straightforward inductive definition of the set of sentences of a first-order language, we will have to adopt a less direct approach.

What complicates the task of defining first-order languages is that we want them to model the role of functions and quantification in first-order propositions. Otherwise we could make do with a language whose sentences were built exclusively with individual constants, predicates, the identity symbol, connectives and brackets. And to define such a language we would only need to replace the base of the inductive definition of *PL* with the following:

(1) For all individual constants $c_1,\ldots,c_n$ of the language and for every n-place predicate P of the language, $Pc_1\ldots c_n$ is a sentence of the language.

(2) For all individual constants a, b of the language, $a \approx b$ is a sentence of the language.

Bringing function symbols into the picture forces us to complicate this approach. We want the base of the definition to treat as sentences tuples such as $Pf(a)$ or $Rh(a, f(b))c$, i.e. predicates followed by the right number of either individual constants or functional terms. The problem is that, whereas individual constants are given with the extralogical vocabulary of the language, functional terms aren't. Function symbols are, but we still need to specify which of the tuples of symbols in which they figure are to count as functional terms. We achieve this with an inductive definition of the set of *terms* of the language, i.e. the tuples of symbols that can be placed after a predicate or on either side of the identity symbol:

1. *Base*: Every individual constant of the language is a term of the language.

2. *Inductive clause*: If f is an m-place function symbol of the language, and $t_1, \ldots, t_m$ are terms of the language, then $f(t_1, \ldots, t_m)$ is a term of the language.

3. Nothing else is a term of the language.

Once we have defined the terms of the language along these lines, we can go on to provide an inductive definition of the sentences of the language. We only need to modify the base that we would use for a language without function symbols (see above) by replacing references to individual constants with references to terms.

Introducing quantifiers requires a further modification of our basic strategy. An inductive definition of the set of sentences of a first-order language would have to include an inductive clause for each of the quantifiers. We would want these clauses to use concatenation functions. Just as the ¬-clause would use the function pairing each tuple of symbols ϕ with the concatenation of ¬ and ϕ, we would want the ∀-clause to use the function pairing each tuple of symbols ϕ and variable x with the concatenation of ∀, x and ϕ. The inductive clause using this concatenation function would look like this:

For every sentence ϕ of the language and every variable x, $\forall x\, \phi$ is a sentence of the language.

The problem with this clause is that a tuple of the form $\forall x\, \phi$ would only be a sentence of the language if ϕ itself were a sentence of the language. Thus, e.g., $\forall x\, Px$ would only be a sentence of the language if Px were one. But we don't want Px to be a sentence. We want to use the sentences of a first-order language to model the syntactic patterns of first-order propositions, and we don't want to use Px in this way. Variables are mere place-holders, to be used in conjunction with quantifiers. We want *Pa* and $\forall x \, Px$, but not *Px*, to be sentences of a first-order language (in which *a* is an individual constant and *P* a one-place predicate).

The most straightforward way of achieving this is to define the intermediary notion of a *formula* of the language. The formulas of a first-order language will be tuples of symbols of the vocabulary including all the sentences, but also tuples like *Px* which we don't want to count as sentences, but which will generate sentences when a quantifier and a variable are concatenated with them. Once we have defined the set of formulas of the language, we shall define the set of sentences by specifying which of the formulas are going to count as sentences.

In light of these considerations, defining a first-order language will be a three-stage process. First, we will define the set of terms of the language. Second, we will define the set of formulas of the language. And third, we will define the set of sentences of the language. Notice, that, strictly speaking, our goal is not to provide a definition of a language, but a schema which will generate a definition of a language for each set of extralogical symbols. Let *V* be a set of extralogical symbols. We want to define the first-order language *L* with *V* as its extralogical vocabulary. First, we define by induction the set of *terms* of *L* (or *L-terms*).

1. *Base*:
   i. Every individual constant of *V* is an *L*-term.
   ii. Every variable is an *L*-term.

2. *Inductive clause*: For all *L*-terms $t_1, \ldots, t_n$, and every *n*-place function symbol *f* of *V*, $f(t_1, \ldots, t_n)$ is an *L*-term.

3. Nothing else is an *L*-term.

Notice that, as always, the inductive clause can be applied repeatedly. If *f* is a one-place function symbol of *V* and *a* is an individual constant of *V*, then *f(a)* is a term of *L*, and so is *f(f(a))*. If *g* is a two-place function symbol of *V*, *g(a, f(x))* is a term of *L*.

Next we define, again by induction, the set of *formulas* of *L* (or *L-formulas*):

1. *Base*:
   i. For all *L*-terms $t_1, \ldots, t_n$, and every *n*-place predicate *P* of *V*, $Pt_1 \ldots t_n$ is an *L*-formula.
   ii. For all *L*-terms *t*, *u*, $t \approx u$ is an *L*-formula.

2. *Inductive clauses*:
   i. For every *L*-formula ϕ, $\neg\phi$ is an *L*-formula.
   ii. For all *L*-formulas ϕ, ψ, $(\phi \wedge \psi)$ is an *L*-formula.
   iii. For all *L*-formulas ϕ, ψ, $(\phi \vee \psi)$ is an *L*-formula.

iv. For all *L*-formulas ϕ, ψ, ($\phi \rightarrow \psi$) is an *L*-formula.

v. For every *L*-formula ϕ and every variable *x*, $\forall x\, \phi$ is an *L*-formula.

vi. For every *L*-formula ϕ and every variable *x*, $\exists x\, \phi$ is an *L*-formula.

3. Nothing else is an *L*-formula.

We shall often identify a first-order language *L* with the set of *L*-formulas.

Let *L* be the first-order language whose extralogical symbols are three individual constants, *a*, *b* and *c*, a one-place predicate, *P*, a two-place predicate, *R*, a one-place function symbol, *f*, and a two-place function symbol, *g*.

EXERCISE 3. 1: Find three *L*-terms, each requiring six applications of the inductive clauses.

EXERCISE 3. 2: Find three *L*-formulas, each requiring six applications of the inductive clauses.

EXERCISE 3. 3: Prove that each of the following tuples is an *L*-term:

(1) $f(a)$

(2) $g(b, f(x))$

(3) $f(g(y, f(c)))$

Hint: Show how they can be obtained by applying the inductive clauses of the definition to the terms in the base.

EXERCISE 3. 4: Prove that each of the following tuples is an *L*-formula:

(1) $\forall x\, (Px \rightarrow Rax)$

(2) $(\forall x\, Px \rightarrow Rax)$

(3) $\exists y\, (y \approx a \wedge \forall x\, Rxf(y))$

Hint: Show how they can be obtained by applying the inductive clauses of the definition to the formulas in the base.

EXERCISE 3. 5: Show that the following tuples are not *L*-terms:

(1) $f(a, x)$

(2) $g(c, f)$

(3) $g(f(c))$

Hint: Show that they cannot be obtained by applying the inductive clauses of the definition to the terms in the base.

EXERCISE 3. 6: Show that the following tuples are not L-formulas:

(1) $\forall x\, f(x)$

(2) $\exists y\, P \approx y$

(3) $(Ra\neg b \vee Pz)$

Hint: Show that they cannot be obtained by applying the inductive clauses of the definition to the formulas in the base.

Having defined the set of terms and the set of formulas of a first-order language by induction will enable us to use the inductive method of proof to establish that every term or every formula has a certain property. The following exercises require simple applications of the inductive method of proof to the set of terms and the set of formulas of a first-order language.

EXERCISE 3. 7: Show that every term of a first-order language has an equal number of left and right brackets.

Hint: Prove by induction on terms.

EXERCISE 3. 8: Show that for every term t of a first-order language, every initial tuple of t (see Exercise 2. 14) more than one symbol long has more left than right brackets.

Hint: Prove by induction on terms. Use Exercise 3. 7.

EXERCISE 3. 9: Show that every formula of a first-order language has an equal number of left and right brackets.

Hint: Use induction on formulas. You can invoke Exercise 3. 7.

EXERCISE 3. 10: Show that for every formula ϕ of a first-order language, every initial tuple of ϕ has at least as many left brackets as right brackets.

Hint: Use induction on formulas. Use Exercise 3. 7, and Exercise 3. 8 for the base, and Exercise 3. 9 in some of the inductive clauses.

EXERCISE 3. 11: Show that for every formula ϕ of a first-order language, every initial tuple of ϕ containing a binary connective has more left than right brackets.

Hint: Use induction on formulas. Invoke Exercise 3. 9 and Exercise 3. 10 for one of the inductive clauses.

Another technique that we will want to use in first-order logic is the recursive method of definition (see Chapter 2, §6). We want to be able to define by recursion functions with the set of terms or the set of formulas of a first-order language as their domain. We know that the fact that both sets have been defined by induction ensures that a definition by recursion on the terms or the formulas of a first-order language will single out at most one function. To establish that at least one function will be singled out in each case, we need to show that the terms and the formulas of a first-order language are uniquely readable. This is expressed by the next two results, which are left as exercises.

EXERCISE 3. 12 (*Unique Readability Theorem for terms*): Show that for every term *t* of a first-order language *L*, at most one of the following holds:

(1) *t* is a variable.
(2) *t* is an individual constant.
(3) *t* is of the form $f(t_1,..., t_n)$ for some *n*-place function symbol *f* and *L*-terms $t_1,..., t_n$.

Furthermore, (3) holds for at most one tuple $\langle t_1,..., t_n \rangle$ of terms.

Hint: Proceed as with *PL*-sentences in Chapter 2. Invoke Exercise 3. 7 and Exercise 3. 8.

EXERCISE 3. 13 (*Unique Readability Theorem for formulas*): Show that for every formula ϕ of a first-order language *L*, at most one of the following holds:

(1) ϕ is of the form $Pt_1...t_n$, for some *n*-place predicate *P* and *L*-terms $t_1,..., t_n$.
(2) ϕ is of the form $t \approx u$, for *L*-terms *t*, *u*.
(3) ϕ is of the form $(\alpha \wedge \beta)$ for some *L*-formulas α, β.
(4) ϕ is of the form $(\alpha \vee \beta)$ for some *L*-formulas α, β.
(5) ϕ is of the form $(\alpha \rightarrow \beta)$ for some *L*-formulas α, β.
(6) ϕ is of the form $\neg\alpha$ for some *L*-formula α.
(7) ϕ is of the form $\forall x\, \alpha$, for some *L*-formula α and variable *x*.
(8) ϕ is of the form $\exists x\, \alpha$, for some *L*-formula α and variable *x*.

Also, (1) holds of ϕ for at most one tuple $\langle t_1,..., t_n \rangle$ of *L*-terms, (2) holds of ϕ for at most two *L*-terms *t*, *u*, each of (3)–(5) holds of ϕ for at most two *L*-formulas α, β, and each of (6)–(8) holds of ϕ for at most one *L*-formula α.

Hint: Proceed as with *PL*. Use Exercise 3. 12, Exercise 3. 9 and Exercise 3. 11.

When one of (2)–(8) holds of a formula ϕ, we shall say that the logical operator which figures in the corresponding schema is the *main logical operator* of ϕ. We shall refer to formulas of the form $Pt_1...t_n$ or $t \approx u$ as *atomic formulas*. Notice that, strictly speaking, to show that a recursive definition on the formulas of a first-order language will single out at least one function, all we need to establish with respect to atomic formulas is that no formula is both atomic and nonatomic. Our formulation of the Unique Readability Theorem goes further than this. It claims, in addition, (i) that no (atomic) formula is such that both (1) and (2) hold of it,

(ii) that (1) holds of an (atomic) formula for at most one tuple $\langle t_1,\ldots, t_n \rangle$ of *L*-terms, and (iii) that (2) holds of an (atomic) formula for at most two terms *t, u*. We will use these additional claims in our definitions by recursion on formulas. Notice that if *f* is a function with the set of formulas of the form $Pt_1\ldots t_n$ as its domain, and *g* is a function with the set of formulas of the form $t \approx u$ as its domain, (i) entails that $f \cup g$ is a function with the set of atomic formulas as its domain (see Exercise 1. 45). Hence, in a definition by recursion on formulas of a function *h*, we will be able to use *f* and *g* to specify the image under *h* of each atomic formula. (ii) will enable us to specify the image under *h* of a formula of the form $Pt_1\ldots t_n$ as the image of $\langle t_1,\ldots, t_n \rangle$ under a function with the set of tuples of terms as its domain. A similar remark applies to (iii).

Let's return now to our main goal in this section. We have already defined the set of terms and the set of formulas of a first-order language. The set of formulas has been so defined that it includes all the tuples that we want to treat as sentences, but it also includes other tuples. To define the set of sentences of a first-order language, we need to specify which formulas we are going to count as sentences. Intuitively, we want to exclude formulas containing occurrences of variables which are not working in conjunction with a quantifier, as, e.g., *Px*, $\forall y\, Px$, or $(Px \wedge \forall x\, Rxa)$. We achieve this with our first application of the recursive method of definition to first-order languages. We define by recursion a function pairing each formula ϕ of a first-order language *L* with a set of variables known as the *free variables* of ϕ (if a variable *x* is an element of the set of free variables of ϕ, we say that *x is free in* ϕ).

DEFINITION: The set of *free variables* of an *L*-formula is its image under the unique function which satisfies the following conditions:

(1) For every *L*-formula of the form $Pt_1\ldots t_n$, *x* is free in $Pt_1\ldots t_n$ if and only if *x* occurs in at least one of $t_1,\ldots, t_n$.

(2) For every *L*-formula of the form $t \approx u$, *x* is free in $t \approx u$ if and only if *x* occurs in at least one of *t, u*.

(3) For every *L*-formula of the form $\neg\phi$, *x* is free in $\neg\phi$ if and only if *x* is free in ϕ.

(4) For every *L*-formula of the form $(\phi \wedge \psi)$, *x* is free in $(\phi \wedge \psi)$ if and only if *x* is free in ϕ or in ψ.

(5) For every *L*-formula of the form $(\phi \vee \psi)$, *x* is free in $(\phi \vee \psi)$ if and only if *x* is free in ϕ or in ψ.

(6) For every *L*-formula of the form $(\phi \rightarrow \psi)$, *x* is free in $(\phi \rightarrow \psi)$ if and only if *x* is free in ϕ or in ψ.

(7) For every *L*-formula of the form $\forall y\, \phi$, *x* is free in $\forall y\, \phi$ if and only if *x* is free in ϕ and $x \neq y$.

(8) For every *L*-formula of the form $\exists y\, \phi$, *x* is free in $\exists y\, \phi$ if and only if *x* is free in ϕ and $x \neq y$.

Notice that it follows from the definition of free variable that every variable which occurs in an atomic formula is free in it, and that the same goes for any quantifier-free formula. A variable which occurs in a formula can only fail to be free in it if the formula contains quantifiers. Thus *x* is free in *Px*, but not in $\forall x\, Px$. And *z* is free in $b \approx z$, but not in $\exists z\; b \approx z$. Notice, however, that the quantifier needs to have the right variable attached to it. *x is* free in $\forall y\, Px$. Notice also that a variable *x* could be free in a formula which contains an *x*-quantifier. Thus take $\forall x\, Px$ and *Rxa*. *x* is not free in the former, but it is free in the latter. Then, by clause (4) of the definition of free variable, *x* is free in $(\forall x\, Px \land Rxa)$, since it is free in one of the conjuncts. However, *x* is not free in $\forall x\, (Px \land Rxa)$.

EXERCISE 3. 14: Indicate which variables are free in each of the following formulas:
(1) $(\forall x\, Px \rightarrow Qx)$
(2) $(\forall x\, Py \rightarrow Qx)$
(3) $\forall x\, (Py \rightarrow Qx)$
(4) $(\forall x \forall y\, Py \rightarrow Qx)$
(5) $\forall x\, (\forall y\, Py \rightarrow Qx)$

Using the notion of free variable, we are finally in a position to define the set of sentences of a first-order language.

DEFINITION: A formula ϕ of a first-order language *L* is a *sentence* of *L* (an *L-sentence*) just in case ϕ has no free variables.

Notice that this definition has the intended effect. If *P* is a one-place predicate of *L*, $\forall x\, Px$ is an *L*-sentence, whereas *Px* is an *L*-formula, but not an *L*-sentence. Notice, however, that the set of *L*-sentences contains tuples that we might as well do without, such as $\forall x\, Pa$ or $\forall y\, \exists y\, Rya$ (provided that *P*, *R* and *a* are symbols of *L* of the right kind). Both tuples are *L*-formulas, and neither of them has free variables. We don't really need sentences like these, but since having them won't do any harm either, we shall not make the effort to exclude them.

If ϕ is a formula of a first-order language L, let's say that the *subformulas* of ϕ are the L-formulas which occur in ϕ, including ϕ itself, and that the *atomic subformulas* of ϕ are the atomic formulas which occur in ϕ. If ϕ is of the form $\neg\alpha$, $\forall x\, \alpha$ or $\exists x\, \alpha$, we shall say that α is the *immediate subformula* of ϕ, and if ϕ is of the form $(\alpha \wedge \beta)$, $(\alpha \vee \beta)$ or $(\alpha \to \beta)$, we shall say that α and β are the *immediate subformulas* of ϕ.

EXERCISE 3. 15: Define by recursion the functions pairing each formula of a first-order language with the set of its subformulas and the set of its atomic subformulas.

From now on, we shall adopt the convention of omitting the outermost brackets of formulas which have them, i.e. formulas of the forms $(\alpha \wedge \beta)$, $(\alpha \vee \beta)$ and $(\alpha \to \beta)$. This will introduce no ambiguity, since, for every formula of one of these forms of a first-order language L, the tuple that we get by dropping the outermost brackets is not an L-formula, and for every L-formula ϕ, the tuple (ϕ) is not an L-formula (see Exercise 3. 16, below). Hence it will always be clear in each case whether we are applying the convention, and, if so, which formula we are referring to.

EXERCISE 3. 16: Show that for every formula of a first-order language L of the form (ϕ), ϕ is not an L-formula, and that for every L-formula ψ, (ψ) is not an L-formula.

Hint: You may want to use Exercise 3. 9 and Exercise 3. 11.

3. Semantics

We have defined first-order languages in such a way that their sentences model the syntactic patterns of first-order propositions. Our next goal is to use first-order languages to model their semantic patterns—the ways in which their truth values depend on which individuals instantiate the properties and relations which figure in them. The way in which the truth value of a proposition depends on which individuals instantiate the properties and relations which figure in it is determined by the syntactic pattern according to which the proposition is built from properties, relations and individuals. Hence, we should expect each syntactic pattern to be associated with a unique semantic pattern. Since each sentence of a first-order language L models a syntactic pattern, we will also want each L-sentence to model the corresponding semantic pattern.

As we saw in Chapter 1, the contribution of a property or a relation to the truth value of a first-order proposition in which it figures can be characterized in terms of set-membership. Thus, e.g., the proposition that

that Mars is a planet is true just in case Mars is an element of the set of planets, and any proposition built from an individual and a property according to the same syntactic pattern will be true just in case the individual is an element of the set of things in which the property is present. In light of this, we can specify the semantic pattern of a first-order proposition by pairing a truth value with each combination of a certain number of individuals, sets, sets of pairs, etc. Thus the semantic pattern of the proposition that Mars is a planet would pair a truth value with each combination of an individual x and a set Y—the value true if x is an element of Y, and the value false otherwise. We can use the same approach to characterize the semantic patterns of more complex propositions. The semantic pattern of the proposition that Mars is a planet no bigger than Venus would assign a truth value to each combination of two individuals, x, y, a set Z and a binary relation W—the value true if x is an element of Z and the pair $\langle x, y \rangle$ is not an element of W, and the value false otherwise. The semantic pattern of the proposition that Princess Stephanie's mother was American would assign a truth value to each combination of an individual x, a one-place function f and a set Y—the value true if the image of x under f is an element of Y, and the value false otherwise.

We can characterize in the same way the semantic patterns of propositions built with universal and existential quantification. Thus, the semantic pattern of the proposition that everything is a planet no bigger than Venus would assign a truth value to each combination of an individual x, a set Y and a binary relation Z—the value true if every individual is an element of Y, and Z contains no pairs with x as the second element, and the value false otherwise. To take into account the possibility of construing quantification as relative to a restricted range of individuals, we could describe the semantic pattern of this proposition as assigning a truth value to each combination of a set W, to be thought of as the range to which quantification is restricted, an element x of W, a subset Y of W, and a binary relation Z in W. It would yield the value true if for every element w of W, w is an element of Y and the pair $\langle w, x \rangle$ is not an element of Z, and the value false otherwise. Similarly, the semantic pattern of the proposition that at least one thing is a planet no bigger than Venus would assign to each of these combinations the value true if at least one element of W satisfies this condition, and the value false otherwise.

Our strategy for modeling in first-order languages the semantic patterns of first-order propositions will be based on these ideas. We introduce for this purpose the notion of a structure for a first-order language. A *structure* $\mathcal{A}$ for a first-order language L (an *L-structure*) consists of a set, A, known as the *universe* of $\mathcal{A}$, and a function pairing each extralogical symbol of L with its *interpretation* in $\mathcal{A}$. For each individual constant

c of L, the interpretation of c in $\mathcal{A}$ will be an element of A, represented as $c_{\mathcal{A}}$. For each n-place predicate P of L, the interpretation of P in $\mathcal{A}$ will be an n-place relation in A, represented as $P_{\mathcal{A}}$ (notice that if P is a one-place predicate, $P_{\mathcal{A}}$ will be a subset of A). And for each n-place function symbol f of L, the interpretation of f in $\mathcal{A}$ will be an n-place function in A, represented as $f_{\mathcal{A}}$.

The universe of a structure is to be thought of as the range to which quantification is restricted. Following a standard convention, we shall assume that the universe of every L-structure is a *nonempty* set. We shall represent structures with the letters $\mathcal{A}$, $\mathcal{B}$, $\mathcal{C}$..., and their universes with the same letter in standard-type upper case—the universe of $\mathcal{A}$ will be the set A, the universe of $\mathcal{B}$ will be the set B, etc.

Notice that, for each L-sentence ϕ, an L-structure will supply the analogue of one of the combinations to which semantic patterns assign truth values—an individual for each individual constant which figures in ϕ, a set for each one-place predicate which figures in ϕ, etc. To model the semantic pattern of the propositions whose syntactic pattern is modeled by an L-sentence ϕ, we just need to assign to ϕ a truth value in each L-structure. We will achieve this for all L-sentences at once if we define, for each L-structure $\mathcal{A}$, a function $v_{\mathcal{A}}$ from the set of L-sentences to the set $\{T, F\}$. As in propositional logic, we shall think of T and F as the truth values true and false, although we shall not make any assumptions about their identity other than that they are different from each other.

The way in which the sentences of a first-order language L model the syntactic patterns of first-order propositions indicates which truth value we will want each L-sentence to receive from $v_{\mathcal{A}}$. Thus, let c, d, P, R and f be two individual constants of L, a one-place and a two-place predicate of L and a one-place function symbol of L, respectively. $v_{\mathcal{A}}$ should yield for the sentence Pc the value T if the individual $c_{\mathcal{A}}$ is an element of the set $P_{\mathcal{A}}$, and the value F otherwise. For the sentence $Pc \wedge \neg Rcd$, $v_{\mathcal{A}}$ should yield the value T if the individual $c_{\mathcal{A}}$ is an element of the set $P_{\mathcal{A}}$ and the pair $\langle c_{\mathcal{A}}, d_{\mathcal{A}} \rangle$ is not an element of the relation $R_{\mathcal{A}}$, and the value F otherwise. For the sentence $Pf(c)$, $v_{\mathcal{A}}$ should yield the value T if the image of the individual $c_{\mathcal{A}}$ under the function $f_{\mathcal{A}}$ is an element of the set $P_{\mathcal{A}}$, and the value F otherwise. For the sentence $\forall x (Px \wedge \neg Rxd)$, $v_{\mathcal{A}}$ should yield the value T if for every element a of the universe of $\mathcal{A}$, a is an element of the set $P_{\mathcal{A}}$, and the pair $\langle a, d_{\mathcal{A}} \rangle$ is not an element of $R_{\mathcal{A}}$, and the value F otherwise. And for the sentence $\exists x (Px \wedge \neg Rxd)$, $v_{\mathcal{A}}$ should yield the value T if at least one element of the universe of $\mathcal{A}$ satisfies this condition, and the value F otherwise.

4. Truth

Our goal in this section is to define, for each structure $\mathcal{A}$ for a first-order language L, the function $v_{\mathcal{A}}$ described in the preceding section from the set of L-sentences to the set $\{T, F\}$. We want to define this function using the recursive method, but as with the definition of first-order languages, we will be forced to take an indirect approach. The difficulties are posed once more by function symbols and quantifiers. For a language without either of these resources, whose sentences are built exclusively from individual constants, predicates, the identity symbol and the connectives, we could define the functions that we are interested in with a straightforward recursion. Thus, let L be such a language, and let $\mathcal{A}$ be an L-structure. We could define $v_{\mathcal{A}}$ as the unique function satisfying the following conditions.

(1) For every L-sentence of the form $Pc_1 \ldots c_n$,

$$v_{\mathcal{A}}(Pc_1 \ldots c_n) = \begin{cases} T \text{ if } \langle c_{1\mathcal{A}}, \ldots, c_{n\mathcal{A}} \rangle \in P_{\mathcal{A}}, \\ F \text{ otherwise.} \end{cases}$$

(2) For every L-sentence of the form $c \approx d$,

$$v_{\mathcal{A}}(c \approx d) = \begin{cases} T \text{ if } c_{\mathcal{A}} = d_{\mathcal{A}}, \\ F \text{ otherwise.} \end{cases}$$

(3) For every L-sentence of the form $\neg\alpha$,

$$v_{\mathcal{A}}(\neg\alpha) = \begin{cases} T \text{ if } v_{\mathcal{A}}(\alpha) = F, \\ F \text{ otherwise.} \end{cases}$$

(4) For every L-sentence of the form $(\alpha \wedge \beta)$,

$$v_{\mathcal{A}}((\alpha \wedge \beta)) = \begin{cases} T \text{ if } v_{\mathcal{A}}(\alpha) = v_{\mathcal{A}}(\beta) = T, \\ F \text{ otherwise.} \end{cases}$$

(5) For every L-sentence of the form $(\alpha \vee \beta)$,

$$v_{\mathcal{A}}((\alpha \vee \beta)) = \begin{cases} F \text{ if } v_{\mathcal{A}}(\alpha) = v_{\mathcal{A}}(\beta) = F, \\ T \text{ otherwise.} \end{cases}$$

(6) For every L-sentence of the form $(\alpha \to \beta)$,

$$v_{\mathcal{A}}((\alpha \to \beta)) = \begin{cases} F \text{ if } v_{\mathcal{A}}(\alpha) = T \text{ and } v_{\mathcal{A}}(\beta) = F, \\ T \text{ otherwise.} \end{cases}$$

Introducing function symbols would force us to modify this simple approach. If f is a function symbol of L, we want the functional terms built with f, like the individual constants of L, to be interpreted in an L-structure with elements of its universe. But these interpretations are not directly given by the definition of the L-structures. To specify them, we need to provide a recursive definition of the function pairing each L-term with the individual with which it is interpreted by an L-structure. We shall refer to the element of the universe with which a term is interpreted in a structure as its *denotation* in the structure. Thus, if L is a quantifier-free first-order language and $\mathcal{A}$ is an L-structure, we can define by recursion the function pairing each L-term with its denotation in $\mathcal{A}$, written $den_{\mathcal{A}}(t)$, as the unique function satisfying the following conditions.

(A) For every individual constant c of L, $den_{\mathcal{A}}(c) = c_{\mathcal{A}}$.

(B) For every L-term of the form $f(t_1,\ldots, t_n)$, $den_{\mathcal{A}}(f(t_1,\ldots, t_n)) = f_{\mathcal{A}}(den_{\mathcal{A}}(t_1),\ldots, den_{\mathcal{A}}(t_n))$.

Thus (B) singles out as the denotation of $f(t_1,\ldots, t_n)$ the image of $\langle den_{\mathcal{A}}(t_1),\ldots, den_{\mathcal{A}}(t_n) \rangle$ under the function with which $\mathcal{A}$ interprets f.

Using the notion of the denotation of an L-term in $\mathcal{A}$, to get a recursive definition of the truth value of an L-sentence in $\mathcal{A}$ we would just need to modify the definition provided above by formulating clauses (1) and (2) as involving the denotations in $\mathcal{A}$ of L-terms, instead of the interpretations in $\mathcal{A}$ of the individual constants of L.

Quantifiers pose a more serious difficulty. For each structure $\mathcal{A}$ for a first-order language L, we would like to define the function $v_{\mathcal{A}}$ by recursion, but we can only use the recursive method to define functions with an inductively defined set as their domain, and we don't have an inductive definition of the set of L-sentences. What we have is an inductive definition of the set of L-*formulas*. This in itself wouldn't be a problem. Every L-sentence is an L-formula. Hence, if we could define $v_{\mathcal{A}}$ by recursion on the L-formulas, we would have specified the image under $v_{\mathcal{A}}$ of each L-sentence. But things are not so simple. We know how we want an L-structure to assign truth values to L-sentences, but we have no notion of what truth values it should assign to L-formulas with free variables. Thus, e.g., we want the truth value of Pc in $\mathcal{A}$ to be T if $c_{\mathcal{A}} \in P_{\mathcal{A}}$, and F otherwise. But we can't specify in the same way the value that we would like $\mathcal{A}$ to assign to Px. There isn't an element of the universe of $\mathcal{A}$ whose presence in, or absence from, $P_{\mathcal{A}}$ should determine the truth value of Px in $\mathcal{A}$. Since variables are not interpreted by structures, we have no nonarbitrary way of assigning a truth value in a structure to a formula with free variables.

We could assign a truth value in a structure to a formula with free variables *relative to an interpretation of its free variables*. Thus, if a is an element of the universe of $\mathcal{A}$ and we interpret x with a, relative to that interpretation, Px will be true in $\mathcal{A}$ if $a \in P_{\mathcal{A}}$, and false otherwise. This suggests that for every structure $\mathcal{A}$ for a first-order language L, we could define a function assigning a truth value in $\mathcal{A}$ to each L-formula relative to each interpretation of the variables. This is the strategy that we are going to adopt.

DEFINITION: If L is a first-order language and $\mathcal{A}$ is an L-structure, a *variable interpretation* in $\mathcal{A}$ is a function from the set of variables to the universe of $\mathcal{A}$.

We can think of the image of a variable under a variable interpretation in $\mathcal{A}$ as a "provisional" denotation of x in $\mathcal{A}$. Our goal now is to define, for each L-structure $\mathcal{A}$, a function pairing each L-formula ϕ with its truth value in $\mathcal{A}$ relative to each variable interpretation in $\mathcal{A}$, i.e. a function from the Cartesian product of the set of L-formulas and the set of variable interpretations to the set $\{T, F\}$. We shall represent this function as $v_{\mathcal{A}}$. Notice that, contrary to our original intentions, $v_{\mathcal{A}}$ will be a two-place function, yielding a truth value for each L-formula and each variable interpretation in $\mathcal{A}$. We can define $v_{\mathcal{A}}$ by recursion on L-formulas. For each of the inductive clauses of the definition of the set of L-formulas, we need to specify how the image under $v_{\mathcal{A}}$ of a formula-variable interpretation pair formed with the output of the inductive clause depends on the image under $v_{\mathcal{A}}$ of the formula-variable interpretation pairs formed with the input of the inductive clause. We start by defining in this way a two-place function $den_{\mathcal{A}}$ pairing each L-term with its denotation in $\mathcal{A}$, relative to each variable interpretation in $\mathcal{A}$. We define $den_{\mathcal{A}}$ by recursion on L-terms.

DEFINITION: If L is a first-order language, and $\mathcal{A}$ an L-structure, the *denotation* in $\mathcal{A}$ of an L-term t relative to a variable interpretation s in $\mathcal{A}$, written $den_{\mathcal{A}}(t, s)$, is the image of t and s under the unique function satisfying the following conditions.

(A) For every variable x, and every variable interpretation s in $\mathcal{A}$, $den_{\mathcal{A}}(x, s) = s(x)$

(B) For every individual constant c of L, and every variable interpretation s in $\mathcal{A}$, $den_{\mathcal{A}}(c, s) = c_{\mathcal{A}}$.

(C) For every L-term of the form $f(t_1,\ldots, t_n)$, and every variable interpretation s in $\mathcal{A}$, $den_{\mathcal{A}}(f(t_1,\ldots, t_n), s) = f_{\mathcal{A}}(den_{\mathcal{A}}(t_1, s),\ldots, den_{\mathcal{A}}(t_n, s))$.

Thus the denotation of a variable in $\mathcal{A}$ relative to s will be its image under s. Individual constants get their denotations directly from the structure. Variable interpretations do not affect which denotation they get. The denotation of a term of the form $f(t_1,\ldots, t_n)$ in $\mathcal{A}$ relative to s will be the image of $\langle den_{\mathcal{A}}(t_1, s),\ldots, den_{\mathcal{A}}(t_n, s)\rangle$ under the interpretation of f in $\mathcal{A}$. Hence, the denotation in $\mathcal{A}$ of a functional term in which no variables occur will be the same for every variable interpretation in $\mathcal{A}$.

We also define $v_{\mathcal{A}}$ by recursion. L-formulas of the forms $Pt_1\ldots t_n$, $t \approx u$, $\neg\alpha$, $(\alpha \wedge \beta)$, $(\alpha \vee \beta)$ and $(\alpha \rightarrow \beta)$ can be dealt with in the same way as in a quantifier-free language. To complete the definition, we only need to find a suitable way of handling formulas of the forms $\forall x\, \alpha$ and $\exists x\, \alpha$. We will need to specify how the image under $v_{\mathcal{A}}$ of a formula-variable interpretation pair built with the output of the relevant inductive clause ($\forall x\, \alpha/\exists x\, \alpha$) is determined by the image under $v_{\mathcal{A}}$ of the formula-variable interpretation pairs built with the input of the clause (α). We can present the intuitive idea behind the clause for the universal quantifier by looking at a specific example. Consider the universal formula $\forall x\, Rxy$. We need to specify how the truth value of this formula in a structure relative to a variable interpretation depends on the truth value of Rxy in a structure relative to a variable interpretation. We could say that $\forall x\, Rxy$ is true in $\mathcal{A}$ relative to s just in case Rxy is true in $\mathcal{A}$ relative to s, *and would remain true no matter what denotation in A we assign to x, while keeping constant the interpretation of R in $\mathcal{A}$, and the interpretation of y relative to s.*

We can base on this idea the clause for the universal quantifier of the definition of $v_{\mathcal{A}}$, with the help of the following piece of notation. If s is a variable interpretation in $\mathcal{A}$, and a is an element of the universe of $\mathcal{A}$, we say that $s_{(x/a)}$ is the variable interpretation in $\mathcal{A}$ which yields the same image as s for every variable except, possibly, for x, which $s_{(x/a)}$ pairs with a. In other words, for every variable y,

$$s_{(x/a)}(y) = \begin{cases} a \text{ if } y = x, \\ s(y) \text{ otherwise.} \end{cases}$$

Notice that, if $s(x)$ is a, s and $s_{(x/a)}$ will be the same variable interpretation.

The clause for the universal quantifier of the definition of $v_{\mathcal{A}}$ will go as follows:

> For every L-formula of the form $\forall x\, \alpha$, and every variable interpretation s in $\mathcal{A}$,
>
> $$v_{\mathcal{A}}(\forall x\, \alpha, s) = \begin{cases} T \text{ if, for every } a \in A,\, v_{\mathcal{A}}(\alpha, s_{(x/a)}) = T, \\ F \text{ otherwise.} \end{cases}$$

It is important to see how this clause expresses the intuitive idea presented above. It tells us that the truth value of $\forall x\, \alpha$ in $\mathcal{A}$ relative to s is determined in the following way. Take the formula α. For all the extralogical symbols and variables that occur in α except for x, keep their interpretations fixed as given by $\mathcal{A}$ and s. Then assign to x each possible denotation in the universe of $\mathcal{A}$. If each such change makes α true, then $\forall x\, \alpha$ is true in $\mathcal{A}$ relative to s. If, on the contrary, at least one of these changes makes α false, then $\forall x\, \alpha$ is false in $\mathcal{A}$ relative to s.

The clause for the existential quantifier uses the same idea:

> For every L-formula of the form $\exists x\, \alpha$, and every variable interpretation s in $\mathcal{A}$,
>
> $$v_{\mathcal{A}}(\exists x\, \alpha, s) = \begin{cases} T \text{ if, for at least one } a \in A,\, v_{\mathcal{A}}(\alpha, s_{(x/a)}) = T, \\ F \text{ otherwise.} \end{cases}$$

Once again, we can imagine that, for all the extralogical symbols and variables that occur in α except for x, we keep their interpretations fixed as given by $\mathcal{A}$ and s. Then we assign to x each possible denotation in the universe of $\mathcal{A}$. If at least one of these changes makes α true, then $\exists x\, \alpha$ is true in $\mathcal{A}$ relative to s. If, on the contrary, each such change makes α false, then $\exists x\, \alpha$ is false in $\mathcal{A}$ relative to s. Now we have all the ingredients that we need to define the truth value of a formula in a structure relative to a variable interpretation.

DEFINITION: If L is a first-order language, and $\mathcal{A}$ an L-structure, the *truth value* in $\mathcal{A}$ of an L-formula ϕ relative to a variable interpretation s in $\mathcal{A}$, written $v_{\mathcal{A}}(\phi, s)$, is the image of ϕ and s under the unique function satisfying the following conditions.

(1) For every L-formula of the form $Pt_1 \ldots t_n$, and every variable interpretation s in $\mathcal{A}$,

$$v_{\mathcal{A}}(Pt_1 \ldots t_n, s) = \begin{cases} T \text{ if } \langle den_{\mathcal{A}}(t_1, s), \ldots, den_{\mathcal{A}}(t_n, s) \rangle \in P_{\mathcal{A}}, \\ F \text{ otherwise.} \end{cases}$$

(2) For every L-formula of the form $t \approx u$, and every variable interpretation s in $\mathcal{A}$,

$$v_{\mathcal{A}}(t \approx u, s) = \begin{cases} T \text{ if } den_{\mathcal{A}}(t, s) = den_{\mathcal{A}}(u, s), \\ F \text{ otherwise.} \end{cases}$$

(3) For every L-formula of the form $\neg\alpha$, and every variable interpretation s in $\mathcal{A}$,

$$v_{\mathcal{A}}(\neg\alpha, s) = \begin{cases} T \text{ if } v_{\mathcal{A}}(\alpha, s) = F, \\ F \text{ otherwise.} \end{cases}$$

(4) For every L-formula of the form $(\alpha \wedge \beta)$, and every variable interpretation s in $\mathcal{A}$,

$$v_{\mathcal{A}}((\alpha \wedge \beta), s) = \begin{cases} T \text{ if } v_{\mathcal{A}}(\alpha, s) = v_{\mathcal{A}}(\beta, s) = T, \\ F \text{ otherwise.} \end{cases}$$

(5) For every L-formula of the form $(\alpha \vee \beta)$, and every variable interpretation s in $\mathcal{A}$,

$$v_{\mathcal{A}}((\alpha \vee \beta), s) = \begin{cases} F \text{ if } v_{\mathcal{A}}(\alpha, s) = v_{\mathcal{A}}(\beta, s) = F, \\ T \text{ otherwise.} \end{cases}$$

(6) For every L-formula of the form $(\alpha \rightarrow \beta)$, and every variable interpretation s in $\mathcal{A}$,

$$v_{\mathcal{A}}((\alpha \rightarrow \beta), s) = \begin{cases} F \text{ if } v_{\mathcal{A}}(\alpha, s) = T \text{ and } v_{\mathcal{A}}(\beta, s) = F, \\ T \text{ otherwise.} \end{cases}$$

(7) For every L-formula of the form $\forall x\, \alpha$, and every variable interpretation s in $\mathcal{A}$,

$$v_{\mathcal{A}}(\forall x\, \alpha, s) = \begin{cases} T \text{ if, for every } a \in A, v_{\mathcal{A}}(\alpha, s_{(x/a)}) = T, \\ F \text{ otherwise.} \end{cases}$$

(8) For every L-formula of the form $\exists x\, \alpha$, and every variable interpretation s in $\mathcal{A}$,

$$v_{\mathcal{A}}(\exists x\, \alpha, s) = \begin{cases} T \text{ if, for at least one } a \in A, v_{\mathcal{A}}(\alpha, s_{(x/a)}) = T, \\ F \text{ otherwise.} \end{cases}$$

Notice that the truth value in $\mathcal{A}$ relative to s of an L-formula of the form $\neg\alpha$, $(\alpha \wedge \beta)$, $(\alpha \vee \beta)$ or $(\alpha \rightarrow \beta)$ is affected only by the truth value of its immediate subformulas in $\mathcal{A}$ relative to s. But the truth value in $\mathcal{A}$ relative to s of an L-formula of the form $\forall x\ \alpha$ or $\exists x\ \alpha$ will be affected, not only by the truth value of its immediate subformula in $\mathcal{A}$ relative to s, but also by its truth value in $\mathcal{A}$ relative to every other variable interpretation in $\mathcal{A}$ which differs from s only in how it interprets x.

For every L-structure $\mathcal{A}$, $v_{\mathcal{A}}$ assigns to each L-formula a truth value in $\mathcal{A}$ relative to each variable interpretation in $\mathcal{A}$. Thus, in particular, $v_{\mathcal{A}}$ assigns to each L-sentence a truth value in $\mathcal{A}$ relative to each variable interpretation in $\mathcal{A}$. This is not quite what we were looking for. We wanted a function assigning to each L-sentence a unique truth value in $\mathcal{A}$. The difference between what we have achieved and what we were looking for arises from the possibility that an L-sentence gets different truth values in $\mathcal{A}$ relative to different variable interpretations. If we could rule out this possibility, we would have shown that $v_{\mathcal{A}}$ assigns to each L-sentence a unique truth value in $\mathcal{A}$, as desired. This would involve showing that, for every L-sentence ϕ, ϕ is paired by $v_{\mathcal{A}}$ with the same truth value relative to each variable interpretation in $\mathcal{A}$.

Notice that this is not in general the case for L-formulas with free variables. If ψ is a formula with free variables and s and s' are two variable interpretations in $\mathcal{A}$, it is possible that $v_{\mathcal{A}}(\psi, s) \neq v_{\mathcal{A}}(\psi, s')$. But for L-sentences this is not so. If ϕ has no free variables, then for every two variable interpretations s, s' in $\mathcal{A}$, we have that $v_{\mathcal{A}}(\phi, s) = v_{\mathcal{A}}(\phi, s')$. We can see intuitively that this is the case with a couple of examples. Consider first a quantifier-free sentence, say, Pc. The truth value of Pc in $\mathcal{A}$ relative to a variable interpretation s in $\mathcal{A}$ is determined by whether $c_{\mathcal{A}}$ is an element of $P_{\mathcal{A}}$. s plays no role whatsoever in determining the truth value of Pc in $\mathcal{A}$ relative to s. Hence, if Pc is true (false) in $\mathcal{A}$ relative to s, it will also be true (false) in $\mathcal{A}$ relative to any other variable interpretation. The same goes for a quantified sentence, say $\exists x\ Px$. Px can be expected to be true in $\mathcal{A}$ relative to some variable interpretations, and false in $\mathcal{A}$ relative to other variable interpretations. But so long as there is at least one variable interpretation s such that Px is true in $\mathcal{A}$ relative to s, $\exists x$ Px will be true in $\mathcal{A}$ relative to *all* variable interpretations. If, on the contrary, there is no variable interpretation s such that Px is true in $\mathcal{A}$ relative to s, then $\exists x\ Px$ will be false in $\mathcal{A}$, again relative to all variable interpretations.

We can replace this intuitive argument with a formal proof of the general principle that variable interpretations don't affect the truth value of a sentence in a structure. This will follow as a corollary of Exercise 3. 18, below. To prove that claim we need to invoke the following result:

EXERCISE 3. 17: Prove that the denotation $den_{\mathcal{A}}(t, s)$ of a term t in a structure $\mathcal{A}$ relative to a variable interpretation s in $\mathcal{A}$ is unchanged if we change the values that s yields for variables not occurring in t.

Hint: Prove by induction on L-terms in the following form: Let $\mathcal{A}$ be an L-structure. For every L-term t, if s, s' are two variable interpretations in $\mathcal{A}$ such that for every variable x that occurs in t, $s(x) = s'(x)$, then $den_{\mathcal{A}}(t, s) = den_{\mathcal{A}}(t, s')$.

Let's say that an L-term is *closed* if it contains no occurrences of variables. It follows from Exercise 3. 17 that a closed L-term t has the same denotation in an L-structure $\mathcal{A}$ relative to every variable interpretation in $\mathcal{A}$. We shall represent the denotation of t in $\mathcal{A}$ as $den_{\mathcal{A}}(t)$.

EXERCISE 3. 18: Prove that the truth value $v_{\mathcal{A}}(\phi, s)$ of a formula ϕ in a structure $\mathcal{A}$ relative to a variable interpretation s in $\mathcal{A}$ is unchanged if we change the values that s yields for variables which are not *free* in ϕ.

Hint: Prove by induction on L-formulas in the following form: Let $\mathcal{A}$ be an L-structure. For every L-formula ϕ, if s and s' are two variable interpretations in $\mathcal{A}$ such that for every variable x that is free in ϕ, $s(x) = s'(x)$, then $v_{\mathcal{A}}(\phi, s) = v_{\mathcal{A}}(\phi, s')$. You'll need to invoke Exercise 3. 17.

Since sentences have no free variables, it follows directly from Exercise 3. 18 that, for any L-structure $\mathcal{A}$ and L-sentence ϕ, either ϕ is true in $\mathcal{A}$ relative to all variable interpretations, or ϕ is false in $\mathcal{A}$ relative to all variable interpretations. Hence, the definition of the truth value of a formula in a structure relative to a variable interpretation gives us, in effect, a definition of the truth value of a sentence in a structure, as desired. We shall refer to the truth value of an L-sentence ϕ in an L-structure $\mathcal{A}$ as $v_{\mathcal{A}}(\phi)$.

We can see with an example how $v_{\mathcal{A}}$ enables us to model in first-order languages the semantic patterns of first-order propositions. Consider the proposition that everyone has beaten everyone by whom they have been beaten, concerning the members of a tennis club. The syntactic pattern of this proposition can be modeled in a first-order language L with a two-place predicate R by the L-sentence $\forall x \forall y \, (Rxy \rightarrow Ryx)$. Consider now the semantic pattern of this proposition. The relation ...*has beaten*... figures in it in such a way that the proposition is true just in case, for all members a, b of the club, if a has beaten b, then b has also beaten a, i.e. just in case the relation ...*has beaten*... defined on the set of club members is a symmetric relation. Every proposition built with a binary relation according to this syntactic pattern will be true just in case the relation, defined on the set of individuals to which quantification is restricted, is a symmetric relation. Hence, the semantic pattern associated with this syntactic pattern assigns a truth value to each combination of a set and a binary relation in the set—the value true if the relation is symmetric, and the value false otherwise. $v_{\mathcal{A}}$ will make the sentence $\forall x \forall y$ $(Rxy \rightarrow Ryx)$ model this semantic pattern. For every L-structure $\mathcal{A}$, $\forall x \forall y$ $(Rxy \rightarrow Ryx)$ will receive the value T from $v_{\mathcal{A}}$ if $R_{\mathcal{A}}$ is a symmetric relation, and the value F otherwise (see Exercise 3. 38, below).

The main ideas of this procedure for modeling in a formal language the semantic patterns of first-order propositions were presented by Alfred Tarski in the 1930s. A definition along the lines of our definition of the truth value of a formula in a structure relative to a variable interpretation is sometimes known as *Tarski's definition of truth*.

EXERCISE 3. 19: Let L be the first-order language whose extralogical vocabulary consists of two one-place predicates, P, Q, and an individual constant, c. Let $\mathcal{A}$ be the L-structure such that $A = \{1, 2, 3, 4\}$, $P_{\mathcal{A}} = \{1, 2\}$, $Q_{\mathcal{A}} = \{2, 3\}$, and $c_{\mathcal{A}} = 1$. Determine the truth value in $\mathcal{A}$ of each of the following sentences. (Since they are sentences, they have the same truth value in $\mathcal{A}$ for every variable interpretation.)

    (1) $\forall x\, (Px \vee Qx)$
    (2) $\exists x\, (Px \wedge \neg Qx)$
    (3) $\forall x\, (Px \rightarrow x \approx c)$
    (4) $\exists x \exists y\, (\neg Px \wedge \neg Qy)$
    (5) $\exists x \exists y\, ((\neg Px \wedge \neg Qy) \wedge \neg x \approx y)$
    (6) $\forall x\, (Px \rightarrow Qx)$
    (7) $\forall x\, Px \rightarrow \forall x\, Qx$
    (8) $\exists x\, Px \rightarrow \forall y\, Py$
    (9) $\exists x\, (Px \rightarrow \forall y\, Py)$

EXERCISE 3. 20: Let L be the first-order language whose extralogical vocabulary consists of one two-place predicate, R. For each of the following L-sentences, describe an L-structure in which it is true and one in which it is false.

    (1) $\forall x \exists y\, Rxy$
    (2) $\exists y \forall x\, Rxy$
    (3) $\forall x \exists y\, Ryx$
    (4) $\exists y \forall x\, Ryx$
    (5) $\forall x\, (Rxx \rightarrow \neg Rxx)$
    (6) $\forall x \forall y\, (Rxy \rightarrow Ryx)$
    (7) $\forall x \forall y\, (Rxy \rightarrow \neg Ryx)$
    (8) $\forall x \forall y\, (\neg Rxy \rightarrow Ryx)$
    (9) $\exists x \exists y \exists z\, (((\neg x \approx y \wedge \neg y \approx z) \wedge \neg x \approx z) \wedge ((Rxy \wedge Rxx) \wedge \neg Rxz))$

5. Logical Consequence and Other Logical Notions

In terms of the truth value of an L-formula in an L-structure relative to a variable interpretation, we can define notions for L-formulas which model the logical properties and relations generated by the structure of first-order propositions.

DEFINITION: If ϕ is a formula of a first-order language L and Γ is a set of L-formulas, ϕ is a *logical consequence* of Γ, written $\Gamma \vDash \phi$, just in case, for every L-structure $\mathcal{A}$ and every variable interpretation s in $\mathcal{A}$, if $v_\mathcal{A}(\gamma, s) = T$ for every $\gamma \in \Gamma$, then $v_\mathcal{A}(\phi, s) = T$. (When ϕ is not a logical consequence of Γ, we write $\nvDash$.)

In other words, if there is an L-structure $\mathcal{A}$, and a variable interpretation s in $\mathcal{A}$, such that all the elements of Γ are true in $\mathcal{A}$ relative to s but ϕ is false in $\mathcal{A}$ relative to s, then ϕ is *not* a logical consequence of Γ. Otherwise ϕ *is* a logical consequence of Γ. Given that variable interpretations don't affect the truth value of a sentence in a structure, it follows from this definition that a *sentence* ϕ is a logical consequence of a set of *sentences* Γ just in case ϕ is true in all structures in which all the elements of Γ are true.

Notice that, if ϕ is a formula of a first-order language, it will also be a formula of every other first-order language whose vocabulary contains all the extralogical symbols which occur in ϕ. If L and L' are first-order languages, and ϕ and all the elements of Γ are both L-formulas and L'-formulas, the question whether ϕ is a logical consequence of Γ can be formulated either in terms of L-structures or in terms of L'-structures. Nevertheless, the answer will be identical in each case. This is a direct consequence of the following exercise:

EXERCISE 3. 21: Let L and L' be first-order languages, and let $\mathcal{A}$ be an L-structure and s a variable interpretation in $\mathcal{A}$. Show that there is an L'-structure $\mathcal{A}'$ and a variable interpretation s' in $\mathcal{A}'$ such that, for every L-formula ϕ which is also an L'-formula, $v_\mathcal{A}(\phi, s) = v_{\mathcal{A}'}(\phi, s')$.

Hint: Describe $\mathcal{A}'$ and s' in terms of $\mathcal{A}$ and s. Show that $\mathcal{A}'$ and s' are related to $\mathcal{A}$ and s in the right way by induction on the L-formulas which are also L'-formulas, i.e. on the formulas of the language whose extralogical vocabulary is the intersection of the extralogical vocabularies of L and L'.

It follows from this that logical consequence claims don't have to be made relative to a specific language.

The claim that an *L*-formula is a logical consequence of a set of *L*-formulas can be seen as a universal implication of the form, for every *L*-structure *A* and every variable interpretation *s* in *A*.... Hence, to establish logical consequence claims we can use the standard procedure for proving universal implications. To see how the procedure works for logical consequence claims, let's apply it to the claim that the *L*-formula *Qc* is a logical consequence of the set of *L*-formulas $\{\forall x (Px \rightarrow Qx), Pc\}$. We want to prove that, for every *L*-structure *A*, and every variable interpretation *s* in *A*, if $v_A(\forall x (Px \rightarrow Qx), s) = v_A(Pc, s) = T$, then $v_A(Qc, s) = T$. Let *A* be an *L*-structure and let *s* be a variable interpretation in *A* such that $v_A(\forall x (Px \rightarrow Qx), s) = v_A(Pc, s) = T$. We want to prove that it follows from this that $v_A(Qc, s) = T$. For this, by the definition of truth, it will suffice to show that $den_A(c, s) \in Q_A$. Also by the definition of truth, from the assumption that $v_A(Pc, s) = T$ it follows that $den_A(c, s) \in P_A$. Hence, to establish that $v_A(Qc, s) = T$, it will suffice to show that it is not the case that $den_A(c, s) \in P_A$ and $den_A(c, s) \notin Q_A$. But this follows from the assumption that $v_A(\forall x (Px \rightarrow Qx), s) = T$, as shown by the following argument:

$v_A(\forall x (Px \rightarrow Qx), s) = T$

⇓   (by the definition of truth)

For every $a \in A$, $v_A(Px \rightarrow Qx, s_{(x/a)}) = T$

⇓   (by the definition of truth)

For every $a \in A$,
it is not the case that $v_A(Px, s_{(x/a)}) = T$ and $v_A(Qx, s_{(x/a)}) = F$

⇓   (by the definition of truth)

For every $a \in A$,
it is not the case that $den_A(x, s_{(x/a)}) \in P_A$ and $den_A(x, s_{(x/a)}) \notin Q_A$

⇓   (by the definition of denotation)

For every $a \in A$, it is not the case that $s_{(x/a)}(x) \in P_A$ and $s_{(x/a)}(x) \notin Q_A$

⇓   (since $s_{(x/a)}(x) = a$)

For every $a \in A$, it is not the case that $a \in P_A$ and $a \notin Q_A$

⇓   (since $den_A(c, s) \in A$)

It is not the case that $den_A(c, s) \in P_A$ and $den_A(c, s) \notin Q_A$

EXERCISE 3. 22: Establish the following claims:
   (1) $\{\forall x\,(Mx \rightarrow Px),\ \forall x\,(Sx \rightarrow Mx)\} \vDash \forall x\,(Sx \rightarrow Px)$
   (2) $\{\forall x\,(Mx \rightarrow \neg Px),\ \exists x\,(Sx \wedge Mx)\} \vDash \exists x\,(Sx \wedge \neg Px)$
   (3) $\{\forall x\,(Px \rightarrow Mx),\ \forall x\,(Sx \rightarrow \neg Mx)\} \vDash \forall x\,(Sx \rightarrow \neg Px)$

Hint: Proceed as in the example provided above. As the reader becomes familiar with the procedure, more and more steps may come to appear too obvious to write out in full.

EXERCISE 3. 23: Establish the following claims:
   (1) $\{\forall x\,Px\} \vDash \exists x\,Px$
   (2) $\{\forall x \forall y\,Rxy\} \vDash \forall x\,Rxx$
   (3) $\{\exists x\,Rxx\} \vDash \exists x \exists y\,Rxy$
   (4) $\{\exists y \forall x\,Rxy\} \vDash \forall x \exists y\,Rxy$
   (5) $\{\forall x\,(Px \rightarrow Qx)\} \vDash \forall x \forall y\,((Px \wedge Rxy) \rightarrow (Qx \wedge Rxy))$
   (6) $\{\forall x\,(Qx \rightarrow Px) \rightarrow \exists x\,(Px \wedge \neg Sx),\ \forall x\,(Px \rightarrow Sx)\} \vDash\ \exists x\,(Qx \wedge \neg Px)$

EXERCISE 3. 24: Show that for all formulas ϕ, ψ of a first-order language, the following claims hold:
   (1) $\{\forall x\,\phi \vee \forall x\,\psi\} \vDash\ \forall x\,(\phi \vee \psi)$
   (2) $\{\exists x\,(\phi \wedge \psi)\} \vDash\ \exists x\,\phi \wedge \exists x\,\psi$
   (3) $\{\forall x\,\phi \wedge \exists x\,\psi\} \vDash\ \exists x\,(\phi \wedge \psi)$
   (4) $\{\forall x\,(\phi \vee \psi)\} \vDash\ \forall x\,\phi \vee \exists x\,\psi$

EXERCISE 3. 25: Show that for all formulas ϕ, ψ of a first-order language, the following claims hold:
   (1) $\{\forall x\,(\phi \rightarrow \psi)\} \vDash \forall x\,\phi \rightarrow \forall x\,\psi$
   (2) $\{\forall x\,(\phi \rightarrow \psi)\} \vDash \exists x\,\phi \rightarrow \exists x\,\psi$
   (3) $\{\exists x\,(\phi \rightarrow \psi)\} \vDash \forall x\,\phi \rightarrow \exists x\,\psi$
   (4) $\{\exists x\,\phi \rightarrow \forall x\,\psi\} \vDash \forall x\,(\phi \rightarrow \psi)$
   (5) $\{\exists x\,\phi \rightarrow \exists x\,\psi\} \vDash \exists x\,(\phi \rightarrow \psi)$

EXERCISE 3. 26: Establish the following claims (t, u and v are arbitrary terms):
   (1) $\{t \approx u\} \vDash f(t) \approx f(u)$
   (2) $\{t \approx u,\ Pt\} \vDash Pu$
   (3) $\{t \approx u\} \vDash u \approx t$
   (4) $\{t \approx u,\ u \approx v\} \vDash t \approx v$

To prove that a formula ϕ is not a logical consequence of a set of formulas Γ, we just need to provide a counterexample to the universal implication expressing the logical consequence claim—a structure $\mathcal{A}$ and a variable interpretation s in $\mathcal{A}$ such that all the elements of Γ are true in $\mathcal{A}$ relative to s but ϕ is false in $\mathcal{A}$ relative to s. Let's see how this works in a

particular case by proving that the formula Pc is not a logical conse-
quence of the set $\{\forall x\ (Px \rightarrow Qx),\ Qc\}$. Consider a structure $\mathcal{A}$ with the
following features: $P_{\mathcal{A}} \subset Q_{\mathcal{A}}$, $c_{\mathcal{A}} \in Q_{\mathcal{A}}$ and $c_{\mathcal{A}} \notin P_{\mathcal{A}}$. We can represent $\mathcal{A}$
with the diagram in Figure 6.

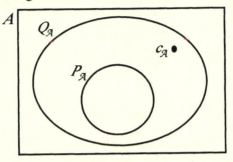

Figure 6

To establish that $\mathcal{A}$ is a counterexample to the claim that $\{\forall x\ (Px \rightarrow$
$Qx),\ Qc\} \models Pc$, we need to show that for at least one variable interpreta-
tion s in $\mathcal{A}$ (i) $v_{\mathcal{A}}(\forall x\ (Px \rightarrow Qx),\ s) = T$, (ii) $v_{\mathcal{A}}(Qc,\ s) = T$ and (iii) $v_{\mathcal{A}}(Pc,$
$s) = F$. But since we are dealing with sentences, which variable
interpretation we choose will make no difference.

For (ii), we have that $c_{\mathcal{A}} \in Q_{\mathcal{A}}$. But by the definition of denotation, $c_{\mathcal{A}}$
$= den_{\mathcal{A}}(c,\ s)$, for any variable interpretation s in $\mathcal{A}$. Hence, $den_{\mathcal{A}}(c,\ s) \in$
$Q_{\mathcal{A}}$. And by the definition of truth, we get $v_{\mathcal{A}}(Qc,\ s) = T$, as desired.

For (iii), we have that $c_{\mathcal{A}} \notin P_{\mathcal{A}}$, i.e. $den_{\mathcal{A}}(c,\ s) \notin P_{\mathcal{A}}$, for every variable
interpretation s in $\mathcal{A}$. Hence, by the definition of truth, we get $v_{\mathcal{A}}(Pc,\ s) =$
F.

That (i) holds for every variable interpretation s in $\mathcal{A}$ follows from the
assumption that $P_{\mathcal{A}}$ is a subset of $Q_{\mathcal{A}}$. We show this with the following
argument.

$P_{\mathcal{A}} \subseteq Q_{\mathcal{A}}$

   $\Downarrow$ (by the definition of $\subseteq$)

For every $a \in A$, it is not the case that $a \in P_{\mathcal{A}}$ and $a \notin Q_{\mathcal{A}}$

   $\Downarrow$ (since $s_{(x/a)}(x)$ is a)

For every $a \in A$, it is not the case that $s_{(x/a)}(x) \in P_{\mathcal{A}}$ and $s_{(x/a)}(x) \notin Q_{\mathcal{A}}$

   $\Downarrow$ (by the definition of denotation)

For every $a \in A$,
it is not the case that $den_{\mathcal{A}}(x,\ s_{(x/a)}) \in P_{\mathcal{A}}$ and $den_{\mathcal{A}}(x,\ s_{(x/a)}) \notin Q_{\mathcal{A}}$

⇓   (by the definition of truth)

For every $a \in A$,
it is not the case that $v_{\mathcal{A}}(Px, s_{(x/a)}) = T$ and $v_{\mathcal{A}}(Qx, s_{(x/a)}) = F$

⇓   (by the definition of truth)

For every $a \in A$, $v_{\mathcal{A}}(Px \rightarrow Qx, s_{(x/a)}) = T$

⇓   (by the definition of truth)

$v_{\mathcal{A}}(\forall x \,(Px \rightarrow Qx), s) = T$

EXERCISE 3. 27: Establish the following claims:
 (1) $\{\exists x\, Px\} \not\vDash \forall x\, Px$
 (2) $\{\forall x\, Px \rightarrow \forall x\, Qx\} \not\vDash \forall x\,(Px \rightarrow Qx)$
 (3) $\{\forall x \exists y\, Rxy\} \not\vDash \exists y \forall x\, Rxy$
 (4) $\{\forall x \exists y\, Rxy\} \not\vDash \forall x \exists y\, Ryx$
 (5) $\{\exists x \forall y\, Rxy\} \not\vDash \exists x \forall y\, Ryx$

Hint: Proceed as in the example provided above. As the reader becomes familiar with the procedure, more and more steps may come to appear too obvious to write out in full.

EXERCISE 3. 28: Show that there are formulas ϕ, ψ, such that
 (1) $\{\exists x\,(\phi \rightarrow \psi)\,\} \not\vDash \exists x\, \phi \rightarrow \exists x\, \psi$
 (2) $\{\forall x\,(\phi \rightarrow \psi)\} \not\vDash \exists x\, \phi \rightarrow \forall x\, \psi$
 (3) $\{\exists x\, \phi \wedge \exists x\, \psi\} \not\vDash \exists x\,(\phi \wedge \psi)$
 (4) $\{\forall x\,(\phi \vee \psi)\} \not\vDash \forall x\, \phi \vee \forall x\, \psi$

We can now use the notion of truth in a structure relative to a variable interpretation to define a few related concepts.

DEFINITION: A formula ϕ of a first-order language L is *logically true*, written $\vDash \phi$, just in case, for every L-structure $\mathcal{A}$, and every variable interpretation s in $\mathcal{A}$, $v_{\mathcal{A}}(\phi, s) = T$.

DEFINITION: Two formulas ϕ, ψ of a first-order language L are *logically equivalent*, written $\phi \doteq \psi$, just in case, for every L-structure $\mathcal{A}$, and every variable interpretation s in $\mathcal{A}$, $v_{\mathcal{A}}(\phi, s) = v_{\mathcal{A}}(\psi, s)$.

DEFINITION: A set of formulas Γ of a first-order language L is *satisfiable* just in case there is an L-structure $\mathcal{A}$, and a variable interpretation s in $\mathcal{A}$, such that for every $\gamma \in \Gamma$ $v_{\mathcal{A}}(\gamma, s) = T$. Otherwise Γ is *unsatisfiable*.

As with logical consequence, we can characterize logical truth, logical equivalence and satisfiability for *sentences* without mentioning variable interpretations. Logically true sentences are true in all structures. Logically equivalent sentences have the same truth value in all structures (they may be true in some structures and false in others, but there are no structures in which one is true and the other is false). And for a satisfiable set of sentences there is at least one structure in which all the elements of the set are true.

EXERCISE 3. 29: Establish the following claims:

(1) $\vDash x \approx x$
(2) $\vDash \forall x \exists y \, x \approx y$
(3) $\vDash \forall x \exists y \, f(x) \approx y$
(4) $\vDash \exists x \, (Px \to \forall y \, Py)$
(5) $\vDash \neg \exists x \forall y \, ((Rxy \to \neg Ryx) \wedge (\neg Ryx \to Rxy))$

Hint: The claim that an *L*-formula ϕ is logically true can be proved by *reductio*, assuming towards a contradiction that there is an *L*-structure $\mathcal{A}$ and a variable interpretation s in $\mathcal{A}$ such that $v_{\mathcal{A}}(\phi, s) = F$.

EXERCISE 3. 30: Show that for all formulas ϕ, ψ of a first-order language the following claims hold:

(1) $\forall x \, \neg \phi \rightleftharpoons \neg \exists x \, \phi$
(2) $\exists x \, \neg \phi \rightleftharpoons \neg \forall x \, \phi$
(3) $\forall x \, \phi \rightleftharpoons \neg \exists x \, \neg \phi$
(4) $\exists x \, \phi \rightleftharpoons \neg \forall x \, \neg \phi$
(5) $\forall x \forall y \, \phi \rightleftharpoons \forall y \forall x \, \phi$
(6) $\exists x \exists y \, \phi \rightleftharpoons \exists y \exists x \, \phi$
(7) $\forall x \, (\phi \wedge \psi) \rightleftharpoons \forall x \, \phi \wedge \forall x \, \psi$
(8) $\exists x \, (\phi \vee \psi) \rightleftharpoons \exists x \, \phi \vee \exists x \, \psi$
(9) $\forall x \, (\phi \to \psi) \rightleftharpoons \neg \exists x \, (\phi \wedge \neg \psi)$

Hint: The claim that two *L*-formulas ϕ, ψ are logically equivalent can be formulated as a universal equivalence—for every *L*-structure $\mathcal{A}$, and every variable interpretation s in $\mathcal{A}$, $v_{\mathcal{A}}(\phi, s) = T$ if and only if $v_{\mathcal{A}}(\psi, s) = T$.

EXERCISE 3. 31: Show that for all formulas ϕ, ψ of a first-order language, if x is not free in ψ, the following claims hold:

(1) $\forall x \, \psi \rightleftharpoons \psi$
(2) $\exists x \, \psi \rightleftharpoons \psi$
(3) $\forall x \, (\phi \vee \psi) \rightleftharpoons \forall x \, \phi \vee \psi$
(4) $\exists x \, (\phi \wedge \psi) \rightleftharpoons \exists x \, \phi \wedge \psi$
(5) $\forall x \, \phi \to \psi \rightleftharpoons \exists x \, (\phi \to \psi)$
(6) $\exists x \, \phi \to \psi \rightleftharpoons \forall x \, (\phi \to \psi)$
(7) $\psi \to \forall x \, \phi \rightleftharpoons \forall x \, (\psi \to \phi)$
(8) $\psi \to \exists x \, \phi \rightleftharpoons \exists x \, (\psi \to \phi)$

EXERCISE 3. 32: Show that, for all formulas ϕ, ψ of a first-order language L, and every set Γ of L-formulas, the following claims hold:
(1) If $\models \phi$, then $\models \forall x\, \phi$ and $\models \exists x\, \phi$
(2) If $\Gamma \cup \{\phi\} \models \psi$, and x is not free in Γ or ψ, then $\Gamma \cup \{\exists x\, \phi\} \models \psi$
(3) If $\Gamma \models \forall x\, \phi$, then $\Gamma \models \phi$
(4) If $\Gamma \cup \{\phi\} \models \psi$, then $\Gamma \cup \{\forall x\, \phi\} \models \psi$
(5) If $\Gamma \models \phi$, and x is not free in Γ, then $\Gamma \models \forall x\, \phi$

Hint: Assume the antecedent and, on this assumption, establish the logical consequence claim in the consequent using the standard procedure.

EXERCISE 3. 33: Show that the following sets of sentences are satisfiable:
(1) $\{\forall x\, (Px \to Qx),\ \forall x\, (Qx \to Tx),\ \exists x\, (Tx \wedge \neg Px)\}$
(2) $\{\exists x\, (Px \wedge Qx),\ \forall x\, (\neg Px \to Qx)\}$
(3) $\{\forall x\, (Px \vee Qx),\ \forall x\, (\neg Px \vee \neg Qx)\}$
(4) $\{\forall x\, (Px \to Qx),\ \forall x\, (Px \to \neg Qx)\}$

Hint: Describe a structure (for a language containing the extralogical symbols occurring in the sentences in the set) in which all the elements of the set are true.

EXERCISE 3. 34: Define logical truth, logical equivalence and satisfiability in terms of logical consequence. Prove that your definitions are correct (i.e. equivalent to the ones given above).

EXERCISE 3. 35: Prove that $\Gamma \models \alpha$ if and only if $\Gamma \cup \{\neg \alpha\}$ is not satisfiable.

There are obvious parallelisms between the syntax and semantics of *PL* and the syntax and semantics of a first-order language. At the syntactic level, the inductive clauses of the definition of *PL* have obvious correlates in the first four inductive clauses of the definition of L-formula for a first-order language L. The main consequence of this is that if $\phi_1, \ldots, \phi_n$ are *PL*-sentences, and $\psi_1, \ldots, \psi_n$ are L-formulas, for every *PL*-sentence that we can build with $\phi_1, \ldots, \phi_n$, we will be able to find an L-formula which is built from $\psi_1, \ldots, \psi_n$ in the same way. At the semantic level, the clauses of the definition of admissible *PL*-assignment can be recognized in clauses (3)–(6) of the definition of truth for first-order formulas. This correspondence generates links between the propositional notions of logical consequence, logical truth, logical equivalence and satisfiability, and their first-order counterparts. Consider claims to the effect that if a *PL*-sentence ϕ and a set of *PL*-sentences Γ are built according to a certain pattern, then ϕ is a logical consequence of Γ, as, e.g., the claim that for all *PL*-sentences ϕ, ψ, $\{\phi \vee \psi, \neg \psi\} \models \phi$, or that for all *PL*-sentences ϕ, ψ,

$\{\phi \lor \psi, \psi\} \vDash \neg\phi$. By virtue of the connection between propositional and first-order semantic notions, a claim of this kind will hold if and only if the same goes for the corresponding claim concerning formulas of a first-order language. Thus, e.g., since $\{\phi \lor \psi, \neg\psi\} \vDash \phi$ holds for all *PL*-sentences ϕ, ψ, it also holds for all formulas ϕ, ψ of a first-order language, and since there are *PL*-sentences ϕ, ψ for which $\{\phi \lor \psi, \psi\} \vDash \neg\phi$ doesn't hold, there are formulas ϕ, ψ of any first-order language for which the claim doesn't hold either. A similar connection obtains between propositional and first-order logical truth, logical equivalence and satisfiability. Hence, since the claims in Exercises 2. 16–19 and 2. 21–26 hold for all *PL*-sentences, they also hold for all formulas of a first-order language. And the arguments that we would use to establish the propositional version of these claims can easily be adapted to establish the first-order versions.

EXERCISE 3. 36: Let $\mathcal{A}$ be a structure of a first-order language L. Show that, for every L-formula ψ, if ϕ, ϕ^* are L-formulas such that, for every variable interpretation s in $\mathcal{A}$, $v_{\mathcal{A}}(\phi, s) = v_{\mathcal{A}}(\phi^*, s)$, and ψ^* is the L-formula which results from replacing every occurrence of ϕ in ψ with an occurrence of ϕ^*, then for every variable interpretation s in $\mathcal{A}$, $v_{\mathcal{A}}(\psi, s) = v_{\mathcal{A}}(\psi^*, s)$.

Hint: By induction.

EXERCISE 3. 37: Show that if ϕ, ϕ^* are formulas of a first-order language L such that $\phi \Leftrightarrow \phi^*$, and ψ, ψ^* are L-formulas such that ψ^* results from replacing every occurrence of ϕ in ψ with an occurrence of ϕ^*, then $\psi \Leftrightarrow \psi^*$.

Hint: Use Exercise 3. 36.

6. Models

So far we have been looking at the connection between syntactic and semantic patterns from the point of view of the syntactic patterns—by considering how the truth values of the propositions with a given syntactic pattern are determined by which individuals instantiate the properties and relations which figure in them. We can also look at this connection from the point of view of the semantic patterns—by asking how we can build with individuals, properties, relations, truth-functional composition devices and universal and existential quantification a proposition corresponding to a given semantic pattern.

We can raise analogous questions in terms of first-order languages. The idea would be to focus on a class C of structures of a first-order language L and to try to find an L-sentence which is true in every L-structure in C, and false in every other L-structure. More generally, we could try to find a set Γ of L-sentences such that every L-structure in C yields the value T for every L-sentence in Γ and every other L-structure yields the value F for at least one L-sentence in Γ. In this section we are going to ask a few questions of this kind, using the following concept.

DEFINITION: An L-structure $\mathcal{A}$ is a *model* of an L-sentence ϕ just in case ϕ is true in $\mathcal{A}$. $\mathcal{A}$ is a *model* of a set of L-sentences Γ just in case every L-sentence in Γ is true in $\mathcal{A}$.

We are going to ask, for a given class C of structures of a first-order language L, whether we can find a set of L-sentences whose models are precisely the structures in C.

i.   *Equivalence Relations*

Let's start by looking at structures for the first-order language L with a two-place predicate R as its only extralogical symbol. An L-structure $\mathcal{A}$ will consist of a set A (the universe) and a two-place relation $R_{\mathcal{A}}$ in A. Some L-structures will interpret R with an equivalence relation in their universe. We can show that the set containing the following three sentences will have precisely these structures as its models.

$\forall x\, Rxx$
$\forall x \forall y\, (Rxy \rightarrow Ryx)$
$\forall x \forall y \forall z\, ((Rxy \wedge Ryz) \rightarrow Rxz)$

To show this, we need to establish that these three sentences are true in an L-structure $\mathcal{A}$ if and only if $R_{\mathcal{A}}$ is an equivalence relation in the universe A of $\mathcal{A}$. For this, it will suffice to prove (i) that for every L-structure $\mathcal{A}$, $v_{\mathcal{A}}(\forall x\, Rxx) = T$ if and only if $R_{\mathcal{A}}$ is reflexive in A, (ii) that for every L-structure $\mathcal{A}$, $v_{\mathcal{A}}(\forall x \forall y\, (Rxy \rightarrow Ryx)) = T$ if and only if $R_{\mathcal{A}}$ is symmetric and (iii) that for every L-structure $\mathcal{A}$, $v_{\mathcal{A}}(\forall x \forall y \forall z\, ((Rxy \wedge Ryz) \rightarrow Rxz)) = T$ if and only if $R_{\mathcal{A}}$ is transitive. For (i), (ii) and (iii) entail that if $R_{\mathcal{A}}$ is an equivalence relation in A, then the three sentences are true in $\mathcal{A}$, and if $R_{\mathcal{A}}$ is not an equivalence relation in A, then at least one of them is false in $\mathcal{A}$.

For (i), we need to show that, for every L-structure $\mathcal{A}$, and every variable interpretation s in $\mathcal{A}$, $v_{\mathcal{A}}(\forall x\, Rxx, s) = T$ if and only if for every $a \in A$, $\langle a, a \rangle \in R_{\mathcal{A}}$. Let $\mathcal{A}$ be an L-structure, and let s be a variable interpretation in $\mathcal{A}$. We argue as follows:

$v_{\mathcal{A}}(\forall x\, Rxx, s) = T$

    $\Updownarrow$ (by the definition of truth)

For every $a \in A$, $v_{\mathcal{A}}(Rxx, s_{(x/a)}) = T$

    $\Updownarrow$ (by the definition of truth)

For every $a \in A$, $\langle den_{\mathcal{A}}(x, s_{(x/a)}), den_{\mathcal{A}}(x, s_{(x/a)})\rangle \in R_{\mathcal{A}}$

    $\Updownarrow$ (by the definition of denotation)

For every $a \in A$, $\langle s_{(x/a)}(x), s_{(x/a)}(x)\rangle \in R_{\mathcal{A}}$

    $\Updownarrow$ (since $s_{(x/a)}(x) = a$)

For every $a \in A$, $\langle a, a \rangle \in R_{\mathcal{A}}$

EXERCISE 3. 38: Prove that for every L-structure $\mathcal{A}$, $\forall x \forall y\ (Rxy \rightarrow Ryx)$ is true in $\mathcal{A}$ if and only if $R_{\mathcal{A}}$ is a symmetric relation and $\forall x \forall y \forall z\ ((Rxy \wedge Ryz) \rightarrow Rxz)$ is true in $\mathcal{A}$ if and only if $R_{\mathcal{A}}$ is a transitive relation.

Hint: Follow the procedure that we have used for reflexivity.

ii.   Orderings

Let L be the language of the preceding section, with a two-place predicate R as its only extralogical symbol. Some L-structures will interpret R with a partial ordering of their universe. We can show that the set containing the following three sentences will have precisely these structures as its models.

    $\forall x\, Rxx$
    $\forall x \forall y\ ((Rxy \wedge Ryx) \rightarrow x \approx y)$
    $\forall x \forall y \forall z\ ((Rxy \wedge Ryz) \rightarrow Rxz)$

We know that $\forall x\, Rxx$ will be true in an L-structure just in case it interprets R with a reflexive relation in its universe, and that $\forall x \forall y \forall z\ ((Rxy \wedge Ryz) \rightarrow Rxz)$ will be true in an L-structure just in case it interprets R with a transitive relation (see Exercise 3. 38). Hence to establish that an L-structure $\mathcal{A}$ is a model of this set of sentences just in case $R_{\mathcal{A}}$ is a partial ordering of A, it will suffice to show that $\forall x \forall y\ ((Rxy \wedge Ryx) \rightarrow x \approx y)$ is true in an L-structure just in case it interprets R with an antisymmetric relation. This is left as an exercise.

EXERCISE 3. 39: Show that for every L-structure $\mathcal{A}$ (and every variable interpretation s in $\mathcal{A}$), $\forall x \forall y\ ((Rxy \wedge Ryx) \rightarrow x \approx y)$ is true in $\mathcal{A}$ (relative to s) just in case $R_{\mathcal{A}}$ is an antisymmetric relation.

Hint: Follow the procedure that we employed for $\forall x\, Rxx$ in the previous section.

EXERCISE 3. 40:   Find a set of L-sentences Γ such that, for every L-structure $\mathcal{A}$, $\mathcal{A}$ is a model of Γ if and only if $R_{\mathcal{A}}$ is a linear (partial) ordering of A with a maximal element. Prove that this holds of Γ.

EXERCISE 3. 41:   Find a set of L-sentences Γ such that, for every L-structure $\mathcal{A}$, $\mathcal{A}$ is a model of Γ if and only if $R_{\mathcal{A}}$ is a strict ordering of A with no minimal element. Prove that this holds of Γ.

EXERCISE 3. 42: A strict ordering ρ of a set A is *dense* just in case for all $x, y \in A$, if $x\rho y$, then there is a $z \in A$ such that $x\rho z$ and $z\rho y$ (see Chapter 1, §8). Find a set of L-sentences Γ such that, for every L-structure $\mathcal{A}$, $\mathcal{A}$ is a model of Γ if and only if $R_{\mathcal{A}}$ is a strict dense linear ordering of A. Prove that this holds of Γ.

iii.   Structures for the First-Order Language with No Extralogical Symbols

Let L now be the first-order language with no extralogical symbols. The L-structures are very rudimentary, consisting only of a universe. We can find sets of L-sentences whose models are the L-structures of a specific size.

EXERCISE 3. 43:   Find an L-sentence ϕ such that ϕ is true in an L-structure just in case its universe has three elements or less. Show that this holds of ϕ.

EXERCISE 3. 44:   Find an L-sentence ϕ such that ϕ is true in an L-structure just in case its universe has two elements or more. Show that this holds of ϕ.

EXERCISE 3. 45:   Find an L-sentence ϕ such that ϕ is true in an L-structure just in case its universe has exactly three elements. Show that this holds of ϕ.

EXERCISE 3. 46:   Find a set of L-sentences whose models are the L-structures whose universes have either two or three elements. Show that this is so.

EXERCISE 3. 47:   Find a set of L-sentences whose models are all the L-structures except those whose universes have exactly two elements. Show that this is so.

iv. Groups

DEFINITION: A two-place function f in a set A is *associative* just in case for all $x, y, z \in A, f(f(x, y), z) = f(x, f(y, z))$.

Examples: The addition of natural numbers is an associative function, since, for all natural numbers $m, n, p, (m + n) + p = m + (n + p)$. Consider the two-place concatenation function used in the inductive clause corresponding to $\rightarrow$ in the definition of a first-order language L, i.e. the function $f_\rightarrow$ such that, for all tuples ϕ, ψ, of symbols of $L, f_\rightarrow(\phi, \psi) = (\phi \rightarrow \psi)$. $f_\rightarrow$ is not an associative function, since for all tuples of symbols of $L, \phi, \psi, \gamma, f_\rightarrow(f_\rightarrow(\phi, \psi), \gamma) = ((\phi \rightarrow \psi) \rightarrow \gamma)$, whereas $f_\rightarrow(\phi, f_\rightarrow(\psi, \gamma)) = (\phi \rightarrow (\psi \rightarrow \gamma))$. And $((\phi \rightarrow \psi) \rightarrow \gamma)$ and $(\phi \rightarrow (\psi \rightarrow \gamma))$ are different tuples.

DEFINITION: If f is a two-place function in a set A, an element e of A is an *identity element* with respect to f just in case the image under f of e and any element of A is that element itself, i.e. just in case for every $x \in A, f(e, x) = f(x, e) = x$.

EXERCISE 3. 48: Show that a set A has at most one identity element with respect to a two-place function in A.

Hint: Show that if e, e' are identity elements, then $e = e'$.

DEFINITION: If f is a two-place function in a set A with an identity element, e, for all $a, b \in A, b$ is an *inverse* of a with respect to f just in case $f(a, b) = f(b, a) = e$.

EXERCISE 3. 49: Let f be an associative two-place function in a set A, and let A have an identity element with respect to f. Show that no element of A has more than one inverse with respect to f.

Hint: Show that if b and c are inverses of a, then $b = c$.

DEFINITION: If f is a two-place function in a set A, A is a *group* with respect to f just in case f is associative, A has an identity element with respect to f and every element of A has an inverse with respect to f.

Examples: The set of integers is a group with respect to the addition function, with 0 as the identity element and, for every integer $x, -x$ as the inverse of x. The set of positive rationals is a group with respect to the multiplication function, with 1 as the identity element and, for every positive rational $m/n, n/m$ as the inverse of m/n. If S is a set, the set of one-to-one correspondences from S to itself is a group with respect to the operation of function composition, with the function pairing each element of S with itself as the identity element, and f^{-1} as the inverse of f.

Let L now be the language whose only extralogical symbols are a two-place function symbol f and an individual constant c. We can find a set of L-sentences Γ such that, for every L-structure $\mathcal{A}$, $\mathcal{A}$ is a model of Γ just in case the universe of $\mathcal{A}$ is a group with respect to $f_{\mathcal{A}}$ in which $c_{\mathcal{A}}$ is the identity element. This is left as an exercise.

EXERCISE 3. 50:   Find a set of L-sentences Γ such that, for every L-structure $\mathcal{A}$, $\mathcal{A}$ is a model of Γ just in case the universe of $\mathcal{A}$ is a group with respect to $f_{\mathcal{A}}$ in which $c_{\mathcal{A}}$ is the identity element. Show that this holds of Γ.

v.   Arithmetic

Let L now be the first-order language whose only extralogical symbols are an individual constant 0, a one-place function symbol s, and two two-place function symbols + and $\cdot$. The natural numbers with the successor, addition and multiplication functions generate an L-structure $\mathcal{N}$. The universe of $\mathcal{N}$ will be ω, $0_{\mathcal{N}}$ will be the number zero, $s_{\mathcal{N}}$ will be the successor function, $+_{\mathcal{N}}$ will be the addition function and $\cdot_{\mathcal{N}}$ the multiplication function. The L-sentences will model the syntactic and semantic patterns of arithmetical propositions. Thus the patterns of the proposition that zero plus one equals one will be modeled by the L-sentence $+(0, s(0)) \approx s(0)$, and the patterns of the proposition that the sum of any two natural numbers equals their product will be modeled by the L-sentence $\forall x \forall y +(x, y) \approx \cdot (x, y)$.

We can now try to find a set of L-sentences having $\mathcal{N}$ as its only model. Let Θ_A be the set whose elements are the following six sentences:

(1) $\forall x \neg s(x) \approx 0$
(2) $\forall x \forall y (s(x) \approx s(y) \rightarrow x \approx y)$
(3) $\forall x +(x, 0) \approx x$
(4) $\forall x \forall y +(x, s(y)) \approx s(+(x, y))$
(5) $\forall x \cdot (x, 0) \approx 0$
(6) $\forall x \forall y \cdot (x, s(y)) \approx +(\cdot (x, y), x),$

and all the (infinitely many) L-sentences of the form

(7) $((\phi)[0/x] \wedge \forall x (\phi \rightarrow (\phi)[s(x)/x])) \rightarrow \forall x \phi,$

where ϕ is an L-formula with x as its only free variable and $(\phi)[t/x]$ is the L-formula that results if we substitute the L-term t for x in ϕ wherever it occurs free (a rigorous definition of this notion will be provided in Chapter 4). The sentences in Θ_A are generally known as the axioms of *Peano arithmetic*.

We can see in intuitive terms that $\mathcal{N}$ is a model of Θ_A. (1) is true in $\mathcal{N}$ because zero is not the successor of any number. (2) is true in $\mathcal{N}$ because no two natural numbers have the same successor. (3) is true in $\mathcal{N}$ because adding zero to any natural number yields that same number. (4) is true in $\mathcal{N}$ because adding a natural number m and the successor of a natural number n yields the successor of $m + n$. (5) is true in $\mathcal{N}$ because any natural number times zero equals zero. (6) is true in $\mathcal{N}$ because multiplying a natural number m by the successor of a natural number n yields m times n plus m (e.g., $3 \cdot s(4) = 3 \cdot 5 = 15 = (3 \cdot 4) + 3$). And the instances of (7) are true in $\mathcal{N}$ because every natural number can be obtained by repeated applications of the successor function to zero. Hence, if zero has a property P, and P is present in the successor of every natural number in which P is present, then all the natural numbers have P.

Furthermore, Θ_A would be a reasonable candidate for a set of L-sentences having $\mathcal{N}$ as its only model. For it seems that to be a model of Θ_A, an L-structure would have to exhibit all the features which define the natural numbers and the successor, addition and multiplication functions defined on them. For any model $\mathcal{A}$ of Θ_A, (1) and (2) seem to guarantee that $s_{\mathcal{A}}$ generates a chain with no loops, starting with $0_{\mathcal{A}}$ and never ending in the other direction. (3) and (4) seem to ensure that $+_{\mathcal{A}}$ has the features which define the addition of natural numbers, as any two elements of the universe of $\mathcal{A}$ will be related to their image under $+_{\mathcal{A}}$ as two natural numbers are related to their sum. The same goes for (5) and (6), $\cdot_{\mathcal{A}}$, and multiplication. And (7) seems to guarantee that the universe of $\mathcal{A}$ contains nothing but $0_{\mathcal{A}}$ and the chain generated from $0_{\mathcal{A}}$ by $s_{\mathcal{A}}$.

Nevertheless, contrary to what these considerations suggest, $\mathcal{N}$ is not the only model of Θ_A. Many other L-structures are also models of Θ_A. The "unintended" models of Θ_A fall in two categories: those which agree with $\mathcal{N}$ in the truth value that they yield for each L-sentence and those which disagree with $\mathcal{N}$ in the truth value that they yield for some L-sentence. Notice that the unintended models of Θ_A of the first kind will also be models of every other set of L-sentences having $\mathcal{N}$ as a model, including the set containing precisely the L-sentences which are true in $\mathcal{N}$. We shall show in Chapter 7 that, in addition to $\mathcal{N}$, this set of L-sentences has other models which are strikingly different from $\mathcal{N}$. This result is an instance of the general phenomenon, to which that chapter is devoted, that, in many cases, for a class C of structures of a first-order language L there won't be a set of L-sentences whose models are just the L-structures in C.

The second category of unintended model of Θ_A poses a different kind of problem. We can certainly find a set of L-sentences having $\mathcal{N}$ as a model and having no models which disagree with $\mathcal{N}$ in the truth value that they yield for any L-sentence, as, e.g., the set containing precisely the L-sentences which are true in $\mathcal{N}$. But every set of L-sentences which satisfies this description will differ from Θ_A in one important respect. Consider the task of determining, for any given L-sentence ϕ, whether ϕ is an element of Θ_A. We could easily describe a general procedure for discharging this task which can in principle be applied *mechanically* in each case—consisting basically in checking whether certain symbols occupy certain positions in ϕ. For the set containing precisely the L-sentences which are true in $\mathcal{N}$, by contrast, a mechanical membership test of this kind is not to be had. And the same goes for every other set of L-sentences having $\mathcal{N}$ as a model and having only models which agree with $\mathcal{N}$ in the truth value that they yield for each L-sentence. We shall not provide a proof of this result, but Chapter 8 will be devoted to exploring this family of issues.

Chapter 4

Deduction

1. Introduction

Logical deduction is a procedure for establishing that a proposition (the conclusion) is a logical consequence of other propositions (the premises)—that if the premises are all true, the conclusion must also be true. It consists in deriving the logical consequence claim that we want to establish from other "more simple" logical consequence claims. Thus, for example, we can establish that a proposition p is a logical consequence of a set of propositions S by showing that p is a logical consequence of a proposition q which is, in turn, a logical consequence of S, or that S has as a logical consequence a disjunctive proposition, each of whose disjuncts has p as a logical consequence. These more simple claims can in turn be derived from other logical consequence claims, but this process must eventually stop, with logical consequence claims whose correctness is taken for granted. Hence, to establish a logical consequence claim by logical deduction we need to use two kinds of tool. First, we need a catalogue of logical consequence claims from which we attempt to derive the claim that we want to establish. Second, we need a collection of principles to underwrite the derivation. We shall refer to these tools as *deductive rules*. We shall classify deductive rules as *categorical* and *hypothetical*, depending on whether they express a sufficient condition for logical consequence or a sufficient condition for a logical consequence claim to follow from other logical consequence claims. We shall refer to a collection of deductive rules as a *deductive system*, and to the process of establishing a logical consequence claim with a deductive system as *deducing* (in the system) the conclusion from the premises. Deducing a conclusion *c* from a set of premises *P* in a deductive system is supposed to show that, in accepting the logical consequence claims expressed by the rules of the system, we would be committed to accepting also that *c* is a logical consequence of *P*. If a deductive system is to serve this purpose, its rules will have to be specified in such a way that to deduce *c* from *P* in the system we don't need to make any further assumptions about logical consequence. One of the traditional aspirations of logic was the provision of a deductive system which, for every set of premises *P*, would allow us to deduce from *P* all its logical consequences and nothing else, i.e. a system in which we could deduce a proposition *c* from *P* if and only if *c* is a logical consequence of *P*. Our main goal in this chapter and the next is to show that, with respect to the instances of logical consequence generated by the structure of first-order propositions, this aspiration can be fulfilled.

In Chapters 2 and 3 we established several results to the effect that whenever a formula ϕ and a set of formulas Γ satisfy a certain condition, ϕ is a logical consequence of Γ. Thus, e.g., we established (i) that any set whose elements are a conditional and its antecedent has its consequent as a logical consequence—or, in more familiar terms, that for all formulas ϕ, ψ, $\{\phi \rightarrow \psi, \phi\} \vDash \psi$ (see Exercise 2. 16 (5)). Notice that this sufficient condition for logical consequence is specified in purely syntactic terms. To determine whether a claim satisfies it we don't need to invoke any semantic assumptions.

We also established conditional results to the effect that a logical consequence claim follows from other logical consequence claims. Thus, e.g., we established that for all formulas ϕ, ψ and for every set of formulas Γ, (ii) if $\Gamma \cup \{\phi\} \vDash \psi$, then $\Gamma \vDash \phi \rightarrow \psi$ (see Exercise 2. 18 (6)), (iii) if $\Gamma \cup \{\phi\} \vDash \psi$, then $\Gamma \cup \{\forall x\, \phi\} \vDash \psi$, and (iv) if $\Gamma \vDash \phi$, and *x* is not free in Γ, then $\Gamma \vDash \forall x\, \phi$ (see Exercise 3. 32 (4) and (5)). These principles express sufficient conditions for a logical consequence claim to follow from other logical consequence claims. And, once again, these conditions are specified in purely syntactic terms. We don't need to make any semantic assumptions to determine whether one of these principles licenses a particular inference.

We can use these two kinds of result to model in first-order languages the process of logical deduction. Results of the first kind generate a catalog of logical consequence claims from which we might attempt to derive other logical consequence claims, and results of the second kind provide principles with which these derivations could be justified. Hence they can play the role of categorical and hypothetical rules in a deductive system with which to establish logical consequence claims concerning formulas of a first-order language.

To deduce a formula from a set of formulas in a deductive system, we derive the claim that the former is a logical consequence of the latter from instances of the categorical rules of the system, using its hypothetical rules to justify the derivation. Consider as an illustration the deductive system whose only categorical rule is (i), and whose hypothetical rules are (ii)–(iv), above. To deduce the formula $\forall x\, Px \rightarrow \forall x\, Qx$ from the set $\{\forall x\, (Px \rightarrow Qx)\}$ in this system, we can argue as follows:

$\{Px \rightarrow Qx, Px\} \vDash Qx$ (by (i))

$\Downarrow$ (by (iii))

$\{\forall x\, (Px \rightarrow Qx), Px\} \vDash Qx$

$\Downarrow$ (by (iii))

$\{\forall x\, (Px \rightarrow Qx), \forall x\, Px\} \vDash Qx$

$\Downarrow$ (by (iv))

$\{\forall x\, (Px \rightarrow Qx), \forall x\, Px\} \vDash \forall x\, Qx$

$\Downarrow$ (by (ii))

$\{\forall x\, (Px \rightarrow Qx)\} \vDash \forall x\, Px \rightarrow \forall x\, Qx$

As we indicated above, we don't need to make any semantic assumptions to determine whether a logical consequence claim is an instance of (i) or whether a derivation is licensed by (ii)–(iv). Hence our argument shows that (i)–(iv) are the only semantic assumptions that we need to make in order to establish $\{\forall x\, (Px \rightarrow Qx)\} \vDash \forall x\, Px \rightarrow \forall x\, Qx$.

Since (i)–(iv) are all true, the deductive system consisting of these rules will not allow us to deduce a formula ϕ from a set of formulas Γ unless ϕ is a logical consequence of Γ. But there are many cases in which a formula ϕ is a logical consequence of a set of formulas Γ but ϕ can't be deduced from Γ in this system. Adding more rules might enable us to deal with some of these cases. And if the semantic principles expressed by the new rules are all true, the expanded system will still allow us to deduce a formula ϕ from a set of formulas Γ only if ϕ is a logical consequence of Γ. This raises the question whether we can provide a deductive system for an arbitrary first-order language L in which we can deduce an L-formula ϕ from a set of L-formulas Γ if and only if ϕ is a logical consequence of Γ. A system with this feature would fulfill, with respect to first-order logic, the traditional aspiration that we mentioned earlier.

Let's say that a deductive system for a first-order language L is *finitary* if it only allows us to deduce L-formulas from finite sets of L-formulas. Obviously a finitary deductive system for L would not allow us to deduce every logical consequence of every set of L-formulas, since infinite sets of L-formulas have logical consequences, and a finitary system would not allow us to deduce anything from such a set. Nevertheless a finitary deductive system for L can still fulfill the traditional aspiration of logic indirectly, if, on the one hand, it allows us to deduce an L-formula ϕ from a set of L-formulas Γ only if ϕ is a logical consequence of Γ, and, on the other, for every set Γ of L-formulas and every L-formula ϕ which is a logical consequence of Γ, the system allows us to deduce ϕ from a finite subset of Γ. We shall refer to the first of these features as *soundness*, and to the second as *completeness*.

DEFINITION: A deductive system for first-order logic is *sound* just in case for every formula ϕ of a first-order language L, and every set Γ of L-formulas, if ϕ is deducible from Γ in the system, then ϕ is a logical consequence of Γ.

DEFINITION: A deductive system for first-order logic is *complete* just in case for every formula ϕ of a first-order language L, and every set Γ of L-formulas, if ϕ is a logical consequence of Γ, then ϕ is deducible in the system from a finite subset of Γ.

Our goal in this chapter will be to present a finitary deductive system for an arbitrary first-order language which is both sound and complete. Proving that the system has these features will be our main goal in Chapter 5.

We shall present the rules of the system as specifying conditions under which a formula is deducible from a set of formulas. When a formula ϕ is deducible in the system from a set of formulas Γ we shall write $\Gamma \vdash \phi$. We shall write $\Gamma \nvdash \phi$ to express that ϕ is not deducible from Γ. The system will contain two rules for each logical operator—an *introduction rule* and an *elimination rule*. The introduction rule for a logical operator * will specify conditions under which we can conclude that a formula with * as its main logical operator is deducible from a set of formulas. The elimination rule for * will specify conditions under which we can derive a deducibility claim from the assumption that a formula with * as its main logical operator is deducible from a set of formulas. Thus, e.g., the introduction rule for $\wedge$ will specify conditions under which we can conclude that a claim of the form $\Gamma \vdash \phi \wedge \psi$ holds, and the elimination rule for ∧ will specify conditions under which a deducibility claim can be derived from a claim of the form $\Gamma \vdash \phi \wedge \psi$.

2. The Basic Rule and the Connective Rules

In this section we introduce the first few rules of our deductive system. The rest will be introduced in §5. The system will only contain one rule which is not an introduction or elimination rule for a logical operator. It models the intuitive principle licensing the deduction of a conclusion from any set of premises containing it. We shall refer to it as the *basic rule*:

(B) For every *L*-formula ϕ and every finite set Γ of *L*-formulas, if $\phi \in \Gamma$, then $\Gamma \vdash \phi$.

The introduction rule for ∧ will model the intuitive principle licensing the deduction of a conjunctive proposition from any set of premises from which both its conjuncts have been deduced:

(∧*I*) For all *L*-formulas ϕ, ψ, and all sets of *L*-formulas Γ, Δ, if $\Gamma \vdash \phi$ and $\Delta \vdash \psi$, then $\Gamma \cup \Delta \vdash \phi \wedge \psi$.

The elimination rule for ∧ will model the intuitive principle that whenever we have deduced a conjunctive proposition from a set of premises, we can deduce each of its conjuncts from the set:

(∧*E*) For all *L*-formulas ϕ, ψ, and every set Γ of *L*-formulas, if $\Gamma \vdash \phi \wedge \psi$, then $\Gamma \vdash \phi$ and $\Gamma \vdash \psi$.

The introduction rule for ∨ will model the principle licensing the deduction of a disjunctive proposition from any set of premises from which either of its disjuncts has been deduced:

(∨*I*) For all *L*-formulas ϕ, ψ, and every set Γ of *L*-formulas, if $\Gamma \vdash \phi$ or $\Gamma \vdash \psi$, then $\Gamma \vdash \phi \vee \psi$.

The elimination rule for ∨ will be based on the principle known as *constructive dilemma*, licensing the deduction from a disjunctive proposition of any conclusion which has been deduced from each of its disjuncts. Our rule will model a more general version of this deductive principle:

(∨*E*) For all *L*-formulas ϕ, ψ, α, and all sets of *L*-formulas Γ, Δ, Σ, if $\Gamma \vdash \phi \vee \psi$, $\Delta \cup \{\phi\} \vdash \alpha$ and $\Sigma \cup \{\psi\} \vdash \alpha$, then $\Gamma \cup \Delta \cup \Sigma \vdash \alpha$.

The introduction rule for → will model the principle of *conditional proof*, licensing the deduction of a material conditional from a set of premises whenever we have deduced its consequent from the union of that set and its antecedent:

($\to$*I*) For all *L*-formulas ϕ, ψ, and every set Γ of *L*-formulas, if $\Gamma \cup \{\phi\}$ $\vdash \psi$, then $\Gamma \vdash \phi \to \psi$.

The elimination rule for $\to$ will be based on the principle of *modus ponens*, licensing the deduction from a material conditional and its antecedent of the consequent of the material conditional. We shall base on this categorical principle the following hypothetical rule:

($\to$*E*) For all *L*-formulas ϕ, ψ, and all sets of *L*-formulas Γ, Δ, if $\Gamma \vdash \phi \to$ ψ and $\Delta \vdash \phi$, then $\Gamma \cup \Delta \vdash \psi$.

The introduction rule for $\neg$ will model the principle known as *ex contradictione quodlibet* (from a contradiction, anything), according to which whenever we have deduced both a proposition and its negation from a set of premises, we can deduce the negation of any of the premises from the set containing the rest:

($\neg$*I*) For all *L*-formulas ϕ, ψ, and all sets of *L*-formulas Γ, Δ, if $\Gamma \cup \{\phi\}$ $\vdash \psi$ and $\Delta \cup \{\phi\} \vdash \neg\psi$, then $\Gamma \cup \Delta \vdash \neg\phi$.

The elimination rule for $\neg$ will be based on the principle of *double negation*, according to which any proposition can be deduced from the negation of its negation. Once again, our system will have a hypothetical rule corresponding to this categorical principle:

($\neg$*E*) For every *L*-formula ϕ, and every set Γ of *L*-formulas, if $\Gamma \vdash \neg\neg\phi$, then $\Gamma \vdash \phi$.

3. Propositional Deduction

Each of the rules that we have introduced in §2 has an obvious correlate for the language *PL* of propositional logic presented in Chapter 2. We concentrate in this section on the deductive system for *PL* that these rules would generate. Our goal is to introduce the technique for establishing deducibility claims in the more simple environment of propositional logic. This deductive system for *PL* is both sound and complete with respect to the relation of logical consequence for *PL*-sentences. We won't establish this result here, since it will be of little independent interest once we have established in Chapter 5 the corresponding result for our deductive system for first-order logic. We shall focus instead on how to establish in particular cases that a *PL*-sentence is deducible from a set of *PL*-sentences of which it is a logical consequence.

To establish a deducibility claim with a deductive system we need to derive it from instances of the categorical rules of the system using its hypothetical rules. Our deductive system for *PL* has only one categorical rule—the basic rule. All the introduction and elimination rules for the connectives are hypothetical. Hence to show that a *PL*-sentence is deducible from a set of *PL*-sentences, we need to derive this claim from instances of the basic rule using the connective rules. To achieve this, we proceed in the following way. Let φ be a *PL*-sentence, and let Γ be a set of *PL*-sentences such that Γ ⊨ φ. To show that Γ ⊢ φ, we first check whether the claim is an instance of the basic rule, i.e. whether φ ∈ Γ. If it is, we are done. Otherwise we need to derive Γ ⊢ φ from other deducibility claims using one of the connective rules, and our next task is to decide which rule we are going to use for this purpose and which deducibility claims we are going to derive Γ ⊢ φ from, using our chosen rule. Now we shift our attention to the deducibility claims from which we have derived Γ ⊢ φ, and we proceed with each of them as we did for Γ ⊢ φ. Those which are instances of the basic rule will be justified by this fact. Each of the others will have to be derived from other deducibility claims using one of the connective rules. We continue this process until we manage to derive Γ ⊢ φ, using the connective rules, from a collection of instances of the basic rule.

Let's apply these general considerations to a specific example, by showing that the *PL*-sentence $a \rightarrow c$ is deducible from the set of *PL*-sentences $\{a \rightarrow b, b \rightarrow c\}$, where a, b and c are different atoms. Notice first that $\{a \rightarrow b, b \rightarrow c\} \vdash a \rightarrow c$ is not an instance of the basic rule, since $a \rightarrow c \notin \{a \rightarrow b, b \rightarrow c\}$. Hence we need to derive it from other deducibility claims using one of the connective rules. $\rightarrow I$ is the only introduction rule we can use. In general, to derive a deducibility claim Γ ⊢ φ, we can use at most one introduction rule—the one corresponding to the main connective of φ. When an introduction rule can be used, this is often (but not always) the best option. Following this strategy, we use $\rightarrow I$ to derive $\{a \rightarrow b, b \rightarrow c\} \vdash a \rightarrow c$ from $\{a \rightarrow b, b \rightarrow c, a\} \vdash c$ (notice that this is the only deducibility claim from which we can derive $\{a \rightarrow b, b \rightarrow c\} \vdash a \rightarrow c$ using $\rightarrow I$). $\{a \rightarrow b, b \rightarrow c, a\} \vdash c$ is not an instance of the basic rule. Hence we need to use a connective rule to derive it from other deducibility claims. Since c is an atom, no introduction rule can be used in this case. Hence we need to use an elimination rule. Notice that c is the consequent of a conditional in $\{a \rightarrow b, b \rightarrow c, a\}$. Its antecedent, b, is the consequent of another conditional in the set, whose antecedent, a, is also in the set. $\rightarrow E$ enables us to conclude that the consequent of a conditional is deducible from the union of two sets from which the conditional and its antecedent are deducible. This suggests that we could derive $\{a \rightarrow b, b \rightarrow c, a\} \vdash c$ with two applications of $\rightarrow E$. We use $\rightarrow E$ first to derive $\{a \rightarrow b, b \rightarrow c, a\} \vdash c$ from $\{b \rightarrow c\} \vdash b \rightarrow c$ and $\{a \rightarrow b, a\} \vdash b$. The former claim is justified by the basic rule. We derive the latter, with another application of $\rightarrow E$, from $\{a \rightarrow b\} \vdash a \rightarrow b$ and $\{a\} \vdash a$. Since both these claims are instances of the basic rule, we have completed the process of deriving $\{a \rightarrow b, b \rightarrow c\} \vdash a \rightarrow c$ with the connective rules from instances of the basic rule. We can conclude that $a \rightarrow c$ is deducible from $\{a \rightarrow b, b \rightarrow c\}$.

Notice that this kind of argument has the structure of a tree, with the claim that we want to establish at its base, and each branch ending with an instance of the basic rule. We can use this fact to provide a more perspicuous representation of these arguments. We arrange the deducibility claims which figure in the argument in tree form. We place the claim that we want to establish at the bottom. If a deducibility claim in the argument is justified by the basic rule, we simply indicate this by writing (*B*) next to it. When a claim is derived from other claims using a connective rule, we indicate which rule we are using next to the claim we are deriving, and place the claims from which we are deriving it above it, separated by a horizontal line. Thus arranged, the argument of the preceding paragraph would look like this:

$$\frac{\{a \rightarrow b\} \vdash a \rightarrow b \ (B) \qquad\qquad \{a\} \vdash a \ (B)}{}$$

$$\frac{\{b \rightarrow c\} \vdash b \rightarrow c \ (B) \qquad\qquad \{a \rightarrow b, a\} \vdash b \ (\rightarrow E)}{}$$

$$\frac{\{a \rightarrow b, b \rightarrow c, a\} \vdash c \ (\rightarrow E)}{}$$

$$\{a \rightarrow b, b \rightarrow c\} \vdash a \rightarrow c \ (\rightarrow I)$$

Notice that, mirroring the arguments that they represent, the natural way to read and build these trees is from the bottom up. We now present in tree form an argument for the claim that, for all *PL*-sentences ϕ, ψ, $\{\phi \rightarrow \psi\} \vdash \neg\psi \rightarrow \neg\phi$.

$$\frac{\{\phi \rightarrow \psi\} \vdash \phi \rightarrow \psi \ (B) \qquad\qquad \{\phi\} \vdash \phi \ (B)}{}$$

$$\frac{\{\phi \rightarrow \psi, \phi\} \vdash \psi \ (\rightarrow E) \qquad\qquad \{\neg\psi, \phi\} \vdash \neg\psi \ (B)}{}$$

$$\frac{\{\phi \rightarrow \psi, \neg\psi\} \vdash \neg\phi \ (\neg I)}{}$$

$$\{\phi \rightarrow \psi\} \vdash \neg\psi \rightarrow \neg\phi \ (\rightarrow I)$$

EXERCISE 4. 1: For each logical consequence claim in Exercise 2. 16 establish the corresponding deducibility claim.

Hint: For (6) use $\neg E$ and $\neg I$.

EXERCISE 4. 2: For each logical consequence claim in Exercise 2. 17 establish the corresponding deducibility claim.

To show that a deducibility claim follows from other deducibility claims, we derive the former from the latter and instances of the categorical rules of the system using its hypothetical rules. Thus, e.g., to show that, for all *PL*-sentences α, β, γ, if $\{\alpha, \beta\} \vdash \gamma$, then $\emptyset \vdash (\alpha \wedge \beta) \rightarrow \gamma$, we assume that α, β, γ are *PL*-sentences such that $\{\alpha, \beta\} \vdash \gamma$ and try to show that it follows from this assumption that $\emptyset \vdash (\alpha \wedge \beta) \rightarrow \gamma$. We can argue as follows:

$\{\alpha, \beta\} \vdash \gamma$ (Assumption)

$\overline{\qquad\qquad\qquad\qquad}$

$\{\alpha\} \vdash \beta \rightarrow \gamma \ (\rightarrow I)$ $\{\alpha \wedge \beta\} \vdash \alpha \wedge \beta \ (B)$

$\overline{\qquad\qquad\qquad\qquad\qquad}$

$\emptyset \vdash \alpha \rightarrow (\beta \rightarrow \gamma) \ (\rightarrow I)$ $\{\alpha \wedge \beta\} \vdash \alpha \ (\wedge E)$ $\{\alpha \wedge \beta\} \vdash \alpha \wedge \beta \ (B)$

$\overline{\qquad\qquad\qquad\qquad\qquad}$ $\overline{\qquad\qquad\qquad\qquad}$

$\{\alpha \wedge \beta\} \vdash \beta \rightarrow \gamma \ (\rightarrow E)$ $\{\alpha \wedge \beta\} \vdash \beta \ (\wedge E)$

$\overline{\qquad\qquad\qquad\qquad\qquad\qquad\qquad\qquad\qquad}$

$\{\alpha \wedge \beta\} \vdash \gamma \ (\rightarrow E)$

$\overline{\qquad\qquad\qquad\qquad\qquad}$

$\emptyset \vdash (\alpha \wedge \beta) \rightarrow \gamma \ (\rightarrow I)$

LEMMA 4. 3: $\Delta \cup \{\gamma_1, \ldots, \gamma_n\} \vdash \phi$ if and only if $\Delta \vdash (\gamma_1 \wedge \ldots \wedge \gamma_n) \rightarrow \phi$.

Proof: We show first that if $\Delta \vdash (\gamma_1 \wedge \ldots \wedge \gamma_n) \rightarrow \phi$, then $\Delta \cup \{\gamma_1, \ldots, \gamma_n\} \vdash \phi$. Assume that $\Delta \vdash (\gamma_1 \wedge \ldots \wedge \gamma_n) \rightarrow \phi$. For every positive integer i less than or equal to n, the basic rule yields $\{\gamma_i\} \vdash \gamma_i$. From $\{\gamma_1\} \vdash \gamma_1$ and $\{\gamma_2\} \vdash \gamma_2$ we can derive, using $\wedge I$, $\{\gamma_1, \gamma_2\} \vdash \gamma_1 \wedge \gamma_2$. If we apply $\wedge I$ $n-1$ times in this way, we get $\{\gamma_1, \ldots, \gamma_n\} \vdash \gamma_1 \wedge \ldots \wedge \gamma_n$. From this, and the assumption that $\Delta \vdash (\gamma_1 \wedge \ldots \wedge \gamma_n) \rightarrow \phi$, using $\rightarrow E$, we derive $\Delta \cup \{\gamma_1, \ldots, \gamma_n\} \vdash \phi$, as desired.

We show now that if $\Delta \cup \{\gamma_1, \ldots, \gamma_n\} \vdash \phi$, then $\Delta \vdash (\gamma_1 \wedge \ldots \wedge \gamma_n) \rightarrow \phi$. Assume that $\Delta \cup \{\gamma_1, \ldots, \gamma_n\} \vdash \phi$. From this, by n applications of $\rightarrow I$, we get $\Delta \vdash \gamma_1 \rightarrow (\gamma_2 \rightarrow (\ldots \rightarrow (\gamma_n \rightarrow \phi) \ldots))$. Using $\wedge E$, we derive $\{\gamma_1 \wedge \ldots \wedge \gamma_n\} \vdash \gamma_i$ for every positive integer i less than or equal to n. Hence, we can apply $\rightarrow E$ n times to get $\Delta \cup \{\gamma_1 \wedge \ldots \wedge \gamma_n\} \vdash \phi$. Using $\rightarrow I$, we derive from this $\Delta \vdash (\gamma_1 \wedge \ldots \wedge \gamma_n) \rightarrow \phi$, as desired. ∎

EXERCISE 4. 4: For each hypothetical logical consequence claim in Exercise 2. 19 establish the corresponding deducibility claim (taking Γ and Δ to be finite sets).

Hint: For (1), use $\rightarrow E$, with the conditional $\phi \rightarrow \phi$. For (2), use $\rightarrow E$, invoking Lemma 4. 3 to obtain the conditional that you need.

EXERCISE 4. 5: Show that every instance of each of the sentence-schemata in Exercise 2. 21 is deducible from the empty set.

EXERCISE 4. 6: For each logical equivalence claim of Exercise 2. 22 establish the corresponding reciprocal deducibility claims.

EXERCISE 4. 7: For each logical equivalence claim of Exercise 2. 23 establish the corresponding reciprocal deducibility claims.

EXERCISE 4. 8: For each logical equivalence claim of Exercise 2. 24 establish the corresponding reciprocal deducibility claims.

4. Substitution

Consider the propositions that everyone is left-handed and that someone is left-handed, concerning the members of a tennis club. The former is true just in case every individual in the range to which quantification is restricted satisfies a certain condition—being left-handed—and the latter is true just in case at least one individual in the range satisfies this condition. Consider now the proposition that Clara, a club member, is left-handed. This proposition is true just in case a specific individual in that range satisfies the same condition. Whenever a proposition is related to a universal or existential proposition in this way, we shall say that the former is an *instance* of the latter.

The relation between quantified propositions and their instances can be used to formulate deductive principles. From a universal proposition we can always deduce any of its instances, and an existential proposition can always be deduced from one of its instances. Also, the strategy that we have been using all along to establish universal implications presupposes that, under certain conditions, a universal proposition can be deduced from one of its instances. And in some proofs we have made use of the fact that, under certain conditions, what can be deduced from an instance of an existential proposition can also be deduced from the existential proposition itself (see, e.g., the proof of Lemma 1. 16, where the idea is introduced). The quantifier rules of our deductive system will be based on these principles. To formulate these rules, we need to find a relation between formulas of a first-order language which models the relation between quantified propositions and their instances. And given the role that we want this relation between formulas to play, we will have to specify it in purely syntactic terms. This will be our goal in this section.

The structure of the propositions that everyone is left-handed, that someone is left-handed, and that Clara is left-handed is modeled in a first-order language by formulas of the form $\forall x\, Px$, $\exists x\, Px$ and Pc. We can try to learn from this example how the formulas which model quantified propositions are related to the formulas which model their instances. Notice that we can get Pc from $\forall x\, Px$ or $\exists x\, Px$ by removing the quantifier and replacing x with c in Px. This seems to suggest that, in general, for every proposition modeled by a formula of the form $\forall x\, \phi$ or $\exists x\, \phi$, its instances will be modeled by the formulas that result when we remove the quantifier and replace every occurrence of x in ϕ with an occurrence of a term of the language.

This is the right general idea, but it needs to be refined in two important respects. The deductive principles invoking the relation between a quantified proposition and its instances are based on the fact that a universal proposition has as a logical consequence any of its instances, and that an existential proposition is a logical consequence of any of its instances. Thus, e.g., the proposition that everyone is left-handed has as a logical consequence the proposition that Clara is left-handed, which, in turn, has as a logical consequence the proposition that someone is left-handed. The formal analogue of this feature is present in $\forall x\, Px$, $\exists x\, Px$ and Pc, since $\{\forall x\, Px\} \models Pc$ and $\{Pc\} \models \exists x\, Px$. But if we extrapolate from this case in the way we have suggested, we generate counterexamples to this general principle.

One family of counterexamples is illustrated by the following exercise.

EXERCISE 4. 9: Show that $\{\forall x\, (Px \rightarrow \exists x\, Tx)\} \not\models Pc \rightarrow \exists x\, Tc$ and that $\{Pc \land \forall x\, Tc\} \not\models \exists x\, (Px \land \forall x\, Tx)$.

The lesson that we can draw from these examples is that, in some cases, to generate a formula which models an instance of a proposition modeled by $\forall x\, \phi$ or $\exists x\, \phi$, some occurrences of x in ϕ should not be replaced by the chosen term. As the following exercise shows, if we don't substitute c for the last occurrence of x in $Px \rightarrow \exists x\, Tx$ or $Px \land \forall x\, Tx$, we get the desired result.

EXERCISE 4. 10: Show that $\{\forall x\, (Px \rightarrow \exists x\, Tx)\} \models Pc \rightarrow \exists x\, Tx$ and that $\{Pc \land \forall x\, Tx\} \models \exists x\, (Px \land \forall x\, Tx)$.

A second family of counterexamples is illustrated by the next exercise.

EXERCISE 4. 11:   Show that $\{\forall x \exists y \ Ryx\} \nvDash \exists y \ Ryf(y)$ and that $\{\forall y$
$Rf(y)y\} \nvDash \exists x \forall y \ Rxy$.

The lesson to be drawn from these examples is that if we replace the
occurrences of x in ϕ with certain terms, the resulting formula does not
model an instance of the proposition modeled by $\forall x \ \phi$ or $\exists x \ \phi$. As the
following exercise shows, if we use $f(x)$ instead of $f(y)$ to replace x in $\exists y$
Ryx and $\forall y \ Rxy$, we get the intended result.

EXERCISE 4. 12:   Show that $\{\forall x \exists y \ Ryx\} \vDash \exists y \ Ryf(x)$ and that $\{\forall y$
$Rf(x)y\} \vDash \exists x \forall y \ Rxy$.

To model in a first-order language the relation between quantified
propositions and their instances, we need to modify our original proposal
to accommodate these two kinds of case.   We shall deal with the first
problem by introducing the notion of the *t/x-substitution* of a formula ϕ
(written $(\phi)[t/x]$), which is a formula in which term t is substituted in ϕ
for the right occurrences of x. Thus, e.g., $Pc \rightarrow \exists x \ Tx$, not $Pc \rightarrow \exists x \ Tc$,
will be the c/x-substitution of $Px \rightarrow \exists x \ Tx$, and $Pc \wedge \forall x \ Tx$, not $Pc \wedge \forall x$
Tc, will be the c/x-substitution of $Px \wedge \forall x \ Tx$. To deal with the second
problem, we shall specify which terms are *substitutable* for a variable in
a formula. Thus, e.g., $f(x)$ will be substitutable for x in $\exists y \ Ryx$ and in $\forall y$
Rxy, but $f(y)$ won't.

The t/x-substitution of a formula ϕ will be a formula which is identical
to ϕ except that t may be substituted for some or all of the occurrences of
x in ϕ. Defining the notion involves specifying which of the occurrences
of x in ϕ will be replaced by t in ϕ's t/x-substitution. Intuitively, we want
to replace all occurrences of x except those which are "affected" by an x-
quantifier.   Thus in the t/x-substitutions of the formulas $Px \rightarrow \exists x \ Tx$ and
$Px \wedge \forall x \ Tx$, we would want t to replace the first occurrence of x, but not
the last one (we never replace occurrences of a variable immediately following a quantifier). We achieve this by defining, for every variable x
and term t, a function which pairs each formula ϕ with its t/x-substitution.
But in order to define the t/x-substitution of a formula, we need to define
first the t/x-substitution of a term. Both functions are defined by recursion.

DEFINITION: Let L be a first-order language. For every variable x and
every L-term t, the *t/x-substitution* of an L-term u, written $(u)[t/x]$, is its
image under the unique function satisfying the following conditions:

(1)   For every individual constant c of L, $(c)[t/x] = c$.

(2)   For every variable y,

$$(y)[t/x] = \begin{cases} t \text{ if } y = x, \\ y \text{ otherwise.} \end{cases}$$

(3) For every L-term of the form $f(u_1,\ldots,u_n)$, $(f(u_1,\ldots,u_n))[t/x] = f((u_1)[t/x],\ldots,(u_n)[t/x])$.

Notice that the effect of this definition is that every occurrence of x in a term u will be replaced by an occurrence of t in the t/x-substitution of u. If x doesn't occur in u, u will be its own t/x-substitution.

DEFINITION: Let L be a first-order language. For every variable x and every L-term t, the t/x-*substitution* of an L-formula α, written $(\alpha)[t/x]$, is its image under the unique function satisfying the following conditions:

(1) For every L-formula of the form $Pu_1\ldots u_n$, $(Pu_1\ldots u_n)[t/x] = P(u_1)[t/x]\ldots(u_n)[t/x]$.

(2) For every L-formula of the form $u \approx u'$, $(u \approx u')[t/x] = (u)[t/x] \approx (u')[t/x]$.

(3) For every L-formula of the form $\neg\phi$, $(\neg\phi)[t/x] = \neg(\phi)[t/x]$.

(4) For every L-formula of the form $\phi \wedge \psi$, $(\phi \wedge \psi)[t/x] = (\phi)[t/x] \wedge (\psi)[t/x]$.

(5) For every L-formula of the form $\phi \vee \psi$, $(\phi \vee \psi)[t/x] = (\phi)[t/x] \vee (\psi)[t/x]$.

(6) For every L-formula of the form $\phi \rightarrow \psi$, $(\phi \rightarrow \psi)[t/x] = (\phi)[t/x] \rightarrow (\psi)[t/x]$.

(7) For every L-formula of the form $\forall y\, \phi$,

$$(\forall y\, \phi)[t/x] = \begin{cases} \forall y\, \phi \text{ if } x = y, \\ \forall y\, (\phi)[t/x] \text{ otherwise.} \end{cases}$$

(8) For every L-formula of the form $\exists y\, \phi$,

$$(\exists y\, \phi)[t/x] = \begin{cases} \exists y\, \phi \text{ if } x = y, \\ \exists y\, (\phi)[t/x] \text{ otherwise.} \end{cases}$$

Notice that the definition yields the intended result. By virtue of clauses (7) and (8), occurrences of x in ϕ which are affected by an x-quantifier will not be replaced by occurrences of t in the t/x-substitution of ϕ. Every other occurrence of x in ϕ will be replaced by an occurrence

of t in the t/x-substitution of ϕ. If Γ is a set of formulas, $\Gamma[t/x]$ will denote the set containing the t/x-substitutions of the elements of Γ.

EXERCISE 4. 13: Provide the following substitutions:
  (1) $(Rxay)[c/x]$
  (2) $(Rxay)[a/z]$
  (3) $(Px \lor Tf(y))[x/y]$
  (4) $(\forall x\, Px \to Ty)[f(a)/x]$
  (5) $(\forall x\, Px \to Ty)[f(a)/y]$
  (6) $(\exists x\, Px \land Tx)[f(a)/x]$
  (7) $(\exists x\,(Px \land Tx))[f(a)/x]$
  (8) $((\forall x\, Px \to Ty)[x/y])[f(a)/x]$
  (9) $((\forall x\,(Px \to Ty))[x/y])[f(a)/x]$
 (10) $((\forall x\, Px \to Ty)[f(x)/y])[f(a)/x]$

EXERCISE 4. 14: Show that if x doesn't occur in a term u, then $(u)[t/x] =$
u.

Hint: By induction on terms.

EXERCISE 4. 15: Show that if x is not free in a formula ϕ, then $(\phi)[t/x] =$
ϕ.

Hint: By induction on formulas. Use Exercise 4. 14 for the base.

EXERCISE 4. 16: Show that if x doesn't occur in a term t, then, for every
term u, x does not occur in $(u)[t/x]$.

Hint: By induction on terms.

EXERCISE 4. 17: Show that if x doesn't occur in a term t, then, for every
formula ϕ, x is not free in $(\phi)[t/x]$.

Hint: By induction on formulas. Use Exercise 4. 16 for the base.

EXERCISE 4. 18: Show that different terms in which an individual constant c doesn't occur have different c/x-substitutions, for every variable x.

Hint: Prove by induction on terms in the following form. For every term
t, if c doesn't occur in t, then for every term u in which c doesn't occur, if
$(t)[c/x] = (u)[c/x]$, then $t = u$.

EXERCISE 4. 19: Show that different formulas in which an individual
constant c doesn't occur have different c/x-substitutions, for every variable x.

Hint: Proceed as with Exercise 4. 18, and invoke that result.

EXERCISE 4. 20: Show that, if y doesn't occur in a term u, then $(u)[t/x]$ is $(u)[y/x][t/y]$.

EXERCISE 4. 21: Show that, if y doesn't occur in a formula ϕ, then $(\phi)[t/x]$ is $(\phi)[y/x][t/y]$.

Our second task is to specify which terms are substitutable for a variable x in a formula ϕ. Notice that we don't need to worry about formulas in which x is not free, since in the t/x-substitutions of these formulas t won't be substituted for any occurrence of x (see Exercise 4. 15). If x is free in ϕ, we want to avoid substituting a term containing a variable y for an occurrence of x that is affected by a y-quantifier. Thus, in $\exists y \, Ryx$ or $\forall y \, Rxy$, we would want $f(x)$, or c, to be substitutable for x, but not $f(y)$ or y.

To achieve this, we define, for each variable x, a function pairing each formula ϕ of a first-order language L with the set of L-terms that are substitutable for x in ϕ. We define this function by recursion.

DEFINITION: Let L be a first-order language. For every variable x, the set of L-terms which are *substitutable* for x in an L-formula ϕ is the image of ϕ under the unique function satisfying the following conditions:

(1) For every L-formula of the form $Pu_1...u_n$, every term is substitutable for x in $Pu_1...u_n$.

(2) For every L-formula of the form $t \approx u$, every term is substitutable for x in $t \approx u$.

(3) For every L-formula of the form $\neg\alpha$, t is substitutable for x in $\neg\alpha$ if and only if t is substitutable for x in α.

(4) For every L-formula of the form $\alpha \wedge \beta$, t is substitutable for x in $\alpha \wedge \beta$ if and only if t is substitutable for x in both α and β.

(5) For every L-formula of the form $\alpha \vee \beta$, t is substitutable for x in $\alpha \vee \beta$ if and only if t is substitutable for x in both α and β.

(6) For every L-formula of the form $\alpha \rightarrow \beta$, t is substitutable for x in $\alpha \rightarrow \beta$ if and only if t is substitutable for x in both α and β.

(7) For every L-formula of the form $\forall y \, \alpha$, t is substitutable for x in $\forall y \, \alpha$ if and only if either x is not free in $\forall y \, \alpha$, or y does not occur in t and t is substitutable for x in α.

(8) For every L-formula of the form $\exists y \, \alpha$, t is substitutable for x in $\exists y \, \alpha$ if and only if either x is not free in $\exists y \, \alpha$, or y does not occur in t and t is substitutable for x in α.

EXERCISE 4. 22: Prove that any term is substitutable in any formula for a variable that isn't free in the formula.

Hint: By induction on formulas.

EXERCISE 4. 23: Show that a term containing none of the variables occurring in a formula is substitutable for any variable in that formula.

Hint: By induction on formulas.

Notice that it follows from Exercise 4. 23 that a term containing no variables is substitutable for any variable in any formula.

EXERCISE 4. 24: Prove that any variable is substitutable for itself in any formula.

Hint: By induction on formulas.

We now have the resources to introduce the necessary refinements in our original proposal. The relation between a quantified proposition and its instances will be modeled in first-order languages by the relation between each formula of the form $\forall x\ \phi$ or $\exists x\ \phi$ and the t/x-substitutions of ϕ, provided that t is substitutable for x in ϕ. We shall use this relation between formulas to model in our deductive system deductive principles involving the relation between quantified propositions and their instances.

5. Quantifier and Identity Rules

In this section we present the remaining rules of our deductive system for an arbitrary first-order language L—the introduction and elimination rules for $\forall$, $\exists$ and $\approx$. The elimination rule for $\forall$ will be based on the principle of *universal instantiation*, according to which from a universal proposition we can deduce any of its instances. We shall base a hypothetical rule on this categorical principle:

($\forall E$) For every L-formula ϕ, every set Γ of L-formulas, every variable x and every L-term t substitutable for x in ϕ, if $\Gamma \vdash \forall x\ \phi$, then $\Gamma \vdash (\phi)[t/x]$.

Notice that this rule models the relation between a universal proposition and its instances with the relation between a formula of the form $\forall x\ \phi$ and the t/x-substitution of ϕ for a term t which is substitutable for x in ϕ.

The introduction rule for $\forall$ will model the principle that whenever we have deduced an instance of a universal proposition from a set of premises, we can deduce from these premises the universal proposition itself, provided that the instance is arbitrary. This proviso can be spelled out as the demand that the individual with which the universal proposition is instantiated doesn't figure in any of the premises or in the universal proposition itself. For if an instance of a universal proposition which satisfies this requirement can be deduced from the premises, we would also be able to deduce from them any other instance of the universal proposition. To model this principle, we need a rule which enables us to derive $\Gamma \vdash \forall x\, \phi$ from $\Gamma \vdash (\phi)[t/x]$ if t is substitutable for x in ϕ and $(\phi)[t/x]$ satisfies an analogue of the arbitrariness requirement with respect to Γ and $\forall x\, \phi$. Since we want our deductive rules to be formulated syntactically, we need to model this requirement in purely syntactic terms. We achieve this by restricting the application of the rule to instances of $\forall x\, \phi$ in which the substituting term is a variable which is not free in any formula in Γ or in $\forall x\, \phi$. Thus the introduction rule for $\forall$ can be formulated as follows:

($\forall I$) For every L-formula ϕ, every set Γ of L-formulas, and all variables x, y such that y is substitutable for x in ϕ, if $\Gamma \vdash (\phi)[y/x]$ and y is not free in Γ or $\forall x\, \phi$, then $\Gamma \vdash \forall x\, \phi$.

Notice that when we use this rule to deduce a formula of the form $\forall x\, (\phi \rightarrow \psi)$ from a set of formulas, we will be modeling the strategy for establishing universal implications that we have been using all along.

The introduction rule for $\exists$ will be based on the principle according to which an existential proposition is deducible form any of its instances. We obtain from this categorical principle the following hypothetical rule:

($\exists I$) For every L-formula ϕ, every set Γ of L-formulas, every variable x and every L-term t substitutable for x in ϕ, if $\Gamma \vdash (\phi)[t/x]$, then $\Gamma \vdash \exists x\, \phi$.

The elimination rule for $\exists$ will be based on the principle that whenever we have deduced a conclusion from an instance of an existential proposition, we can deduce the same conclusion from the existential proposition itself, provided that the instance is arbitrary. The arbitrariness proviso can be understood once more as the demand that the individual with which the existential proposition is instantiated doesn't figure in the conclusion or in the existential proposition. This would ensure that we would have been able to deduce the same conclusion from any other instance of the existential proposition. The elimination rule for $\exists$ will model a more general version of this deductive principle. To model the arbitrariness requirement, we adopt the same strategy as in $\forall I$:

(∃*E*) For every *L*-formula φ, all sets of *L*-formulas Γ, Δ, and all variables
        x, *y* such that *y* is substitutable for *x* in φ, if Γ ⊢ ∃*x* φ, Δ ∪
        {(φ)[*y*/*x*]} ⊢ ψ and *y* is not free in Δ, ∃*x* φ or ψ, then Γ ∪ Δ ⊢ ψ.

The introduction rule for ≈ will model the principle that the proposition
that an individual is identical with itself can be deduced from any set of
premises (including the empty set):

(≈*I*) For every *L*-term *t* and every finite set Γ of *L*-formulas, Γ ⊢ *t* ≈ *t*.

Consider the propositions that Clara is left-handed and that Alicia's
doubles partner is left-handed. The former is true just in case an individual, Clara, satisfies a certain condition—being left-handed—and the latter is true just in case this condition is satisfied by an individual, Alicia's
doubles partner, which may or may not be identical with Clara. When
two propositions are related in this way, we shall say that they are *coinstances*. The elimination rule for ≈ will be based on the principle that a
proposition can be deduced from any of its coinstances and the proposition that the instantiating individuals of the two coinstances are identical
to each other. The principle allows us to deduce the proposition that
Alicia's doubles partner is left-handed from the propositions that Clara is
left-handed and that she is Alicia's doubles partner. Once more, we shall
base on this categorical principle a hypothetical rule. To model the relation between coinstances, we shall use the relation between the *t*/*x*-
substitution and the *u*/*x*-substitution of a formula φ, where *t* and *u* are
terms which are substitutable for *x* in φ:

(≈*E*) For every *L*-formula φ, all sets of *L*-formulas Γ, Δ, every variable *x*
        and all *L*-terms *t*, *u* substitutable for *x* in φ, if Γ ⊢ (φ)[*t*/*x*] and Δ ⊢
        t ≈ *u*, then Γ ∪ Δ ⊢ (φ)[*u*/*x*].

6. Establishing (First-Order) Deducibility Claims

We have now presented all the rules of our deductive system for first-
order logic. They are collected in Figure 7 for easy reference. The procedure for establishing a deducibility claim in first-order logic is identical to the procedure that we presented in §3 for propositional logic. We
need to derive the claim from instances of the categorical rules of the
system using its hypothetical rules. The system contains only two categorical rules—the basic rule and the introduction rule for ≈. Hence to
show that a formula of a first-order language *L* is deducible from a set of
L-formulas, we need to derive this claim from instances of *B* and ≈*I* using
the remaining rules of the system.

(B) $\Gamma \vdash \phi$ whenever $\phi \in \Gamma$	
$(\wedge I)$ $\Gamma \vdash \phi, \Delta \vdash \psi$ ⎯⎯⎯⎯⎯⎯ $\Gamma \cup \Delta \vdash \phi \wedge \psi$	$(\wedge E)$ $\Gamma \vdash \phi \wedge \psi$ $\qquad$ $\Gamma \vdash \phi \wedge \psi$ ⎯⎯⎯⎯ $\qquad$ ⎯⎯⎯⎯ $\Gamma \vdash \phi$ $\qquad\qquad$ $\Gamma \vdash \psi$
$(\vee I)$ $\Gamma \vdash \phi$ $\qquad$ $\Gamma \vdash \psi$ ⎯⎯⎯⎯ $\quad$ ⎯⎯⎯⎯ $\Gamma \vdash \phi \vee \psi$ $\quad$ $\Gamma \vdash \phi \vee \psi$	$(\vee E)$ $\Gamma \vdash \phi \vee \psi, \Delta \cup \{\phi\} \vdash \alpha, \Sigma \cup \{\psi\} \vdash \alpha$ ⎯⎯⎯⎯⎯⎯⎯⎯⎯⎯ $\Gamma \cup \Delta \cup \Sigma \vdash \alpha$
$(\rightarrow I)$ $\Gamma \cup \{\phi\} \vdash \psi$ ⎯⎯⎯⎯⎯⎯ $\Gamma \vdash \phi \rightarrow \psi$	$(\rightarrow E)$ $\Gamma \vdash \phi, \Delta \vdash \phi \rightarrow \psi$ ⎯⎯⎯⎯⎯⎯⎯ $\Gamma \cup \Delta \vdash \psi$
$(\neg I)$ $\Gamma \cup \{\phi\} \vdash \psi, \Delta \cup \{\phi\} \vdash \neg\psi$ ⎯⎯⎯⎯⎯⎯⎯⎯⎯ $\Gamma \cup \Delta \vdash \neg\phi$	$(\neg E)$ $\Gamma \vdash \neg\neg\phi$ ⎯⎯⎯⎯ $\Gamma \vdash \phi$
$(\forall I)$ $\Gamma \vdash (\phi)[y/x]$ ⎯⎯⎯⎯⎯ $\Gamma \vdash \forall x\, \phi$ If y is substitutable for x in ϕ and not free in Γ or $\forall x\, \phi$.	$(\forall E)$ $\Gamma \vdash \forall x\, \phi$ ⎯⎯⎯⎯⎯ $\Gamma \vdash (\phi)[t/x]$ If t is substitutable for x in ϕ
$(\exists I)$ $\Gamma \vdash (\phi)[t/x]$ ⎯⎯⎯⎯⎯ $\Gamma \vdash \exists x\, \phi$ If t is substitutable for x in ϕ	$(\exists E)$ $\Gamma \vdash \exists x\, \phi, \Delta \cup \{(\phi)[y/x]\} \vdash \psi$ ⎯⎯⎯⎯⎯⎯⎯ $\Gamma \cup \Delta \vdash \psi$ If y is substitutable for x in ϕ and not free in Δ, $\exists x\, \phi$ or ψ
$(\approx I)$ $\Gamma \vdash t \approx t$	$(\approx E)$ $\Gamma \vdash (\phi)[t/x], \Delta \vdash t \approx u$ ⎯⎯⎯⎯⎯⎯⎯ $\Gamma \cup \Delta \vdash (\phi)[u/x]$ If t and u are substitutable for x in ϕ

Figure 7

We can present first-order deducibility arguments with the same trees that we used for propositional logic. We show first that the formula $\forall x\, Px \rightarrow \forall x\, Qx$ is deducible form the set $\{\forall x\, (Px \rightarrow Qx)\}$.

$$\frac{\{\forall x\, Px\} \vdash \forall x\, Px \ (B)}{\{\forall x\, Px\} \vdash Px \ (\forall E)}$$ $$\frac{\{\forall x\, (Px \to Qx)\} \vdash \forall x\, (Px \to Qx) \ (B)}{\{\forall x\, (Px \to Qx)\} \vdash Px \to Qx \ (\forall E)}$$

$$\frac{\{\forall x\, (Px \to Qx),\, \forall x\, Px\} \vdash Qx \ (\to E)}{\{\forall x\, (Px \to Qx),\, \forall x\, Px\} \vdash \forall x\, Qx \ (\forall I)}$$

$$\{\forall x\, (Px \to Qx)\} \vdash \forall x\, Px \to \forall x\, Qx \ (\to I)$$

Notice that we can apply $\forall E$ to derive $\{\forall x\, Px\} \vdash Px$ from $\{\forall x\, Px\} \vdash \forall x\, Px$, and $\{\forall x\, (Px \to Qx)\} \vdash Px \to Qx$ from $\{\forall x\, (Px \to Qx)\} \vdash \forall x\, (Px \to Qx)$ because every variable is substitutable for itself in every formula (see Exercise 4. 24) and every formula is its own x/x-substitution. The same remarks explain the derivation of $\{\forall x\, (Px \to Qx),\, \forall x\, Px\} \vdash \forall x\, Qx$ from $\{\forall x\, (Px \to Qx),\, \forall x\, Px\} \vdash Qx$ using $\forall I$, given that x is not free in any element of $\{\forall x\, (Px \to Qx),\, \forall x\, Px\}$ or in $\forall x\, Qx$. It is often convenient to use x/x-substitutions in this way to apply quantifier rules.

We show now that $\exists x\, Px \to \exists x\, Qx$ is deducible from $\{\forall x\, (Px \to Qx)\}$.

$$\frac{\{\forall x\, (Px \to Qx)\} \vdash \forall x\, (Px \to Qx) \ (B)}{\{\forall x\, (Px \to Qx)\} \vdash Px \to Qx \ (\forall E)} \qquad \{Px\} \vdash Px \ (B)$$

$$\frac{\{\forall x\, (Px \to Qx),\, Px\} \vdash Qx \ (\to E)}{\{\forall x\, (Px \to Qx),\, Px\} \vdash \exists x\, Qx \ (\exists I)}$$

$$\{\exists x\, Px\} \vdash \exists x\, Px \ (B) \qquad \{\forall x\, (Px \to Qx),\, Px\} \vdash \exists x\, Qx \ (\exists I)$$

$$\frac{\{\forall x\, (Px \to Qx),\, \exists x\, Px\} \vdash \exists x\, Qx \ (\exists E)}{\{\forall x\, (Px \to Qx)\} \vdash \exists x\, Px \to \exists x\, Qx \ (\to I)}$$

We show now that $\forall x \forall y\, (x \approx y \to f(x) \approx f(y))$ is deducible from the empty set.

$$\varnothing \vdash f(x) \approx f(x) \ (\approx I) \qquad\qquad\qquad \{x \approx y\} \vdash x \approx y \ (B)$$

$$\frac{\{x \approx y\} \vdash f(x) \approx f(y) \ (\approx E)}{\varnothing \vdash x \approx y \to f(x) \approx f(y) \ (\to I)}$$

$$\varnothing \vdash \forall y\, (x \approx y \to f(x) \approx f(y)) \ (\forall I)$$

$$\varnothing \vdash \forall x \forall y\, (x \approx y \to f(x) \approx f(y)) \ (\forall I)$$

To understand the application of $\approx E$ in this argument, notice that $f(x) \approx f(x)$ is $(f(x) \approx f(y))[x/y]$, $f(x) \approx f(y)$ is $(f(x) \approx f(y))[y/y]$, and both x and y are substitutable for y in $f(x) \approx f(y)$.

Notice that although the deducibility claims of Exercises 4. 1–2, Lemma 4. 3 and Exercises 4. 4–8 concern *PL*-sentences, they have direct analogues for formulas of a first-order language *L*. And if they hold for *PL*-sentences, they also hold for *L*-formulas, since the deductive system for *L* contains all the rules of the deductive system for *PL* that we used in §3.

EXERCISE 4. 25: For each logical consequence claim in Exercise 3. 22 establish the corresponding deducibility claim.

Hint: Proceed as in the examples provided above. For (2), use $\exists E$ to obtain $\{\forall x \ (Mx \rightarrow \neg Px), \exists x \ (Sx \wedge Mx)\} \vdash \exists x \ (Sx \wedge \neg Px)$. Notice that using $\exists I$ to derive this claim from $\{\forall x \ (Mx \rightarrow \neg Px), \exists x \ (Sx \wedge Mx)\} \vdash Sx \wedge \neg Px$ wouldn't be a good idea, since, for every term t, $St \wedge \neg Pt$ is not a logical consequence of $\{\forall x \ (Mx \rightarrow \neg Px), \exists x \ (Sx \wedge Mx)\}$. Hence, if our deductive system is sound, we will not be able to derive $\{\forall x \ (Mx \rightarrow \neg Px), \exists x \ (Sx \wedge Mx)\} \vdash Sx \wedge \neg Px$. In particular, we won't be able to use $\exists E$ to derive this claim from $\{\exists x \ (Sx \wedge Mx)\} \vdash \exists x \ (Sx \wedge Mx)$ and $\{\forall x \ (Mx \rightarrow \neg Px), Sx \wedge Mx\} \vdash Sx \wedge \neg Px$, since the fact that x is free in $Sx \wedge \neg Px$ violates one of the restrictions on the application of this rule. The general lesson is that if $\exists E$ and $\exists I$ are to be used in a derivation, $\exists E$ should normally be used before (i.e. closer to the bottom than) $\exists I$.

EXERCISE 4. 26: For each logical consequence claim in Exercise 3. 23 establish the corresponding deducibility claim.

Hint: For (3) and (4), see the hint for Exercise 4. 25 (2). (6) is very long. Don't use $\exists I$ right away. Use $\neg E$ and $\neg I$ instead.

EXERCISE 4. 27: For each logical consequence claim in Exercise 3. 24 establish the corresponding deducibility claim.

Hint: (4) is hard. Use the reasoning of Exercise 4. 4 (8) to derive $\{\forall x \ (\phi \vee \psi)\} \vdash \forall x \ \phi \vee \exists x \ \psi$ from $\{\forall x \ (\phi \vee \psi), \neg \exists x \ \psi\} \vdash \forall x \ \phi$.

EXERCISE 4. 28: For each logical consequence claim in Exercise 3. 25 establish the corresponding deducibility claim.

Hint: (5) is hard. Use ($\neg E$ and then) $\neg I$, deducing $\forall x \ \neg \psi$ and $\neg \forall x \ \neg \psi$ from $\{\exists x \ \phi \rightarrow \exists x \ \psi, \neg \exists x \ (\phi \rightarrow \psi)\}$.

EXERCISE 4. 29: For each logical consequence claim in Exercise 3. 26 establish the corresponding deducibility claim.

EXERCISE 4. 30: Show that every formula in Exercise 3. 29 is deducible from the empty set.

Hint: (5) is long. Use ¬*I*, deducing, say, $z \approx z$ and ¬$z \approx z$ from $\{\exists x \forall y$ $((Rxy \rightarrow \neg Ryx) \wedge (\neg Ryx \rightarrow Rxy))\}$.

EXERCISE 4. 31: For each logical equivalence claim of Exercise 3. 30 establish the corresponding reciprocal deducibility claims.

EXERCISE 4. 32: For each logical equivalence claim of Exercise 3. 31 establish the corresponding reciprocal deducibility claims, subject to the proviso that x is not free in ψ.

EXERCISE 4. 33: For each hypothetical logical consequence claim in Exercise 3. 32 establish the corresponding deducibility claim (taking Γ to be a finite set).

LEMMA 4. 34: If $\{\gamma_1,..., \gamma_n\}[y/x] \vdash (\phi)[y/x]$ and y does not occur in $\gamma_1,..., \gamma_n$ or ϕ, then $\{\gamma_1,..., \gamma_n\} \vdash \phi$.

Proof: Assume that $\{\gamma_1,..., \gamma_n\}[y/x] \vdash (\phi)[y/x]$ and that y does not occur in $\gamma_1,..., \gamma_n$ or ϕ. From this, by Lemma 4. 3, we get $\varnothing \vdash ((\gamma_1)[y/x] \wedge...\wedge (\gamma_n)[y/x]) \rightarrow (\phi)[y/x]$. By the definition of t/x-substitution, $((\gamma_1)[y/x] \wedge...\wedge (\gamma_n)[y/x]) \rightarrow (\phi)[y/x]$ is $((\gamma_1 \wedge...\wedge \gamma_n) \rightarrow \phi)[y/x]$. Hence we have $\varnothing \vdash ((\gamma_1 \wedge...\wedge \gamma_n) \rightarrow \phi)[y/x]$. Since y doesn't occur in $(\gamma_1 \wedge...\wedge \gamma_n) \rightarrow \phi$, we have, by Exercise 4. 23, that y is substitutable for x in $(\gamma_1 \wedge...\wedge \gamma_n) \rightarrow \phi$. And since y is not free in $\forall x ((\gamma_1 \wedge...\wedge \gamma_n) \rightarrow \phi)$ or, trivially, in $\varnothing$, we can apply $\forall I$ to derive $\varnothing \vdash \forall x ((\gamma_1 \wedge...\wedge \gamma_n) \rightarrow \phi)$. From this, using $\forall E$, we derive $\varnothing \vdash (\gamma_1 \wedge...\wedge \gamma_n) \rightarrow \phi$. Applying Lemma 4. 3 once more we get $\{\gamma_1,..., \gamma_n\} \vdash \phi$, as desired. ∎

EXERCISE 4. 35: Show that, if y doesn't occur in ϕ, then $\{\exists x \phi\} \vdash \exists y$ $(\phi)[y/x]$ and $\{\forall x \phi\} \vdash \forall y (\phi)[y/x]$.

7. The Definition of Deducibility

We have presented our deductive system as a collection of rules governing the process of logical deduction in a first-order language. This is the natural way of looking at the system when we use it to establish claims to the effect that a formula is deducible from a set of formulas. But we will also want to establish results *about* the system, including the fact that it is both sound and complete. For this purpose, it is better to consider the deductive system, not as a collection of rules, but as a definition of a binary relation, for each first-order language L, pairing finite sets of L-

formulas with L-formulas. We shall refer to this relation as *deducibility* (in L), written D_L.

Let's say that an *L-sequent* is an ordered pair $\langle \Gamma, \phi \rangle$, where Γ is a finite set of L-formulas and ϕ an L-formula (thus the set of L-sequents is the Cartesian product of the set of finite sets of L-formulas and the set of L-formulas). Then we can characterize our deductive system as a definition of a set of L-sequents, i.e. the set D_L such that $\langle \Gamma, \phi \rangle \in D_L$ if and only if $\Gamma \vdash \phi$. It defines D_L by induction, with the categorical rules of the system providing the base of the definition and the hypothetical rules its inductive clauses. We can formulate the definition of D_L along the following lines:

1. *Base*:

(B) For every finite set Γ of L-formulas, and every L-formula ϕ such that $\phi \in \Gamma$, $\langle \Gamma, \phi \rangle \in D_L$.

($\approx$*I*) For every finite set Γ of L-formulas, and every L-term t, $\langle \Gamma, t \approx t \rangle \in D_L$.

2. *Inductive Clauses*:

($\wedge$*I*) For all L-sequents $\langle \Gamma, \phi \rangle$, $\langle \Delta, \psi \rangle \in D_L$, $\langle \Gamma \cup \Delta, \phi \wedge \psi \rangle \in D_L$.

($\wedge$*E*) For every L-sequent $\langle \Gamma, \phi \wedge \psi \rangle \in D_L$, $\langle \Gamma, \phi \rangle$, $\langle \Gamma, \psi \rangle \in D_L$.

($\vee$*I*) For every L-sequent $\langle \Gamma, \phi \rangle \in D_L$, $\langle \Gamma, \phi \vee \psi \rangle$, $\langle \Gamma, \psi \vee \phi \rangle \in D_L$, for every L-formula ψ.

($\vee$*E*) For all L-sequents $\langle \Gamma, \phi \vee \psi \rangle$, $\langle \Delta \cup \{\phi\}, \alpha \rangle$, $\langle \Sigma \cup \{\psi\}, \alpha \rangle \in D_L$, $\langle \Gamma \cup \Delta \cup \Sigma, \alpha \rangle \in D_L$.

($\rightarrow$*I*) For every L-sequent $\langle \Gamma \cup \{\phi\}, \psi \rangle \in D_L$, $\langle \Gamma, \phi \rightarrow \psi \rangle \in D_L$.

($\rightarrow$*E*) For all L-sequents $\langle \Gamma, \phi \rightarrow \psi \rangle$, $\langle \Delta, \phi \rangle \in D_L$, $\langle \Gamma \cup \Delta, \psi \rangle \in D_L$.

($\neg$*I*) For all L-sequents $\langle \Gamma \cup \{\phi\}, \psi \rangle$, $\langle \Delta \cup \{\phi\}, \neg\psi \rangle \in D_L$, $\langle \Gamma \cup \Delta, \neg\phi \rangle \in D_L$.

($\neg$*E*) For every L-sequent $\langle \Gamma, \neg\neg\phi \rangle \in D_L$, $\langle \Gamma, \phi \rangle \in D_L$.

($\forall$*I*) For every L-sequent $\langle \Gamma, (\phi)[y/x] \rangle \in D_L$, such that y is substitutable for x in ϕ and not free in Γ or $\forall x \phi$, $\langle \Gamma, \forall x \phi \rangle \in D_L$.

($\forall$*E*) For every L-sequent $\langle \Gamma, \forall x \phi \rangle \in D_L$, $\langle \Gamma, (\phi)[t/x] \rangle \in D_L$, for every L-term t substitutable for x in ϕ.

($\exists$*I*) For every L-sequent $\langle \Gamma, (\phi)[t/x] \rangle \in D_L$, such that t is substitutable for x in ϕ, $\langle \Gamma, \exists x \phi \rangle \in D_L$.

($\exists$*E*) For all L-sequents $\langle \Gamma, \exists x \phi \rangle$, $\langle \Delta \cup \{(\phi)[y/x]\}, \psi \rangle \in D_L$, such that y is substitutable for x in ϕ and not free in Δ, ψ, or $\exists x \phi$, $\langle \Gamma \cup \Delta, \psi \rangle \in D_L$.

($\approx$*E*) For all L-sequents $\langle \Gamma, (\phi)[t/x] \rangle$, $\langle \Delta, t \approx u \rangle \in D_L$, such that t and u are substitutable for x in ϕ, $\langle \Gamma \cup \Delta, (\phi)[u/x] \rangle \in D_L$.

3. Nothing else is in D_L.

According to our characterization of inductive definitions, each inductive clause of the definition of D_L would have to use a function in the set of L-sequents, stipulating that if an L-sequent is in D_L (or, for an n-place function, if all the L-sequents in an n-tuple are in D_L), then its image under the function is also in D_L. In some cases, it is easy to see which function is being used. Thus, e.g., $\wedge I$ uses the binary function f in the set of L-sequents defined as follows: $f(\langle \Gamma, \phi \rangle, \langle \Delta, \psi \rangle) = \langle \Gamma \cup \Delta, \phi \wedge \psi \rangle$. But other cases are not so straightforward. Thus we want $\wedge E$ to use two functions. One would pair a sequent $\langle \Gamma, \phi \rangle$ with the sequent $\langle \Gamma, \alpha \rangle$, where α is the first conjunct of ϕ, if ϕ is a conjunction (the other function would do the same with respect to the second conjunct of ϕ). But a function in the set of sequents would also have to assign an image to $\langle \Gamma, \phi \rangle$ when ϕ doesn't have this form, although we wouldn't want to add new sequents to D_L when we apply $\wedge E$ in these cases. We achieve this with the functions l, r in the set of L-sequents defined as follows:

$$l(\langle \Gamma, \phi \rangle) = \begin{cases} \langle \Gamma, \alpha \rangle \text{ if } \phi \text{ is of the form } \alpha \wedge \beta \text{ for some } L\text{-formulas } \alpha, \beta, \\ \langle \Gamma, \phi \rangle \text{ otherwise.} \end{cases}$$

$$r(\langle \Gamma, \phi \rangle) = \begin{cases} \langle \Gamma, \beta \rangle \text{ if } \phi \text{ is of the form } \alpha \wedge \beta \text{ for some } L\text{-formulas } \alpha, \beta, \\ \langle \Gamma, \phi \rangle \text{ otherwise.} \end{cases}$$

Other clauses would have to be construed as using infinitely many functions in the set of L-sequents. Thus, e.g., $\rightarrow I$ could be construed as using, for each L-formula ϕ, the function g_ϕ in the set of L-sequents defined as follows:

$$g_\phi(\langle \Gamma, \psi \rangle) = \begin{cases} \langle \Gamma - \{\phi\}, \phi \rightarrow \psi \rangle \text{ if } \phi \in \Gamma, \\ \langle \Gamma, \psi \rangle \text{ otherwise.} \end{cases}$$

Similarly, $\forall I$ could be construed as using, for each L-formula ϕ and each variable x, the function $h_{\phi,x}$ in the set of L-sequents defined as follows:

$$h_{\phi,x}(\langle \Gamma, \psi \rangle) = \begin{cases} \langle \Gamma, \forall x\, \phi \rangle \text{ if } \psi \text{ is } (\phi)[y/x] \text{ for some variable } y \\ \text{substitutable for } x \text{ in } \phi \text{ which is not free in } \Gamma \text{ or in } \forall x\, \phi, \\ \langle \Gamma, \psi \rangle \text{ otherwise.} \end{cases}$$

EXERCISE 4. 36: Find functions in the set of L-sequents which could be used to construe the remaining inductive clauses of the definition of D_L.

Hint: Use the strategies of the examples provided. You will need to use two functions for each L-formula for $\vee I$, one function for each L-formula for $\neg I$, $\forall E$, $\exists E$ and $\approx E$, and one function for each L-formula and variable for $\exists I$.

8. Deducibility in Different Languages

Let L be a first-order language, and let $L*$ be a language which results from adding new extralogical symbols to the vocabulary of L. Consider the relationship between deducibility in $L*$ and deducibility in L with respect to L-formulas. Clearly, if an L-formula ϕ is deducible in L from a set of L-formulas Γ, ϕ will also be deducible from Γ in $L*$. But the converse is less straightforward, since some of the arguments that we can use to deduce in $L*$ an L-formula ϕ from a set of L-formulas Γ will involve $L*$-formulas not in L, and hence cannot be used to deduce ϕ from Γ in L. Thus, e.g., if $\phi \wedge \psi$ is deducible from Γ in $L*$, we can apply $\wedge E$ to deduce ϕ from Γ in $L*$, but if ψ is an $L*$-formula not in L, we cannot use this argument to deduce ϕ from Γ in L. The new symbols provide additional tools for deducing L-formulas from sets of L-formulas. This raises the question, whether an L-formula could be deducible from a set of L-formulas in $L*$ but not in L. Our goal in this section is to show that this is not a possibility. We proceed in two stages. We show first that if we add new predicates and function symbols to the vocabulary of L, an L-formula ϕ won't be deducible from a set of L-formulas Γ in the expanded language unless ϕ is deducible from Γ in L itself. Then we show that the same situation obtains if we add new individual constants to L. We shall write $\Gamma \vdash_L \phi$ to express that ϕ is deducible from Γ in language L.

Let Π be a set of predicates and function symbols not in the vocabulary of L, and let $L+\Pi$ be the language which results from adding all the symbols in Π to the vocabulary of L. We want to show that if an L-formula ϕ is deducible in $L+\Pi$ from a set of L-formulas Γ, then ϕ is also deducible from Γ in L. But instead of establishing this claim directly, we prove a result from which the claim will follow as a corollary. The intuitive idea behind our reasoning is that if we can deduce an L-formula ϕ from a set of L-formulas Γ with an argument which involves $L+\Pi$-formulas not in L, we can also deduce ϕ from Γ with an argument in which those formulas are replaced by L-formulas. We shall refer to the L-formula which replaces an $L+\Pi$-formula ψ in the new argument as the Π-*purge* of ψ, written $(\psi)_L$. We shall represent the set containing the Π-purges of the elements of a set Γ of $L+\Pi$-formulas as Γ_L.

We first define by recursion on terms the Π-purge of an $L+\Pi$-term.

DEFINITION: The Π-*purge* of an $L+\Pi$-term t, written $(t)_L$, is the image of t under the unique function satisfying the following conditions:

(A) For every variable x, $(x)_L = x$.

(B) For every individual constant c of $L+\Pi$, $(c)_L = c$.

(C) For every $L+\Pi$-term of the form $f(t_1,\ldots, t_n)$,

$$(f(t_1,\ldots,t_n))_L = \begin{cases} (t_1)_L \text{ if } f \in \Pi, \\ f((t_1)_L,\ldots,(t_n)_L) \text{ otherwise.} \end{cases}$$

We now define by recursion on formulas the Π-purge of an $L+\Pi$-formula.

DEFINITION: The Π-*purge* of an $L+\Pi$-formula ϕ, written $(\phi)_L$, is the image of ϕ under the unique function satisfying the following conditions:

(1) For every $L+\Pi$-formula of the form $Pt_1\ldots t_n$,

$$(Pt_1\ldots t_n)_L = \begin{cases} \exists x\, x \approx x \text{ if } P \in \Pi, \\ P(t_1)_L\ldots(t_n)_L \text{ otherwise.} \end{cases}$$

(2) For every $L+\Pi$-formula of the form $t \approx u$, $(t \approx u)_L = (t)_L \approx (u)_L$.

(3) For every $L+\Pi$-formula of the form $\neg\alpha$, $(\neg\alpha)_L = \neg(\alpha)_L$.

(4) For every $L+\Pi$-formula of the form $\alpha \wedge \beta$, $(\alpha \wedge \beta)_L = (\alpha)_L \wedge (\beta)_L$.

(5) For every $L+\Pi$-formula of the form $\alpha \vee \beta$, $(\alpha \vee \beta)_L = (\alpha)_L \vee (\beta)_L$.

(6) For every $L+\Pi$-formula of the form $\alpha \rightarrow \beta$, $(\alpha \rightarrow \beta)_L = (\alpha)_L \rightarrow (\beta)_L$.

(7) For every $L+\Pi$-formula of the form $\forall x\, \alpha$, $(\forall x\, \alpha)_L = \forall x\, (\alpha)_L$.

(8) For every $L+\Pi$-formula of the form $\exists x\, \alpha$, $(\exists x\, \alpha)_L = \exists x\, (\alpha)_L$.

It will soon become clear that any other L-sentence could have played the role of $\exists x\, x \approx x$ in (1). We are going to invoke the following results about the notion of Π-purge.

EXERCISE 4. 37: Show that for every $L+\Pi$-term t and every $L+\Pi$-formula ϕ, $(t)_L$ is an L-term and $(\phi)_L$ is an L-formula.

Hint: By induction on $L+\Pi$-terms and on $L+\Pi$-formulas, in that order.

EXERCISE 4. 38: Show that every L-term and every L-formula is its own Π-purge.

Hint: Reformulate and prove by induction on $L+\Pi$-terms and on $L+\Pi$-formulas, in that order.

EXERCISE 4. 39: Show that for every $L+\Pi$-term t, if x doesn't occur in t, then x doesn't occur in $(t)_L$, and that for every $L+\Pi$-formula ϕ, if x is not free in ϕ, then x is not free in $(\phi)_L$.

Hint: By induction on $L+\Pi$-formulas.

EXERCISE 4. 40: Show that for every $L+\Pi$-term t and every $L+\Pi$-formula ϕ, if u is an $L+\Pi$-term, then $((t)[u/x])_L = ((t)_L)[(u)_L/x]$, and $((\phi)[u/x])_L = ((\phi)_L)[(u)_L/x]$.

Hint: By induction on $L+\Pi$-terms and on $L+\Pi$-formulas, in that order.

EXERCISE 4. 41: Show that for every $L+\Pi$-formula ϕ, if t is substitutable for x in ϕ, then $(t)_L$ is substitutable for x in $(\phi)_L$.

Hint: By induction on $L+\Pi$-formulas.

We now prove that if an $L+\Pi$-formula ϕ is deducible in $L+\Pi$ from a set of $L+\Pi$-formulas Γ, then the Π-purge of ϕ is deducible in L from the Π-purge of Γ. In light of Exercise 4. 38, this will entail that if an L-formula ϕ is deducible in $L+\Pi$ from a set of L-formulas Γ, then ϕ is also deducible from Γ in L, as desired.

LEMMA 4. 42: For every $L+\Pi$-formula ϕ, and every set of $L+\Pi$-formulas Γ, if $\Gamma \vdash_{L+\Pi} \phi$, then $\Gamma_L \vdash_L (\phi)_L$.

Proof: As we saw in the preceding section, our deductive system provides, for every first-order language L, an inductive definition of the deducibility relation for L, D_L. This lemma is a universal claim about the $L+\Pi$-sequents in $D_{L+\Pi}$. Hence, we can prove it by induction on deducibility in $L+\Pi$.

   Base:
   B. We need to show that for every $L+\Pi$-formula ϕ, and every finite set of $L+\Pi$-formulas Γ, if $\phi \in \Gamma$, then $\Gamma_L \vdash_L (\phi)_L$. Let ϕ be an $L+\Pi$-formula, and Γ a finite set of $L+\Pi$-formulas such that $\phi \in \Gamma$. Then $(\phi)_L \in \Gamma_L$, and since, by Exercise 4. 37, $(\phi)_L$ is an L-formula and Γ_L is a finite set of L-formulas, we can apply the basic rule to conclude that $\Gamma_L \vdash_L (\phi)_L$, as desired.
   $\approx I$. We need to show that for every finite set of $L+\Pi$-formulas Γ, and every $L+\Pi$-term t, $\Gamma_L \vdash_L (t \approx t)_L$. Let Γ be a finite set of $L+\Pi$-formulas and let t be an $L+\Pi$-term. By the definition of Π-purge, $(t \approx t)_L$ is $(t)_L \approx (t)_L$. Since, by Exercise 4. 37, $(t)_L$ is an L-term and Γ_L is a finite set of L-formulas, we can apply $\approx I$ to conclude that $\Gamma_L \vdash_L (t \approx t)_L$, as desired.

Inductive Step: We shall deal with $\wedge E$, $\forall I$ and $\approx E$, leaving the remaining clauses as an exercise.

$\wedge E$. Let $\phi \wedge \psi$ be an $L+\Pi$-formula, and Γ a set of $L+\Pi$-formulas such that $\Gamma \vdash_{L+\Pi} \phi \wedge \psi$. We need to show that if the lemma holds for $\langle\Gamma, \phi \wedge \psi\rangle$, then it also holds for $\langle\Gamma, \phi\rangle$ and $\langle\Gamma, \psi\rangle$. We assume (IH) that $\Gamma_L \vdash_L (\phi \wedge \psi)_L$. We need to show that it follows from this that $\Gamma_L \vdash_L (\phi)_L$ and $\Gamma_L \vdash_L (\psi)_L$. By the definition of Π-purge, $(\phi \wedge \psi)_L$ is $(\phi)_L \wedge (\psi)_L$, and, by Exercise 4. 37, $(\phi)_L \wedge (\psi)_L$ is an L-formula and Γ_L is a set of L-formulas. Hence we can apply $\wedge E$ to derive $\Gamma_L \vdash_L (\phi)_L$ and $\Gamma_L \vdash_L (\psi)_L$, as desired.

$\forall I$. Let Γ be a set of $L+\Pi$-formulas, ϕ an $L+\Pi$-formula, and x, y variables such that $\Gamma \vdash_{L+\Pi} (\phi)[y/x]$, and y is substitutable for x in ϕ and not free in Γ or in $\forall x\ \phi$. We need to show that if the lemma holds for $\langle\Gamma, (\phi)[y/x]\rangle$, then it also holds for $\langle\Gamma, \forall x\ \phi\rangle$. We assume (IH) that $\Gamma_L \vdash_L ((\phi)[y/x])_L$. We need to show that it follows from this that $\Gamma_L \vdash_L (\forall x\ \phi)_L$. By Exercise 4. 40, we have that $((\phi)[y/x])_L = ((\phi)_L)[(y)_L/x] = ((\phi)_L)[y/x]$. Hence we get $\Gamma_L \vdash_L ((\phi)_L)[y/x]$. By Exercise 4. 37, $((\phi)_L)[y/x]$ is an L-formula and Γ_L is a set of L-formulas. Since $(y)_L$ is y, we have, by Exercise 4. 41, that y is substitutable for x in $(\phi)_L$. Also, by Exercise 4. 39, y is not free in Γ_L or in $\forall x\ (\phi)_L$. Hence we can apply $\forall I$ to derive $\Gamma_L \vdash_L \forall x\ (\phi)_L$, i.e. $\Gamma_L \vdash_L (\forall x\ \phi)_L$, as desired.

$\approx E$. Let Γ, Δ be sets of $L+\Pi$-formulas, ϕ an $L+\Pi$-formula, t, u $L+\Pi$-terms, and x a variable such that $\Gamma \vdash_{L+\Pi} (\phi)[t/x]$, $\Delta \vdash_{L+\Pi} t \approx u$, and t and u are substitutable for x in ϕ. We need to show that if the lemma holds for $\langle\Gamma, (\phi)[t/x]\rangle$, $\langle\Delta, t \approx u\rangle$, then it also holds for $\langle\Gamma \cup \Delta, (\phi)[u/x]\rangle$. Assume (IH) that $\Gamma_L \vdash_L ((\phi)[t/x])_L$, $\Delta_L \vdash_L (t \approx u)_L$. We need to show that $\Gamma_L \cup \Delta_L \vdash_L ((\phi)[u/x])_L$. By Exercise 4. 40, $((\phi)[t/x])_L$ is $((\phi)_L)[(t)_L/x]$. By the definition of Π-purge, $(t \approx u)_L$ is $(t)_L \approx (u)_L$. By Exercise 4. 37, Γ_L and Δ_L are sets of L-formulas, and $((\phi)_L)[(t)_L/x]$ and $(t)_L \approx (u)_L$ are L-formulas, and by Exercise 4. 41, $(t)_L$ and $(u)_L$ are substitutable for x in $(\phi)_L$. Hence we can apply $\approx E$ to derive $\Gamma_L \cup \Delta_L \vdash_L ((\phi)_L)[(u)_L/x]$, i.e., again by Exercise 4. 40, $\Gamma_L \cup \Delta_L \vdash_L ((\phi)[u/x])_L$, as desired. ∎

EXERCISE 4. 43: Complete the proof of Lemma 4. 42 dealing with the remaining inductive clauses.

Our next goal is to show that if we add new individual constants to the vocabulary of L, an L-formula ϕ won't be deducible from a set of L-formulas Γ in the expanded language unless ϕ is deducible from Γ in L itself. Let L be a first-order language, C a set of individual constants not in the vocabulary of L, and $L+C$ the language which results from adding all the individual constants in C to the vocabulary of L. We want to show that if an L-formula ϕ is deducible in $L+C$ from a set of L-formulas

Γ, then ϕ is also deducible from Γ in L. We follow, with some modifications, the same strategy as with $L+\Pi$.

DEFINITION: If $\langle\Gamma, \phi\rangle$ is an $L+C$-sequent, and f is a one-to-one function from the set of constants from C which occur in Γ or ϕ to the set of variables which don't occur in Γ or ϕ, the C-*purge* of $\langle\Gamma, \phi\rangle$ generated by f is the sequent that results from replacing every occurrence in Γ or ϕ of an individual constant from C with its image under f.

If g is a function from a subset of C to the set of variables, then for every $L+C$-formula ϕ, $(\phi)|g|$ will denote the formula that results from replacing every occurrence in ϕ of an individual constant in the domain of g with its image under g. Similarly, for every set of $L+C$-formulas Γ, $\Gamma|g|$ will denote the set containing the formulas which result from replacing every occurrence in an element of Γ of an individual constant in the domain of g with its image under g. Using this notation, we can represent the C-purge of $\langle\Gamma, \phi\rangle$ generated by f as $\langle\Gamma|f|, (\phi)|f|\rangle$.

Notice that every C-purge of an $L+C$-sequent is an L-sequent, and that every L-sequent is its own C-purge. Hence the following lemma will have as a corollary the result that we want to establish: if an L-formula ϕ is deducible in $L+C$ from a set of L-formulas Γ, then ϕ is also deducible from Γ in L.

LEMMA 4. 44: For every $L+C$-sequent $\langle\Gamma, \phi\rangle$, if $\langle\Gamma, \phi\rangle$ is an element of D_{L+C}, then every C-purge of $\langle\Gamma, \phi\rangle$ is an element of D_L.

Proof: By induction on deducibility in $L+C$.
   Base:
   B. Let ϕ be an $L+C$-formula and Γ a finite set of $L+C$-formulas such that $\phi \in \Gamma$. We need to show that every C-purge of $\langle\Gamma, \phi\rangle$ is in D_L. Let f be a one-to-one function from the set of constants from C which occur in Γ or ϕ to the set of variables which don't occur in Γ or ϕ. Then $(\phi)|f|$ is an L-formula, $\Gamma|f|$ is a finite set of L-formulas, and $(\phi)|f| \in \Gamma|f|$. Hence, by the basic rule, we get $\Gamma|f| \vdash_L (\phi)|f|$, as desired.
   $\approx I$. Let Γ be a finite set of $L+C$-formulas, and let t be an $L+C$-term. We need to show that every C-purge of $\langle\Gamma, t \approx t\rangle$ is in D_L. Let f be a one-to-one function from the set of constants from C which occur in Γ or $t \approx t$ to the set of variables which don't occur in Γ or $t \approx t$. Then $(t \approx t)|f|$ is an L-formula and $\Gamma|f|$ a finite set of L-formulas, and since $(t \approx t)|f|$ is $(t)|f| \approx (t)|f|$, by $\approx I$, we get $\Gamma|f| \vdash_L (t \approx t)|f|$, as desired.
   Inductive Step: We shall deal with $\wedge I$, $\wedge E$ and $\forall I$, leaving the rest as an exercise.
   $\wedge I$. Let Γ, Δ be sets of $L+C$-formulas, and ϕ, ψ $L+C$-formulas such that $\Gamma \vdash_{L+C} \phi$ and $\Delta \vdash_{L+C} \psi$. We need to show that if every C-purge of $\langle\Gamma,$

$\phi\rangle$ or $\langle\Delta, \psi\rangle$ is an element of D_L, then every C-purge of $\langle\Gamma \cup \Delta, \phi \wedge \psi\rangle$ is an element of D_L. We assume (IH) that every C-purge of $\langle\Gamma, \phi\rangle$ or $\langle\Delta, \psi\rangle$ is an element of D_L, and try to show that it follows from this that every C-purge of $\langle\Gamma \cup \Delta, \phi \wedge \psi\rangle$ is an element of D_L. Let f be a one-to-one function from the set of constants from C which occur in $\Gamma \cup \Delta$ or $\phi \wedge \psi$ to the set of variables which don't occur in $\Gamma \cup \Delta$ or $\phi \wedge \psi$. We need to show that $(\Gamma \cup \Delta)|f| \vdash_L (\phi \wedge \psi)|f|$. We have that $\langle\Gamma|f|, (\phi)|f|\rangle$ is a C-purge of $\langle\Gamma, \phi\rangle$, and $\langle\Delta|f|, (\psi)|f|\rangle$ is a C-purge of $\langle\Delta, \psi\rangle$. Hence IH yields $\Gamma|f| \vdash_L (\phi)|f|$, $\Delta|f| \vdash_L (\psi)|f|$. Now we can use $\wedge I$ to derive $\Gamma|f| \cup \Delta|f| \vdash_L (\phi)|f| \wedge (\psi)|f|$, i.e. $(\Gamma \cup \Delta)|f| \vdash_L (\phi \wedge \psi)|f|$, as desired.

$\wedge E$. Let Γ be a set of $L+C$-formulas, and $\phi \wedge \psi$ an $L+C$-formula such that $\Gamma \vdash_{L+C} \phi \wedge \psi$. We need to show that if every C-purge of $\langle\Gamma, \phi \wedge \psi\rangle$ is an element of D_L, then every C-purge of $\langle\Gamma, \phi\rangle$ or $\langle\Gamma, \psi\rangle$ is an element of D_L. We assume (IH) that every C-purge of $\langle\Gamma, \phi \wedge \psi\rangle$ is an element of D_L, and try to show that it follows from this that every C-purge of $\langle\Gamma, \phi\rangle$ or $\langle\Gamma, \psi\rangle$ is an element of D_L. We present the argument for $\langle\Gamma, \phi\rangle$. $\langle\Gamma, \psi\rangle$ can be dealt with in the same way. Let f be a one-to-one function from the set of constants from C which occur in Γ or ϕ to the set of variables which don't occur in Γ or ϕ. We need to show that $\Gamma|f| \vdash_L (\phi)|f|$.

Notice that $\langle\Gamma|f|, (\phi \wedge \psi)|f|\rangle$ is not in general a C-purge of $\langle\Gamma, \phi \wedge \psi\rangle$. For, on the one hand, any individual constants from C which might occur in ψ but not in Γ or ϕ will not be replaced by variables in $(\phi \wedge \psi)|f|$, and, on the other, some of the variables with which f pairs individual constants might occur in ψ. Hence we can't apply the inductive hypothesis to $\langle\Gamma|f|, (\phi \wedge \psi)|f|\rangle$, and we need to adopt a different strategy.

Let g be a one-to-one function from the set of constants from C which occur in Γ or $\phi \wedge \psi$ to the set of variables which don't occur in Γ or $\phi \wedge \psi$ and which are not in the range of f. Then, $\langle\Gamma|g|, (\phi \wedge \psi)|g|\rangle$ is a C-purge of $\langle\Gamma, \phi \wedge \psi\rangle$, and, by IH, we get $\Gamma|g| \vdash_L (\phi \wedge \psi)|g|$. Since $(\phi \wedge \psi)|g|$ is $(\phi)|g| \wedge (\psi)|g|$, we can apply $\wedge E$ to derive $\Gamma|g| \vdash_L (\phi)|g|$. However, what we need to show is not this, but $\Gamma|f| \vdash_L (\phi)|f|$. We argue as follows. Let $c_1,..., c_n$ be the individual constants from C which occur in Γ or ϕ, and, for every positive integer i less than or equal to n, let x_i be the image of c_i under f, and y_i its image under g. It follows from our assumptions about f and g that $(\phi)|g|$ is $((\phi)|f|)[y_1/x_1]...[y_n/x_n]$ and that $\Gamma|g|$ is $\Gamma|f|[y_1/x_1]...[y_n/x_n]$. Hence we have that $\Gamma|f|[y_1/x_1]...[y_n/x_n] \vdash_L ((\phi)|f|)[y_1/x_1]...[y_n/x_n]$. Notice also that y_1 doesn't occur in $\Gamma|f|$ or $(\phi)|f|$, and, for every positive integer i between 2 and n, y_i doesn't occur in $((\phi)|f|)[y_1/x_1]...[y_{i-1}/x_{i-1}]$ or in $\Gamma|f|[y_1/x_1]...[y_{i-1}/x_{i-1}]$. Hence, with n applications of Lemma 4. 34 we obtain $\Gamma|f| \vdash_L (\phi)|f|$, as desired.

$\forall I$. Let Γ be a set of $L+C$-formulas, ϕ an $L+C$-formula and x, y variables such that $\Gamma \vdash_L (\phi)[y/x]$, and y is substitutable for x in ϕ and not free in Γ or $\forall x\ \phi$. We need to show that if every C-purge of $\langle\Gamma, (\phi)[y/x]\rangle$ is an element of D_L, then every C-purge of $\langle\Gamma, \forall x\ \phi\rangle$ is an element of D_L. We assume (IH) that every C-purge of $\langle\Gamma, (\phi)[y/x]\rangle$ is an element of D_L, and try to show that it follows from this that every C-purge of $\langle\Gamma, \forall x\ \phi\rangle$ is an element of D_L. Let f be a one-to-one function from the set of constants from C which occur in Γ or $\forall x\ \phi$ to the set of variables which don't occur in Γ or $\forall x\ \phi$. We need to show that $\Gamma|f| \vdash_L (\forall x\ \phi)|f|$.

Here we face one of the problems that we encountered in $\wedge E$. $\langle\Gamma|f|,$ $((\phi)[y/x])|f|\rangle$ may not be a C-purge of $\langle\Gamma, (\phi)[y/x]\rangle$, since y might be one of the variables with which f pairs individual constants, and it might occur in $(\phi)[y/x]$. Hence we can't apply the inductive hypothesis to $\langle\Gamma|f|,$ $((\phi)[y/x])|f|\rangle$. To circumvent this problem, we use the same strategy as in $\wedge E$. Let g be a one-to-one function from the set of constants from C which occur in Γ or $(\phi)[y/x]$ to the set of variables other than x or y which don't occur in Γ or $(\phi)[y/x]$ and which are not in the range of f. Then $\langle\Gamma|g|, ((\phi)[y/x])|g|\rangle$ is a C-purge of $\langle\Gamma, (\phi)[y/x]\rangle$, and, by IH, we get $\Gamma|g|$ $\vdash_L ((\phi)[y/x])|g|$. Since x is not in the range of g, we have that $((\phi)[y/x])|g|$ is $((\phi)|g|)[y/x]$. Since y is substitutable for x in ϕ, it is also substitutable for x in $(\phi)|g|$. And since y is not free in Γ or in $\forall x\ \phi$, and is not in the range of g, it is not free in $\Gamma|g|$ or in $\forall x\ (\phi)|g|$ either. Hence we can apply $\forall I$ to derive $\Gamma|g| \vdash_L \forall x\ (\phi)|g|$, i.e. $\Gamma|g| \vdash_L (\forall x\ \phi)|g|$. Using the same reasoning as in $\wedge E$, we obtain from this $\Gamma|f| \vdash_L (\forall x\ \phi)|f|$, as desired. ∎

EXERCISE 4. 45: Complete the proof of Lemma 4. 44, dealing with the remaining inductive clauses.

Before we proceed, we establish a consequence of Lemma 4. 44 which will be of use later on.

LEMMA 4. 46: Let ϕ be an L-formula, and Γ a finite set of L-formulas, and let $c_1,\dots, c_n$ be different individual constants from C, and $x_1,\dots, x_n$ different variables. If $\Gamma[c_1/x_1]\dots[c_n/x_n] \vdash_{L+C} (\phi)[c_1/x_1]\dots[c_n/x_n]$, then $\Gamma \vdash_L \phi$.

Proof: Assume that $\Gamma[c_1/x_1]\dots[c_n/x_n] \vdash_{L+C} (\phi)[c_1/x_1]\dots[c_n/x_n]$. Let f be a one-to-one function from $\{c_1,\dots, c_n\}$ to the set of variables which don't occur in Γ or ϕ. Then $\langle\Gamma[c_1/x_1]\dots[c_n/x_n]|f|, (\phi)[c_1/x_1]\dots[c_n/x_n]|f|\rangle$ is the C-purge of $\langle\Gamma[c_1/x_1]\dots[c_n/x_n], (\phi)[c_1/x_1]\dots[c_n/x_n]\rangle$ generated by f. Hence, by Lemma 4. 44, we have that $\Gamma[c_1/x_1]\dots[c_n/x_n]|f| \vdash_L (\phi)[c_1/x_1]\dots[c_n/x_n]|f|$. For every positive integer i less than or equal to n, let's refer to the image of c_i under f as y_i. Then $\Gamma[c_1/x_1]\dots[c_n/x_n]|f|$ is $\Gamma[y_1/x_1]\dots[y_n/x_n]$, and $(\phi)[c_1/x_1]\dots[c_n/x_n]|f|$ is $(\phi)[y_1/x_1]\dots[y_n/x_n]$. Hence we have that $\Gamma[y_1/x_1]\dots[y_n/x_n] \vdash_L (\phi)[y_1/x_1]\dots[y_n/x_n]$. And since $y_1,\dots,$

y_n are all different from each other and don't occur in Γ or ϕ, n applications of Lemma 4. 34 yield $\Gamma \vdash_L \phi$, as desired.   ■

We can now combine Lemma 4. 42 and Lemma 4. 44 to show that by adding extralogical symbols to the vocabulary of a first-order language L we won't make an L-formula ϕ deducible from a set of L-formulas Γ, unless ϕ is already deducible from Γ before the additions.

LEMMA 4. 47: Let L be a first-order language, and let L^* be a language which results from adding new extralogical symbols to the vocabulary of L. For every L-formula ϕ and every set of L-formulas Γ, if $\Gamma \vdash_{L^*} \phi$, then $\Gamma \vdash_L \phi$.

Proof: Let Π be the set of predicates and function symbols in the vocabulary of L^* but not in the vocabulary of L, and let C be the set of individual constants in the vocabulary of L^* but not in the vocabulary of L. Let ϕ be an L-formula, and Γ a set of L-formulas such that $\Gamma \vdash_{L^*} \phi$. Since L^* is $L+C+\Pi$, Lemma 4. 42 gives us $\Gamma_{L+C} \vdash_{L+C} (\phi)_{L+C}$. But since every L-formula is an $L+C$-formula, we have, by Exercise 4. 38, that $(\phi)_{L+C}$ is ϕ, and Γ_{L+C} is Γ. Hence we get $\Gamma \vdash_{L+C} \phi$. Now, by Lemma 4. 44, every C-purge of $\langle \Gamma, \phi \rangle$ is in D_L. But since ϕ is an L-formula and Γ a set of L-formulas, $\langle \Gamma, \phi \rangle$ is its own C-purge. Therefore $\Gamma \vdash_L \phi$, as desired.   ■

Chapter 5

Soundness and Completeness

1. Soundness

Our main goal in this chapter is to establish that the deductive system for first-order languages presented in Chapter 4 is both sound and complete. We prove the soundness of the system in this section. Establishing that the system is complete will occupy us for much of the remainder of the chapter. We start then by proving that our deductive system is sound—that it will only allow us to deduce a formula ϕ from a set of formulas Γ if ϕ is a logical consequence of Γ.

SOUNDNESS THEOREM: For every formula ϕ of a first-order language L and every set Γ of L-formulas, if $\Gamma \vdash \phi$, then $\Gamma \vDash \phi$.

Proof: By induction on deducibility in L. In the inductive clauses corresponding to the quantifier rules, we shall invoke a result about substitution which we will only establish after we have completed the present proof.

Base:

B. Let ϕ be an L-formula and Γ a finite set of L-formulas such that $\phi \in \Gamma$. We need to show that $\Gamma \vDash \phi$, i.e. that for every L-structure $\mathcal{A}$ and every variable interpretation s in $\mathcal{A}$, if $v_{\mathcal{A}}(\gamma, s) = T$ for every $\gamma \in \Gamma$, then $v_{\mathcal{A}}(\phi, s) = T$. This follows directly from the assumption that $\phi \in \Gamma$.

$\approx I$. Let Γ be a finite set of L-formulas, and t an L-term. We need to show that $\Gamma \vDash t \approx t$, i.e. that for every L-structure $\mathcal{A}$ and every variable interpretation s in $\mathcal{A}$, if $v_{\mathcal{A}}(\gamma, s) = T$ for every $\gamma \in \Gamma$, then $v_{\mathcal{A}}(t \approx t, s) = T$. Let $\mathcal{A}$ be an L-structure and s a variable interpretation in $\mathcal{A}$ such that $v_{\mathcal{A}}(\gamma, s) = T$ for every $\gamma \in \Gamma$. We have that $den_{\mathcal{A}}(t, s) = den_{\mathcal{A}}(t, s)$. Hence, by the definition of truth, $v_{\mathcal{A}}(t \approx t, s) = T$, as desired.

Inductive Step: We shall deal with $\vee E$, $\forall E$, $\forall I$ and $\exists E$, leaving the rest as an exercise.

$\vee E$. Let ϕ, ψ, α be L-formulas and Γ, Δ, Σ sets of L-formulas such that $\Gamma \vdash \phi \vee \psi$, $\Delta \cup \{\phi\} \vdash \alpha$, and $\Sigma \cup \{\psi\} \vdash \alpha$. We need to show that if the theorem holds for $\langle \Gamma, \phi \vee \psi \rangle$, $\langle \Delta \cup \{\phi\}, \alpha \rangle$ and $\langle \Sigma \cup \{\psi\}, \alpha \rangle$, then it also holds for $\langle \Gamma \cup \Delta \cup \Sigma, \alpha \rangle$, i.e. that if $\Gamma \vDash \phi \vee \psi$, $\Delta \cup \{\phi\} \vDash \alpha$, and $\Sigma \cup \{\psi\} \vDash \alpha$, then $\Gamma \cup \Delta \cup \Sigma \vDash \alpha$. We assume (IH) that $\Gamma \vDash \phi \vee \psi$, $\Delta \cup \{\phi\} \vDash \alpha$, and $\Sigma \cup \{\psi\} \vDash \alpha$, and try to prove that it follows from this that $\Gamma \cup \Delta \cup \Sigma \vDash \alpha$. Let $\mathcal{A}$ be an L-structure, and s a variable interpretation in $\mathcal{A}$ such that for every $\gamma \in \Gamma \cup \Delta \cup \Sigma$, $v_{\mathcal{A}}(\gamma, s) = T$. We need to show that $v_{\mathcal{A}}(\alpha, s) = T$. By the definition of $\cup$, we have that (i), for every $\gamma \in \Gamma$, $v_{\mathcal{A}}(\gamma, s) = T$, (ii) for every $\delta \in \Delta$, $v_{\mathcal{A}}(\delta, s) = T$, and (iii) for every $\sigma \in \Sigma$, $v_{\mathcal{A}}(\sigma, s) = T$. From (i) and IH, it follows that $v_{\mathcal{A}}(\phi \vee \psi, s) = T$, and, by the definition of truth, we have that either $v_{\mathcal{A}}(\phi, s) = T$ or $v_{\mathcal{A}}(\psi, s) = T$. If, on the one hand, $v_{\mathcal{A}}(\phi, s) = T$, then, from (ii), we have that, for every $\delta \in \Delta \cup \{\phi\}$, $v_{\mathcal{A}}(\delta, s) = T$, and hence, by IH, that $v_{\mathcal{A}}(\alpha, s) = T$. If, on the other hand, $v_{\mathcal{A}}(\psi, s) = T$, we can reason in the same way to derive $v_{\mathcal{A}}(\alpha, s) = T$ once more. Hence either way we have that $v_{\mathcal{A}}(\alpha, s) = T$, as desired.

$\forall E$. Let $\forall x\, \phi$ be an L-formula, and Γ a set of L-formulas such that $\Gamma \vdash \forall x\, \phi$. We want to show that if the theorem holds for $\langle \Gamma, \forall x\, \phi \rangle$, then it also holds for $\langle \Gamma, (\phi)[t/x] \rangle$, for every L-term t which is substitutable for x in ϕ. We assume (IH) that $\Gamma \vDash \forall x\, \phi$, and try to show that it follows from this that if t is an L-term which is substitutable for x in ϕ, then $\Gamma \vDash (\phi)[t/x]$. Let t be an L-term which is substitutable for x in ϕ, and let $\mathcal{A}$ be an L-structure and s a variable interpretation in $\mathcal{A}$ such that $v_{\mathcal{A}}(\gamma, s) = T$ for every $\gamma \in \Gamma$. By IH, it follows that $v_{\mathcal{A}}(\forall x\, \phi, s) = T$. By the definition of truth, it follows from this that, for every $a \in A$, $v_{\mathcal{A}}(\phi, s_{(x/a)}) = T$. Since $den_{\mathcal{A}}(t, s) \in A$, we have, in particular, that $v_{\mathcal{A}}(\phi, s_{(x/den_{\mathcal{A}}(t, s))}) = T$. We want to derive from this that $v_{\mathcal{A}}((\phi)[t/x], s) = T$. Intuitively, we should be able to do this. To get $(\phi)[t/x]$ from ϕ, we replace every occurrence of x in ϕ which is not affected by an x-quantifier with an occurrence of t. But $s_{(x/den_{\mathcal{A}}(t, s))}$ interprets those occurrences of x as if they were occurrences of t. The remaining occurrences of x in ϕ are not replaced by t in $(\phi)[t/x]$, but for those occurrences of x in ϕ, the difference between s and $s_{(x/den_{\mathcal{A}}(t, s))}$ has no effect. This connection is expressed by the following lemma.

SUBSTITUTION LEMMA: For every formula ϕ of a first-order language L, if t is an L-term which is substitutable for x in ϕ, then for every L-structure $\mathcal{A}$ and every variable interpretation s in $\mathcal{A}$, $v_{\mathcal{A}}((\phi)[t/x], s) = v_{\mathcal{A}}(\phi, s_{(x/den_{\mathcal{A}}(t, s))})$.

We are going to complete the proof of the Soundness Theorem on the assumption that the Substitution Lemma holds. Then we shall discharge this assumption with a proof of the Substitution Lemma itself. With our first application of the Substitution Lemma, we complete the reasoning for the $\forall E$-clause by concluding that $v_{\mathcal{A}}((\phi)[t/x], s) = T$, as desired.

$\forall I$. Let ϕ be an L-formula, Γ a set of L-formulas, and x, y variables such that $\Gamma \vdash (\phi)[y/x]$ and y is substitutable for x in ϕ and not free in Γ or $\forall x \, \phi$. We assume (IH) that $\Gamma \models (\phi)[y/x]$, and try to show that it follows from this that $\Gamma \models \forall x \, \phi$. Let $\mathcal{A}$ be an L-structure and s a variable interpretation in $\mathcal{A}$ such that $v_{\mathcal{A}}(\gamma, s) = T$ for every $\gamma \in \Gamma$. We need to show that $v_{\mathcal{A}}(\forall x \, \phi, s) = T$. For this, by the definition of truth, it will suffice to show that, for every $a \in A$, $v_{\mathcal{A}}(\phi, s_{(x/a)}) = T$. Let $a \in A$. To show that $v_{\mathcal{A}}(\phi, s_{(x/a)}) = T$ we argue as follows:

$v_{\mathcal{A}}(\gamma, s) = T$ for every $\gamma \in \Gamma$

$\Downarrow$ (by Exercise 3. 18, from the assumption that y is not free in Γ)

$v_{\mathcal{A}}(\gamma, s_{(y/a)}) = T$ for every $\gamma \in \Gamma$

$\Downarrow$ (by IH)

$v_{\mathcal{A}}((\phi)[y/x], s_{(y/a)}) = T$

$\Downarrow$ (by the Substitution Lemma)

$v_{\mathcal{A}}(\phi, s_{(y/a)(x/den_{\mathcal{A}}(y, s_{(y/a)}))}) = T$

$\Downarrow$ (since, by the definition of denotation, $den_{\mathcal{A}}(y, s_{(y/a)}) = s_{(y/a)}(y)$)

$v_{\mathcal{A}}(\phi, s_{(y/a)(x/s_{(y/a)}(y))}) = T$

$\Downarrow$ (since $s_{(y/a)}(y) = a$)

$v_{\mathcal{A}}(\phi, s_{(y/a)(x/a)}) = T$

$\Downarrow$ (since $s_{(y/a)(x/a)} = s_{(x/a)(y/a)}$)

$v_{\mathcal{A}}(\phi, s_{(x/a)(y/a)}) = T$

⇓ (since, if y is not free in ϕ, then, by Exercise 3. 18, $v_{\mathcal{A}}(\phi, s_{(x/a)(y/a)}) = v_{\mathcal{A}}(\phi, s_{(x/a)})$, and, if y is free in ϕ, from the assumption that y is not free in $\forall x\ \phi$, it follows that $y = x$, and hence $s_{(x/a)(y/a)} = s_{(x/a)}$)

$v_{\mathcal{A}}(\phi, s_{(x/a)}) = T$

$\exists E$. Let ϕ, ψ be L-formulas, Γ, Δ, sets of L-formulas, and y, x variables such that $\Gamma \vdash \exists x\ \phi$, $\Delta \cup \{(\phi)[y/x]\} \vdash \psi$, and y is substitutable for x in ϕ and not free in Δ, $\exists x\ \phi$, or ψ. We assume (IH) that $\Gamma \vDash \exists x\ \phi$, $\Delta \cup \{(\phi)[y/x]\} \vDash \psi$, and try to show that it follows from this that $\Gamma \cup \Delta \vDash \psi$. Let $\mathcal{A}$ be an L-structure and s a variable interpretation in $\mathcal{A}$ such that $v_{\mathcal{A}}(\gamma, s) = T$ for every $\gamma \in \Gamma \cup \Delta$. We need to show that $v_{\mathcal{A}}(\psi, s) = T$. Notice that, since y is not free in ψ, we have, by Exercise 3. 18, that for every $a \in A$, $v_{\mathcal{A}}(\psi, s) = v_{\mathcal{A}}(\psi, s_{(y/a)})$. Hence, to show that $v_{\mathcal{A}}(\psi, s) = T$, it will suffice to show that for at least one $a \in A$, $v_{\mathcal{A}}(\psi, s_{(y/a)}) = T$. For this, in turn, by IH, it will suffice to establish that for at least one $a \in A$, (i) $v_{\mathcal{A}}(\delta, s_{(y/a)}) = T$ for every $\delta \in \Delta$ and (ii) $v_{\mathcal{A}}((\phi)[y/x], s_{(y/a)}) = T$. Since y is not free in Δ, the assumption that $v_{\mathcal{A}}(\delta, s) = T$ for every $\delta \in \Delta$ entails, again by Exercise 3. 18, that (i) holds for every $a \in A$. Hence, to show that $v_{\mathcal{A}}(\psi, s) = T$, it will suffice to establish that (ii) holds for at least one $a \in A$. But this follows from the assumption that $v_{\mathcal{A}}(\gamma, s) = T$ for every $\gamma \in \Gamma$, as shown by the following argument.

$v_{\mathcal{A}}(\gamma, s) = T$ for every $\gamma \in \Gamma$

⇓ (by IH)

$v_{\mathcal{A}}(\exists x\ \phi, s) = T$

⇓ (by the definition of truth)

For at least one $a \in A$, $v_{\mathcal{A}}(\phi, s_{(x/a)}) = T$

⇓ (since, if y is not free in ϕ, then, by Exercise 3. 18, $v_{\mathcal{A}}(\phi, s_{(x/a)(y/a)}) = v_{\mathcal{A}}(\phi, s_{(x/a)})$, and, if y is free in ϕ, from the assumption that y is not free in $\exists x\ \phi$, it follows that $y = x$, and hence $s_{(x/a)(y/a)} = s_{(x/a)}$)

For at least one $a \in A$, $v_{\mathcal{A}}(\phi, s_{(x/a)(y/a)}) = T$

⇓ (since $s_{(x/a)(y/a)} = s_{(y/a)(x/a)}$)

For at least one $a \in A$, $v_{\mathcal{A}}(\phi, s_{(y/a)(x/a)}) = T$

$\Downarrow$ (since $a = s_{(y/a)}(y)$)

For at least one $a \in A$, $v_{\mathcal{A}}(\phi, s_{(y/a)(x/s_{(y/a)}(y))}) = T$

$\Downarrow$ (since, by the definition of denotation, $den_{\mathcal{A}}(y, s_{(y/a)}) = s_{(y/a)}(y)$)

For at least one $a \in A$, $v_{\mathcal{A}}(\phi, s_{(y/a)(x/den_{\mathcal{A}}(y, s_{(y/a)}))}) = T$

$\Downarrow$ (by the Substitution Lemma)

For at least one $a \in A$, $v_{\mathcal{A}}((\phi)[y/x], s_{(y/a)}) = T$ ∎

We can see now that the restrictions imposed by $\forall I$ and $\exists E$ on the instantiating variable y in $(\phi)[y/x]$ are not gratuitous, since we have had to invoke each of them in order to show that $\forall I$ and $\exists E$ preserve logical consequence.

EXERCISE 5. 1: Complete the proof of the Soundness Theorem dealing with the remaining inductive clauses, using the Substitution Lemma when necessary.

Hint: For the connective clauses, see Exercise 2. 18.

We have proved the Soundness Theorem on the assumption that the Substitution Lemma holds. Our next item of business is to discharge this assumption with a proof of this result. First we need to establish a related result concerning the t/x-substitutions of terms.

SUBSTITUTION LEMMA FOR TERMS: For all terms t, u of a first-order language L, every variable x, every L-structure $\mathcal{A}$, and every variable interpretation s in $\mathcal{A}$, $den_{\mathcal{A}}((t)[u/x], s) = den_{\mathcal{A}}(t, s_{(x/den_{\mathcal{A}}(u, s))})$.

Proof: By induction on terms.
  Base:
  (i) Let x, y be variables, u an L-term, $\mathcal{A}$ an L-structure and s a variable interpretation in $\mathcal{A}$. We need to show that $den_{\mathcal{A}}((y)[u/x], s) = den_{\mathcal{A}}(y, s_{(x/den_{\mathcal{A}}(u, s))})$. We have to consider two cases. Suppose, first, that $x = y$. We present our argument as a string of identities.

$den_{\mathcal{A}}((y)[u/x], s)$

   =   (by the definition of the t/x-substitution of a term)

$den_{\mathcal{A}}(u, s)$

   =   (by the definition of $s_{(x/den_{\mathcal{A}}(u, s))}$, since $x = y$)

$s_{(x/den_{\mathcal{A}}(u, s))}(y)$

   =   (by the definition of denotation)

$den_{\mathcal{A}}(y, s_{(x/den_{\mathcal{A}}(u, s))})$

Suppose now that $x \neq y$. We argue as follows:

$den_{\mathcal{A}}((y)[u/x], s)$

> = (by the definition of the t/x-substitution of a term)

$den_{\mathcal{A}}(y, s)$

> = (by the definition of denotation)

$s(y)$

> = (by the definition of $s_{(x/den_{\mathcal{A}}(u, s))}$, since $x \neq y$)

$s_{(x/den_{\mathcal{A}}(u, s))}(y)$

> = (by the definition of denotation)

$den_{\mathcal{A}}(y, s_{(x/den_{\mathcal{A}}(u, s))})$

Hence, either way we have that $den_{\mathcal{A}}((y)[u/x], s) = den_{\mathcal{A}}(y, s_{(x/den_{\mathcal{A}}(u, s))})$, as desired.

(ii) Let c be an individual constant of L, x a variable and u an L-term, and let $\mathcal{A}$ be an L-structure and s a variable interpretation in $\mathcal{A}$. We need to show that $den_{\mathcal{A}}((c)[u/x], s) = den_{\mathcal{A}}(c, s_{(x/den_{\mathcal{A}}(u, s))})$. We argue as follows:

$den_{\mathcal{A}}((c)[u/x], s)$

> = (by the definition of the t/x-substitution of a term)

$den_{\mathcal{A}}(c, s)$

> = (by the definition of denotation)

$c_{\mathcal{A}}$

> = (by the definition of denotation)

$den_{\mathcal{A}}(c, s_{(x/den_{\mathcal{A}}(u, s))})$

Inductive Step: Let f be an n-place function symbol of L, and $t_1, \ldots, t_n$ L-terms. We need to show that if the lemma holds for $t_1, \ldots, t_n$, then it also holds for $f(t_1, \ldots, t_n)$. We assume (IH) that for every positive integer i less than or equal to n, and every L-term u, variable x, L-structure $\mathcal{A}$ and variable interpretation s in $\mathcal{A}$, $den_{\mathcal{A}}((t_i)[u/x], s) = den_{\mathcal{A}}(t_i, s_{(x/den_{\mathcal{A}}(u, s))})$. We need to show that it follows from this that for every L-term u, variable x, L-structure $\mathcal{A}$ and variable interpretation s in $\mathcal{A}$, $den_{\mathcal{A}}((f(t_1, \ldots, t_n))[u/x], s) = den_{\mathcal{A}}(f(t_1, \ldots, t_n), s_{(x/den_{\mathcal{A}}(u, s))})$. We argue as follows:

$den_{\mathcal{A}}((f(t_1,\ldots, t_n))[u/x], s)$

    =   (by the definition of the t/x-substitution of a term)

$den_{\mathcal{A}}(f((t_1)[u/x],\ldots, (t_n)[u/x]), s)$

    =   (by the definition of denotation)

$f_{\mathcal{A}}(den_{\mathcal{A}}((t_1)[u/x], s),\ldots, den_{\mathcal{A}}((t_n)[u/x], s))$

    =   (by IH)

$f_{\mathcal{A}}(den_{\mathcal{A}}(t_1, s_{(x/den_{\mathcal{A}}(u, s))}),\ldots, den_{\mathcal{A}}(t_n, s_{(x/den_{\mathcal{A}}(u, s))}))$

    =   (by the definition of denotation)

$den_{\mathcal{A}}(f(t_1,\ldots, t_n), s_{(x/den_{\mathcal{A}}(u, s))})$ ■

SUBSTITUTION LEMMA (for formulas): For every formula ϕ of a first-order language L, if t is an L-term which is substitutable for x in ϕ, then for every L-structure $\mathcal{A}$ and every variable interpretation s in $\mathcal{A}$, $v_{\mathcal{A}}((\phi)[t/x], s) = v_{\mathcal{A}}(\phi, s_{(x/den_{\mathcal{A}}(t, s))})$.

Proof: By induction on formulas.

    Base: We deal with atomic formulas of the form $Pt_1\ldots t_n$, leaving formulas of the form $t \approx u$ as an exercise.

    Let P be an n-place L-predicate, and $t_1,\ldots, t_n$ L-terms. Let x be a variable and u an L-term which is substitutable for x in $Pt_1\ldots t_n$, and let $\mathcal{A}$ be an L-structure and s a variable interpretation in $\mathcal{A}$. We need to show that $v_{\mathcal{A}}((Pt_1\ldots t_n)[u/x], s) = v_{\mathcal{A}}(Pt_1\ldots t_n, s_{(x/den_{\mathcal{A}}(u, s))})$. We argue as follows:

$v_{\mathcal{A}}((Pt_1\ldots t_n)[u/x], s) = T$

    ⇕   (by the definition of t/x-substitution)

$v_{\mathcal{A}}(P(t_1)[u/x]\ldots(t_n)[u/x], s) = T$

    ⇕   (by the definition of truth)

$\langle den_{\mathcal{A}}((t_1)[u/x], s),\ldots, den_{\mathcal{A}}((t_n)[u/x], s)\rangle \in P_{\mathcal{A}}$

    ⇕   (by the Substitution Lemma for terms)

$\langle den_{\mathcal{A}}(t_1, s_{(x/den_{\mathcal{A}}(u, s))}),\ldots, den_{\mathcal{A}}(t_n, s_{(x/den_{\mathcal{A}}(u, s))})\rangle \in P_{\mathcal{A}}$

    ⇕   (by the definition of truth)

$v_{\mathcal{A}}(Pt_1\ldots t_n, s_{(x/den_{\mathcal{A}}(u, s))}) = T$

    Inductive Step: We deal with the clauses for $\wedge$ and $\forall$, leaving the rest as an exercise.

∧. Let α, β be L-formulas. We need to show that if the lemma holds for α, β, then it also holds for $\alpha \wedge \beta$. We assume (IH) that if t is an L-term which is substitutable for x in α, then for every L-structure $\mathcal{A}$ and every variable interpretation s in $\mathcal{A}$, $v_{\mathcal{A}}((\alpha)[t/x], s) = v_{\mathcal{A}}(\alpha, s_{(x/den_{\mathcal{A}}(t, s))})$, and that if t is an L-term which is substitutable for x in β, then for every L-structure $\mathcal{A}$ and every variable interpretation s in $\mathcal{A}$, $v_{\mathcal{A}}((\beta)[t/x], s) = v_{\mathcal{A}}(\beta, s_{(x/den_{\mathcal{A}}(t, s))})$. We have to show that it follows from this that if t is an L-term which is substitutable for x in $\alpha \wedge \beta$, then for every L-structure $\mathcal{A}$ and every variable interpretation s in $\mathcal{A}$, $v_{\mathcal{A}}((\alpha \wedge \beta)[t/x], s) = v_{\mathcal{A}}(\alpha \wedge \beta, s_{(x/den_{\mathcal{A}}(t, s))})$. Let t be an L-term which is substitutable for x in $\alpha \wedge \beta$, and let $\mathcal{A}$ be an L-structure and s a variable interpretation in $\mathcal{A}$. We argue as follows:

$v_{\mathcal{A}}((\alpha \wedge \beta)[t/x], s) = T$

⇕   (by the definition of t/x-substitution)

$v_{\mathcal{A}}((\alpha)[t/x] \wedge (\beta)[t/x], s) = T$

⇕   (by the definition of truth)

$v_{\mathcal{A}}((\alpha)[t/x], s) = v_{\mathcal{A}}((\beta)[t/x], s) = T$

⇕   (by IH, since the assumption that t is substitutable for x in $\alpha \wedge \beta$ entails that t is substitutable for x in α and in β)

$v_{\mathcal{A}}(\alpha, s_{(x/den_{\mathcal{A}}(t, s))}) = v_{\mathcal{A}}(\beta, s_{(x/den_{\mathcal{A}}(t, s))}) = T$

⇕   (by the definition of truth)

$v_{\mathcal{A}}(\alpha \wedge \beta, s_{(x/den_{\mathcal{A}}(t, s))}) = T$

∀. Let α be an L-formula. We need to show that if the lemma holds for α, then it also holds for $\forall y\, \alpha$. We assume (IH) that if t is an L-term which is substitutable for x in α, then for every L-structure $\mathcal{A}$ and every variable interpretation s in $\mathcal{A}$, $v_{\mathcal{A}}((\alpha)[t/x], s) = v_{\mathcal{A}}(\alpha, s_{(x/den_{\mathcal{A}}(t, s))})$. We need to show that if t is an L-term which is substitutable for x in $\forall y\, \alpha$, then for every L-structure $\mathcal{A}$ and every variable interpretation s in $\mathcal{A}$, $v_{\mathcal{A}}((\forall y\, \alpha)[t/x], s) = v_{\mathcal{A}}(\forall y\, \alpha, s_{(x/den_{\mathcal{A}}(t, s))})$. Let t be an L-term which is substitutable for x in $\forall y\, \alpha$, and let $\mathcal{A}$ be an L-structure and s a variable interpretation in $\mathcal{A}$. x may or may not be free in $\forall y\,\alpha$, and we need to consider each of these cases separately.

Suppose, first, that x is not free in $\forall y\,\alpha$. We argue as follows:

$v_{\mathcal{A}}((\forall y\,\alpha)[t/x], s) = T$

$\quad\Updownarrow$ (by Exercise 4. 15)

$v_{\mathcal{A}}(\forall y\,\alpha, s) = T$

$\quad\Updownarrow$ (by Exercise 3. 18)

$v_{\mathcal{A}}(\forall y\,\alpha, s_{(x/den_{\mathcal{A}}(t,\,s))}) = T$

Suppose, now, that x is free in $\forall y\,\alpha$. Since t is substitutable for x in $\forall y\,\alpha$, it follows by the definition of substitutability that t is substitutable for x in α and that y does not occur in t. And since y is not free in $\forall y\,\alpha$, it also follows that $x \neq y$. We argue as follows:

$v_{\mathcal{A}}((\forall y\,\alpha)[t/x], s) = T$

$\quad\Updownarrow$ (by the definition of t/x-substitution, since $x \neq y$)

$v_{\mathcal{A}}(\forall y\,(\alpha)[t/x], s) = T$

$\quad\Updownarrow$ (by the definition of truth)

For every $a \in A$, $v_{\mathcal{A}}((\alpha)[t/x], s_{(y/a)}) = T$

$\quad\Updownarrow$ (by IH, since t is substitutable for x in α)

For every $a \in A$, $v_{\mathcal{A}}(\alpha, s_{(y/a)(x/den_{\mathcal{A}}(t,\,s_{(y/a)}))}) = T$

$\quad\Updownarrow$ (since the assumption that y doesn't occur in t entails that $den_{\mathcal{A}}(t,\,s_{(y/a)}) = den_{\mathcal{A}}(t,\,s)$ (Exercise 3. 17))

For every $a \in A$, $v_{\mathcal{A}}(\alpha, s_{(y/a)(x/den_{\mathcal{A}}(t,\,s))}) = T$

$\quad\Updownarrow$ (since $s_{(y/a)(x/den_{\mathcal{A}}(t,\,s))}$ is $s_{(x/den_{\mathcal{A}}(t,\,s))(y/a)}$, given that $x \neq y$ and y doesn't occur in t)

For every $a \in A$, $v_{\mathcal{A}}(\alpha, s_{(x/den_{\mathcal{A}}(t,\,s))(y/a)}) = T$

$\quad\Updownarrow$ (by the definition of truth)

$v_{\mathcal{A}}(\forall y\,\alpha, s_{(x/den_{\mathcal{A}}(t,\,s))}) = T$

Either way we have that $v_{\mathcal{A}}((\forall y\,\alpha)[t/x], s) = T$ if and only if $v_{\mathcal{A}}(\forall y\,\alpha, s_{(x/den_{\mathcal{A}}(t,\,s))}) = T$, as desired. ∎

EXERCISE 5. 2: Complete the proof of the Substitution Lemma dealing with formulas of the form $t \approx u$ and the remaining inductive clauses.

2. Completeness, Consistency and Model Existence

We turn now to the task of establishing that our deductive system is complete—that if a formula ϕ is a logical consequence of a set of formulas Γ, then ϕ is deducible from some finite subset of Γ.

COMPLETENESS THEOREM: For every formula ϕ of a first-order language L and every set Γ of L-formulas, if $\Gamma \vDash \phi$, then there is a finite subset Γ_0 of Γ such that $\Gamma_0 \vdash \phi$.

We are not going to prove the completeness of the system directly in this form. Most of our efforts will be devoted to establishing a different result, from which the Completeness Theorem, by comparison, will follow easily.

DEFINITION: A set Γ of formulas of a first-order language L is *inconsistent* just in case there is an L-formula ϕ and finite subsets Γ_1, Γ_2 of Γ such that $\Gamma_1 \vdash \phi, \Gamma_2 \vdash \neg\phi$. If Γ is not inconsistent, we say that it is *consistent*.

Using the notion of consistency, we can formulate the result from which we shall derive the Completeness Theorem.

MODEL EXISTENCE THEOREM: Every consistent set of sentences of a first-order language has a model.

To establish the Completeness Theorem, we shall prove the Model Existence Theorem and show that the Completeness Theorem follows from it. The latter will be our goal in the remainder of this section. In fact, we are going to show that the Completeness Theorem and the Model Existence Theorem are equivalent to each other. We achieve this by showing that both results are equivalent to the following:

SATISFACTION LEMMA: Every consistent set of formulas of a first-order language is satisfiable.

LEMMA 5. 3: The Completeness Theorem is equivalent to the Satisfaction Lemma.

Proof: We show first that the Completeness Theorem follows from the Satisfaction Lemma. We assume the Satisfaction Lemma, and try to show that it follows from this that, for every formula ϕ of a first-order language L and every set Γ of L-formulas such that $\Gamma \vDash \phi$, there is a finite subset Γ_0 of Γ such that $\Gamma_0 \vdash \phi$. Let ϕ be an L-formula, and Γ a set of L-formulas such that $\Gamma \vDash \phi$. It follows from this, by Exercise 3. 35, that $\Gamma \cup \{\neg\phi\}$ is not satisfiable. Hence, by the Satisfaction Lemma, $\Gamma \cup \{\neg\phi\}$ is inconsistent, i.e. there is an L-formula ψ and finite subsets Γ_1, Γ_2 of $\Gamma \cup \{\neg\phi\}$, such that $\Gamma_1 \vdash \psi$ and $\Gamma_2 \vdash \neg\psi$. From this, by Exercise 4. 4 (1), it follows that $\Gamma_1 \cup \{\neg\phi\} \vdash \psi$ and $\Gamma_2 \cup \{\neg\phi\} \vdash \neg\psi$, and, by Lemma 1. 13, that $(\Gamma_1 - \{\neg\phi\}) \cup \{\neg\phi\} \vdash \psi$ and $(\Gamma_2 - \{\neg\phi\}) \cup \{\neg\phi\} \vdash \neg\psi$. Using $\neg I$, we can derive from this $(\Gamma_1 - \{\neg\phi\}) \cup (\Gamma_2 - \{\neg\phi\}) \vdash \neg\neg\phi$, which, by $\neg E$, yields $(\Gamma_1 - \{\neg\phi\}) \cup (\Gamma_2 - \{\neg\phi\}) \vdash \phi$. Since $(\Gamma_1 - \{\neg\phi\}) \cup (\Gamma_2 - \{\neg\phi\})$ is a finite subset of Γ, we have shown that ϕ is deducible from a finite subset of Γ, as desired.

We prove now that the Satisfaction Lemma follows from the Completeness Theorem. We assume the Completeness Theorem, and try to prove that it follows from this that if a set of formulas is not satisfiable, then it is inconsistent. Let Γ be a set of formulas of a first-order language L which is not satisfiable, i.e. there is no L-structure $\mathcal{A}$ and variable interpretation s in $\mathcal{A}$ such that $v_{\mathcal{A}}(\gamma, s) = T$ for every $\gamma \in \Gamma$. Let ϕ be an L-formula. It follows that there is no L-structure $\mathcal{A}$ and variable interpretation s in $\mathcal{A}$ such that $v_{\mathcal{A}}(\gamma, s) = T$ for every $\gamma \in \Gamma$ *and* $v_{\mathcal{A}}(\phi, s) = F$, and no L-structure $\mathcal{A}$ and variable interpretation s in $\mathcal{A}$ such that $v_{\mathcal{A}}(\gamma, s) = T$ for every $\gamma \in \Gamma$ *and* $v_{\mathcal{A}}(\neg\phi, s) = F$, i.e. $\Gamma \vDash \phi$ and $\Gamma \vDash \neg\phi$. Then, by the Completeness Theorem, Γ has finite subsets Γ_1, Γ_2 such that $\Gamma_1 \vdash \phi$ and $\Gamma_2 \vdash \neg\phi$, i.e. Γ is inconsistent, as desired. ∎

LEMMA 5. 4: The Model Existence Theorem is equivalent to the Satisfaction Lemma.

Proof: The Model Existence Theorem follows from the Satisfaction Lemma as a special case. For if Γ is a consistent set of sentences of a first-order language L, Γ is also a consistent set of L-formulas. And if $\mathcal{A}$ is an L-structure and s a variable interpretation in $\mathcal{A}$ such that $v_{\mathcal{A}}(\gamma, s) = T$ for every $\gamma \in \Gamma$, then $\mathcal{A}$ is a model of Γ.

It remains to show that the Model Existence Theorem entails the Satisfaction Lemma. Our proof will be based on the idea that for any consistent set of formulas Γ, we can find a set of sentences Γ' that is also consistent, and such that if Γ' has a model, then Γ is satisfiable. Thus let Γ be a consistent set of formulas of a first-order language L. We proceed in two steps. First (i) we define a set of sentences Γ' and show that the assumption that Γ is consistent entails that Γ' is also consistent. Then (ii) we show that if Γ' has a model, then Γ is satisfiable. The structure of our reasoning is represented by the diagram in Figure 8.

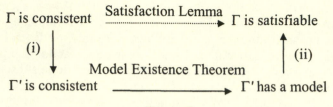

Figure 8

(i) We get Γ' from Γ by substituting for the free variables of Γ different individual constants which don't occur in Γ. We can't assume that the vocabulary of L will contain enough constants to perform these substitutions. Hence Γ' will have to be a set of sentences of an expanded language. Let C be an infinite set of individual constants not in the vocabulary of L, and let $L+C$ be the language which results from adding to the vocabulary of L all the individual constants in C.

Now, let f be a one-to-one function from the set of free variables of Γ to C. And let Γ' be the set of $L+C$-sentences which result if, for every free variable x of Γ, we substitute $f(x)$ for x in every formula in Γ. Hence, if γ is a formula in Γ, whose free variables are $x_1,\ldots, x_n$, and if, for every i less than or equal to n, c_i is the constant from C with which f pairs x_i, the corresponding sentence in Γ' will be $(\gamma)[c_1/x_1]\ldots[c_n/x_n]$.

Our goal is to show that the assumption that Γ is consistent entails that Γ' is also consistent. Assume, towards a contradiction, that Γ' is inconsistent. Then there is an $L+C$-formula ϕ and finite subsets Γ'_1 and Γ'_2 of Γ' such that $\Gamma'_1 \vdash_{L+C} \phi$ and $\Gamma'_2 \vdash_{L+C} \neg\phi$. Then, by Lemma 4. 4 (1), we have that $\Gamma'_1 \cup \{\exists x\, x \approx x\} \vdash_{L+C} \phi$ and $\Gamma'_2 \cup \{\exists x\, x \approx x\} \vdash_{L+C} \neg\phi$. From this, using $\neg I$, we derive $\Gamma'_1 \cup \Gamma'_2 \vdash_{L+C} \neg\exists x\, x \approx x$. Let $c_1,\ldots, c_m$ be the constants from C which occur in $\Gamma'_1 \cup \Gamma'_2$, and for every i less than or equal to m, let x_i be the variable whose image under f is c_i. Then there is a finite subset Γ_0 of Γ such that $\Gamma'_1 \cup \Gamma'_2$ is $\Gamma_0[c_1/x_1]\ldots[c_m/x_m]$. Since $\neg\exists x\, x \approx x$ has no free variables, we also have, by Exercise 4. 15, that $\neg\exists x\, x \approx x$ is $(\neg\exists x\, x \approx x)[c_1/x_1]\ldots[c_m/x_m]$. Hence we have that $\Gamma_0[c_1/x_1]\ldots[c_m/x_m] \vdash_{L+C} (\neg\exists x\, x \approx x)[c_1/x_1]\ldots[c_m/x_m]$. Therefore, by Lemma 4. 46, we have that $\Gamma_0 \vdash_L \neg\exists x\, x \approx x$. But using $\approx I$ and $\exists I$ we can deduce $\exists x\, x \approx x$ (in L) from any finite subset of Γ. Therefore Γ is inconsistent, which contradicts our assumption.

(ii) Now we need to show that the existence of a model for Γ' entails that Γ is satisfiable, i.e. that there is an L-structure $\mathcal{A}$ and a variable interpretation s in $\mathcal{A}$ making all the formulas in Γ true. If L_1, L_2 are two languages such that the extralogical vocabulary of L_1 is a subset of the extralogical vocabulary of L_2, then for every L_2-structure $\mathcal{A}$, we say that the *reduct* of A to L_1, written $A \mid L_1$, is the L_1-structure with the same universe as A in which the extralogical symbols of L_1 have the same interpretations as in A. Notice that every variable interpretation in an L_2-structure is a variable interpretation in its reduct to L_1, and that, for every L_2-structure A, variable interpretation s in A, and L_1-formula ϕ, $v_A(\phi, s) = v_{A \mid L_1}(\phi, s)$.

Now, let A be an $L+C$-structure which is a model of Γ', and let s^* be a variable interpretation in A pairing each free variable x of Γ with the interpretation in A of the individual constant with which f pairs x. We want to show that, for every $\gamma \in \Gamma$, $v_{A \mid L}(\gamma, s^*) = T$. Let $\gamma \in \Gamma$. Let $x_1, \ldots, x_p$ be the free variables of γ, and, for every i less than or equal to p, let c_i be the individual constant from C with which f pairs x_i. We argue as follows:

$\gamma \in \Gamma$

$\Downarrow$ (by the definition of Γ')

$(\gamma)[c_1/x_1]\ldots[c_p/x_p] \in \Gamma'$

$\Downarrow$ (since A is a model of Γ')

$v_A((\gamma)[c_1/x_1]\ldots[c_p/x_p], s^*) = T$

$\Downarrow$ (by the Substitution Lemma)

$v_A(\gamma, s^*(x_1/den_A(c_1, s^*))\ldots(x_p/den_A(c_p, s^*))) = T$

$\Downarrow$ (by the definition of denotation)

$v_A(\gamma, s^*(x_1/c_{1A})\ldots(x_p/c_{pA})) = T$

$\Downarrow$

$v_{A \mid L}(\gamma, s^*(x_1/c_{1A})\ldots(x_p/c_{pA})) = T$

$\Downarrow$ (since $s^*(x_1/c_{1A})\ldots(x_p/c_{pA}) = s^*$)

$v_{A \mid L}(\gamma, s^*) = T$ ∎

EXERCISE 5. 5: Show that no inconsistent set of sentences has a model.

The completeness of a deductive system for first-order logic was first established by Kurt Gödel in 1930, but the proof of the Model Existence Theorem that we are going to present is due, in its essentials, to Leon Henkin. The best way to understand Henkin's proof is to think of it as deriving the theorem from two results concerning a type of sets of sentences to which we shall refer as *well-rounded sets*. The first result is that every well-rounded set has a model, the second, that every consistent set is a subset of a well-rounded set. Since a model of a set of sentences is a model of each of its subsets, these two results entail the Model Existence Theorem. The proof, which will occupy us for most of the remainder of the chapter, is of a different order of magnitude from the proofs that we have considered so far. It can be regarded as consisting of several independent results, and should be studied at two levels. One should try to understand, on the one hand, how each of these partial results is established, and, on the other, how they can be combined to establish the Model Existence Theorem. The proof that we are going to provide here applies only to first-order languages which satisfy a certain condition. In Chapter 6 we shall indicate how the reasoning would have to be modified in order to generalize the result to all first-order languages.

3. Canonical Structures and Well-Rounded Sets, I: First-Order Languages without Identity

A central ingredient of Henkin's proof of the Model Existence Theorem is a technique for generating a structure from a given set of sentences of a first-order language, to which we shall refer as *Henkin's technique*. The central idea of the technique can be more clearly presented in connection with first-order languages which differ from the ones we are considering in lacking the identity symbol. We present Henkin's technique for first-order languages without identity in this section. In §4, we shall discuss how the technique has to be modified in order to accommodate the identity symbol.

When we define a first-order language, we use a set of objects, its vocabulary, to define other sets, as, for example, the set of terms of the language and the set of formulas. Then, when we define a structure for the language, we designate a set of objects as its universe, and interpret the extralogical symbols of the language with the elements of this set. Henkin's technique for generating a structure from a set of sentences is based on the idea that among the sets which we can designate as the universe of a structure for a first-order language are the sets which result from the syntactic definitions of the language. Thus, e.g., a structure for a first-order language L can have as its universe the set of functional terms of L, or the set of L-formulas with more than three quantifiers.

Let L be a first-order language without identity whose extralogical vocabulary contains at least one individual constant. The structure generated by Henkin's technique from any set of L-sentences will have as its universe the set of closed terms of L. This suggests an obvious interpretation for the individual constants of L. Since individual constants are closed terms and hence in the universe of the structure, they can be interpreted as denoting themselves. A similar idea yields an interpretation for each function symbol of L. Let f be an n-place function symbol of L. As we know, f is interpreted in an L-structure with an n-place function in its universe. Hence, in the L-structures generated by Henkin's technique, f will be interpreted with an n-place function in the set of closed terms of L. If $t_1,\ldots, t_n$ are closed terms of L, then $f(t_1,\ldots, t_n)$ is also a closed term of L. Hence the function pairing $\langle t_1,\ldots, t_n \rangle$ with $f(t_1,\ldots, t_n)$ for all closed terms $t_1,\ldots, t_n$ of L is a function in the set of closed terms of L. The L-structures generated by Henkin's technique interpret f with this function. Notice that it follows from this that closed functional terms, like individual constants, will denote themselves. Thus, e.g., if c is an individual constant of L and g is a one-place function symbol of L, the term $g(c)$ will denote the image of the denotation of c under the function with which g is interpreted. Since c denotes itself and g is interpreted with the function pairing each closed term t of L with the term $g(t)$, $g(c)$ will denote $g(c)$.

All the L-structures generated by Henkin's technique will have the same universe, and they will interpret the individual constants and function symbols of L in the same way—according to the procedure presented in the preceding paragraph. But the L-structures that the technique generates from different sets of L-sentences will differ in general in how they interpret the L-predicates. Let P be an n-place predicate of L, and let Γ be a set of L-sentences. An L-structure will interpret P with a set of n-tuples of elements of its universe. Hence, in an L-structure generated by Henkin's technique, P will be interpreted with a set of n-tuples of closed terms of L. The interpretation of P in the L-structure generated from Γ by Henkin's technique will be determined directly by which sentences of the form $Pt_1\ldots t_n$ are in Γ. For all closed terms $t_1,\ldots, t_n$ of L, $\langle t_1,\ldots, t_n \rangle$ will be in the set with which P is interpreted just in case the sentence $Pt_1\ldots t_n$ is in Γ.

We shall refer to the structure generated from a set of sentences Γ by Henkin's technique as its *canonical structure*.

DEFINITION: If Γ is a set of sentences of a first-order language L without identity with at least one individual constant in its vocabulary, the *canonical structure* of Γ is the L-structure $\mathcal{A}$ defined as follows:

(i) The universe of $\mathcal{A}$ is the set of closed terms of L.

(ii) For every individual constant c of L, $c_{\mathcal{A}} = c$.

(iii) For every n-place function symbol f of L, and all closed terms $t_1,\ldots, t_n$ of L, $f_{\mathcal{A}}(t_1,\ldots, t_n) = f(t_1,\ldots, t_n)$.

(iv) For every m-place predicate P of L, and all closed terms $t_1,\ldots, t_m$ of L, $\langle t_1,\ldots, t_m \rangle \in P_{\mathcal{A}}$ if and only if $Pt_1\ldots t_m \in \Gamma$.

Thus, in a canonical structure, each closed term denotes itself, and the truth value of a sentence in the canonical structure of Γ will be determined by which atomic sentences Γ contains.

Every set of L-sentences has a canonical structure, but we are mainly interested in the canonical structures of sets of sentences of a particular kind, to which we shall refer as *well rounded*.

DEFINITION: A set of sentences Γ of a language L without identity is *well rounded* just in case it satisfies the following conditions:

(1) For every L-sentence of the form $\neg\phi$, $\neg\phi \in \Gamma$ if and only if $\phi \notin \Gamma$.

(2) For every L-sentence of the form $\phi \wedge \psi$, $\phi \wedge \psi \in \Gamma$ if and only if $\phi \in \Gamma$ and $\psi \in \Gamma$.

(3) For every L-sentence of the form $\phi \vee \psi$, $\phi \vee \psi \in \Gamma$ if and only if $\phi \in \Gamma$ or $\psi \in \Gamma$.

(4) For every L-sentence of the form $\phi \rightarrow \psi$, $\phi \rightarrow \psi \in \Gamma$ if and only if $\phi \notin \Gamma$ or $\psi \in \Gamma$.

(5) For every L-sentence of the form $\exists x\, \phi$, $\exists x\, \phi \in \Gamma$ if and only if for at least one closed term t of L, $(\phi)[t/x] \in \Gamma$.

(6) For every L-sentence of the form $\forall x\, \phi$, $\forall x\, \phi \in \Gamma$ if and only if for every closed term t of L, $(\phi)[t/x] \in \Gamma$.

Notice that the canonical structure of a set of L-sentences Γ need not be a model of Γ. For one thing, sets of sentences with no models have canonical structures. But even if a set of sentences has models, its canonical structure may not be one of them. Take, e.g., $\{Pa, Pa \wedge Pb\}$. Let $\mathcal{A}$ be the canonical structure of this set. Since $Pb \notin \{Pa, Pa \wedge Pb\}$, we have that $b \notin P_{\mathcal{A}}$. Hence Pb is false in $\mathcal{A}$, and so is $Pa \wedge Pb$. What makes well-rounded sets of sentences interesting for our purposes is that, if Γ is a well-rounded set of sentences, then the canonical structure of Γ is guaranteed to be a model of Γ. In fact we can make a stronger claim about the relationship between well-rounded sets of sentences and their canonical structures. If Γ is a well-rounded set of L-sentences, and $\mathcal{A}$ is the canonical structure of Γ, every sentence in Γ will be true in $\mathcal{A}$ *and* every L-sentence outside Γ will be false in $\mathcal{A}$. We can reformulate this claim in terms of the following notion:

DEFINITION: If $\mathcal{A}$ is a structure of a first-order language L, the *theory of* $\mathcal{A}$, written *Th* $\mathcal{A}$, is the set whose elements are the L-sentences which are true in $\mathcal{A}$.

Obviously every structure is a model of its theory, but the theory of an L-structure $\mathcal{A}$ won't be the only set of L-sentences having $\mathcal{A}$ as a model, since $\mathcal{A}$ will also be a model of every subset of its theory. The claim that we are making is that every well-rounded set of sentences is the theory of its canonical structure.

We shall not establish a result to this effect until we have adapted the notions of canonical structure and well-rounded set of sentences to first-order languages with identity. Nevertheless, we can see in intuitive terms that the claim has some plausibility. Let Γ be a well-rounded set of L-sentences, and let $\mathcal{A}$ be the canonical structure of Γ. It follows directly from the definition of canonical structure that an atomic L-sentence will be true in $\mathcal{A}$ if and only if it is in Γ. And we can see with a couple of examples that we should expect the result to hold also for nonatomic L-sentences. Thus, let $Pa \vee Rf(b)c$ be an L-sentence. Suppose first that $Pa \vee Rf(b)c$ is in Γ. Then, by the definition of well-roundedness, either Pa or $Rf(b)c$ is in Γ. But then, by the definition of canonical structure, either Pa or $Rf(b)c$ is true in $\mathcal{A}$, and, by the definition of truth, $Pa \vee Rf(b)c$ is true in $\mathcal{A}$. Suppose now that $Pa \vee Rf(b)c$ is not in Γ. Then, by the definition of well-roundedness, neither Pa nor $Rf(b)c$ is in Γ. But then, by the definition of canonical structure, neither Pa nor $Rf(b)c$ is true in $\mathcal{A}$, and, by the definition of truth, $Pa \vee Rf(b)c$ is false in $\mathcal{A}$. Hence $Pa \vee Rf(b)c$ is true in $\mathcal{A}$ if and only if $Pa \vee Rf(b)c$ is in Γ. Consider now the L-sentence $\forall x\, Px$. Suppose, first, that $\forall x\, Px$ is in Γ. Then, by the definition of well-roundedness, for every closed term t of L, the L-sentence Pt is in Γ. Then, by the definition of canonical structure, we have that every closed term of L (i.e. every element of the universe of $\mathcal{A}$) is an element of $P_{\mathcal{A}}$. Hence $\forall x\, Px$ is true in $\mathcal{A}$. Suppose now that $\forall x\, Px$ is not in Γ. Then, by the definition of well-roundedness, for at least one closed term t of L, the L-sentence Pt is not in Γ. Then, by the definition of canonical structure, we have that at least one closed term of L (i.e. an element of the universe of $\mathcal{A}$) is not an element of $P_{\mathcal{A}}$. Hence $\forall x\, Px$ is false in $\mathcal{A}$. Therefore $\forall x\, Px$ is true in $\mathcal{A}$ if and only if it is an element of Γ.

4. Canonical Structures and Well-Rounded Sets, II: First-Order Languages with Identity

We closed the preceding section with the suggestion that every well-rounded set of sentences of a first-order language without identity is the theory of its canonical structure. We can also apply our definitions of well-rounded set of sentences and canonical structure to first-order languages with identity, but the claim that every well-rounded set of sentences of a first-order language with identity is the theory of its canonical structure will not hold in general.

There are two different ways in which identity sentences can prevent a well-rounded set of sentences of a first-order language L with identity from being the theory of its canonical structure. Notice first that the definition of well-roundedness doesn't rule out the possibility that a well-rounded set of L-sentences contains sentences of the form $t \approx u$, where t and u are different terms. But since in a canonical structure closed terms denote themselves, different terms will have different denotations. Hence if t and u are different closed terms of L, the sentence $t \approx u$ will be false in every canonical structure, and any well-rounded set of L-sentences containing it will not have its canonical structure as a model.

The second difficulty doesn't concern canonical structures specifically. Identity sentences could prevent a well-rounded set of L-sentences from being the theory of any L-structure. Thus, e.g., a well-rounded set of L-sentences could fail to contain the sentence $t \approx t$, for some closed term t of L, but $t \approx t$ is true in every L-structure. Similarly, a well-rounded set of L-sentences could contain the sentence $\neg t \approx t$, but this sentence is false in every L-structure. Also, a well-rounded set of L-sentences could contain a sentence of the form $t \approx u$ without containing $u \approx t$, but these two sentences have the same truth value in every L-structure. Or it might contain $t \approx u$ and Pt, but not Pu, but the third sentence cannot be false in a structure in which the first two are true.

With our present definitions of well-rounded set of sentences and canonical structure, the claim that every well-rounded set of sentences is the theory of its canonical structure doesn't hold for first-order languages with identity. The claim will only hold for these languages if we reform our definitions in order to overcome the difficulties posed by identity sentences. We are going to act on two fronts. On the one hand, we are going to strengthen our definition of well-roundedness to ensure that a well-rounded set of sentences is not prevented from being the theory of any structure by which identity sentences it contains. On the other, we are going to modify our definition of canonical structure to allow canonical structures to yield the value true for identity sentences involving different terms.

DEFINITION: A set Γ of sentences of a first-order language L with identity is *well rounded* just in case it satisfies the following conditions:

(1)–(6) As in first-order languages without identity.

(7) For every closed term t of L, $t \approx t \in \Gamma$.

(8) For all closed terms t, u of L, if $t \approx u \in \Gamma$, then $u \approx t \in \Gamma$.

(9) For all closed terms t, u, v of L, if $t \approx u$, $u \approx v \in \Gamma$, then $t \approx v \in \Gamma$.

(10) For every n-place function symbol f of L and all closed terms $t_1,\ldots,$ t_n, $u_1,\ldots,$ u_n of L, if $t_1 \approx u_1,\ldots,$ $t_n \approx u_n \in \Gamma$, then $f(t_1,\ldots, t_n) \approx f(u_1,\ldots, u_n) \in \Gamma$.

(11) For every m-place predicate P of L and all closed terms $t_1,\ldots, t_m$, $u_1,\ldots, u_m$ of L, if $t_1 \approx u_1,\ldots,$ $t_m \approx u_m \in \Gamma$, and $Pt_1\ldots t_m \in \Gamma$, then $Pu_1\ldots u_m \in \Gamma$.

We can see, intuitively, that the new clauses of the definition solve some of the difficulties posed by identity sentences for our original definition. Thus, e.g., if Γ is a well-rounded set of L-sentences, we have, by Clause (7), that Γ will contain every L-sentence of the form $t \approx t$, and, by Clause (1), Γ will not contain any L-sentence of the form $\neg t \approx t$. Similarly, by Clause (8), Γ will contain either both $t \approx u$ and $u \approx t$ or neither of these sentences. And by Clause (11), if Γ contains $t \approx u$ and Pt, it will also contain Pu.

Notice, however, that the new definition still allows well-rounded sets to contain sentences of the form $t \approx u$, where t and u are different closed terms, and, as we saw above, any sentence of this form will be false in every canonical structure. To deal with this difficulty, we modify Henkin's technique for generating a structure from a set of sentences. The new version of Henkin's technique, unlike the original one, will not generate a canonical structure from every set of sentences, but it will generate a canonical structure from every well-rounded set of sentences, and that's as much as we need. In what follows, we shall restrict our attention to well-rounded sets of sentences.

Let Γ be a well-rounded set of sentences of a first-order language L with identity. We define a binary relation $\sim_\Gamma$ in the set of closed terms of L as follows. For all closed terms t, u of L, $t \sim_\Gamma u$ if and only if $t \approx u \in \Gamma$. Notice that it follows directly from clauses (7)–(9) of the definition of well-roundedness that $\sim_\Gamma$ is an equivalence relation in the set of closed terms of L. Using the notions introduced in Chapter 1, §6i, we can define, for every closed term t of L, the equivalence class generated by t with $\sim_\Gamma$, written «t»$_\Gamma$, i.e. the set of closed terms of L to which t bears $\sim_\Gamma$. The main respect in which we are going to modify Henkin's technique for generating a structure from a well-rounded set Γ of L-sentences is by designating as its universe, not the set of closed terms of L, but the set of equivalence classes generated with $\sim_\Gamma$ by the closed terms of L.

The interpretation of the extralogical symbols of L in the canonical structure of Γ will be adjusted accordingly. First, an individual constant will no longer denote itself, but the equivalence class that it generates with $\sim_\Gamma$. Second, an n-place function symbol f will have to be interpreted with an n-place function in the set of equivalence classes generated with $\sim_\Gamma$ by the closed terms of L. We will use for this purpose the function which pairs, for all closed terms $t_1,\ldots, t_n$ of L, the tuple $\langle$«t_1»$_\Gamma,\ldots,$ «t_n»$_\Gamma\rangle$ with «$f(t_1,\ldots, t_n)$»$_\Gamma$—i.e. with the equivalence class generated with $\sim_\Gamma$ by $f(t_1,\ldots, t_n)$. Hence, if c is an individual constant of L and g is a one-place function symbol of L, the term $g(c)$ will denote «$g(c)$»$_\Gamma$, and, in general, every closed term of L will denote the equivalence class that it generates with $\sim_\Gamma$. Finally, if P is an m-place L-predicate, for all closed terms $t_1,\ldots, t_m$ of L, the m-tuple $\langle$«t_1»$_\Gamma,\ldots,$ «t_m»$_\Gamma\rangle$ will be in the set with which P is interpreted if and only if the sentence $Pt_1\ldots t_m$ is in Γ. Thus, e.g., if c is an individual constant of L and S is a one-place L-predicate, «c»$_\Gamma$ will be in the set with which S is interpreted just in case the sentence Sc is in Γ.

We use these ideas to define the canonical structure of a set of sentences of a first-order language with identity.

DEFINITION: If L is a first-order language with identity with at least one individual constant in its vocabulary, the *canonical structure* of a well-rounded set of L-sentences Γ is the L-structure $\mathcal{A}$ defined as follows:

(i) The universe of $\mathcal{A}$ is the set of equivalence classes generated with $\sim_\Gamma$ by the closed terms of L.

(ii) For every individual constant c of L, $c_\mathcal{A} =$ «c»$_\Gamma$.

(iii) For every n-place function symbol f of L, and all closed terms $t_1,\ldots, t_n$ of L, $f_\mathcal{A}($«t_1»$_\Gamma,\ldots,$ «t_n»$_\Gamma) =$ «$f(t_1,\ldots, t_n)$»$_\Gamma$.

(iv) For every m-place predicate P of L, and all closed terms $t_1,\ldots, t_m$ of L, $\langle$«t_1»$_\Gamma,\ldots,$ «t_m»$_\Gamma\rangle \in P_\mathcal{A}$ if and only if $Pt_1\ldots t_m \in \Gamma$.

Before we proceed, we need to make sure that (iii) succeeds in singling out a function as the interpretation of f in $\mathcal{A}$, and that (iv) succeeds in singling out a set as the interpretation of P in $\mathcal{A}$. Let g be a one-place function symbol of L. (iii) specifies the image under $g_{\mathcal{A}}$ of an element of the universe of $\mathcal{A}$ in terms of which closed term of L generates it. But different closed terms of L can generate the same equivalence class with $\sim_\Gamma$. Hence we need to make sure that if $\langle\!\langle t\rangle\!\rangle_\Gamma = \langle\!\langle u\rangle\!\rangle_\Gamma$, (iii) doesn't assign to $\langle\!\langle t\rangle\!\rangle_\Gamma$ and $\langle\!\langle u\rangle\!\rangle_\Gamma$ different images under $g_{\mathcal{A}}$. This result, in its general form, is expressed by the following lemma.

LEMMA 5. 6: For every n-place function symbol f of L, and all closed terms $t_1,\ldots, t_n, u_1,\ldots, u_n$, of L, if $\langle\!\langle t_1\rangle\!\rangle_\Gamma = \langle\!\langle u_1\rangle\!\rangle_\Gamma,\ldots, \langle\!\langle t_n\rangle\!\rangle_\Gamma = \langle\!\langle u_n\rangle\!\rangle_\Gamma$, then $\langle\!\langle f(t_1,\ldots, t_n)\rangle\!\rangle_\Gamma = \langle\!\langle f(u_1,\ldots, u_n)\rangle\!\rangle_\Gamma$.

Proof: Let f be an n-place function symbol of L, and let $t_1,\ldots, t_n, u_1,\ldots, u_n$ be closed terms of L. We argue as follows:

$\langle\!\langle t_1\rangle\!\rangle_\Gamma = \langle\!\langle u_1\rangle\!\rangle_\Gamma,\ldots, \langle\!\langle t_n\rangle\!\rangle_\Gamma = \langle\!\langle u_n\rangle\!\rangle_\Gamma$

$\Downarrow$ (since objects which generate the same equivalence class with $\sim_\Gamma$ are $\sim_\Gamma$-related (see Exercise 1. 32))

$t_1 \sim_\Gamma u_1,\ldots, t_n \sim_\Gamma u_n$

$\Downarrow$ (by the definition of $\sim_\Gamma$)

$t_1 \approx u_1,\ldots, t_n \approx u_n \in \Gamma$

$\Downarrow$ (by the well-roundedness of Γ)

$f(t_1,\ldots, t_n) \approx f(u_1,\ldots, u_n) \in \Gamma$

$\Downarrow$ (by the definition of $\sim_\Gamma$)

$f(t_1,\ldots, t_n) \sim_\Gamma f(u_1,\ldots, u_n)$

$\Downarrow$ (since objects which are $\sim_\Gamma$-related generate the same equivalence class with $\sim_\Gamma$ (see Lemma 1. 30))

$\langle\!\langle f(t_1,\ldots, t_n)\rangle\!\rangle_\Gamma = \langle\!\langle f(u_1,\ldots, u_n)\rangle\!\rangle_\Gamma$ ∎

We face a similar situation with (iv). Let S be a one-place predicate of L. (iv) specifies whether an element of the universe of $\mathcal{A}$ is in $S_{\mathcal{A}}$ in terms of which closed term of L generates it. But different closed terms of L can generate the same equivalence class with $\sim_\Gamma$. Hence we need to make sure that if $\langle\!\langle t\rangle\!\rangle_\Gamma = \langle\!\langle u\rangle\!\rangle_\Gamma$, the definition doesn't place $\langle\!\langle t\rangle\!\rangle_\Gamma$ in $S_{\mathcal{A}}$ but $\langle\!\langle u\rangle\!\rangle_\Gamma$ outside it. This result, in its general form, is expressed by the following exercise:

EXERCISE 5. 7: Show that, for every n-place L-predicate P and all closed terms $t_1,\ldots, t_n, u_1,\ldots, u_n$ of L, such that $\langle\!\langle t_1\rangle\!\rangle_\Gamma = \langle\!\langle u_1\rangle\!\rangle_\Gamma,\ldots, \langle\!\langle t_n\rangle\!\rangle_\Gamma = \langle\!\langle u_n\rangle\!\rangle_\Gamma$, if $\langle\langle\!\langle t_1\rangle\!\rangle_\Gamma,\ldots, \langle\!\langle t_n\rangle\!\rangle_\Gamma\rangle \in P_{\mathcal{A}}$, then $\langle\langle\!\langle u_1\rangle\!\rangle_\Gamma,\ldots, \langle\!\langle u_n\rangle\!\rangle_\Gamma\rangle \in P_{\mathcal{A}}$.

5. A Well-Rounded Set of Sentences Is the Theory of its Canonical Structure

The modifications of the definitions of well-rounded set of sentences and canonical structure introduced in §4 were meant to ensure that every well-rounded set of sentences of a first-order language with identity is the theory of its canonical structure. Our goal in this section is to establish this result. The claim is expressed by the following lemma.

LEMMA 5. 8: If Γ is a well-rounded set of sentences of a first-order language L, and $\mathcal{A}$ is the canonical structure of Γ, then, for every L-sentence ϕ, $v_{\mathcal{A}}(\phi) = T$ if and only if $\phi \in \Gamma$.

The best way to establish this result will be to find a claim about all L-formulas which can be established by induction, from which Lemma 5. 8 follows as a special case. If ϕ is an L-formula, let's say that a *closure* of ϕ is a formula which results from substituting in ϕ a closed term of L for each free variable of ϕ. Thus, e.g., if $x_1, \ldots, x_n$ are the free variables of ϕ, and $t_1, \ldots, t_n$ are closed terms of L, then $(\phi)[t_1/x_1]\ldots[t_n/x_n]$ is a closure of ϕ. Notice that every closure of every L-formula is an L-sentence, and that L-sentences are their own closures. Let Γ be a well-rounded set of sentences of a first-order language L, and let $\mathcal{A}$ be the canonical structure of Γ. Suppose that for every L-formula ϕ we could find, for every closure ψ of ϕ, a variable interpretation s in $\mathcal{A}$ such that ϕ is true in $\mathcal{A}$ relative to s if and only if ψ is in Γ. Then, in particular, since L-sentences are their own closures, we would have found, for every L-sentence ϕ, a variable interpretation s such that ϕ is true in $\mathcal{A}$ relative to s if and only if ϕ is in Γ. Hence we would be able to conclude that every L-sentence is true in $\mathcal{A}$ if and only if it is in Γ, as desired.

This is the strategy that we are going to adopt. If ϕ is an L-formula and σ is a function from the set of variables to the set of closed terms of L, we say that the *closure of ϕ generated by* σ, written $(\phi)[\sigma]$, is the L-formula which results if we substitute in ϕ for each free variable of ϕ its image under σ. Thus if $x_1, \ldots, x_n$ are the free variables of ϕ, then the closure of ϕ generated by σ, $(\phi)[\sigma]$, is $(\phi)[\sigma(x_1)/x_1]\ldots[\sigma(x_n)/x_n]$. To implement our strategy, we need to find, for every L-formula ϕ and every function σ from the set of variables to the set of closed terms of L, a variable interpretation s in $\mathcal{A}$ such that ϕ is true in $\mathcal{A}$ relative to s if and only if $(\phi)[\sigma]$ is in Γ. We claim that this condition will be satisfied by the variable interpretation which pairs each variable x with $\langle\!\langle\sigma(x)\rangle\!\rangle_\Gamma$, i.e. with the equivalence class generated with $\sim_\Gamma$ by the closed term of L with which σ pairs x. Thus if σ is a function from the set of variables to the set of closed terms of L, we define σ* as the variable interpretation in $\mathcal{A}$ such that, for every variable x, σ*(x) = «σ(x)»$_\Gamma$. Then we can formulate our claim by saying that, for every L-formula φ and every function σ from the set of variables to the set of closed terms of L, φ is true in $\mathcal{A}$ relative to σ* if and only if (φ)[σ] is in Γ. As we saw in the preceding paragraph, Lemma 5. 8 follows from this result as a special case, since, if φ is a sentence, (φ)[σ] = φ. As usual, to establish this result about L-formulas, we first need to establish a related result about L-terms. If t is an L-term and σ is a function from the set of variables to the set of closed terms of L, we say that the *closure of t generated by* σ, written (t)[σ], is the term that results if for every variable x which occurs in t, we substitute σ(x) for x in t.

LEMMA 5. 9: Let $\mathcal{A}$ be the canonical structure of a well-rounded set Γ of L-sentences, and σ a function from the set of variables to the set of closed terms of L. For every L-term t, $den_{\mathcal{A}}(t, σ*) = $ «(t)[σ]»$_\Gamma$.

Proof: By induction on terms.
   Base:
   (i) Let c be an individual constant of L. We need to show that $den_{\mathcal{A}}(c, σ*) = $ «(c)[σ]»$_\Gamma$. We argue as follows:

$den_{\mathcal{A}}(c, σ*)$

   =   (definition of denotation)

$c_{\mathcal{A}}$

   =   (definition of canonical structure)

«c»$_\Gamma$

   =   (since $c = (c)[σ]$)

«(c)[σ]»$_\Gamma$

   (ii) Let x be a variable. We need to show that $den_{\mathcal{A}}(x, σ*) = $ «(x)[σ]»$_\Gamma$. We argue as follows:

$den_{\mathcal{A}}(x, σ*)$

   =   (definition of denotation)

σ*(x)

   =   (definition of σ*)

«σ(x)»$_\Gamma$

$\quad = \quad$ (since $(x)[\sigma(x)/x] = \sigma(x)$)

$\langle\langle(x)[\sigma(x)/x]\rangle\rangle_\Gamma$

$\quad = \quad$ (since $(x)[\sigma(x)/x] = (x)[\sigma]$)

$\langle\langle(x)[\sigma]\rangle\rangle_\Gamma$

Inductive Step: Let f be an n-place function symbol of L, and $t_1,\ldots, t_n$ L-terms. We need to show that if the lemma holds for $t_1,\ldots, t_n$, then it also holds for $f(t_1,\ldots, t_n)$. Assume (IH) that $den_{\mathcal{A}}(t_1, \sigma^*) = \langle\langle(t_1)[\sigma]\rangle\rangle_\Gamma,\ldots,$ $den_{\mathcal{A}}(t_n, \sigma^*) = \langle\langle(t_n)[\sigma]\rangle\rangle_\Gamma$. We want to prove that it follows from this that $den_{\mathcal{A}}(f(t_1,\ldots, t_n), \sigma^*) = \langle\langle(f(t_1,\ldots, t_n))[\sigma]\rangle\rangle_\Gamma$. We argue as follows:

$den_{\mathcal{A}}(f(t_1,\ldots, t_n), \sigma^*)$

$\quad = \quad$ (definition of denotation)

$f_{\mathcal{A}}(den_{\mathcal{A}}(t_1, \sigma^*),\ldots, den_{\mathcal{A}}(t_n, \sigma^*))$

$\quad = \quad$ (IH)

$f_{\mathcal{A}}(\langle\langle(t_1)[\sigma]\rangle\rangle_\Gamma,\ldots, \langle\langle(t_n)[\sigma]\rangle\rangle_\Gamma)$

$\quad = \quad$ (definition of canonical structure)

$\langle\langle f_{\mathcal{A}}((t_1)[\sigma],\ldots, (t_n)[\sigma])\rangle\rangle_\Gamma$

$\quad = \quad$ (definition of closure)

$\langle\langle(f(t_1,\ldots, t_n))[\sigma]\rangle\rangle_\Gamma$ $\qquad\qquad\qquad\qquad\qquad$ ■

LEMMA 5. 10: Let Γ be a well-rounded set of L-sentences, and let $\mathcal{A}$ be the canonical structure of Γ. For every L-formula ϕ, and for every function σ from the set of variables to the set of closed terms of L, $v_{\mathcal{A}}(\phi, \sigma^*)$ $= T$ if and only if $(\phi)[\sigma] \in \Gamma$.

Proof: By induction on formulas.

Base: We deal with formulas of the form $t \approx u$, leaving formulas of the form $Pt_1\ldots t_n$ as an exercise. Let t, u be L-terms, and let σ be a function from the set of variables to the set of closed terms of L. We need to show that $v_{\mathcal{A}}(t \approx u, \sigma^*) = T$ if and only if $(t \approx u)[\sigma] \in \Gamma$. We argue as follows:

$v_{\mathcal{A}}(t \approx u, \sigma^*) = T$

$\quad \Updownarrow \quad$ (definition of truth)

$den_{\mathcal{A}}(t, \sigma^*) = den_{\mathcal{A}}(u, \sigma^*)$

$\quad \Updownarrow \quad$ (Lemma 5. 9)

$«(t)[\sigma]»_\Gamma = «(u)[\sigma]»_\Gamma$

⇕   (since terms generate the same equivalence class with $\sim_\Gamma$ if and only if they are $\sim_\Gamma$-related (see Lemma 1. 30 and Exercise 1. 32))

$(t)[\sigma] \sim_\Gamma (u)[\sigma]$

⇕   (definition of $\sim_\Gamma$)

$(t)[\sigma] \approx (u)[\sigma] \in \Gamma$

⇕   (definition of closure)

$(t \approx u)[\sigma] \in \Gamma$

Inductive Step: We deal with the clauses for ∧ and ∃, leaving the rest as an exercise.

∧. Let ϕ, ψ be *L*-formulas. We need to show that if the lemma holds for ϕ and ψ, then it also holds for $\phi \wedge \psi$. Assume (IH) that for every function σ from the set of variables to the set of closed terms of *L*, $v_{\mathcal{A}}(\phi, \sigma^*) = T$ if and only if $(\phi)[\sigma] \in \Gamma$, and $v_{\mathcal{A}}(\psi, \sigma^*) = T$ if and only if $(\psi)[\sigma] \in \Gamma$. We want to prove that it follows from this that, for every σ, $v_{\mathcal{A}}(\phi \wedge \psi, \sigma^*) = T$ if and only if $(\phi \wedge \psi)[\sigma] \in \Gamma$. Let σ be a function from the set of variables to the set of closed terms of *L*. We argue as follows:

$v_{\mathcal{A}}(\phi \wedge \psi, \sigma^*) = T$

⇕   (definition of truth)

$v_{\mathcal{A}}(\phi, \sigma^*) = v_{\mathcal{A}}(\psi, \sigma^*) = T$

⇕   (IH)

$(\phi)[\sigma] \in \Gamma$ and $(\psi)[\sigma] \in \Gamma$

⇕   (well-roundedness of Γ)

$(\phi)[\sigma] \wedge (\psi)[\sigma] \in \Gamma$

⇕   (definition of closure)

$(\phi \wedge \psi)[\sigma] \in \Gamma$

∃. Let ϕ be an *L*-formula. We need to show that if the lemma holds for ϕ, then it also holds for $\exists x \, \phi$. Assume (IH) that for every function σ from the set of variables to the set of closed terms of *L*, $v_{\mathcal{A}}(\phi, \sigma^*) = T$ if and only if $(\phi)[\sigma] \in \Gamma$. We want to prove that it follows from this that for every function σ from the set of variables to the set of closed terms of *L*, $v_{\mathcal{A}}(\exists x \, \phi, \sigma^*) = T$ if and only if $(\exists x \, \phi)[\sigma] \in \Gamma$. Let σ be a function from the set of variables to the set of closed terms of *L*. We argue as follows:

$v_\mathcal{A}(\exists x\ \phi, \sigma^*) = T$

    ⇕   (definition of truth)

For at least one $a \in A$, $v_\mathcal{A}(\phi, \sigma^*_{(x/a)}) = T$

    ⇕   (since the elements of A are the equivalence classes generated with $\sim_\Gamma$ by the closed terms of L)

For at least one closed term t of L, $v_\mathcal{A}(\phi, \sigma^*_{(x/\ll t\gg_\Gamma)}) = T$

    ⇕   (since $\sigma^*_{(x/\ll t\gg_\Gamma)} = \sigma_{(x/t)}^*$)

For at least one closed term t of L, $v_\mathcal{A}(\phi, \sigma_{(x/t)}^*) = T$

    ⇕   (IH)

For at least one closed term t of L, $(\phi)[\sigma_{(x/t)}] \in \Gamma$

    ⇕   (Let $(\phi)[\sigma-x]$ be the formula which differs from $(\phi)[\sigma]$ only in that $\sigma(x)$ has not been substituted for x in ϕ. Then we have that $(\phi)[\sigma_{(x/t)}] = (\phi)[\sigma-x][t/x])$

For at least one closed term t of L, $(\phi)[\sigma-x][t/x] \in \Gamma$

    ⇕   (by the well-roundedness of Γ)

$\exists x\ (\phi)[\sigma-x] \in \Gamma$

    ⇕   (definition of substitution)

$(\exists x\ \phi)[\sigma-x] \in \Gamma$

    ⇕   (by Exercise 4. 15, since x is not free in $\exists x\ \phi$ and $(\exists x\ \phi)[\sigma]$ is $(\exists x\ \phi)[\sigma-x][\sigma(x)/x])$

$(\exists x\ \phi)[\sigma] \in \Gamma$ ■

EXERCISE 5. 11: Complete the proof of Lemma 5. 10 by dealing with atomic formulas of the form $Pt_1...t_n$ and supplying the remaining inductive clauses.

6. Negation Completeness

We have established that every well-rounded set of sentences is the theory of its canonical structure. It follows from this that every well-rounded set of sentences has a model. We know that every model of a set of sentences is also a model of any of its subsets. Hence, to show that every consistent set of sentences has a model, it will suffice to show that every consistent set of sentences is a subset of a well-rounded set. This will be our goal for the remainder of the proof of the Model Existence Theorem. If Γ is a set of sentences and Δ is a subset of Γ, we say that Γ is an *extension* of Δ, or that Γ *extends* Δ. Our goal is to show that every consistent set of sentences has a well-rounded extension. We are going to draw this conclusion from the combination of two results. One is presented in this section, and the other in the next.

DEFINITION: A set of sentences Γ of a first-order language *L* is *negation-complete* just in case, for every *L*-sentence φ, either φ ∈ Γ or ¬φ ∈ Γ.

Notice that, by virtue of Clause (1) of the definition of well-roundedness, for every *L*-sentence φ, a well-rounded set of *L*-sentences must contain either φ or ¬φ. Hence negation completeness is a necessary condition for well-roundedness. The result that well-rounded sets of sentences have models and the fact (Exercise 5. 5) that inconsistent sets of sentences don't have models yield another necessary condition for well-roundedness: a set of sentences won't be well-rounded unless it is consistent.

Negation completeness and consistency are not only necessary conditions for well-roundedness. They also come very close to providing a jointly sufficient condition for well-roundedness. As we shall see presently, there is only one feature of well-rounded sets of sentences that a consistent, negation-complete set could lack. Hence if we can show that every consistent set of sentences has a negation-complete extension which is also consistent, we will have taken an important step towards showing that every consistent set of sentences has a well-rounded extension. This will be our goal in this section.

We want to prove that for every consistent set Γ of sentences of a first-order language *L*, there is a consistent, negation-complete set of *L*-sentences which extends Γ. Our proof of this result will rest on an important assumption about *L*. The proof will invoke an *enumeration* of the *L*-sentences, i.e. a one-to-one correspondence between the set of positive integers and the set of *L*-sentences which enables us to arrange the *L*-sentences in a linear sequence, according to which number each of them has been paired with. Hence our proof will rest on the assumption that the *L*-sentences can be enumerated. We shall see in Chapter 6 what this assumption comes to. We shall also see there that if we drop this assumption the result can still be established, provided that we accept a general set-theoretic principle known as the Axiom of Choice.

In the proof we are going to use for the first time a technique that we shall apply extensively later on. It is based on the fact that the set of positive integers can be defined by induction, with number 1 as the base

and an inductive clause to the effect that the result of adding 1 to a positive integer is also a positive integer (see Chapter 2, §2). Notice that this
definition satisfies the conditions that would make it possible to use the
recursive method to define a function with the set of positive integers as
its domain, since the set of positive integers is freely generated from the
base of the definition by its inductive clause (see Chapter 2, §6). On the
one hand, if we add 1 to two different positive integers we never get the
same number. On the other, if we start with number 1, adding 1 any
number of times will never yield number 1 again. Hence we can define a
function f with the positive integers as its domain by specifying the image of 1 under f and, for every positive integer n, how the image under f
of $n + 1$ is determined by the image under f of n.

LEMMA 5. 12: Let L be a first-order language whose sentences can be
enumerated. Every consistent set of L-sentences is extended by a consistent, negation-complete set of L-sentences.

Proof: Let f be an enumeration of the L-sentences, and, for every positive integer n, let α_n be the L-sentence which f pairs with n—i.e. the n-th
sentence in the sequence defined by f. Let Γ be a consistent set of L-
sentences. We define, by recursion on the positive integers, a function
pairing each positive integer n with a set Γ^n of L-sentences, as the unique
function satisfying the following conditions:

$\Gamma^1 = \Gamma$.

For every positive integer n,

$$\Gamma^{n+1} = \begin{cases} \Gamma^n \text{ if } \Gamma^n \cup \{\alpha_n\} \text{ is inconsistent,} \\ \Gamma^n \cup \{\alpha_n\} \text{ otherwise.} \end{cases}$$

Notice that we can see this function as defining a sequence Γ^1, Γ^2,
Γ^3,... of extensions of Γ. At each stage in this sequence, we consider
whether to extend the set produced at the preceding stage by adding a
new L-sentence, and we add it just in case doing so doesn't result in an
inconsistent set. Since every L-sentence is α_n for some positive integer
n, each L-sentence is eventually considered for membership in one of the
extensions of Γ in this sequence.

Let Γ^* be the collection containing all the sets in this sequence. Then
$\bigcup\Gamma^*$ is the set containing all the L-sentences from each of the sets in the
sequence. We establish the lemma by showing that $\bigcup\Gamma^*$ is a consistent,
negation-complete extension of Γ.

To see that $\bigcup\Gamma^*$ is an extension of Γ, notice that, since Γ is Γ^1, we have that $\Gamma \in \Gamma^*$, and hence, by the definition of union, that $\Gamma \subseteq \bigcup\Gamma^*$.

To show that $\bigcup\Gamma^*$ is consistent, notice first that every set in the sequence Γ^1, Γ^2, Γ^3,... is consistent. This can be established with a very simple argument by induction on the positive integers, which is left as an exercise. Now we assume, towards a contradiction, that $\bigcup\Gamma^*$ is inconsistent. Then there is an L-formula ϕ, and finite subsets Δ_1, Δ_2 of $\bigcup\Gamma^*$ such that $\Delta_1 \vdash \phi$, $\Delta_2 \vdash \neg\phi$. Let n be the greatest positive integer such that $\alpha_n \in \Delta_1$ or $\alpha_n \in \Delta_2$. Then Δ_1 and Δ_2 are finite subsets of Γ^{n+1}, and Γ^{n+1} is inconsistent, which contradicts the claim that every set in the sequence of extensions of Γ is consistent (see Exercise 5. 13, below).

It only remains to be shown that $\bigcup\Gamma^*$ is negation-complete. For this, it will suffice to establish that the negation of every L-sentence outside $\bigcup\Gamma^*$ is deducible from a finite subset of $\bigcup\Gamma^*$. For then, if we assume, towards a contradiction, that there is an L-sentence ϕ such that ϕ, $\neg\phi \notin \bigcup\Gamma^*$, we can conclude that $\neg\phi$ and $\neg\neg\phi$ are deducible from finite subsets of $\bigcup\Gamma^*$, which contradicts the fact that $\bigcup\Gamma^*$ is consistent.

To show that the negation of every sentence outside $\bigcup\Gamma^*$ is deducible from a finite subset of $\bigcup\Gamma^*$ we argue as follows. Let ϕ be an L-sentence such that $\phi \notin \bigcup\Gamma^*$. Let n be the positive integer such that ϕ is α_n. Since $\Gamma^{n+1} \subseteq \bigcup\Gamma^*$, we have that $\alpha_n \notin \Gamma^{n+1}$. But then, by the definition of the sequence of extensions of Γ, $\Gamma^n \cup \{\alpha_n\}$ is inconsistent, i.e. there is an L-formula ψ and finite subsets Δ_1, Δ_2 of $\Gamma^n \cup \{\alpha_n\}$ such that $\Delta_1 \vdash \psi$, $\Delta_2 \vdash \neg\psi$. Then, by Exercise 4. 4 (1), we have that $\Delta_1 \cup \{\alpha_n\} \vdash \psi$, $\Delta_2 \cup \{\alpha_n\} \vdash \neg\psi$. Since $X \cup Y = (X - Y) \cup Y$ (see Lemma 1. 13), it follows that $(\Delta_1 - \{\alpha_n\}) \cup \{\alpha_n\} \vdash \psi$, $(\Delta_2 - \{\alpha_n\}) \cup \{\alpha_n\} \vdash \neg\psi$. Hence, by $\neg I$, we can derive $(\Delta_1 - \{\alpha_n\}) \cup (\Delta_2 - \{\alpha_n\}) \vdash \neg\alpha_n$. $(\Delta_1 - \{\alpha_n\}) \cup (\Delta_2 - \{\alpha_n\})$ is a finite subset of $\bigcup\Gamma^*$, and $\neg\alpha_n$ is $\neg\phi$. Hence we have shown that $\neg\phi$ is deducible form a finite subset of $\bigcup\Gamma^*$, as desired. ■

EXERCISE 5. 13: Show that, for every positive integer n, Γ^n is consistent.

DEFINITION: A set of L-sentences is *deductively closed* just in case it contains every L-sentence which is deducible from one of its finite subsets.

We are going to make extensive use of the fact that every consistent, negation-complete set of sentences is deductively closed.

LEMMA 5. 14: Every consistent, negation-complete set of sentences is deductively closed.

Proof: Let Γ be a consistent, negation-complete set of L-sentences, and let ϕ be an L-sentence such that $\phi \notin \Gamma$. We need to show that it follows from this that ϕ is not deducible from any finite subset of Γ. We argue as follows:

$\phi \notin \Gamma$

$\qquad \Downarrow$ (since Γ is negation-complete)

$\neg \phi \in \Gamma$

$\qquad \Downarrow$ (by the definition of $\subseteq$)

$\{\neg \phi\} \subseteq \Gamma$

$\qquad \Downarrow$ (since $\{\neg \phi\} \vdash \neg \phi$)

$\neg \phi$ is deducible from a finite subset of Γ

$\qquad \Downarrow$ (since Γ is consistent)

ϕ is not deducible from any finite subset of Γ ∎

7. Henkin Constants and Henkin Axioms

As we indicated in the preceding section, consistency and negation-completeness come very close to constituting a jointly sufficient condition for well-roundedness—a consistent negation-complete set of sentences is guaranteed to satisfy almost all the clauses of the definition of well-rounded set. The only exceptions are the left-to-right direction of Clause (5) and the right-to-left direction of Clause (6). According to the former, if a well-rounded set of L-sentences contains a sentence of the form $\exists x\ \phi$, it will also contain a sentence of the form $(\phi)[t/x]$, for some closed L-term t. According to the latter, if a well-rounded set of L-sentences contains every sentence of the form $(\phi)[t/x]$, where t is a closed L-term, it will also contain the sentence $\forall x\ \phi$. A consistent, negation-complete set of sentences could fail to exhibit these features. Take, e.g., the left-to-right direction of Clause (5). A set Γ of L-sentences can contain a sentence of the form $\exists x\ \phi$ but no sentence of the form $(\phi)[t/x]$, and still be consistent and negation-complete. To be negation-complete, Γ will have to contain every L-sentence of the form $\neg(\phi)[t/x]$, where t is a closed L-term, but this is compatible with Γ being consistent—$\neg\exists x\ \phi$ might still not be deducible from any finite subset of Γ. A similar situation obtains with respect to the right-to-left direction of Clause (6).

Lemma 5. 12 tells us that if Γ is a consistent set of sentences (of a language whose sentences can be enumerated), it will be extended by a consistent, negation-complete set of sentences, but these considerations suggest that a consistent, negation-complete extension of Γ could fail to be well rounded. However, there is a kind of sets of sentences, to which we shall refer as Henkin sets, for which this situation doesn't arise—every consistent, negation-complete extension of a Henkin set is well rounded.

DEFINITION: A set Γ of sentences of a first-order language L is a *Henkin set* just in case, for every L-sentence of the form $\exists x\ \phi$ (whether or not $\exists x\ \phi$ is in Γ), Γ contains a sentence of the form $\exists x\ \phi \to (\phi)[t/x]$, where t is a closed term of L.

We can see in intuitive terms that the aspects of well-roundedness that a consistent, negation-complete set of sentences could fail to exhibit will be present in any consistent, negation-complete extension of a Henkin set. Let Γ be a Henkin set, and let Γ^* be a consistent, negation-complete extension of Γ. Suppose that Γ^* contains a sentence of the form $\exists x\ \phi$. Since Γ^* extends a Henkin set, it contains the sentence $\exists x\ \phi \to (\phi)[t/x]$, for some closed L-term t. Hence $\{\exists x\ \phi \to (\phi)[t/x], \exists x\ \phi\}$ is a (finite) sub-set of Γ^*. But we have that $\{\exists x\ \phi \to (\phi)[t/x], \exists x\ \phi\} \vdash (\phi)[t/x]$. Hence, since, by Lemma 5. 14, Γ^* is deductively closed, we have that $(\phi)[t/x] \in \Gamma^*$. A similar piece of reasoning would establish that Γ^* also satisfies the right-to-left direction of Clause (6).

In §8, we shall establish that every consistent, negation-complete extension of a Henkin set is indeed well rounded. From this and Lemma 5. 12, we will be able to conclude that, if L is a language whose sentences can be enumerated, every consistent Henkin set of L-sentences has a well-rounded extension. Hence, to show that a consistent set of sentences has a well-rounded extension, it will suffice to show that it is extended by a consistent Henkin set—in a language whose sentences can be enumerated. Our goal in this section is to show that every consistent set of sentences is extended by a consistent Henkin set.

This task is made complicated by the fact that a consistent set Γ of sentences of a language L may not be extended by any consistent Henkin set of L-sentences. Suppose, e.g., that Γ contains a sentence of the form $\exists x\ \phi$ and, for every closed term t of L, the sentence $\neg(\phi)[t/x]$. Then adding to Γ any sentence of the form $\exists x\ \phi \to (\phi)[t/x]$, where t is a closed term of L, will generate an inconsistency, since both $(\phi)[t/x]$ and $\neg(\phi)[t/x]$ will be deducible from finite subsets of the resulting set.

Notice, however, that no obvious inconsistency would result if we expanded the vocabulary of L with a new individual constant c, and added to Γ the sentence $\exists x\ \phi \to (\phi)[c/x]$ of the expanded language. This will be the basic idea of our strategy for extending an arbitrary consistent set of sentences to a Henkin set of sentences which is also consistent. For this purpose, we introduce the following notions. For every first-order language L, let $L+HC$ be the language which results if we add to the vocabulary of L, for each L-sentence of the form $\exists x\ \phi$, a different new individual constant $c_{\exists x\ \phi}$. And let $HA(L)$ be the set of $L+HC$-sentences containing, for every L-sentence of the form $\exists x\ \phi$, the sentence $\exists x\ \phi \rightarrow (\phi)[c_{\exists x\ \phi}/x]$. Let's refer to the new constants of $L+HC$ as *Henkin constants*, and to the sentences in $HA(L)$ as *Henkin axioms*.

Needless to say, if we add Henkin axioms to a set Γ of sentences of a first-order language L, we might be able to deduce from the resulting set $L+HC$-formulas which are not deducible from Γ alone. Nevertheless, adding Henkin axioms to Γ won't boost the deductive power of Γ *within* L. If we can deduce (in $L+HC$) an L-formula ψ from the union of Γ and a set of Henkin axioms, then ψ is also deducible (in L) from Γ alone. This result is going to play a crucial role in our subsequent reasoning. It is expressed by the following lemma.

LEMMA 5. 15: For every finite set Γ of sentences of a first-order language L, and every L-formula ψ, if there is a finite subset Δ of $HA(L)$ such that $\Gamma \cup \Delta \vdash_{L+HC} \psi$, then $\Gamma \vdash_L \psi$.

Proof: Let Γ be a finite set of sentences of a first-order language L, ϕ an L-formula, and Δ a finite set of Henkin Axioms for L such that $\Gamma \cup \Delta \vdash_{L+HC} \psi$. We want to show that it follows from this that $\Gamma \vdash_L \psi$. Let $\exists x_1\ \phi_1 \rightarrow (\phi_1)[c_{\exists x_1 \phi_1}/x_1], \ldots, \exists x_n\ \phi_n \rightarrow (\phi_n)[c_{\exists x_n\ \phi_n}/x_n]$ be the elements of Δ. Let $y_1, \ldots, y_n$ be different variables none of which occurs in Δ or is free in ψ. Then, for every positive integer i less than or equal to n, we have that $(\phi_i)[c_{\exists x_i\ \phi_i}/x_i]$ is $(\phi_i)[y_i/x_i][c_{\exists x_i\ \phi_i}/y_i]$ (see Exercise 4. 21). Also, since $\exists x_i\ \phi_i$ has no free variables, $\exists x_i\ \phi_i$ is $(\exists x_i\ \phi_i)[c_{\exists x_i\ \phi_i}/y_i]$. We can conclude that $\exists x_i\ \phi_i \rightarrow (\phi_i)[c_{\exists x_i\ \phi_i}/x_i]$ is $(\exists x_i\ \phi_i)[c_{\exists x_i\ \phi_i}/y_i] \rightarrow (\phi_i)[y_i/x_i][c_{\exists x_i\ \phi_i}/y_i]$, i.e., by the definition of t/x-substitution, $(\exists x_i\ \phi_i \rightarrow (\phi_i)[y_i/x_i])[c_{\exists x_i\ \phi_i}/y_i]$. Now, since y_i is the only free variable in $\exists x_i\ \phi_i \rightarrow (\phi_i)[y_i/x_i]$, and all of $y_1, \ldots, y_n$ are different from each other, it follows that $(\exists x_i\ \phi_i \rightarrow (\phi_i)[y_i/x_i])[c_{\exists x_i\ \phi_i}/y_i]$ is $(\exists x_i\ \phi_i \rightarrow (\phi_i)[y_i/x_i])[c_{\exists x_1\ \phi_1}/y_1] \ldots [c_{\exists x_n \phi_n}/y_n]$. And since Γ has no free variables, and none of $y_1, \ldots, y_n$ is free in ψ, we have that Γ is $\Gamma[c_{\exists x_1\ \phi_1}/y_1] \ldots [c_{\exists x_n\ \phi_n}/y_n]$ and ψ is $(\psi)[c_{\exists x_1 \phi_1}/y_1] \ldots [c_{\exists x_n\ \phi_n}/y_n]$. We can conclude that $\Gamma \cup \Delta \vdash_{L+HC} \psi$ entails $\Gamma[c_{\exists x_1\phi_1}/y_1]...[c_{\exists x_n\phi_n}/y_n] \cup \{\exists x_1\ \phi_1 \rightarrow (\phi_1)[y_1/x_1],..., \exists x_n\ \phi_n \rightarrow (\phi_n)[y_n/x_n]\}[c_{\exists x_1\phi_1}/y_1]...[c_{\exists x_n\phi_n}/y_n] \vdash_{L+HC} (\psi)[c_{\exists x_1\phi_1}/y_1]...[c_{\exists x_n\phi_n}/y_n]$. And from this, by Lemma 4. 46, we can derive $\Gamma \cup \{\exists x_1\ \phi_1 \rightarrow (\phi_1)[y_1/x_1],..., \exists x_n\ \phi_n \rightarrow (\phi_n)[y_n/x_n]\} \vdash_L \psi$. Now we can argue as follows (the details of some steps of the reasoning are left as exercises):

$\Gamma \cup \{\exists x_1\ \phi_1 \rightarrow (\phi_1)[y_1/x_1],..., \exists x_n\ \phi_n \rightarrow (\phi_n)[y_n/x_n]\} \vdash_L \psi$

$\Downarrow$ (by Lemma 4. 3)

$\Gamma \vdash_L (\exists x_1\ \phi_1 \rightarrow (\phi_1)[y_1/x_1] \wedge...\wedge \exists x_n\ \phi_n \rightarrow (\phi_n)[y_n/x_n]) \rightarrow \psi$

$\Downarrow$ (by n applications of $\forall I$)

$\Gamma \vdash_L \forall y_1...\forall y_n ((\exists x_1\ \phi_1 \rightarrow(\phi_1)[y_1/x_1] \wedge...\wedge \exists x_n\ \phi_n \rightarrow(\phi_n)[y_n/x_n]) \rightarrow \psi)$

$\Downarrow*$ (since, if z is not free in β, we have that $\{\forall z\ (\alpha \rightarrow \beta)\} \vdash \exists z\ \alpha \rightarrow \beta$ (see Exercise 4. 32 (6)))

$\Gamma \vdash_L \exists y_1...\exists y_n (\exists x_1\ \phi_1 \rightarrow (\phi_1)[y_1/x_1] \wedge...\wedge \exists x_n\ \phi_n \rightarrow (\phi_n)[y_n/x_n]) \rightarrow \psi$

$\Downarrow*$ (since, if z is not free in β, we have that $\{\exists z\ (\alpha \wedge \beta)\} \vdash \exists z\ \alpha \wedge \beta$ (see Exercise 4. 32 (4)))

$\Gamma \vdash_L (\exists y_1\ (\exists x_1\ \phi_1 \rightarrow (\phi_1)[y_1/x_1]) \wedge...\wedge \exists y_n\ (\exists x_n\ \phi_n \rightarrow (\phi_n)[y_n/x_n])) \rightarrow \psi$

$\Downarrow*$ (since, if z is not free in α, we have that $\{\alpha \rightarrow \exists z\ \beta\} \vdash \exists z\ (\alpha \rightarrow \beta)$ (see Exercise 4. 32 (8)))

$\Gamma \vdash_L (\exists x_1\ \phi_1 \rightarrow \exists y_1\ (\phi_1)[y_1/x_1] \wedge...\wedge \exists x_n\ \phi_n \rightarrow \exists y_n\ (\phi_n)[y_n/x_n]) \rightarrow \psi$

$\Downarrow*$ (since, if z doesn't occur in α, $\{\exists w\ \alpha\} \vdash \exists z\ (\alpha)[z/w]$ (see Exercise 4. 35))

$\Gamma \vdash_L \psi$ ∎

EXERCISE 5. 16: Fill in the details of the steps of the argument in the proof of Lemma 5. 15 marked with asterisks, using in each case the facts invoked to justify them.

Let's go back to the problem of generating a consistent Henkin extension of an arbitrary consistent set Γ of sentences of a first-order language L. As a first approximation, we can use the notions that we have just introduced to define the set $\Gamma \cup HA(L)$ of sentences of language $L+HC$. $\Gamma \cup HA(L)$ is certainly an extension of Γ, and it wouldn't be hard to show that it is consistent. Nevertheless, it is not the set we are looking for, since, contrary to what may seem, it is not a Henkin set. For $\Gamma \cup$

$HA(L)$ contains an $L+HC$-sentence of the form $\exists x \, \phi \to (\phi)[t/x]$, where t is a closed term, for each L-sentence of the form $\exists x \, \phi$. But there are many $L+HC$-sentences of the form $\exists x \, \phi$ which are not L-sentences, because they contain occurrences of Henkin constants, and for those, $\Gamma \cup HA(L)$ contains no $L+HC$-sentence of the form $\exists x \, \phi \to (\phi)[t/x]$, for any closed term t.

What we want is a language L' whose vocabulary contains, in addition to the extralogical symbols of L, a different constant for each L'-sentence of the form $\exists x \, \phi$, whether or not it is an L-sentence, and an extension of Γ containing a Henkin axiom for each L'-sentence of the form $\exists x \, \phi$, whether or not it is an L-sentence. To achieve this, we proceed as follows. First we define, for each positive integer n, the language L_n, as the image of n under the unique function satisfying the following conditions:

$L_1 = L.$

For every positive integer n, $L_{n+1} = L_n + HC$.

Then we define, for each positive integer n, the set of L_n-sentences Γ^n, as the image of n under the unique function satisfying the following conditions:

$\Gamma^1 = \Gamma.$

For every positive integer n, $\Gamma^{n+1} = \Gamma^n \cup HA(L_n)$.

Now let L^+ be the collection containing all the languages in the sequence $L_1, L_2, \ldots$, and let Γ^+ be the collection containing all the sets of sentences in the sequence $\Gamma^1, \Gamma^2, \ldots$. Then the following lemma expresses the result that $\bigcup L^+$ and $\bigcup \Gamma^+$ are the language and the set of sentences that we are looking for.

LEMMA 5. 17: If Γ is a consistent set of sentences of a first-order language L, then $\bigcup \Gamma^+$ is a consistent Henkin set of $\bigcup L^+$-sentences which extends Γ.

Proof: Let Γ be a consistent set of L-sentences. We need to show that $\bigcup \Gamma^+$ is (i) an extension of Γ, (ii) a Henkin set of $\bigcup L^+$-sentences and (iii) consistent (in $\bigcup L^+$).

For (i), notice that, since Γ is Γ^1, we have that $\Gamma \in \Gamma^+$ and, by the definition of $\bigcup$, $\Gamma \subseteq \bigcup \Gamma^+$.

For (ii), let $\exists x \, \phi$ be a $\bigcup L^+$-sentence. Then, for some positive integer n, $\exists x \, \phi \in L_n$. Then there is an individual constant c of L_{n+1} such that $\exists x \, \phi$

$\rightarrow (\phi)[c/x] \in HA(L_n)$. Hence $\exists x\ \phi \rightarrow (\phi)[c/x] \in \Gamma^{n+1}$, and $\exists x\ \phi \rightarrow (\phi)[c/x] \in \bigcup\Gamma^+$, as desired.

For (iii), it will suffice to show that, for every positive integer n, Γ^n is consistent. For, if $\bigcup\Gamma^+$ were inconsistent, there would be a $\bigcup L^+$-formula ψ and finite subsets Δ_1, Δ_2 of $\bigcup\Gamma^+$ such that $\Delta_1 \vdash \psi$, $\Delta_2 \vdash \neg\psi$. But since Δ_1 and Δ_2 are finite, there is a positive integer n such that ψ is an L_n-formula and $\Delta_1, \Delta_2 \subseteq \Gamma^n$. Hence Γ^n would be inconsistent.

We show that for every positive integer n, Γ^n is consistent with an argument by induction on the positive integers. The base is trivial, since Γ^1 is Γ, which we are assuming to be consistent. For the inductive clause, we need to show, for every positive integer n, that if Γ^n is consistent, then Γ^{n+1} is also consistent. We assume that Γ^{n+1} is inconsistent, and try to prove that it follows from this that Γ^n is also inconsistent. If Γ^{n+1} is inconsistent, then there is an L^{n+1}-formula ϕ and finite subsets Δ_1, Δ_2 of Γ^{n+1} such that $\Delta_1 \vdash_{L_{n+1}} \phi$, $\Delta_2 \vdash_{L_{n+1}} \neg\phi$. Then, by Lemma 4. 4 (1), we have that $\Delta_1 \cup \{x \approx x\} \vdash_{L_{n+1}} \phi$, $\Delta_2 \cup \{x \approx x\} \vdash_{L_{n+1}} \neg\phi$. Hence, by $\neg I$, we can derive $\Delta_1 \cup \Delta_2 \vdash_{L_{n+1}} \neg x \approx x$. We have that $\Delta_1 \cup \Delta_2 \subseteq \Gamma^{n+1}$, Γ^{n+1} is $\Gamma^n \cup HA(L_n)$, and Γ^n is a set of L_n-sentences. Hence $\Delta_1 \cup \Delta_2$ is the union of a finite set of L_n-sentences (i.e. $(\Delta_1 \cup \Delta_2) \cap \Gamma^n$) and a finite set of Henkin axioms for L_n (i.e. $(\Delta_1 \cup \Delta_2) \cap HA(L_n)$). Since, in addition, $\neg x \approx x$ is an L_n-formula, we have, by Lemma 5. 15, that $(\Delta_1 \cup \Delta_2) \cap \Gamma^n \vdash_{L_n} \neg x \approx x$. But we also have that $\emptyset \vdash_{L_n} x \approx x$. Therefore Γ^n is inconsistent, as desired. ∎

EXERCISE 5. 18: Show that if Γ is a Henkin set of sentences of a first-order language L, and Γ^* is a set of L-sentences which extends Γ, then Γ^* is also a Henkin set of L-sentences.

8. Consistent, Negation-Complete Henkin Sets Are Well Rounded

Let's say that a first-order language L is *small* just in case the sentences of the language $\bigcup L^+$ defined in the previous section can be enumerated. Using the results of §§6 and 7 we can show that every consistent set of sentences of a small first-order language has a consistent, negation-complete Henkin extension. Furthermore, we established in §5 that every well-rounded set of sentences has a model. Hence, to show that every consistent set of sentences of a small language has a model, it will suffice to show that every consistent, negation-complete Henkin set of sentences is well rounded. The goal of this section is to establish this result.

LEMMA 5. 19: Every consistent, negation-complete Henkin set of sentences is well rounded.

Proof: Let Γ be a consistent, negation-complete Henkin set of sentences of a first-order language L. We need to show that Γ satisfies every clause of the definition of well-roundedness. We shall deal with Clauses (1), (3), (6) and (10), leaving the rest as an exercise.

(1) (i) We show first that if $\neg\phi \in \Gamma$, then $\phi \notin \Gamma$. Let $\neg\phi \in \Gamma$. Then, since $\{\neg\phi\} \vdash \neg\phi$, $\neg\phi$ is deducible from a finite subset of Γ. Then, since Γ is consistent, ϕ is not deducible from any finite subset of Γ. But $\{\phi\} \vdash \phi$. Therefore $\phi \notin \Gamma$, as desired.

(ii) We show now that if $\phi \notin \Gamma$, then $\neg\phi \in \Gamma$. This follows directly from the negation-completeness of Γ.

(3) (i) We show first that if $\phi, \psi \notin \Gamma$, then $\phi \vee \psi \notin \Gamma$. Assume that ϕ, $\psi \notin \Gamma$. Then, by the negation-completeness of Γ, $\neg\phi, \neg\psi \in \Gamma$. But, as the following argument shows, $\{\neg\phi, \neg\psi\} \vdash \neg(\phi \vee \psi)$.

$\{\phi, x \approx x\} \vdash \phi\ (B)\ \{\neg\phi, x \approx x\} \vdash \neg\phi\ (B)$

$$\frac{\{\neg\phi, \phi\} \vdash \neg x \approx x\ (\neg I) \qquad\qquad \{\psi, x \approx x\} \vdash \psi\ (B)\ \ \{\neg\psi, x \approx x\} \vdash \neg\psi\ (B)}{\begin{array}{cc} & \{\phi \vee \psi\} \vdash \phi \vee \psi\ (B) \qquad \{\neg\psi, \psi\} \vdash \neg x \approx x\ (\neg I)\end{array}}$$

$$\frac{\{\neg\phi, \neg\psi, \phi \vee \psi\} \vdash \neg x \approx x\ (\vee E) \qquad \{\phi \vee \psi\} \vdash x \approx x\ (\approx I)}{\{\neg\phi, \neg\psi\} \vdash \neg(\phi \vee \psi)\ (\neg I)}$$

Hence $\neg(\phi \vee \psi)$ is deducible from a finite subset of Γ, and, by the consistency of Γ, $\phi \vee \psi$ is not deducible from any finite subset of Γ. But $\{\phi \vee \psi\} \vdash \phi \vee \psi$. Hence $\phi \vee \psi \notin \Gamma$, as desired.

(ii) We show now that if $\phi \in \Gamma$ or $\psi \in \Gamma$, then $\phi \vee \psi \in \Gamma$. Assume that $\phi \in \Gamma$. We have that $\{\phi\} \vdash \phi$, and from this, using $\vee I$, we can derive $\{\phi\} \vdash \phi \vee \psi$. Hence $\phi \vee \psi$ is deducible from a finite subset of Γ, and, since Γ is deductively closed, $\phi \vee \psi \in \Gamma$. We obtain this conclusion in the same way from the assumption that $\psi \in \Gamma$.

(6) (i) We show first that if $\forall x\ \phi \notin \Gamma$, there is a closed term t of L such that $(\phi)[t/x] \notin \Gamma$. Assume that $\forall x\ \phi \notin \Gamma$. Then, by the negation-completeness of Γ, $\neg\forall x\ \phi \in \Gamma$. Since Γ is a Henkin set, there is a closed

term t of L such that the sentence $\exists x \, \neg\phi \to (\neg\phi)[t/x] \in \Gamma$. But, by the following argument, $\{\neg\forall x \, \phi, \exists x \, \neg\phi \to (\neg\phi)[t/x]\} \vdash (\neg\phi)[t/x]$.

$\{\neg\phi\} \vdash \neg\phi$ (B)

$\{\neg\phi\} \vdash \exists x \, \neg\phi$ 　(∃I) 　　　　　 $\{\neg\exists x \, \neg\phi, \neg\phi\} \vdash \neg\exists x \, \neg\phi$ (B)

$\{\neg\exists x \, \neg\phi\} \vdash \neg\neg\phi$ (¬I)

$\{\neg\exists x \, \neg\phi\} \vdash \phi$ (¬E)

$\{\neg\exists x \, \neg\phi\} \vdash \forall x \, \phi$ (∀I) 　 $\{\neg\forall x \, \phi, \neg\exists x \, \neg\phi\} \vdash \neg\forall x \, \phi$ (B)

$\{\neg\forall x \, \phi\} \vdash \neg\neg\exists x \, \neg\phi$ (¬I)

$\{\exists x \, \neg\phi \to (\neg\phi)[t/x]\} \vdash \exists x \, \neg\phi \to (\neg\phi)[t/x]$ (B) 　 $\{\neg\forall x \, \phi\} \vdash \exists x \, \neg\phi$ (¬E)

$\{\neg\forall x \, \phi, \exists x \, \neg\phi \to (\neg\phi)[t/x]\} \vdash (\neg\phi)[t/x]$ (→E)

Hence $(\neg\phi)[t/x]$ is deducible from a finite subset of Γ. But $(\neg\phi)[t/x]$ is $\neg(\phi)[t/x]$. Hence, by the consistency of Γ, $(\phi)[t/x]$ is not deducible from any finite subset of Γ. But $\{(\phi)[t/x]\} \vdash (\phi)[t/x]$. Therefore $(\phi)[t/x] \notin \Gamma$, as desired.

(ii) We show now that if $\forall x \, \phi \in \Gamma$, then, for every closed term t of L, $(\phi)[t/x] \in \Gamma$. Assume that $\forall x \, \phi \in \Gamma$, and let t be a closed term of L. We have that $\{\forall x \, \phi\} \vdash \forall x \, \phi$, and since, by Exercise 4. 23, t is substitutable for x in ϕ, we can derive from this $\{\forall x \, \phi\} \vdash (\phi)[t/x]$. Hence $(\phi)[t/x]$ is deducible from a finite subset of Γ, and, since Γ is deductively closed, we can conclude that $(\phi)[t/x] \in \Gamma$, as desired.

(10) We need to show that, if $t_1 \approx u_1, \ldots, t_n \approx u_n \in \Gamma$, then $f(t_1, \ldots, t_n) \approx f(u_1, \ldots, u_n) \in \Gamma$. Assume that $t_1 \approx u_1, \ldots, t_n \approx u_n \in \Gamma$. We have that $\varnothing \vdash f(t_1, \ldots, t_n) \approx f(t_1, \ldots, t_n)$ and, for every i less than or equal to n, $\{t_i \approx u_i\} \vdash t_i \approx u_i$. But if $x_1, \ldots, x_n$ are different variables, $f(t_1, \ldots, t_n) \approx f(t_1, \ldots, t_n)$ is $(f(t_1, \ldots, t_n) \approx f(x_1, \ldots, x_n))[t_1/x_1] \ldots [t_n/x_n]$, $f(t_1, \ldots, t_n) \approx f(u_1, \ldots, u_n)$ is $(f(t_1, \ldots, t_n) \approx f(x_1, \ldots, x_n))[u_1/x_1] \ldots [u_n/x_n]$, and, for every i less than or equal to n, t_i is substitutable for x_i in $(f(t_1, \ldots, t_n) \approx f(x_1, \ldots, x_n))[t_1/x_1] \ldots [t_{i-1}/x_{i-1}]$, and u_i is substitutable for x_i in $(f(t_1, \ldots, t_n) \approx f(x_1, \ldots, x_n))[u_1/x_1] \ldots [u_{i-1}/x_{i-1}]$. Hence, by n applications of $\approx E$ we get $\{t_1 \approx u_1, \ldots, t_n \approx u_n\} \vdash f(t_1, \ldots, t_n) \approx f(u_1, \ldots, u_n)$. Therefore, since Γ is deductively closed, $f(t_1, \ldots, t_n) \approx f(u_1, \ldots, u_n) \in \Gamma$, as desired. ∎

EXERCISE 5. 20: Complete the proof of Lemma 5. 17 dealing with the remaining clauses of the definition of well-roundedness.

We now have all the necessary ingredients to prove the Model Existence Theorem for small languages. The reasoning is outlined in Figure 9.

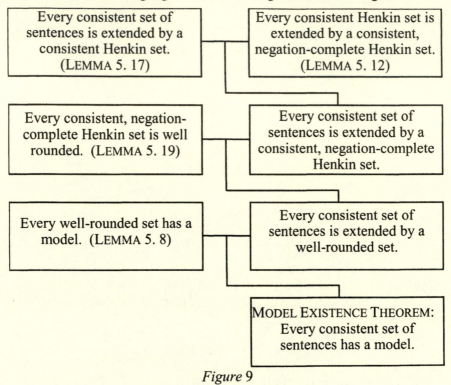

Figure 9

MODEL EXISTENCE THEOREM (for small languages): Every consistent set of sentences of a small first-order language has a model.

Proof: Let Γ be a consistent set of sentences of a small first-order language L. Then by Lemma 5. 17, Γ is extended by a consistent Henkin set Γ' of sentences of a language L', whose sentences can be enumerated. Then, by Lemma 5. 12, Γ' is extended by a consistent, negation-complete set $\Gamma^\#$ of L'-sentences. Since $\Gamma^\#$ extends Γ', by Exercise 5. 18, $\Gamma^\#$ is, in addition, a Henkin set of L'-sentences. Hence, by Lemma 5. 19, $\Gamma^\#$ is well rounded, and, by Lemma 5. 10, there is an L'-structure $\mathcal{A}$ which is a model of $\Gamma^\#$. Since Γ is a subset of $\Gamma^\#$, $\mathcal{A}$ is also a model of Γ, and the reduct of $\mathcal{A}$ to L is an L-structure which is a model of Γ, as desired.   ∎

EXERCISE 5. 21: Show that if L is a small first-order language, then for every L-formula ϕ, and every finite set of L-formulas Γ, $\Gamma \vDash \phi$ if and only if $\Gamma \vdash \phi$.

9. Compactness

Using the connection between logical consequence and deducibility expressed by the Soundness and Completeness Theorems, we can establish a very important fact about the notion of first-order logical consequence: A formula cannot be a logical consequence of an infinite set of formulas unless it is also a logical consequence of some finite subset of this set. This feature of first-order logic is known as *compactness*.

COMPACTNESS THEOREM: For every formula ϕ of a first-order language L and every set Γ of L-formulas, if $\Gamma \vDash \phi$, then there is a finite subset Γ_0 of Γ such that $\Gamma_0 \vDash \phi$.

Proof: Let $\Gamma \vDash \phi$. By the Completeness Theorem, there is a finite subset Γ_0 of Γ such that $\Gamma_0 \vdash \phi$. But then, by the Soundness Theorem, $\Gamma_0 \vDash \phi$, as desired. ∎

Obviously this reasoning shows that the Compactness Theorem holds for those languages for which the Completeness Theorem holds. Hence all we are entitled to assert so far is that compactness holds for small languages. We will have a general proof of the Compactness Theorem only when we show, in Chapter 6, §13, that completeness holds for every language.

Notice that, although the proof of the Compactness Theorem exploits the connection between logical consequence and deducibility, the theorem is not a result about this connection, but about logical consequence itself. It can also be formulated as a result about satisfiability.

COMPACTNESS THEOREM (reformulation): For every set Γ of formulas of a first-order language, if every finite subset of Γ is satisfiable, then Γ is satisfiable.

To prove that the first formulation of the theorem entails the second, we shall invoke the following result.

EXERCISE 5. 22: Show that a set Γ of formulas is satisfiable if and only if $\Gamma \nvDash \neg x \approx x$.

LEMMA 5. 23: The first formulation of the Compactness Theorem entails the second.

Proof: Assume the first formulation of the theorem, and let Γ be a set of formulas which is not satisfiable. Then, by Exercise 5. 22, $\Gamma \vDash \neg x \approx x$. Then, by the first formulation of compactness, there is a finite subset Γ_0 of Γ such that $\Gamma_0 \vDash \neg x \approx x$. Hence, again by Exercise 5. 22, Γ_0 is not satisfiable, as desired. ∎

The proof that the second formulation entails the first is left as an exercise.

EXERCISE 5. 24: Show that the second formulation of compactness entails the first.

Hint: Use Exercise 3. 35.

Chapter 6

Cardinality

1. The Size of Infinity

In Chapter 1 we introduced a family of notions with which sets can be characterized. Thus, e.g., we can characterize a set A as a subset of a set B, or as the union of sets C and D. The application of these notions is based on the identity of the elements of the sets involved. A is a subset of B just in case every element of A is identical to an element of B, and A is the union of C and D just in case every element of A is identical to an element of C or to an element of D and every element of C and every element of D is identical to an element of A.

If we abstract from the identity of their elements, we can still characterize sets with respect to *how many* elements they have—with respect to their *size*. If a and b are different objects, we can say that the set $\{a, b\}$ has two elements, independently of which particular objects a and b are. And if c, d and e are different objects, we can say that the set $\{c, d, e\}$ has more elements, is bigger, than the set $\{a, b\}$, independently of whether any element of one set is identical to any element of the other. We can also use arithmetical notions to compare the sizes of sets. We can say, for example, that the size of the set $\{c, d, e\}$ is the sum of the sizes of the sets $\{a, b\}$ and $\{f\}$, independently, once more, of whether the elements of one of these sets are identical to the elements of the other two.

Our intuitive understanding of the notion of size affords a much more precise and sophisticated characterization of the size of finite sets than of infinite ones. All we seem capable of saying about the size of an infinite set is that it has more elements than any finite set. Attempts to compare the sizes of infinite sets lead to conflicts of intuitions. Take, for example, the set of positive integers and the set containing the perfect squares, 1, 4, 9, 16,.... On the one hand, we want to say that the set of positive integers has more elements than the set of perfect squares, since the former contains all the elements of the latter plus infinitely many others. In fact, as we advance in the sequence of positive integers, the proportion of perfect squares to other positive integers tends to 0. On the other hand, we want to say that both sets are the same size. For the elements of each of them form a series in which every element is followed by infinitely many, and it is hard to see why it would make a difference to the size of the set of objects in a series of this form which particular object occupies each position.

One of the fundamental components of set theory, as developed by Georg Cantor in the final decades of the 19th century, was a proposal as to how to extend our notion of size that would enable us to characterize the sizes of infinite sets with the same precision and sophistication as finite ones. This notion, known as *cardinality*, plays a central role in the aspects of the theory of logic that we are going to present in subsequent chapters. The goal of the present chapter is to introduce the basic ideas of the theory of cardinality and to establish the results concerning the cardinality of infinite sets that we are going to invoke later on.

There may be an issue as to whether the notion of cardinality constitutes a genuine extension of our notion of size or an altogether different notion, which happens to agree with the notion of size with respect to finite sets. In order to avoid this question, we shall introduce cardinality as an independent notion, but we shall show that the ensuing characterization of the cardinality of finite sets provides a perfect match for all the basic facts about their size.

2. Criteria for Size Claims

Suppose that you are working at an ice-cream parlor, and you want to establish that the number of cones you have equals the number of customers in the shop. One way to do this would be to determine how many cones and how many customers you have, e.g., by counting them, and to check that the number of cones equals the number of customers. But you could approach the problem in a different way. Suppose, e.g., that you could distribute all the cones among the customers, with everyone getting exactly one cone and no one having to share. This would not tell you how many cones or customers you have. Nevertheless, you would be able to conclude that you have the same number of each, whatever that number is.

This illustration indicates that we have two different kinds of criteria for claims to the effect that a set A has the same size as a set B. The first criterion is whether the sizes of A and B are represented by the same natural number. The second criterion is whether there is a one-to-one correspondence between A and B. These criteria are related in the following way: For claims concerning the sizes of finite sets, as we shall see presently, both criteria yield the same results. But for claims concerning the sizes of infinite sets the situation is very different. The first criterion is simply not applicable to infinite sets, as their sizes are not represented by natural numbers. But the applicability of the second criterion is not restricted in this way. The question whether there is a one-to-one correspondence between sets A and B is in principle just as meaningful when A and B are infinite sets as when they are finite.

We are going to see that with respect to each basic type of claim concerning the sizes of sets the same situation obtains. In each case we will have a *numerical* criterion, based on which natural number represents the size of each set, and a *functional* criterion, based on relations between the sets themselves. And in each case the numerical and functional criteria will be related in the same way. They will yield the same results for claims concerning the sizes of finite sets, but whereas the application of the numerical criterion will be restricted to finite sets, the functional criterion will be applicable to finite and infinite sets alike.

The notion of cardinality will arise from this situation. We are going to introduce it in such a way that the truth value of claims about the cardinality of sets is determined by the functional criteria for size claims. Hence, every claim about the cardinality of finite sets will have the same truth value as the corresponding claim about their size, but we will also have precise criteria for determining the truth value of claims concerning the cardinality of infinite sets.

3. Counting

Our immediate goal is to show that, in addition to numerical criteria for size claims, we have functional criteria which yield the same results as numerical criteria for claims involving finite sets, but are also applicable to claims involving infinite sets. In order to establish the equivalence of functional and numerical criteria with respect to finite sets, we will need to have a precise account of the numerical criteria. This will be our goal in this section.

The numerical criteria for size claims are based on the assumption that, for every finite set, there is a unique natural number representing its size. We shall take the domain of natural numbers as given, and consider how each finite set is paired with the natural number which represents its size. Intuitively, the way to determine the number of elements of a finite set is to count them. Counting the elements of a set consists in pairing them with positive integers according to certain rules. All elements have to be counted, and none can be counted more than once. Also, the numbers have to be taken in the right order, starting with 1 and taking each number after its predecessor, without skipping any or taking any more than once. If these conditions are satisfied, the highest number paired with an element of the set will represent the size of the set.

We can use this basic idea to provide a precise account of which number represents the size of each finite set. For this purpose, we define by recursion a function pairing each natural number with a set of positive integers to which we shall refer as its counting sequence.

DEFINITION: For every natural number n, the *counting sequence* of n (abbreviated $CS(n)$) is the image of n under the unique function satisfying the following conditions:

$CS(0) = \emptyset$.

For every natural number n, $CS(n + 1) = CS(n) \cup \{n + 1\}$.

Thus the counting sequence of a positive integer n is the set of numbers involved in counting to n, i.e. all positive integers up to and including n. We shall represent the counting sequence of an arbitrary natural number n as $\{1,..., n\}$. When we count the elements of a set S, we conclude that it has n elements just in case the elements of S can be paired with the elements of $\{1,..., n\}$ in such a way that each element of either set is paired with one and only one element of the other, i.e. when there is a one-to-one correspondence between S and $\{1,..., n\}$.

The existence of one-to-one correspondences between sets is going to play a major role in our discussion of size.

DEFINITION: A set A is *similar* to a set B, written $A \sim B$, just in case there is a one-to-one correspondence between A and B. (When A is not similar to B, we write $A \nsim B$.)

Similarity is an equivalence relation. This result will be of some importance to us later on. It is expressed by the following exercise.

EXERCISE 6. 1: Show that, for all sets X, Y, Z, (i) $X \sim X$, (ii) if $X \sim Y$, then $Y \sim X$, and (iii) if $X \sim Y$ and $Y \sim Z$, then $X \sim Z$.

The following exercises express features of the similarity relation that we will invoke later on in the proofs of more involved results.

EXERCISE 6. 2: Let set A be disjoint with set B, and let set A' be disjoint with set B'. Show that if $A \sim A'$, $B \sim B'$, then $A \cup B \sim A' \cup B'$.

EXERCISE 6. 3: Let A, B be sets, and let $a \in A$, $b \in B$. Show that if $A \sim B$, then $A - \{a\} \sim B - \{b\}$.

We are going to use the notion of similarity in our account of how each finite set is paired with the natural number which represents its size: the number of elements of a finite set A (abbreviated #(A)) is n just in case A is similar to the counting sequence of n, i.e., for every finite set A, #(A) = n if and only if $A \sim \{1,..., n\}$. We want this definition to single out a unique natural number as the size of each finite set. This requires, on the one hand, that every finite set is similar to at least one counting sequence and, on the other, that every finite set is similar to at most one counting sequence. So far we have been relying on our intuitive understanding of the notion of a finite set. But in order to show that these two require-ments are satisfied, we need to provide an explicit definition of the no-tion.

DEFINITION: A set is *finite* just in case it is similar to a counting se-quence.

This definition takes care of the first requirement immediately. The second requirement will be a corollary of the following lemma.

LEMMA 6. 4: No counting sequence is similar to a proper subset of itself.

Proof: Let S be a counting sequence, and let $S^* \subset S$. Assume, towards a contradiction, that S is similar to S^*. Then there is a one-to-one corre-spondence between S and S^*. Hence there is a function f from S to S^* which is one-to-one. f is also a one-to-one function from S to itself, but since the range of f is S^*, and S^* is a proper subset of S, it follows that there is at least one element of S which is not in the range of f. We shall establish the lemma by showing that this is not a possibility. Every one-to-one function from a counting sequence to itself has the whole count-ing sequence as its range. In other words, every one-to-one function from a counting sequence to itself is a one-to-one correspondence. We prove this claim by induction on the natural numbers, using the recursive definition of counting sequence.

Base: The claim is trivially satisfied by the base. There is only one function from $\emptyset$ to $\emptyset$, namely $\emptyset$ itself (see Lemma 1. 50). And, by Lemma 1. 49, $\emptyset$ is a one-to-one correspondence between $\emptyset$ and $\emptyset$.

Inductive Step: We assume (IH) that every one-to-one function from $\{1,..., n\}$ to itself has the whole of $\{1,..., n\}$ as its range. We need to show that it follows from this that every one-to-one function from $\{1,..., n + 1\}$ to itself has the whole of $\{1,..., n + 1\}$ as its range.

Let f be a one-to-one function from $\{1,..., n + 1\}$ to itself. We need to show that f has the whole of $\{1,..., n + 1\}$ as its range. We have that $f \restriction \{1,..., n\}$ is a one-to-one function from $\{1,..., n\}$ to $\{1,..., n + 1\}$. We have two cases to consider.

Suppose first that for every $x \in \{1,..., n\}, f(x) \in \{1,..., n\}$. Then $f \restriction \{1,..., n\}$ is a one-to-one function from $\{1,..., n\}$ to $\{1,..., n\}$, and, by IH, it has (the whole of) $\{1,..., n\}$ as its range. Hence, since f is one-to-one, $f(n + 1) = n + 1$, and the range of f is $\{1,..., n\} \cup \{n + 1\}$, i.e. $\{1,..., n + 1\}$, as desired.

Suppose now that there is a $p \in \{1,..., n\}$ such that $f(p) = n + 1$. We can define a function f^* from $\{1,..., n + 1\}$ to itself as follows:

$$\text{For every } x \in \{1,..., n + 1\}, \ f^*(x) = \begin{cases} f(n+1) \text{ if } x = p, \\ f(p) \text{ (i.e. } n+1) \text{ if } x = n+1, \\ f(x) \text{ otherwise.} \end{cases}$$

Thus f and f^* only differ in that the images of p and $n + 1$ have been swapped. Notice that $f^* \restriction \{1,..., n\}$ is a one-to-one function from $\{1,..., n\}$ to itself. Hence, by IH, $f^* \restriction \{1,..., n\}$ has the whole of $\{1,..., n\}$ as its range, and, since $f^*(n + 1) = f(p) = n + 1$, the range of f^* is $\{1,..., n + 1\}$. But given the way in which f^* is related to f, it follows that $\{1,..., n + 1\}$ is also the range of f, as desired. ∎

EXERCISE 6. 5: Show that if $\{1,..., m\} \sim \{1,..., n\}$, then $m = n$.

EXERCISE 6. 6: Show that if $A \sim \{1,..., m\}$ and $A \sim \{1,..., n\}$, then $m = n$.

Exercise 6. 6 gives us the result that we were looking for. Our definition of # pairs each set with at most one natural number. Since we know that the definition pairs each finite set with at least one natural number, we can conclude that for each finite set A there is a unique natural number #(A). We shall treat this number as the size of A.

EXERCISE 6. 7: Show that no finite set is similar to a proper subset of itself.

LEMMA 6. 8: If $S \subset \{1,..., n\}$, then for some $m < n, S \sim \{1,..., m\}$.

Proof: We prove this result by induction on n. The base is trivial, as the counting sequence of 0 is Ø, and Ø has no proper subsets.

Inductive Step: We assume (IH) that for every $S \subset \{1,\ldots, n\}$, there is a natural number $m < n$, such that $S \sim \{1,\ldots, m\}$. We need to prove that for every $T \subset \{1,\ldots, n + 1\}$, there is a natural number $p < n + 1$, such that $T \sim \{1,\ldots, p\}$. There are three cases to consider: (*a*) $T = \{1,\ldots, n\}$, (*b*) $T \subset \{1,\ldots, n\}$ and (*c*) $T \nsubseteq \{1,\ldots, n\}$.

Case (*a*) is straightforward, as $n < n + 1$, and every set is similar to itself. For case (*b*), the existence of a natural number p less than n (and hence less than $n + 1$) such that $T \sim \{1,\ldots, p\}$ follows from the inductive hypothesis. In case (*c*) we have that $n + 1 \in T$. Since T is a proper subset of $\{1,\ldots, n + 1\}$, it follows that $T - \{n + 1\}$ is a proper subset of $\{1,\ldots, n\}$. Hence, by the inductive hypothesis, for some natural number p less than n, $T - \{n + 1\} \sim \{1,\ldots, p\}$. Notice that, since p is less than n, $p + 1$ is less than $n + 1$. Let f be a one-to-one correspondence between $T - \{n + 1\}$ and $\{1,\ldots, p\}$. If we extend f by pairing $n + 1$ with $p + 1$, we obtain a one-to-one correspondence between T and $\{1,\ldots, p + 1\}$, as desired. ∎

EXERCISE 6. 9: Show that every subset of a finite set is finite.

4. Functional Criteria

We turn now to the task of presenting functional criteria for each basic type of size claim and showing that they are equivalent with respect to finite sets to the corresponding numerical criteria.

i. Same Size

We start with claims to the effect that a set A has the same size as a set B. We have suggested in §2 that a functional criterion for this kind of claim is provided by the similarity of A and B, i.e. by the existence of a one-to-one correspondence between A and B. The following lemma expresses the result that this criterion is equivalent to the corresponding numerical criterion with respect to finite sets.

LEMMA 6. 10: If A and B are finite sets, then $\#(A) = \#(B)$ if and only if $A \sim B$.

Proof: Assume first that $\#(A) = \#(B)$, and let $\#(A) = \#(B) = n$. Then $A \sim \{1,\ldots, n\}$, $B \sim \{1,\ldots, n\}$. From here, by Exercise 6. 1, we get $A \sim B$, as desired.

Assume now that $A \sim B$, and let $\#(A) = m$, $\#(B) = n$. We have that $A \sim \{1,\ldots, m\}$, $B \sim \{1,\ldots, n\}$. By Exercise 6. 1 we get $\{1,\ldots, m\} \sim \{1,\ldots, n\}$, and from this, by Exercise 6. 5, it follows that $m = n$. Therefore $\#(A) = \#(B)$, as desired. ∎

ii. Big and Small

Suppose again that you are working in an ice-cream parlor, and you want to make sure that you have at least as many cones as customers. One way to do this would be to determine how many of each you have and check that the number of customers is less than or equal to the number of cones. But once again we can adopt a different strategy which bypasses numbers altogether, e.g., by giving a cone to each customer, with no one having to share. In this case it doesn't matter if there are cones left over. So long as each customer gets a different cone, you'll be able to conclude that you have no more customers than cones.

The second procedure suggests a functional criterion for claims to the effect that a set A has no more elements than a set B—namely the existence of a one-to-one function from A to B. By giving a different cone to each customer you show that there is a function of this kind from the set of customers to the set of cones, i.e. the function pairing each customer with the cone he or she gets.

DEFINITION: A set A is *dominated* by a set B, written $A \preceq B$, just in case there is a one-to-one function from A to B.

The criterion that we are considering for A having no more elements than B is whether A is dominated by B. Before we show that this functional criterion is equivalent to the numerical criterion with respect to finite sets, we shall establish a couple of claims about domination.

EXERCISE 6. 11: Show that a set dominates each of its subsets; i.e., if $A \subseteq B$, then $A \preceq B$.

EXERCISE 6. 12: Show that if $A \sim A'$, $B \sim B'$ and $A \preceq B$, then $A' \preceq B'$.

The following lemma expresses the claim that the domination criterion is equivalent to the corresponding numerical criterion with respect to finite sets.

LEMMA 6. 13: If A and B are finite sets, then $\#(A) \leq \#(B)$ if and only if $A \preceq B$.

Proof: Let $\#(A) = m$, $\#(B) = n$. Assume first that $\#(A) \leq \#(B)$, i.e. $m \leq n$. Then $\{1,\ldots, m\} \subseteq \{1,\ldots, n\}$. By Exercise 6. 11, it follows that $\{1,\ldots, m\}$

$\preceq \{1,\ldots, n\}$. But since $A \sim \{1,\ldots, m\}$, $B \sim \{1,\ldots, n\}$, we have, by Exercise 6. 12, that $A \preceq B$, as desired.

Assume now that $A \preceq B$. We have that $A \sim \{1,\ldots, m\}$, $B \sim \{1,\ldots, n\}$, and it follows from this, by Exercise 6. 12, that $\{1,\ldots, m\} \preceq \{1,\ldots, n\}$. Let f be a one-to-one function from $\{1,\ldots, m\}$ to $\{1,\ldots, n\}$. We have that f is a one-to-one correspondence between $\{1,\ldots, m\}$ and a subset S of $\{1,\ldots, n\}$. Assume, towards a contradiction, that $m \not\preceq n$. Then we have that $n < m$, and $\{1,\ldots, n\} \subset \{1,\ldots, m\}$. Since $S \subseteq \{1,\ldots, n\}$, we have that $S \subset \{1,\ldots, m\}$, and f is a one-to-one correspondence between $\{1,\ldots, m\}$ and a proper subset of itself, which contradicts Lemma 6. 4, as desired. ∎

EXERCISE 6. 14: Show that a set A is dominated by a set B if and only if A is similar to a subset of B.

A related notion that we shall use later on is strict domination.

DEFINITION: A set A is *strictly dominated* by a set B, written $A \prec B$, just in case $A \preceq B$ but $A \nsim B$.

EXERCISE 6. 15: Show that, for all sets A, B, $A \preceq B$ if and only if $A \prec B$ or $A \sim B$.

iii. Addition

Let's go back to the ice-cream parlor. Suppose that you want to establish that the number of customers in the shop is the sum of the number of cones and the number of spoons you have. One way to achieve this is to determine how many customers, cones and spoons you have, and to check that the number representing the size of the set of customers is the sum of the numbers representing the size of the set of cones and the size of the set of spoons. But once again you could adopt an alternative strategy which doesn't involve finding out which number represents the size of each set. Suppose that you could distribute all the cones and all the spoons among the customers, in such a way that everyone gets exactly one item and no one has to share. This procedure would not tell you how many customers, cones or spoons you have, but you would still be able to conclude that the number of customers is the sum of the number of cones and the number of spoons.

The second procedure in this illustration suggests a functional criterion for claims to the effect that the size of a set C is the sum of the sizes of sets A and B—namely, whether there is a one-to-one correspondence between C and the union of A and B. Notice however that this criterion can only be expected to work when A and B are disjoint sets. If you have four friends, I have three, and my wife has two, there could still be a one-to-one correspondence between the set of your friends and the union of the set of my wife's friends and the set of mine, provided that my wife and I have one friend in common.

Nevertheless, the proposed criterion can be easily modified in order to take care of nondisjoint sets. The idea is to use as our functional criterion for the size of C being the sum of the sizes of A and B the similarity of C, not with the union of A and B, but with the union of sets A' and B' which are similar to A and B, respectively, and disjoint. It follows from the following two exercises that such sets will always exist.

EXERCISE 6. 16: Show that the Cartesian product of a set A and a one-element set is similar to A.

EXERCISE 6. 17: Show that, for any sets A, B, if $a \neq b$, then $A \times \{a\}$ and $B \times \{b\}$ are disjoint.

The equivalence of the proposed functional criterion with the corresponding numerical criterion with respect to finite sets will be a direct consequence of the following lemma.

LEMMA 6. 18: If A, B are disjoint finite sets, then $\#(A \cup B) = \#(A) + \#(B)$.

Proof: Given that every finite set has a natural number as its image under $\#$, the lemma can be reformulated as a universal claim about pairs of natural numbers: For all natural numbers x, y, if A and B are disjoint sets such that $\#(A) = x$, $\#(B) = y$, then $\#(A \cup B) = x + y$. This, in turn, can be reformulated as the claim that for every natural number x the following holds: for every natural number y, if A and B are disjoint sets such that $\#(A) = x$, $\#(B) = y$, then $\#(A \cup B) = x + y$. Let m be an arbitrary natural number. We need to show that, for every natural number y, if A and B are disjoint sets such that $\#(A) = m$, $\#(B) = y$, then $\#(A \cup B) = m + y$. We establish this claim by induction on y.

Base ($y = 0$): Let A and B be disjoint sets such that $\#(A) = m$, $\#(B) = 0$. We have to show that $\#(A \cup B) = m + 0 = m$. Since $\#(B) = 0$, we have that B is $\emptyset$. For the counting sequence of 0 is $\emptyset$, and no other set is similar to $\emptyset$. Hence $A \cup B = A \cup \emptyset = A$. Therefore $\#(A \cup B) = \#(A) = m$, as desired.

Inductive Step: We have to show that, for every natural number y, if for all disjoint sets A, B such that $\#(A) = m$, $\#(B) = y$ we have that $\#(A \cup B) = m + y$, then for all disjoint sets A, B such that $\#(A) = m$, $\#(B) = y + 1$ we have that $\#(A \cup B) = m + (y + 1)$. Let n be a natural number. We assume (IH) that if A, B are disjoint sets such that $\#(A) = m$, $\#(B) = n$, then $\#(A \cup B) = m + n$. We need to show that it follows from this that if

A, B are disjoint sets such that $\#(A) = m$, $\#(B) = n + 1$, then $\#(A \cup B) = m + (n + 1)$. Let *A, B* be disjoint sets such that $\#(A) = m$, $\#(B) = n + 1$. We have to show that $A \cup B \sim \{1,\ldots, m + (n + 1)\}$. We have that $B \sim \{1,\ldots, n + 1\}$. Therefore, by Exercise 6. 3, if $b \in B$, we have that $B - \{b\} \sim \{1,\ldots, n\}$, i.e. $\#(B - \{b\}) = n$. By IH, we have that $\#(A \cup (B - \{b\})) = m + n$, i.e. $A \cup (B - \{b\}) \sim \{1,\ldots, m + n\}$. Notice also that $\{b\} \sim \{m + (n + 1)\}$. But we have that $A \cup B$ is $(A \cup (B - \{b\})) \cup \{b\}$, and $A \cup (B - \{b\})$ and $\{b\}$ are disjoint. Similarly $\{1,\ldots, m + (n + 1)\}$ is $\{1,\ldots, m + n\} \cup \{m + (n + 1)\}$, and $\{1,\ldots, m + n\}$ and $\{m + (n + 1)\}$ are disjoint. Hence, by Exercise 6. 2, it follows that $A \cup B \sim \{1,\ldots, m + (n + 1)\}$, as desired. ∎

We can now show that our functional criterion for the size of *C* to be the sum of the sizes of *A* and *B* is equivalent to the corresponding numerical criterion when *A, B* and *C* are finite sets.

LEMMA 6. 19: If *A, B, C* are finite sets, then $\#(A) + \#(B) = \#(C)$ if and only if there are disjoint sets *A', B'* such that $A \sim A'$, $B \sim B'$ and $A' \cup B' \sim C$.

Proof: Let *A', B'* be disjoint sets such that $A \sim A'$, $B \sim B'$. We argue as follows:

$\#(A) + \#(B) = \#(C)$

⇕ (by Lemma 6. 10)

$\#(A') + \#(B') = \#(C)$

⇕ (by Lemma 6. 18)

$\#(A' \cup B') = \#(C)$

⇕ (by Lemma 6. 10)

$A' \cup B' \sim C$ ∎

iv. Multiplication

Let's go back to the ice-cream parlor. Suppose you want to establish now that the number of customers is the number of ice-cream flavors times the number of toppings. One way to do this would be to determine how many customers, flavors and toppings you have, multiply the number of flavors by the number of toppings and check that the number you get equals the number of customers. But you could also take a different approach. Suppose that you could distribute ice cream and toppings among the customers in such a way that everyone gets exactly one flavor and exactly one topping, every flavor-topping combination is used, and none is repeated. You would not learn from this how many customers, flavors or toppings you have, but you would still be able to conclude that the number of customers is the number of flavors times the number of toppings.

The second procedure in this illustration suggests a functional criterion for whether the size of a set C is the product of the sizes of sets A and B—namely whether there is a one-to-one correspondence between C and the Cartesian product of A and B. The equivalence of this criterion with the corresponding numerical criterion with respect to finite sets is a direct consequence of the following lemma.

LEMMA 6. 20: If A and B are finite sets, then $\#(A \times B) = \#(A) \cdot \#(B)$

Proof: As with Lemma 6. 18, this result can be formulated as a claim about pairs of natural numbers: for all natural numbers x, y, if A, B are sets such that $\#(A) = x$, $\#(B) = y$, then $\#(A \times B) = x \cdot y$. We proceed as in the proof of Lemma 6. 18. Let m be an arbitrary natural number. We prove by induction on y that, for every natural number y, if A, B are sets such that $\#(A) = m$, $\#(B) = y$, then $\#(A \times B) = m \cdot y$.

Base ($y = 0$): Let A, B be sets such that $\#(A) = m$, $\#(B) = 0$. We have to show that $\#(A \times B) = m \cdot 0 = 0$. Since $\#(B) = 0$, we have, by the reasoning provided in the proof of Lemma 6. 18, that B is $\emptyset$. But $A \times \emptyset = \emptyset$ (see Exercise 1. 27 (4)). Therefore $\#(A \times B) = \#(\emptyset) = 0$, as desired.

Inductive Step: Let n be a natural number. We assume (IH) that if A, B are sets such that $\#(A) = m$, $\#(B) = n$, then $\#(A \times B) = m \cdot n$. We have to show that it follows from this that if A, B are sets such that $\#(A) = m$, $\#(B) = n + 1$, then $\#(A \times B) = m \cdot (n + 1)$. We shall make use of the fact that $m \cdot (n + 1) = (m \cdot n) + m$.

Let A, B be sets such that $\#(A) = m$, $\#(B) = n + 1$. We have to show that $A \times B \sim \{1,..., m \cdot (n + 1)\}$. We have that $B \sim \{1,..., n + 1\}$. Hence, by Exercise 6. 3, if $b \in B$, we have that $B - \{b\} \sim \{1,..., n\}$, i.e. $\#(B - \{b\}) = n$. By IH, we have that $\#(A \times (B - \{b\})) = m \cdot n$, i.e. $A \times (B - \{b\}) \sim \{1,..., m \cdot n\}$. Notice that $A \times B$ is $A \times (B - \{b\}) \cup A \times \{b\}$ (see Exercise 1. 27 (1)), and $A \times (B - \{b\})$ and $A \times \{b\}$ are disjoint. Similarly, $\{1,..., m \cdot (n + 1)\}$ is $\{1,..., m \cdot n\} \cup \{(m \cdot n) + 1,..., (m \cdot n) + m\}$, and $\{1,..., m \cdot n\}$ and $\{(m \cdot n) + 1,..., (m \cdot n) + m\}$ are disjoint. Hence, by Exercise 6. 2, to establish that $A \times B \sim \{1,..., m \cdot (n + 1)\}$ it will suffice to show that $A \times \{b\} \sim \{(m \cdot n) + 1,..., (m \cdot n) + m\}$. This is left as an exercise. ∎

EXERCISE 6. 21: Show that if $\#(A) = m$, then $A \times \{b\} \sim \{(m \cdot n) + 1,..., (m \cdot n) + m\}$.

We can now show that the two criteria for whether the size of C is the product of the sizes of A and B are equivalent with respect to finite sets.

LEMMA 6. 22: If A, B and C are finite sets, then $\#(A) \cdot \#(B) = \#(C)$ if and only if $A \times B \sim C$.

Proof: Substituting from Lemma 6. 20, we get $\#(A) \cdot \#(B) = \#(C)$ if and only if $\#(A \times B) = \#(C)$. And from Lemma 6. 10 we get $\#(A \times B) = \#(C)$ if and only if $A \times B \sim C$, as desired. ■

v.   Exponentiation

Let's consider the ice-cream parlor one more time. Suppose that you want to show that the number of customers is the number of toppings raised to the power of the number of ice-cream flavors. One way to do this would be to determine how many customers, flavors and toppings you have, raise the number of toppings to the number of flavors and check that the number you get equals the number of customers. But you could also take a different approach. Suppose that you could distribute ice cream among the customers in such a way that everyone gets exactly one scoop of each flavor, each scoop with a topping, and every way of assigning toppings to flavors is used and none is repeated. You would not learn from this how many customers, flavors or toppings you have, but you would still be able to conclude that the number of customers is the number of toppings raised to the number of flavors.

Notice that if you follow the second procedure, the combination that each customer gets corresponds to a different function from the set of flavors to the set of toppings. This suggests a functional criterion for whether the size of a set C is the size of a set B raised to the power of the size of a set A—namely whether there is a one-to-one correspondence between C and the set $^A B$ of functions from A to B. The equivalence of this criterion with the corresponding numerical criterion with respect to finite sets is a direct consequence of the following lemma.

LEMMA 6. 23: If A and B are finite sets, then $\#(^A B) = \#(B)^{\#(A)}$.

Proof: As with Lemma 6. 18 and Lemma 6. 20, we can formulate this result as a claim about pairs of natural numbers: for all natural numbers x, y, if A, B are sets such that $\#(A) = x$, $\#(B) = y$, then $\#(^A B) = y^x$. We proceed as in the proofs of Lemma 6. 18 and Lemma 6. 20. Let n be a natural number. We prove by induction on x that for every natural number x, if A, B are sets such that $\#(A) = x$, $\#(B) = n$, then $\#(^A B) = n^x$.

Base ($x = 0$): Let A, B be sets such that $\#(B) = n$, $\#(A) = 0$. We have to show that $\#(^A B) = n^0 = 1$. Since $\#(A) = 0$, we have, by the reasoning provided in the proof of Lemma 6. 18, that A is $\emptyset$. From Lemma 1. 50, we know that $^{\emptyset}B = \{\emptyset\}$. We also have that $\{\emptyset\} \sim \{1\}$. Therefore $\#(^{A}B) = 1$, as desired.

Inductive Step: Let m be a natural number. We assume (IH) that if A, B are sets such that $\#(A) = m$, $\#(B) = n$, then $\#(^{A}B) = n^{m}$. We want to show that it follows from this that if A, B are sets such that $\#(A) = m + 1$, $\#(B) = n$, then $\#(^{A}B) = n^{m+1}$. We shall use the fact that $n^{m+1} = n^{m} \cdot n = ((n-1) \cdot n^{m}) + n^{m}$.

Let A, B be sets such that $\#(A) = m + 1$, $\#(B) = n$. We have to show that $^{A}B \sim \{1,..., n^{m+1}\}$. We have that $A \sim \{1,..., m + 1\}$. Therefore, by Exercise 6. 3, if $a \in A$, we have that $A - \{a\} \sim \{1,..., m\}$, i.e. $\#(A - \{a\}) = m$. By IH, we have that $\#(^{A-\{a\}}B) = n^{m}$, i.e. $^{A-\{a\}}B \sim \{1,..., n^{m}\}$. We also have that $B \sim \{1,..., n\}$. Let F be a one-to-one correspondence between $^{A-\{a\}}B$ and $\{1,..., n^{m}\}$, and let g be a one-to-one correspondence between B and $\{1,..., n\}$. We are going to use functions F and g to define a one-to-one correspondence F^* between ^{A}B and $\{1,..., n^{m+1}\}$, thus establishing the similarity of these sets. Bear in mind that the objects in the domain of F, and of the function F^* that we are going to define, are themselves functions, not all of which are one-to-one correspondences.

	$F(\phi \restriction A-\{a\}) = 1$	$F(\phi \restriction A-\{a\}) = 2$	$...$	$F(\phi \restriction A-\{a\}) = n^{m}$
$g(\phi(a))=1$	1	2	$...$	n^{m}
$g(\phi(a))=2$	$n^{m} + 1$	$n^{m} + 2$	$...$	$n^{m} + n^{m}$
$g(\phi(a))=3$	$2n^{m} + 1$	$2n^{m} + 2$	$...$	$2n^{m} + n^{m}$
$\vdots$	$\vdots$	$\vdots$		$\vdots$
$g(\phi(a))=n$	$(n-1)\,n^{m} + 1$	$(n-1)\,n^{m} + 2$	$...$	$(n-1)\,n^{m} + n^{m}$

Figure 10

We can present the intuitive idea behind the definition in terms of the table in Figure 10. Notice that the cells of the table contain all the elements of $\{1,..., n^{m+1}\}$, listed consecutively in ascending order without repetitions, from left to right and from top to bottom. Suppose we can define a function from ^{A}B to $\{1,..., n^{m+1}\}$ such that, for every $\phi \in {}^{A}B$, the column occupied by the image of ϕ is determined by the value of $F(\phi \restriction A - \{a\})$, and the row that it occupies is determined by the value of $g(\phi(a))$, as entered across the top and on the left-hand side of the table; i.e. if $F(\phi \restriction A - \{a\}) = j$, $g(\phi(a)) = i$, the image of ϕ is the number in the i-th row and j-th column of the table. We can show that any function which satisfies this description will be a one-to-one correspondence between ^{A}B and $\{1,..., n^{m+1}\}$. Let Φ^* be such a function. We have to show (i) that Φ^* is a function from ^AB to $\{1,\ldots, n^{m+1}\}$, (ii) that Φ^* is one-to-one, and (iii) that the range of Φ^* is the whole of $\{1,\ldots, n^{m+1}\}$.

For (i), let $\phi \in {}^AB$. Then $\phi \restriction A - \{a\} \in {}^{A-\{a\}}B$. Hence, since F is a function from $^{A-\{a\}}B$ to $\{1,\ldots, n^m\}$, $\phi \restriction A - \{a\}$ will have a unique image under F in $\{1,\ldots, n^m\}$. Also, since $\phi(a) \in B$ and g is a function from B to $\{1,\ldots, n\}$, $\phi(a)$ will have a unique image under g in $\{1,\ldots, n\}$. Therefore Φ^* will pair ϕ with a unique column and row, and hence with a unique element of $\{1,\ldots, n^{m+1}\}$, as desired.

For (ii), notice that both F and g are one-to-one. Hence if $\phi, \psi \in {}^AB$, and $\phi \restriction A - \{a\} \neq \psi \restriction A - \{a\}$, then $F(\phi \restriction A - \{a\}) \neq F(\psi \restriction A - \{a\})$. And if $\phi(a) \neq \psi(a)$, then $g(\phi(a)) \neq g(\psi(a))$. But if ϕ and ψ are different functions, either $\phi \restriction A - \{a\} \neq \psi \restriction A - \{a\}$ or $\phi(a) \neq \psi(a)$. Therefore Φ^* will pair different elements of ^AB with different columns or with different rows, and hence with different elements of $\{1,\ldots, n^{m+1}\}$, as desired.

For (iii), notice that the range of F is the whole of $\{1,\ldots, n^m\}$, and the range of g is the whole of $\{1,\ldots, n\}$. Hence for every $p \in \{1,\ldots, n^m\}$, there is a function in $^{A-\{a\}}B$ having p as its image under F. And for every $q \in \{1,\ldots, n\}$, there is an element of B having q as its image under g. But for every $\psi \in {}^{A-\{a\}}B$, and every $b \in B$, there is a function ϕ in ^AB such that $\phi \restriction A - \{a\} = \psi$, $\phi(a) = b$; i.e. ϕ extends ψ by pairing a with b. Therefore every column-row combination, and hence every element of $\{1,\ldots, n^{m+1}\}$, will be paired by Φ^* with a function in ^AB, as desired.

To define a function that satisfies the description of Φ^*, we use the fact that the element of $\{1,\ldots, n^{m+1}\}$ which occupies the i-th row and the j-th column in the table can be expressed as $(i-1)\, n^m + j$. This suggest that the function $F^*(\phi) = (g(\phi(a)) - 1)\, n^m + F(\phi \restriction A - \{a\})$ will do the job. We can show that F^* is a one-to-one correspondence between ^AB and $\{1,\ldots, n^{m+1}\}$. The proof is left as an exercise. ∎

EXERCISE 6. 24: Show that F^*, in the proof of Lemma 6. 23, is a one-to-one correspondence between ^AB and $\{1,\ldots, n^{m+1}\}$.

LEMMA 6. 25: If A, B and C are finite sets, then $\#(B)^{\#(A)} = \#(C)$ if and only if $^AB \sim C$.

Proof: From Lemma 6. 23, we have that $\#(B)^{\#(A)} = \#(C)$ if and only if $\#(^AB) = \#(C)$. And from Lemma 6. 10 we have that $\#(^AB) = \#(C)$ if and only if $^AB \sim C$. ∎

5. Cardinality

In the preceding section we have shown that, for each basic type of claim concerning the sizes of finite sets, in addition to a numerical criterion we have a functional criterion, and that in each case the two criteria are equivalent. We have also indicated that, whereas the numerical criteria can only be applied to finite sets, the functional criteria are in principle applicable to finite and infinite sets alike. Hence, if we introduce the notion of cardinality in such a way that the truth value of cardinality claims is determined by the functional criteria for size claims, claims about the cardinality of finite sets will have the same truth value as the corresponding claims concerning their size, but we will be able to apply the same criteria to determine the truth value of claims concerning the cardinality of infinite sets.

We introduce the notion of cardinality by postulating a domain of objects and a pairing of each (finite or infinite) set X with a unique object in this domain—the cardinality of X, written *Card X*. We shall refer to the cardinalities of sets as *cardinals*. We make no assumptions about the identity of cardinals. We simply stipulate that the pairing of sets with their cardinalities has to satisfy the following principle:

(1) For all sets X, Y, *Card X* = *Card Y* if and only if $X \sim Y$.

Notice that, since identity is an equivalence relation, the pairing of sets with their cardinalities can only satisfy this principle if similarity is also an equivalence relation, but we have already established that this is so (see Exercise 6. 1).

Now we define a binary relation $\leq$ in the cardinals as follows:

(2) For all cardinals κ, λ, $\kappa \leq \lambda$ if and only if $K \preceq L$, where K and L are sets such that *Card K* = κ and *Card L* = λ.

Notice that (2) will only determine, for two cardinals κ, λ, whether or not $\kappa \leq \lambda$ if either all sets of cardinality κ are dominated by all sets of cardinality λ or no set of cardinality κ is dominated by any set of cardinality λ. But since, by (1), sets of the same cardinality are similar to each other, it follows from Exercise 6. 12 that this condition holds.

Next, we define three binary functions in the cardinals as follows:

(3) For all cardinals κ, λ, $\kappa + \lambda$ = *Card* $(K \cup L)$, where K and L are disjoint sets such that *Card K* = κ and *Card L* = λ.

(4) For all cardinals κ, λ, $\kappa \cdot \lambda = Card\ (K \times L)$, where K and L are sets such that $Card\ K = \kappa$ and $Card\ L = \lambda$.

(5) For all cardinals κ, λ, $\kappa^\lambda = Card\ {}^LK$, where K and L are sets such that $Card\ K = \kappa$ and $Card\ L = \lambda$.

Notice that (3) will single out a unique image for two cardinals κ, λ only if the union of two disjoint sets, one of cardinality κ, and one of cardinality λ, always has the same cardinality. But since sets of the same cardinality are similar to each other, this is a direct consequence of Exercise 6. 2.

Likewise, (4) will single out a unique image for two cardinals κ and λ only if the Cartesian product of two sets, one of cardinality κ, and one of cardinality λ, always has the same cardinality. This is a direct consequence of the following exercise.

EXERCISE 6. 26: Show that, for all sets X, X', Y, Y', such that $X \sim X'$ and $Y \sim Y'$, $X \times Y \sim X' \times Y'$.

Finally, (5) will single out a unique image for two cardinals κ and λ only if the set of functions from a set of cardinality λ to a set of cardinality κ always has the same cardinality. This follows immediately from the following lemma.

LEMMA 6. 27: For all sets X, X', Y, Y', such that $X \sim X'$ and $Y \sim Y'$, ${}^XY \sim {}^{X'}Y'$.

Proof: Let A, A', B, B' be sets such that $A \sim A'$, $B \sim B'$. We need to show that there is a one-to-one correspondence between the set of functions from A to B and the set of functions from A' to B'. Let f_A be a one-to-one correspondence between A and A', and let f_B be a one-to-one correspondence between B and B'. For every function f from A to B, we say, for the purposes of this proof, that a function f' from A' to B' is the *clone* of f just in case it has the following feature: if f pairs an element a of A with an element b of B, then f' pairs the image of a under f_A with the image of b under f_B. As the diagram in Figure 11 suggests, the image under the clone of f of an element a of A' is $f_B(f(f_A^{-1}(a)))$. In other words, the clone of f is the function $f_B \circ f \circ f_A^{-1}$. Let F be the function which pairs each function in ${}^AB$ with its clone; i.e., for every $\phi \in {}^AB$, $F(\phi) = f_B \circ \phi \circ f_A^{-1}$. We can show that F is a one-to-one correspondence between ${}^AB$ and ${}^{A'}B'$. This is left as an exercise. ∎

EXERCISE 6. 28: Show that F, in the proof of Lemma 6. 27, is a one-to-one correspondence between ${}^AB$ and ${}^{A'}B'$.

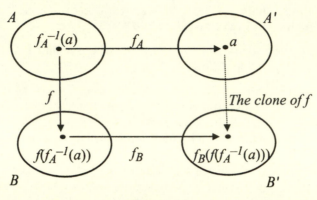

Figure 11

As we indicated above, we want the notion of cardinality to mirror the notion of size with respect to finite sets. This requires that every claim about the cardinality of finite sets has the same truth value as the corresponding claim about their size. Notice that we can conclude that size and cardinality are connected in this way from our results concerning the equivalence of numerical and functional criteria for size claims, since the truth value of each claim concerning the cardinality of finite sets is directly determined by the functional criterion associated with the corresponding size claim. Thus, Lemma 6. 10 entails that, for all finite sets X, Y, $\#(X) = \#(Y)$ if and only if *Card X = Card Y*. Lemma 6. 13 entails that, for all finite sets X, Y, $\#(X) \leq \#(Y)$ if and only if *Card X $\leq$ Card Y*. Lemma 6. 19 entails that, for all finite sets X, Y, Z, $\#(X) + \#(Y) = \#(Z)$ if and only if *Card X + Card Y = Card Z*. And Lemma 6. 22 and Lemma 6. 25 establish a similar connection between the multiplication and exponentiation of the sizes of finite sets and the multiplication and exponentiation of their cardinalities.

We can take advantage of this situation by stipulating that any numeral referring to the size of a finite set will also refer to its cardinality. If the notion of cardinality is not an extension of the notion of size, numerals will denote different things in different contexts, but given the parallelisms between the two notions that we have just highlighted, this ambiguity will be harmless.

6. Contextual Definition

Introducing the notion of cardinality amounts to expanding the language that we use to talk about sets by adding five new symbols to our vocabulary—the one-place function symbol "*Card*," the binary predicate "$\leq$," and the two-place function symbols representing cardinal addition, multiplication and exponentiation. (1)–(5) can be seen as defining these new symbols in terms of the old language. Notice that, on a traditional account of definition, (1)–(5) would be completely inadequate. On this account, a successful definition of the function symbol "*Card*" should enable us to identify, in terms of the old language, the object denoted by each functional term of the form "*Card X*," where "*X*" denotes a set. Likewise, a successful definition of the binary predicate "$\leq$" or of the function symbol for cardinal addition, multiplication or exponentiation should enable us to identify in terms of the old language the pairs in the relation represented by the predicate or in the function represented by each of the function symbols. Let's refer to definitions which satisfy this criterion as *explicit definitions*.

Clearly (1)–(5) don't satisfy this criterion. (1) doesn't enable us to identify the object denoted by, say, the functional term "*Card* $\{1, 2\}$" in terms of the old language. It only enables us to identify this object with other new functional terms, as, e.g., "*Card* {Mars, the Moon}." And since we can't use the old language to identify cardinals, (2)–(5) can't tell us how to identify in terms of the old language the relation and the functions that they purport to define. (1)–(5) are not explicit definitions.

(1)–(5) provide instead what is sometimes known as *contextual definitions* of the new symbols. What they do is to specify, in terms of the old language, truth conditions for sentences which can be formed with the new symbols. (1) doesn't identify with the old language the object denoted by a term of the form "*Card X*," but it specifies, in terms of the old language, necessary and sufficient conditions for the truth of sentences of the form "*Card X* = *Card Y*." Similarly, (2)–(5) don't identify in terms of the old language the pairs in the relation represented by "$\leq$," or in the functions represented by the function symbols for cardinal addition, multiplication and exponentiation. But they specify in terms of the old language necessary and sufficient conditions for the truth of sentences of the forms "$\kappa \leq \lambda$," "$\kappa + \lambda = \mu$," "$\kappa \cdot \lambda = \mu$" and "$\kappa^\lambda = \mu$," where "$\kappa$," "$\lambda$" and "$\mu$" denote cardinals.

This is not the place to discuss the status of contextual definitions. But it should be pointed out that none of the basic notions that we have introduced in this book has been defined explicitly. Thus, the principles with which we introduced the notion of set in Chapter 1 do not enable us to identify, in terms of the old language, the object to which we are referring, say, with the term "the set of planets." All they do is to specify in terms of the old language truth conditions for sentences concerning these objects. The same goes for our definition of ordered tuple, and for our definitions of formal languages in Chapters 2 and 3.

Once we have expanded our language with a contextual definition of a new symbol, we can use the expanded language to provide explicit definitions of other symbols. Thus, having defined the predicate "$\in$" contextually, we go on to define "$\subseteq$" explicitly in terms of it, and having defined the function symbol "*Card*" contextually, we can use it to define explicitly the individual constant "0," in its new use, as denoting *Card* $\varnothing$. An extraordinary fact about set theory is that, once we have provided a suitable contextual definition of set and set membership, we can use these notions to provide explicit definitions of every other notion that we have introduced contextually, and, in fact, of all the basic notions of classical mathematics, including all the number systems that we are treating as given.

We can use the notion of ordered pair to illustrate this phenomenon. Ordered pairs can be defined explicitly in set-theoretic terms as follows: for all objects x, y, $\langle x, y \rangle = \{\{x\}, \{x, y\}\}$. By defining ordered pairs in this way, we ascribe to them all the features that we want them to have. For it follows from this definition that two ordered pairs are different just in case they have different first members or different second members, given that, as the following exercise shows, the sets in terms of which ordered pairs have been defined have the corresponding property.

EXERCISE 6. 29: Show that, for all objects x, y, w, z, $\{\{x\}, \{x, y\}\} = \{\{w\}, \{w, z\}\}$ if and only if $x = w$ and $y = z$.

Notice, however, that this definition would also ascribe to ordered pairs properties that we didn't intend them to have. Thus, e.g., it turns out now that the ordered pair $\langle x, y \rangle$ has the set $\{x, y\}$ as an element. Nevertheless, for practical purposes, this definition of ordered pair would be entirely satisfactory.

Similar set-theoretic definitions can be provided for the notion of natural number, integer, rational number, real number, and even cardinal, as well as the standard relations and operations in these domains. Thus, an explicit definition of cardinality in set-theoretic terms singles out a set as the object denoted by each term of the form "*Card X*," in such a way that (1) comes out true. Then the predicate "$\leq$" and the function symbols for cardinal addition, multiplication and exponentiation can be interpreted with a set-theoretic relation and three set-theoretic functions in the domain of sets playing the role of cardinals, in such a way that (2)–(5) also come out true.

That so many notions can be explicitly defined in set-theoretic terms is no doubt an extremely important fact, which justifies the "foundational" status that set theory enjoys within mathematics. Nevertheless, it is by no means clear that an explicit set-theoretic definition of ordered pairs, rational numbers or cardinals comes closer to revealing "what these objects really are" than the corresponding contextual definition.

7. Continuities

We know that claims about the cardinalities of finite sets have the same truth values as the corresponding claims about their images under #. Hence all the features of the ordering, addition, multiplication and exponentiation of natural numbers carry over to the ordering, addition, multiplication and exponentiation of finite cardinals (a cardinal is *finite* if it is the cardinality of a finite set, and *infinite* if it is the cardinality of an infinite set). In this section we are going to see that some of these features are exhibited by the ordering, addition, multiplication and exponentiation of all cardinals.

Let's consider first the relation $\leq$. It follows from Lemma 6. 13, that $\leq$, defined on the finite cardinals, is a linear (partial) ordering, with 0 (i.e. *Card* Ø) as minimal element and with no maximal element. We begin to characterize $\leq$ as a relation in all the cardinals by showing that it is a partial ordering of them. Reflexivity and transitivity are straightforward, and left as exercises.

EXERCISE 6. 30: Show that for every cardinal κ, $\kappa \leq \kappa$.

Hint: To prove a claim of the form $\kappa \leq \lambda$, establish the corresponding claim about domination.

EXERCISE 6. 31: Show that for all cardinals κ, λ, μ, if $\kappa \leq \lambda$ and $\lambda \leq \mu$, then $\kappa \leq \mu$.

The antisymmetry of $\leq$ is a much more involved result. It is a corollary of the following theorem.

SCHRÖDER-BERNSTEIN THEOREM: For all sets X, Y, if $X \preceq Y$ and $Y \preceq X$, then $X \sim Y$.

We shall prove the Schröder-Bernstein Theorem by showing how, using an arbitrary one-to-one function from a set A to a set B, and an arbitrary one-to-one function from B to A, we can define a one-to-one correspondence between A and B. We can present the intuitive idea behind the procedure with an example. Consider the set $\mathbf{Z}^+$ of the positive integers, and the set $\mathbf{Z}^-$ of the negative integers. Let f be the function pairing each positive integer x with $-x-1$, and g the function pairing each negative integer x with $2-x$. f is a one-to-one function from $\mathbf{Z}^+$ to $\mathbf{Z}^-$, and g is a one-to-one function from $\mathbf{Z}^-$ to $\mathbf{Z}^+$. The patterns of pairings that f and g generate are represented by the diagram in Figure 12.

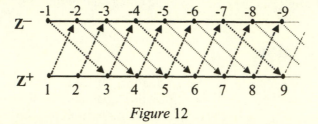

Figure 12

Suppose that we want to define a one-to-one correspondence h between $\mathbf{Z}^+$ and $\mathbf{Z}^-$ pairing each element of $\mathbf{Z}^+$ either with its image under f or with its image under g^{-1}. Notice that in some cases f is the only function we can use for this purpose. 1 and 2 will have to be paired by h with their images under f, since they have no image under g^{-1}. But these pairings force us to use f for other positive integers as well. 4 and 5 will also have to be paired by h with their images under f, since, if h paired them with their images under g^{-1}, h wouldn't be one-to-one. These pairings, in turn, force us to use f for 7 and 8 as well, since, again, otherwise h wouldn't be one-to-one. Notice that there is a pattern to this sequence of forced choices. The positive integers which have to be paired by h with their images under f are (i) those which are not in the range of g (1 and 2) and (ii) those which are the images under g of the images under f of positive integers which have already been paired by h with their images under f (4 is $g(f(1))$, 5 is $g(f(2))$, 7 is $g(f(4))$, 8 is $g(f(5))$, etc.). If we let h pair these positive integers with their images under f, and all the others with their images under g^{-1}, the pairings generated by h will follow the pattern represented by the diagram in Figure 13. The proof of the Schröder-Bernstein Theorem is based on the idea that any function that we define according to this procedure will be a one-to-one correspondence.

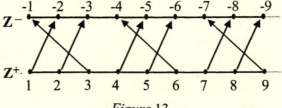

Figure 13

Proof of the Schröder-Bernstein Theorem: Let A, B be sets such that $A \preceq B$ and $B \preceq A$, and let f be a one-to-one function from A to B and g a one-to-one function from B to A. Our goal is to use f and g^{-1} to define a one-to-one correspondence h between A and B, following the procedure that we used in the example.

For every positive integer n, we define by recursion the set A_n, as the image of n under the unique function satisfying the following conditions:

A_1 is the difference of A and the range of g.

For every positive integer n, A_{n+1} is the range of $(g \circ f) \restriction A_n$.

As we are about to see, the elements of these sets are the elements of A which our one-to-one correspondence will pair with their images under f.

Now let A^* be the collection containing all the sets in the sequence A_1, A_2, A_3,... We define h as follows:

$$\text{For every } x \in A, \ h(x) = \begin{cases} f(x) \text{ if } x \in \bigcup A^*, \\ g^{-1}(x) \text{ otherwise.} \end{cases}$$

To complete the proof, it will suffice to show (i) that h is a function from A to B, (ii) that h is one-to-one, and (iii) that the range of h is the whole of B.

For (i), notice that, since every element of $\bigcup A^*$ is in the domain of f, and every element of $A - \bigcup A^*$ is in the domain of g^{-1}, every element of A has an image under h, and since f and g^{-1} are both functions, this image will be unique.

For (ii), notice, first, that, since f is one-to-one, the images under h of the elements of $\bigcup A^*$ will be distinct from each other, and, since g^{-1} is one-to-one, the same goes for the elements of A outside $\bigcup A^*$. Hence, to show that h is one-to-one, it will suffice to show that the image under h of each element of $\bigcup A^*$ is different from the image under h of every element of A outside $\bigcup A^*$. Let $a \in \bigcup A^*$, and let $b \in A - \bigcup A^*$. We need to show that $h(a) \neq h(b)$. Assume, towards a contradiction, that $h(a) = h(b)$. We have, by the definition of h, that $h(a) = f(a)$, and $h(b) = g^{-1}(b)$. It follows that $f(a) = g^{-1}(b)$. Since $a \in \bigcup A^*$, we have, by the definition of A_n, that $g(f(a)) \in \bigcup A^*$. It follows that $g(g^{-1}(b)) \in \bigcup A^*$. But we have that $g(g^{-1}(b))$ is b (see Exercise 1. 43). Therefore $b \in \bigcup A^*$, which contradicts our assumption.

For (iii), it will suffice to show that any element of B which is not the image under h of any element of $\bigcup A^*$ is the image under h of an element of A outside $\bigcup A^*$. Let b be an element of B which is not the image under h of any element of $\bigcup A^*$. We want to show that there is an element of A

outside $\bigcup A^*$ whose image under h is b. For this, it will suffice to show that $g(b) \notin \bigcup A^*$. For then, by the definition of h, $h(g(b)) = g^{-1}(g(b))$. But then, since $g^{-1}(g(b))$ is b (see Exercise 1. 43), b will be the image under h of $g(b)$.

To show that $g(b) \notin \bigcup A^*$, we show, by induction on the positive integers, that, for every positive integer n, $g(b) \notin A_n$. For the base, notice that, since the elements of A_1 are outside the range of g, $g(b)$ can't be in A_1. For the inductive step, we assume (IH) that $g(b) \notin A_n$, and try to show that it follows from this that $g(b) \notin A_{n+1}$. Assume, towards a contradiction, that $g(b) \in A_{n+1}$. Then, by the definition of A_{n+1}, there is an $a \in A_n$ such that $g(f(a)) = g(b)$. Then, since g is one-to-one, $f(a) = b$, and, since $a \in \bigcup A^*$, we have, by the definition of h, that $h(a) = f(a) = b$, which contradicts the assumption that b is not the image under h of any element of $\bigcup A^*$. ∎

The following exercises express results to the effect that some of the features of the addition, multiplication and exponentiation of natural numbers, and hence of finite cardinals, are also exhibited by the corresponding operations on all cardinals.

EXERCISE 6. 32: Show that the following claims hold for all cardinals κ, λ, μ:
  (1) $\kappa + \lambda = \lambda + \kappa$
  (2) $\kappa + (\lambda + \mu) = (\kappa + \lambda) + \mu$
  (3) If $\kappa \leq \lambda$, then $\kappa + \mu \leq \lambda + \mu$
  (4) $\kappa + 0 = 0 + \kappa = \kappa$

EXERCISE 6. 33: Show that the following claims hold for all cardinals κ, λ, μ:
  (1) $\kappa \cdot \lambda = \lambda \cdot \kappa$
  (2) $\kappa \cdot (\lambda \cdot \mu) = (\kappa \cdot \lambda) \cdot \mu$
  (3) $\kappa \cdot (\lambda + \mu) = (\kappa \cdot \lambda) + (\kappa \cdot \mu)$
  (4) If $\kappa \leq \lambda$, then $\kappa \cdot \mu \leq \lambda \cdot \mu$
  (5) $\kappa \cdot 0 = 0 \cdot \kappa = 0$
  (6) $\kappa \cdot 1 = 1 \cdot \kappa = \kappa$
  (7) $\kappa + \kappa = 2 \cdot \kappa$

EXERCISE 6. 34: Show that the following claims hold for all cardinals κ, λ, μ:
  (1) $\kappa^{\lambda + \mu} = \kappa^\lambda \cdot \kappa^\mu$
  (2) $(\kappa \cdot \lambda)^\mu = \kappa^\mu \cdot \lambda^\mu$
  (3) $(\kappa^\lambda)^\mu = \kappa^{\lambda \cdot \mu}$
  (4) If $\kappa \leq \lambda$, then $\kappa^\mu \leq \lambda^\mu$
  (5) If $\kappa \leq \lambda$ and either $\kappa \neq 0$ or $\mu \neq 0$, then $\mu^\kappa \leq \mu^\lambda$

(6) $\kappa^0 = 1$
(7) If $\kappa \neq 0$, then $0^\kappa = 0$

The next four exercises establish that infinite cardinals are related to finite cardinals as we would expect.

EXERCISE 6. 35: Show that, for every finite cardinal n, and every infinite cardinal κ, $n < \kappa$.

Hint: To show that $n \leq \kappa$, prove by induction on n that, if X is an infinite set, then there is a one-to-one function from the counting sequence of n to X.

EXERCISE 6. 36: Show that, for all finite cardinals m, n, $m + n$, $m \cdot n$ and m^n are finite cardinals.

EXERCISE 6. 37: Show that, for every cardinal κ and every infinite cardinal λ, $\kappa + \lambda$ and $\lambda + \kappa$ are infinite.

EXERCISE 6. 38: Show that, for every infinite cardinal κ, and every cardinal $\lambda \neq 0$, $\kappa \cdot \lambda$, $\lambda \cdot \kappa$, and κ^λ are infinite.

8. Denumerable Sets

We turn now to the task of comparing the cardinalities of specific infinite sets. We shall use the set $\mathbf{Z}^+$ of the positive integers as a reference point, asking how the cardinalities of other infinite sets are related to the cardinality of $\mathbf{Z}^+$. This section is devoted to a series of results to the effect that a wide variety of infinite sets have the same cardinality as $\mathbf{Z}^+$. We shall refer to the cardinality of $\mathbf{Z}^+$ as $\aleph_0$ ("$\aleph$" is aleph, the first letter of the Hebrew alphabet).

DEFINITION: A set A is *denumerable* just in case $A \sim \mathbf{Z}^+$, i.e. just in case *Card* $A = \aleph_0$.

First we shall consider several results to the effect that the set of positive integers has the same cardinality as some of its proper subsets.

EXERCISE 6. 39: Show that the cardinality of the set $\mathbf{Z}^+ - \{1, 2\}$ is $\aleph_0$.

Hint: Find a one-to-one correspondence between $\mathbf{Z}^+ - \{1, 2\}$ and $\mathbf{Z}^+$.

EXERCISE 6. 40: Show that the cardinality of the set of odd positive integers is $\aleph_0$.

EXERCISE 6. 41: Show that the cardinality of the set of perfect squares is $\aleph_0$.

We consider now sets having $\mathbf{Z}^+$ as a proper subset, and show that many of them also have the same cardinality as $\mathbf{Z}^+$.

EXERCISE 6. 42: Show that the cardinality of ω is $\aleph_0$.

EXERCISE 6. 43: Show that the union of the set of positive integers and the set of days of the week has cardinality $\aleph_0$.

LEMMA 6. 44: The cardinality of the set $\mathbf{Z}$ of the integers is $\aleph_0$.

Proof: We need to find a one-to-one correspondence between $\mathbf{Z}^+$ and $\mathbf{Z}$. Consider the function which assigns integers to positive integers taking the positive integers in increasing order and the integers in increasing order of absolute value, starting with 0 and then alternating between negative and positive integers, i.e. in the sequence 0, −1, 1, −2, 2, −3, 3,.... We can define this function as follows:

$$\text{For every positive integer } n, \ f(n) = \begin{cases} \dfrac{-n}{2} & \text{if } n \text{ is even,} \\ \dfrac{n-1}{2} & \text{if } n \text{ is odd.} \end{cases}$$

f is a one-to-one correspondence between $\mathbf{Z}^+$ and $\mathbf{Z}$. ∎

The direct procedure for establishing that a set A is dominated by $\mathbf{Z}^+$ is to show that there is a one-to-one function from A to $\mathbf{Z}^+$. The first part of the next result gives us an alternative procedure for attaining this goal.

LEMMA 6. 45: (*a*) For every set X, if there is a function from $\mathbf{Z}^+$ to X with the whole of X as its range, then $X \preceq \mathbf{Z}^+$. (*b*) For every nonempty set X, if $X \preceq \mathbf{Z}^+$, then there is a function from $\mathbf{Z}^+$ to X with the whole of X as its range.

Proof: For (*a*), let A be a set, and let f be a function from $\mathbf{Z}^+$ to A with the whole of A as its range. To show that $A \preceq \mathbf{Z}^+$, we need to find a one-to-one function from A to $\mathbf{Z}^+$. For every $x \in A$, let $g(x) = n$ if and only if $f(n) = x$ and for every $m \in \mathbf{Z}^+$, if $f(m) = x$, then $n \leq m$; i.e. $g(x)$ is the least of the positive integers paired with x by f. We can show that g is a one-to-one function from A to $\mathbf{Z}^+$ (this is left as an exercise), as desired.

For (*b*), let A be a nonempty set dominated by $\mathbf{Z}^+$, and let f be a one-to-one function from A to $\mathbf{Z}^+$. We need to find a function from $\mathbf{Z}^+$ to A with the whole of A as its range. Let a be an element of A. For every $n \in \mathbf{Z}^+$, let

$$g(n) = \begin{cases} f^{-1}(n) & \text{if } n \text{ is in the range of } f, \\ a & \text{otherwise.} \end{cases}$$

g is a function from $\mathbf{Z}^+$ to A, since every positive integer has an image under g in A. And since the range of f^{-1} is the whole of A, the same goes for g, as desired. ∎

EXERCISE 6. 46: Show that the function g in the proof of Lemma 6. 45 (a) is a one-to-one function from A to $\mathbf{Z}^+$.

EXERCISE 6. 47: Show that, for every set X, if there is a function from a denumerable set to X with the whole of X as its range, then $X \preceq \mathbf{Z}^+$.

Hint: Use Lemma 6. 45 (a).

Lemma 6. 45 (a) and Exercise 6. 47 provide an alternative strategy for showing that a set is dominated by $\mathbf{Z}^+$, and hence that its cardinality is at most $\aleph_0$. We use this strategy in the proof of the following theorem.

THEOREM 6. 48: The cardinality of the set $\mathbf{Q}^+$ of positive rational numbers is $\aleph_0$.

Proof: We want to show that $\mathbf{Q}^+$ is similar to $\mathbf{Z}^+$. By the Schröder-Bernstein Theorem, it will suffice to show that these two sets dominate each other.

Notice first that since every positive integer is a positive rational number, it follows that $\mathbf{Z}^+ \preceq \mathbf{Q}^+$ (see Exercise 6. 11).

$$\langle 1, 1 \rangle \ \langle 1, 2 \rangle \ \langle 1, 3 \rangle \ \langle 1, 4 \rangle \quad \cdots$$

$$\langle 2, 1 \rangle \ \langle 2, 2 \rangle \ \langle 2, 3 \rangle$$

$$\langle 3, 1 \rangle \ \langle 3, 2 \rangle$$

$$\langle 4, 1 \rangle$$

$$\vdots$$

Figure 14

To show that $\mathbf{Q}^+ \preceq \mathbf{Z}^+$, by Lemma 6. 45, it will suffice to find a function from $\mathbf{Z}^+$ to $\mathbf{Q}^+$ whose range is the whole of $\mathbf{Q}^+$. To introduce our procedure for defining this function, notice that the elements of $\mathbf{Q}^+$ can be represented by ordered pairs of positive integers (taking the elements of each pair as the numerator and denominator of a fraction), and these pairs can be arranged in the table in Figure 14. The cells of the table contain all the ordered pairs of positive integers, i.e. all the elements of $\mathbf{Z}^+ \times \mathbf{Z}^+$. Hence if we find a way of assigning a different positive integer to each pair in the table, we will be able to define a function from $\mathbf{Z}^+$ to $\mathbf{Z}^+ \times \mathbf{Z}^+$ with the whole of $\mathbf{Z}^+ \times \mathbf{Z}^+$ as its range. One way to do this is to cover the table in diagonals as indicated in the diagram of Figure 15. We just need to find a function which pairs elements of $\mathbf{Z}^+$ with elements of $\mathbf{Z}^+ \times \mathbf{Z}^+$ in this way. We define by recursion the function f from $\mathbf{Z}^+$ to $\mathbf{Z}^+ \times \mathbf{Z}^+$, as the unique function satisfying the following conditions:

$f(1) = \langle 1, 1 \rangle$.

For every $n \in \mathbf{Z}^+$,

$$f(n+1) = \begin{cases} \langle p+1, q-1 \rangle \text{ if } f(n) = \langle p,q \rangle \text{ for some } q \neq 1, \\ \langle 1, p+1 \rangle \text{ if } f(n) = \langle p,1 \rangle. \end{cases}$$

Notice that the first case of the second condition makes us move one step down a diagonal. The second case applies when we have reached the end of a diagonal, making us jump to the next. We can now define in terms of f a function f^* from $\mathbf{Z}^+$ to $\mathbf{Q}^+$. For every $n \in \mathbf{Z}^+$, $f^*(n) = p/q$ if and only if $f(n) = \langle p, q \rangle$. It can be easily shown that the range of f^* is the whole of $\mathbf{Q}^+$ (this is left as an exercise), as desired.   ∎

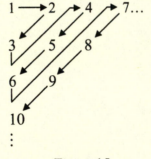

Figure 15

EXERCISE 6. 49: Show that the range of f^*, in the proof of Theorem 6. 48, is the whole of $\mathbf{Q}^+$. Show that f^* is not one-to-one.

EXERCISE 6. 50: Show that the cardinality of the set $\mathbf{Q}$ of the rational numbers is $\aleph_0$.

Hint: You can use a modified version of the procedure that we have employed to establish Theorem 6. 48.

EXERCISE 6. 51: Show that, for every finite cardinal n, $n + \aleph_0 = \aleph_0$.

Hint: Find a one-to-one correspondence between $\mathbf{Z}^+$ and $\mathbf{Z}^+ \cup (\{1,...,n\} \times \{a\})$.

EXERCISE 6. 52: Show that, for every finite cardinal n other than 0, $n \cdot \aleph_0 = \aleph_0$.

Hint: Find a one-to-one correspondence between $\mathbf{Z}^+$ and $\{1,\ldots,n\} \times \mathbf{Z}^+$.

LEMMA 6. 53: $\aleph_0 + \aleph_0 = \aleph_0$.

Proof: We need to find two disjoint sets A, B of cardinality $\aleph_0$ such that $A \cup B \sim \mathbf{Z}^+$. We know (Exercise 6. 40) that the cardinality of the set of odd positive integers is $\aleph_0$. By the same reasoning we can establish that the cardinality of the set of even positive integers is $\aleph_0$. But these sets are disjoint, and their union is identical with, and hence similar to, $\mathbf{Z}^+$, as desired. ∎

EXERCISE 6. 54: Show that $\aleph_0 \cdot \aleph_0 = \aleph_0$.

Hint: You need to show that $\mathbf{Z}^+ \times \mathbf{Z}^+ \sim \mathbf{Z}^+$. You can use for this purpose the function f defined in the proof of Theorem 6. 48.

In the following two results, we use some of these principles of cardinal arithmetic to determine the cardinalities of sets.

LEMMA 6. 55: The union of two denumerable sets is denumerable.

Proof: Let A, B be sets such that *Card* A = *Card* $B = \aleph_0$. We need to show that *Card* $A \cup B = \aleph_0$, i.e. that $A \cup B \sim \mathbf{Z}^+$. By the Schröder-Bernstein Theorem, it will suffice to show (i) that $\mathbf{Z}^+ \preceq A \cup B$ and (ii) that $A \cup B \preceq \mathbf{Z}^+$.

For (i), notice that, since $A \subseteq A \cup B$, we have, by Exercise 6. 11, that $A \preceq A \cup B$. And since $A \sim \mathbf{Z}^+$, it follows by Exercise 6. 12 that $\mathbf{Z}^+ \preceq A \cup B$, as desired.

For (ii), we have from Exercise 6. 52 that $\{1, 2\} \times \mathbf{Z}^+ \sim \mathbf{Z}^+$. Hence it will suffice to show that $A \cup B \preceq \{1, 2\} \times \mathbf{Z}^+$. Let f_A be a one-to-one correspondence between $\mathbf{Z}^+$ and A, and let f_B be a one-to-one correspondence between $\mathbf{Z}^+$ and B. We now define a function F from $\{1, 2\} \times \mathbf{Z}^+$ to $A \cup B$ as follows:

$$\text{For every } \langle m, n \rangle \in \{1, 2\} \times \mathbf{Z}^+, \ F(\langle m, n \rangle) = \begin{cases} f_A(n) \text{ if } m = 1, \\ f_B(n) \text{ if } m = 2. \end{cases}$$

It is easy to verify that the range of F is the whole of $A \cup B$ (this is left as an exercise). Hence, by Exercise 6. 47, we have that $A \cup B \preceq \{1, 2\} \times \mathbf{Z}^+$, as desired. ∎

EXERCISE 6. 56: Show that the range of F in the proof of Lemma 6. 55 is the whole of $A \cup B$.

EXERCISE 6. 57: Show that the union of a finite collection of denumerable sets is denumerable.

Hint: Show by induction on n that if A is a collection of denumerable sets and $A \sim \{1,\ldots, n\}$, then $\bigcup A$ is denumerable. For the inductive clause use Lemma 6. 55.

DEFINITION: A set A is *countable* just in case $A \preceq Z^+$.

EXERCISE 6. 58: Show that the union of two countable sets is countable.

9. Diagonals

The results of the previous section may make the cardinality of infinite sets appear rather uninteresting. All infinite sets seem to have the same cardinality, and applying arithmetical operations to that cardinal always seems to yield the same cardinal again. As we are about to see, this impression is completely mistaken. There are infinite sets of many different cardinalities, and infinite cardinals form an enormously rich structure (sometimes known as Cantor's paradise) many aspects of which we are still trying to understand. In this section, we take our first steps in Cantor's paradise by showing that there are infinite sets whose cardinality is not $\aleph_0$. The method that Cantor discovered for establishing results to this effect is the cornerstone of the theory of cardinality. We apply it for the first time in the proof of the following theorem:

THEOREM 6. 59: The cardinality of the set $\Re$ of the real numbers is greater than $\aleph_0$.

Proof: We need to show that $Z^+ \prec \Re$. We have that $Z^+ \subseteq \Re$. Hence, by Exercise 6. 11, $Z^+ \preceq \Re$. Therefore all that remains to be shown is that $Z^+ \not\sim \Re$, i.e. that there isn't a one-to-one correspondence between Z^+ and $\Re$. We establish this by showing that for every function f from Z^+ to $\Re$, there is at least one real number outside the range of f.

Let f be a function from Z^+ to $\Re$. Our goal is to find a real number which is not the image under f of any positive integer. Let d^f be the real number represented by the following decimal expansion: $0.d^f_1 \, d^f_2 \, d^f_3\ldots$, where

$$d^f_n = \begin{cases} 6 \text{ if the } n\text{-th decimal of } f(n) \text{ is } 5, \\ 5 \text{ otherwise.} \end{cases}$$

It is easy to see that df is not the image under f of any positive integer. Thus suppose that the successive values of f are expressed by the following list of decimal expansions:

$$f(1) = \quad 458.\,\underline{7}\,3\,5\,6\,9\,2...$$
$$f(2) = \quad -2.8\,5\,\underline{7}\,2\,3\,9...$$
$$f(3) = \quad 0.2\,5\,0\,\underline{0}\,0\,0...$$
$$f(4) = 82736.3\,2\,3\,\underline{2}\,3\,2...$$
$$\vdots$$

Then the decimal expansion of df will start as follows: $0.5655...$. You can see that the decimal expansion of df will differ from the decimal expansion of $f(1)$ in the first decimal place, from the decimal expansion of $f(2)$ in the second, from the decimal expansion of $f(3)$ in the third.... In general, the decimal expansion of df will differ from the decimal expansion of $f(n)$ in the n-th decimal place; i.e. the decimal expansion of df will differ from the decimal expansion of the image under f of each positive integer in at least one decimal place. Therefore df won't be the image under f of any positive integer, as desired. ■

One could try to resist this proof with the following reasoning. We could "add df to the list of values of f," by defining a function that differs from f only in this respect, as, for example, the function $f*$ defined as follows:

For every positive integer n, $f*(n) = \begin{cases} d^f & \text{if } n=1, \\ f(n-1) & \text{otherwise.} \end{cases}$

Then the successive values of $f*$ will be expressed by the following list of decimal expansions:

$$f*(1) = \quad 0.\,\underline{5}\,6\,5\,5...$$
$$f*(2) = \quad 458.7\,\underline{3}\,5\,6\,9\,2...$$
$$f*(3) = \quad -2.8\,5\,7\,\underline{2}\,3\,9...$$
$$f*(4) = \quad 0.2\,5\,0\,0\,\underline{0}\,0...$$
$$f*(5) = 82736.3\,2\,3\,2\,3\,\underline{2}...$$
$$\vdots$$

Clearly df is the image under $f*$ of a positive integer (1). But this is of no consequence, as we can use the same procedure once more to find a real number $df*$ $(0.65555...)$ which is not the image under $f*$ of any positive integer, because its decimal expansion differs from the decimal expansion of $f*(n)$ in the n-th decimal place, thus showing that $f*$ doesn't have the whole of $\Re$ as its range either.

Notice also that for any function g from $\mathbf{Z}^+$ to $\mathfrak{R}$ we can generate, not just one, but infinitely many different real numbers which are not the image under g of any positive integer. Thus, e.g., for any natural number m, take the real number e^g represented by the following decimal expansion: $0.e^g_1 \, e^g_2 \, e^g_3...$, where, for every positive integer n,

$$e^g_n = \begin{cases} 6 \text{ if the } m+n\text{-th decimal of } g(n) \text{ is 5,} \\ 5 \text{ otherwise.} \end{cases}$$

It is easy to see that, for every positive integer n, e^g will differ from $g(n)$ in the $m + n$-th decimal place.

The form of reasoning exemplified by the proof of Theorem 6. 59 is known as *Cantor's diagonal argument* (notice that the decimal places of the values of f from which d^f differs form a diagonal). We have used it to establish that there is at least one set whose cardinality is greater than $\aleph_0$. Another application of Cantor's diagonal argument will show that for any given set A, there is another set whose cardinality is greater than that of A.

THEOREM 6. 60: For every set X, $X \prec \wp X$.

Proof: Let A be a set. For every $a \in A$, we have that $\{a\} \in \wp A$. Hence the function $f(x) = \{x\}$ is a one-to-one function from A to $\wp A$, which shows that $A \preceq \wp A$. Hence to show that $A \prec \wp A$, we only need to establish that $A \not\sim \wp A$, i.e. that there isn't a one-to-one correspondence between A and $\wp A$. We establish this by showing that, for every function f from A to $\wp A$, there is at least one subset of A (i.e. an element of $\wp A$) outside the range of f.

Let f be a function from A to $\wp A$. Let B_f be the subset of A defined as follows: For every $b \in A$, $b \in B_f$ if and only if $b \notin f(b)$. We have that, for every $a \in A$, B_f differs from $f(a)$ in at least one element, namely a itself. If $a \in f(a)$, then $a \notin B_f$, and if $a \notin f(a)$, then $a \in B_f$. Either way, $B_f \neq f(a)$. Hence B_f is an element of $\wp A$ which is different from the image under f of every element of A, i.e. B_f is not in the range of f, as desired. ∎

We know from Theorem 6. 59 that there are at least two different infinite cardinals. Theorem 6. 60 shows that there are infinitely many of them. In fact we can go beyond saying that *Card* $\wp A$ is greater than *Card A*. We can say "how much bigger" it is by representing the former as the result of applying a specific arithmetical operation on the latter, as expressed by the following theorem.

THEOREM 6. 61: For every set X, *Card* $\wp X = 2^{Card \, X}$.

Proof: Let A be a set. We need to find a one-to-one correspondence between $\wp\, A$ and $^A\{1, 2\}$. For every subset B of A, let the *characteristic function* of B be the function f_B from A to $\{1, 2\}$ which pairs every element of B with 1 and every other element of A with 2; i.e., for every $x \in A$,

$$f_B(x) = \begin{cases} 1 \text{ if } x \in B, \\ 2 \text{ otherwise.} \end{cases}$$

We can easily verify that the function pairing each subset of A with its characteristic function is a one-to-one correspondence between $\wp\, A$ and $^A\{1, 2\}$. This is left as an exercise. ∎

EXERCISE 6. 62: Show that the function pairing each subset of a set A with its characteristic function (see Theorem 6. 61) is a one-to-one correspondence between $\wp\, A$ and $^A\{1, 2\}$.

If κ and λ are cardinals such that $\kappa \leq \lambda$ and $\kappa \neq \lambda$, we say that κ is *less than* λ, or that λ is *greater than* κ, written $\kappa < \lambda$. The following result is a direct consequence of Theorem 6. 60 and Theorem 6. 61.

COROLLARY 6. 63: For every cardinal κ, $\kappa < 2^\kappa$.

It follows from Theorem 6. 61 that *Card* $\wp\, \mathbf{Z}^+ = 2^{\aleph_0}$. We show now that this is also the cardinality of other familiar sets.

THEOREM 6. 64: The set $[0, 1)$ of real numbers between 0 and 1 (including 0 and excluding 1) has cardinality $2^{\aleph_0}$.

Proof: We need to show that $[0, 1) \sim\, ^{\mathbf{Z}^+}\{1, 2\}$. By the Schröder-Bernstein Theorem, it will suffice to show (i) that $[0, 1) \preceq\, ^{\mathbf{Z}^+}\{1, 2\}$ and (ii) that $^{\mathbf{Z}^+}\{1, 2\} \preceq [0, 1)$.

For (i), we need to find a one-to-one function from $[0, 1)$ to $^{\mathbf{Z}^+}\{1, 2\}$—i.e. to pair each element of $[0, 1)$ with a different function from $\mathbf{Z}^+$ to $\{1, 2\}$. To understand the method that we are going to use to define this pairing, notice that tables like the one in Figure 16 can be used to represent infinite sequences of digits, and hence decimal expansions. Each row in the table will contain one 1 and nine 2's. Each row represents one decimal place, and each column one digit. The n-th decimal place of the decimal expansion represented by one of these tables will be the digit whose column contains the 1 in the n-th row. If we now assign positive integers to the cells in one of these tables, and we pair each positive integer with the number (1 or 2) in the cell to which it has been assigned, we obtain a function from $\mathbf{Z}^+$ to $\{1, 2\}$. If we assign positive integers to cells in a uniform way, different tables will generate different functions

from $\mathbf{Z}^+$ to $\{1, 2\}$. Hence, since each table represents a unique element
of $[0, 1)$, by pairing each table with the function that it generates in this
way, we will have paired each element of $[0, 1)$ with a different function
from $\mathbf{Z}^+$ to $\{1, 2\}$.

	0	1	2	3	4	5	6	7	8	9
1st decimal	2	2	2	1	2	2	2	2	2	2
2nd decimal	2	1	2	2	2	2	2	2	2	2
3rd decimal	2	2	2	2	2	2	2	2	1	2
$\vdots$	$\vdots$	$\vdots$	$\vdots$	$\vdots$	$\vdots$	$\vdots$	$\vdots$	$\vdots$	$\vdots$	$\vdots$

Figure 16

    To implement this strategy, we assign positive integers to the cells of a
table, taking the positive integers in ascending order and the cells from
left to right and top to bottom. We use the fact that for every positive
integer n there is a unique pair of positive integers d_n, r_n, with r_n less
than or equal to 10, such that $n = 10(d_n - 1) + r_n$. Thus, e.g., 325 is
$10(33 - 1) + 5$, 7 is $10(1 - 1) + 7$, and 60 is $10(6 - 1) + 10$. Now, for
every element of $[0, 1)$, let the *binary representation* of e be the function
f_e from $\mathbf{Z}^+$ to $\{1, 2\}$ defined as follows:

    For every positive integer n,

$$f_e(n) = \begin{cases} 1 \text{ if } r_n - 1 \text{ is the } d_n\text{-th decimal of } e, \\ 2 \text{ otherwise.} \end{cases}$$

Notice that the image under f_e of a positive integer n will be found in the
d_n-th row and the r_n-th column of the table. We can easily verify that the
function pairing each element of $[0, 1)$ with its binary representation is a
one-to-one function from $[0, 1)$ to $^{\mathbf{Z}^+}\{1, 2\}$. This is left as an exercise.

    For (ii), let f be a function from $\mathbf{Z}^+$ to $\{1, 2\}$. Let the *decimal repre-
sentative* of f be the real number whose whole part is 0, and whose n-th
decimal, for every n, is the image of n under f. It is easy to show that if
we pair each function from $\mathbf{Z}^+$ to $\{1, 2\}$ with its decimal representative
we get a one-to-one function from $^{\mathbf{Z}^+}\{1, 2\}$ to $[0, 1)$. This is left as an
exercise.   ∎

EXERCISE 6. 65: Show that the function pairing each element of $[0, 1)$
with its binary representation (as defined in the proof of Theorem 6. 64)
is a one-to-one function from $[0, 1)$ to $^{\mathbf{Z}^+}\{1, 2\}$. Explain why this function is not a one-to-one correspondence between $[0, 1)$ and $^{\mathbf{Z}^+}\{1, 2\}$.

EXERCISE 6. 66: Show that the function pairing each element of $Z^+\{1, 2\}$ with its decimal representative (as defined in the proof of Theorem 6. 64) is a one-to-one function from $Z^+\{1, 2\}$ to $[0, 1)$. Explain why this function is not a one-to-one correspondence between $Z^+\{1, 2\}$ and $[0, 1)$.

LEMMA 6. 67: $\aleph_0 \cdot 2^{\aleph_0} = 2^{\aleph_0}$.

Proof: By the antisymmetry of $\leq$, it will suffice to show (i) that $2^{\aleph_0} \leq \aleph_0 \cdot 2^{\aleph_0}$ and (ii) that $\aleph_0 \cdot 2^{\aleph_0} \leq 2^{\aleph_0}$.

For (i) we need to show that $\wp\, Z^+ \preceq Z^+ \times \wp\, Z^+$. This follows from the fact that the function $f(x) = \langle 1, x \rangle$ is a one-to-one function from $\wp\, Z^+$ to $Z^+ \times \wp\, Z^+$.

For (ii), notice that it follows from Lemma 6. 53 that $2^{\aleph_0} = 2^{\aleph_0 + \aleph_0}$. And by Exercise 6. 34 (1) we have that $2^{\aleph_0 + \aleph_0} = 2^{\aleph_0} \cdot 2^{\aleph_0}$. Hence it will suffice to show that $\aleph_0 \cdot 2^{\aleph_0} \leq 2^{\aleph_0} \cdot 2^{\aleph_0}$, i.e. $Z^+ \times \wp\, Z^+ \preceq \wp\, Z^+ \times \wp\, Z^+$. This follows from the fact that the function $f(\langle x, y \rangle) = \langle \{x\}, y \rangle$ is a one-to-one function from $Z^+ \times \wp\, Z^+$ to $\wp\, Z^+ \times \wp\, Z^+$. ∎

THEOREM 6. 68: *Card* $\Re = 2^{\aleph_0}$.

Proof: We know (Lemma 6. 44) that the set Z of the integers has cardinality $\aleph_0$. We also know (Theorem 6. 64) that the set $[0, 1)$ of real numbers between 0 and 1 (including 0 but excluding 1) has cardinality $2^{\aleph_0}$. Hence, the Cartesian product of these two sets has cardinality $\aleph_0 \cdot 2^{\aleph_0}$, which, by Lemma 6. 67, equals $2^{\aleph_0}$. Hence it will suffice to show that $\Re$ is similar to $Z \times [0, 1)$. We get a one-to-one correspondence between these two sets if we assign to each real number the pair formed by its whole part and its decimal part. ∎

Corollary 6. 63 tells us that $2^{\aleph_0}$ is greater than $\aleph_0$, and that there are still greater cardinals. We may wonder at this point whether there are any cardinals between $\aleph_0$ and $2^{\aleph_0}$, i.e. cardinals greater $\aleph_0$ but less than $2^{\aleph_0}$. Cantor was convinced that there was no such cardinal, and spent a good deal of effort trying, unsuccessfully, to settle the issue. The principle in question can be formulated as follows.

(CANTOR'S) CONTINUUM HYPOTHESIS: There is no cardinal κ such that $\aleph_0 < \kappa$ and $\kappa < 2^{\aleph_0}$.

Notice that Cantor's Continuum Hypothesis is a special case of the general claim that, for any infinite cardinal λ, there are no cardinals between λ and 2^λ, which can be formulated as follows.

GENERALIZED CONTINUUM HYPOTHESIS: For every infinite cardinal λ, there is no cardinal κ such that $\lambda < \kappa$ and $\kappa < 2^\lambda$.

To characterize the status of these hypotheses, and of other important principles that we shall encounter later on, we need to consider in some detail how sets are introduced.

10. ZF

In Chapter 1, we introduced the notions of set and set membership using the Principles of Extensionality, Determinacy and Specification. As we indicated in §6 of this chapter, these principles do not provide an explicit definition of set-theoretic notions. We could see them instead as defining these notions contextually. Thus, set and set membership would be introduced by postulating a domain of objects, the sets, and a binary relation, $\in$, which satisfy the Principles of Extensionality, Determinacy and Specification. But a definition along these lines would be completely inadequate. The problem has to do with the Principle of Specification, according to which, whenever we can specify a determinate totality of objects, we can say that there is a set whose elements are precisely those objects. The Principle of Specification seems entirely natural, and was treated as a basic principle of set theory by many of its early proponents. But, as we announced in Chapter 1, the principle cannot be accepted, because it leads to contradiction. The difficulty on which we are going to focus is known as *Russell's paradox*, after Bertrand Russell, who presented the problem to Gottlob Frege in a letter of 1902. Russell's paradox is remarkably simple. One of the determinate totalities that we seem capable of specifying consists of the sets which are not members of themselves. According to the Principle of Specification, there is a set whose elements are precisely these objects. But there can be no such set, since, if it existed, it would be a member of itself if and only if it weren't a member of itself—a contradiction. It follows that a contextual definition of set and set membership which employs the Principle of Specification is bound to fail—we cannot postulate without contradiction a domain of objects and a binary relation which satisfy this principle.

We can examine the situation using ideas from first-order logic that we presented in earlier chapters. At the end of Chapter 3, we set ourselves the task of finding sets of first-order sentences having as their models precisely structures of a certain kind—equivalence relations, partially ordered sets, etc. This procedure can be seen as modeling the method of contextual definition—we define partially ordered sets contextually by finding a set of sentences which are true in structures in which a binary relation partially orders the universe, and false in every other structure. We can use this procedure to model the task of defining set contextually.

We could do this with the first-order language whose extralogical vocabulary contains one one-place predicate, S, and one two-place predicate, $\in$. Our goal would be to find a set of sentences of this language which has a structure $\mathcal{A}$ as a model just in case the elements of the universe in $S_{\mathcal{A}}$ behave like sets with respect to the relation $\in_{\mathcal{A}}$, seen as the set-membership relation. But a different approach is more commonly adopted. Let's say that a set is *pure* if all its elements are sets, all the elements of each of its elements are sets, and so on, all the way down. Thus, e.g., $\varnothing$, $\{\varnothing\}$ and $\{\{\{\varnothing\}, \varnothing\}, \{\{\varnothing\}\}\}$ are pure sets. Restricting our attention to pure sets would simplify matters with no significant loss of power—pure sets are all that is required for the set-theoretic definitions of mathematical notions mentioned in §6. The task of defining pure sets contextually can be modeled in the first-order language $L_{\in}$ with a two-place predicate, $\in$, as its only extralogical symbol. Our goal would be to find a set Γ of $L_{\in}$-sentences such that an $L_{\in}$-structure $\mathcal{A}$ is a model of Γ just in case the elements of the universe of $\mathcal{A}$ behave like (pure) sets with respect to the relation $\in_{\mathcal{A}}$, seen as the set-membership relation. We shall depart from our standard practice by placing $\in$ between the two terms involved in the atomic formulas in which it figures.

We can now try to find $L_{\in}$-sentences which model the principles with which we introduced sets in Chapter 1. The Principle of Extensionality will be modeled by the following sentence:

(E) $\quad \forall x \forall y \, (\forall z \, ((z \in x \to z \in y) \wedge (z \in y \to z \in x)) \to x \approx y)$

The Principle of Determinacy would be modeled by the sentence $\forall x \forall y$ $(x \in y \vee \neg x \in y)$, but there would be no point in using it to model in $L_{\in}$ a contextual definition of set-theoretic notions, since it is true in every $L_{\in}$-structure.

The Principle of Specification can be modeled with the following sentence schema:

(S) $\quad \exists y \forall x \, ((\phi \to x \in y) \wedge (\neg \phi \to \neg x \in y))$,

where ϕ is an $L_{\in}$-formula with x as its only free variable. Notice that each instance of this schema asserts the existence of a set whose elements are precisely the elements of the universe of an $L_{\in}$-structure which satisfy the condition represented by ϕ.

We can see now how Russell's paradox arises. Since $\neg x \in x$ is an $L_{\in}$-formula with x as its only free variable, the following sentence is an instance of (S):

$$\exists y \forall x \, ((\neg x \in x \to x \in y) \wedge (\neg \neg x \in x \to \neg x \in y))$$

The problem with this sentence is that it is false in every $L_\in$-structure. One way to see this is to show that its negation is deducible from the empty set, and hence, by the Soundness Theorem, true in every $L_\in$-structure. This is left as an exercise.

EXERCISE 6. 69: Show that $\varnothing \vdash \neg\exists y\forall x\,((\neg x \in x \rightarrow x \in y) \wedge (\neg\neg x \in x \rightarrow \neg x \in y))$.

Hint: Use $\neg I$, deducing, say, $z \approx z$ and $\neg z \approx z$ from $\{\exists y\forall x\,((\neg x \in x \rightarrow x \in y) \wedge (\neg\neg x \in x \rightarrow \neg x \in y))\}$. To derive $\{\exists y\forall x\,((\neg x \in x \rightarrow x \in y) \wedge (\neg\neg x \in x \rightarrow \neg x \in y))\} \vdash \neg z \approx z$, use $\exists E$, with $\forall x\,((\neg x \in x \rightarrow x \in y) \wedge (\neg\neg x \in x \rightarrow \neg x \in y))$ as your instance. To deduce $\neg z \approx z$ from this, apply $\neg I$ once more, with $y \in y$ and $\neg y \in y$ as your contradiction.

Thus, if our goal is to find a set of $L_\in$-sentences which has an $L_\in$-structure as a model just in case the elements of its universe behave like (pure) sets with respect to the relation with which $\in$ is interpreted, the set containing (*E*) and all the instances of schema (*S*) won't do the job. This set of $L_\in$-sentences simply has no models.

The principles which figure in a contextual definition of set-theoretic notions are known as *axioms of set theory*. An adequate set of axioms of set theory has to capture our intuitive conception of set to the extent that this can be achieved without generating inconsistencies. In the aftermath of the discovery of Russell's paradox, several sets of axioms were proposed which seem to be adequate in this sense. Perhaps the most popular of them is the one known as *Zermelo-Fraenkel Set Theory*, or by the initials ZF. Like other axiomatizations of set theory, ZF includes among its axioms the Principle of Extensionality and selected instances of the Principle of Specification. The selection is informed, on the one hand, by our intuitions as to which sets there are, and, on the other, by the need to avoid inconsistencies. ZF is widely considered reasonably adequate on the first count, and to satisfy the consistency criterion.

If we treat ZF as our contextual definition of set, we have a clear criterion for assessing claims about sets: We should accept those claims which are logical consequences of ZF and reject those whose negations are logical consequences of ZF. If we apply this criterion to Cantor's Continuum Hypothesis and the Generalized Continuum Hypothesis we encounter the following situation. On the one hand, the negation of the Generalized Continuum Hypothesis (and hence of Cantor's restricted version) is not a logical consequence of ZF (if ZF is consistent). On the other hand, Cantor's Continuum Hypothesis (and hence the generalized version) is not a logical consequence of ZF either (again, if ZF is consistent). The former result was established by Gödel in 1939, and the latter by Paul Cohen in 1963. It follows from these results that our criterion for assessing claims about sets yields no verdict in this case.

Once again, this situation has a formal correlate in $L_\in$, since the axioms of ZF can be modeled with $L_\in$-sentences. Let Θ_{ZF} be a set of $L_\in$-sentences modeling the axioms of ZF. Treating ZF as a contextual definition of set-theoretic notions would yield the following criterion for assessing set-theoretic claims: We should accept a proposition if it is modeled by an $L_\in$-sentence which is true in every model of Θ_{ZF}, and reject it if it is modeled by an $L_\in$-sentence which is false in every model of Θ_{ZF}. But this criterion yields no verdict for either version of the Continuum Hypothesis, since the $L_\in$-sentences which model them are true in some models of Θ_{ZF} and false in others (if Θ_{ZF} has models).

This situation seems to leave our intuitions about sets as our only guide for deciding the fate of the Continuum Hypothesis. If we thought that a domain of objects and a binary relation can only be treated as the set-theoretic universe if they satisfy the Continuum Hypothesis, we could add it to ZF as an extra axiom. If we thought that a domain of objects and a binary relation can only be treated as the set-theoretic universe if they don't satisfy the Continuum Hypothesis, we could treat its negation as an additional axiom. And if we thought that a domain of objects and a binary relation can be treated as the set-theoretic universe whether or not they satisfy the Continuum Hypothesis, we could simply leave things as they are, accepting that the universe of sets is indeterminate in this respect, or hoping that the issue will be settled indirectly by the adoption of other axioms.

The nature of this decision is a controversial matter among philosophers of set theory. For some, the universe of sets is a fully determinate reality in which the Continuum Hypothesis, and every other set-theoretic claim, is either true or false, and our intuitions as to which axioms to choose are answerable to how things stand in this realm. For others, sets have only those properties which we bestow on them with our axiomatizations, and, so long as consistency is preserved, and our intuitions satisfied, there is no such thing as going wrong in our choice of axioms. We shall not go into this issue here. We shall simply record the fact that the standard position with respect to the Continuum Hypothesis among practicing set-theorists is not to consider it (in either version) or its negation as an axiom of set theory.

11. Choice

DEFINITION: A *choice function* for a set A is a function pairing each non-empty subset of A with one of its elements—i.e. a function f from $(\wp\, A)$ $-\{\varnothing\}$ to A such that for every $B \in (\wp\, A) - \{\varnothing\}, f(B) \in B$.

We can think of a choice function for A as "choosing" a unique element from each nonempty subset of A. It is easy to find choice functions for many sets, as in the following exercise.

EXERCISE 6. 70: Find a choice function for the set $\{a, b, c\}$.

In fact we can show that every finite set has a choice function.

LEMMA 6. 71: Every finite set has a choice function.

Proof: Let A be a finite set. Then, for some natural number n, $A \sim \{1,...,$ $n\}$. Let f be a one-to-one correspondence between A and $\{1,...,n\}$. We now use f to define a function g from $(\wp\, A) - \{\varnothing\}$ to A as follows: For every $B \in (\wp\, A) - \{\varnothing\}$, $g(B) = b$ if and only if $b \in B$ and for every $c \in$ $B, f(b) \leq f(c)$; i.e., for each nonempty subset B of A, we consider the elements of $\{1,...,n\}$ with which the elements of B are paired by f, and take the element of B paired with the *least* of these as the image under g of B. It is easy to see that g is a choice function for A. This is left as an exercise. ∎

EXERCISE 6. 72: Show that the function g in the proof of Lemma 6. 71 is a choice function for A.

The following exercise extends this result to denumerable sets.

EXERCISE 6. 73: Show that every denumerable set has a choice function.

Hint: Proceed as in the proof of Lemma 6. 71, using a one-to-one correspondence between A and $\mathbf{Z}^+$.

Having established that finite and denumerable sets have choice functions, we may consider whether every set has one. The claim that this is so is known as the *Axiom of Choice*.

AXIOM OF CHOICE: Every set has a choice function.

Is the Axiom of Choice true? This question has been a subject of controversy among philosophers and mathematicians since the principle was first explicitly formulated in the first decade of the twentieth century. Notice first that the strategy employed to establish Lemma 6. 71 and

Exercise 6. 73 cannot be adapted to prove the Axiom of Choice. In those cases, to establish that a set has a choice function we describe a procedure for constructing one. But we don't have a general procedure for constructing a choice function for a set A which is neither finite nor denumerable—for picking one element of each (nonempty) subset of A to act as its image under a choice function.

As we did with the Continuum Hypothesis, we can try to use ZF as a criterion for deciding on the status of the Axiom of Choice, but we would face once more the same situation that we encountered in that case. When Gödel proved that the negation of the Continuum Hypothesis is not a logical consequence of ZF (if ZF is consistent), he proved also that the same goes for the negation of the Axiom of Choice. And when Cohen proved that the Continuum Hypothesis is not a logical consequence of ZF (if ZF is consistent), he established a parallel result for the Axiom of Choice. In short, ZF has neither the Axiom of Choice, nor its negation as a logical consequence (provided that ZF is consistent)—or, in terms of $L_\in$-sentences, an $L_\in$-sentence modeling the Axiom of Choice will be true in some models of Θ_{ZF} and false in others (if Θ_{ZF} has models).

This means that, as with the Continuum Hypothesis, we have to make a decision as to whether we should add the Axiom of Choice or its negation to ZF as an extra axiom, or leave things as they are, accepting that the universe of sets is indeterminate in this respect. The debate on the status of the Axiom of Choice turns on fundamental issues concerning how the notion of set should be understood. Suppose, on the one hand, that for a set to exist there has to be an act of collecting certain objects, its elements—that only from such an act of collecting can the set, a further object, be generated. It would be natural to think of this act of collecting as something we do—a mental operation of putting together the elements of the set. And then we wouldn't be able to assert in general that every set A has a choice function. For a choice function for A is a set of pairs, and the mental operation that would be required to generate it is not in general one that we can perform. This mental operation could only consist either in picking one by one the pairs that the choice function will contain, or in finding a general principle to select them. And if A is neither finite nor denumerable, both kinds of operation will be unavailable.

Suppose, on the other hand, that the existence of a set does not require a mental operation of collecting its elements—that sets don't need our participation in any way in order to "come into existence." Then one could hardly object to the thought that, for any set X, and any totality of elements of X, there is a set (a subset of X) whose elements are precisely those objects, whether or not it is within our powers to specify the elements of this set. Then, if we accepted the existence of the power set of any set, and of the Cartesian product of any two sets (both of which are consequences of ZF), we would have to accept the Axiom of Choice, since a choice function for a set A is a subset of $(\wp\ A) \times A$.

Our verdict on the Axiom of Choice has important repercussions for the theory of cardinality. As we know, the truth value of cardinality claims depends on the existence of certain functions. And for many important general claims about the cardinality of sets, the existence of the functions that would make them true follows from the Axiom of Choice, but cannot be established in its absence. In what follows, we shall continue to develop the theory of cardinality on the assumption that the Axiom of Choice is true, bearing in mind the preceding remarks about the conception of sets to which this assumption seems to commit us.

There is a wide range of propositions known to be equivalent to the Axiom of Choice. Some of them are so close to the principle to which we have assigned this label that they can be considered as alternative formulations of the Axiom. In other cases, the equivalence is much less obvious, as the propositions in question seem to have a completely different subject matter, having nothing to do with choosing elements from sets. The following is one of the many propositions which fall naturally under the heading of reformulations of the Axiom of Choice.

AXIOM OF CHOICE (second formulation): If A is a collection of nonempty disjoint sets, then there is a set C which shares exactly one element with each set in A.

LEMMA 6. 74: The two formulations of the Axiom of Choice are equivalent.

Proof: We show first that the first formulation entails the second. Let A be a collection of nonempty disjoint sets. Consider the set $(\wp\ \bigcup A) - \{\varnothing\}$. Notice that every set in A is also in $(\wp\ \bigcup A) - \{\varnothing\}$ (see Exercise 1. 25). By the first formulation of the Axiom of Choice, there is a function f pairing each set in $(\wp\ \bigcup A) - \{\varnothing\}$ with one of its elements. We can easily show that the range of $f \restriction A$ contains exactly one element of each set in A. This is left as an exercise.

We show now that the second formulation entails the first. For the purposes of this proof, we say that the *set-element product* of a nonempty set B is the set $\{B\} \times B$ of ordered pairs of the form $\langle B, b \rangle$, where b is an element of B. Let A be a set, and let A^* be the collection of the set-element products of the nonempty subsets of A, i.e. $A^* = \{\{B\} \times B \mid B$ is a nonempty subset of $A\}$. Notice that the elements of A^* are disjoint, since the pairs in the set-element products of different sets have different first members. Since $A*$ is a collection of nonempty disjoint sets, by the second formulation of the Axiom of Choice, there is a set C having exactly one element in common with each element of $A*$. It is easy to verify that C is a choice function for A (this is left as an exercise), as desired. ∎

EXERCISE 6. 75: Show that the range of $f \restriction A$ (see the first part of the proof of Lemma 6. 74) contains exactly one element of each set in A.

EXERCISE 6. 76: Show that the set C in the second part of the proof of Lemma 6. 74 is a choice function for A.

The involvement of the Axiom of Choice in a proof can easily go unnoticed. We shall use our next result to illustrate this point.

LEMMA 6. 77: The union of a denumerable collection of denumerable sets is denumerable.

Proof: Let A be a denumerable collection of denumerable sets. We need to show that $\bigcup A \sim \mathbf{Z}^+$. By the Schröder-Bernstein Theorem it will suffice to show (i) that $\mathbf{Z}^+ \preceq \bigcup A$ and (ii) that $\bigcup A \preceq \mathbf{Z}^+$.

For (i), let $B \in A$. The function pairing each element of B with itself is a one-to-one function from B to $\bigcup A$. But $B \sim \mathbf{Z}^+$. Hence we have that $\mathbf{Z}^+ \preceq \bigcup A$, as desired.

For (ii), we have from Exercise 6. 54 that $\mathbf{Z}^+ \times \mathbf{Z}^+$ is denumerable. Hence, by Exercise 6. 47, it will suffice to show that there is a function from $\mathbf{Z}^+ \times \mathbf{Z}^+$ to $\bigcup A$ with the whole of $\bigcup A$ as its range. Let f be a one-to-one correspondence between $\mathbf{Z}^+$ and A. Let's refer to the image of n under f as A_n. We have that $A_1, A_2,\dots$ are all denumerable. Hence, for every $n \in \mathbf{Z}^+$, there is a one-to-one correspondence f_n between $\mathbf{Z}^+$ and A_n. Now we define a function F from $\mathbf{Z}^+ \times \mathbf{Z}^+$ to $\bigcup A$ as follows: For all $m, n \in \mathbf{Z}^+$, $F(\langle m, n \rangle) = f_m(n)$. We can easily verify that F is a function from $\mathbf{Z}^+ \times \mathbf{Z}^+$ to $\bigcup A$ with the whole of $\bigcup A$ as its range (this is left as an exercise), as desired. ∎

EXERCISE 6. 78: Show that F in the proof of Lemma 6. 77 is a function from $\mathbf{Z}^+ \times \mathbf{Z}^+$ to $\bigcup A$ with the whole of $\bigcup A$ as its range.

The proof of Lemma 6. 77 makes no explicit appeal to the Axiom of Choice, but, as we are about to see, the reasoning can only be accepted if the Axiom of Choice is assumed. The proof is based on the assertion that there is a function F from $\mathbf{Z}^+ \times \mathbf{Z}^+$ to $\bigcup A$ with the whole of $\bigcup A$ as its range. By the Principle of Specification, we can assert that F exists if we can specify which pairs we are going to count as its elements. We do so by stipulating that, for all $m, n \in \mathbf{Z}^+$, F contains the pair $\langle\langle m, n\rangle, f_m(n)\rangle$. Hence we will have succeeded in specifying which pairs we are going to count as elements of F just in case we have succeeded in specifying which functions $f_1, f_2, f_3, \ldots$ are. But we have done no such thing. We have asserted that, for every positive integer n, there is at least one one-to-one correspondence from $\mathbf{Z}^+$ to A_n. But if there is one there are infinitely many, and we have no general procedure for picking out the function among these which we are going to treat as f_n, for each n. And if we can't do this we haven't specified either which pairs we are going to count as elements of F—we have failed to support our assertion that F exists.

It is at this point that the Axiom of Choice is tacitly invoked. For every positive integer n, let ϕ_n be the set of one-to-one correspondences between $\mathbf{Z}^+$ and A_n, and let Φ be the collection $\{\phi_n \mid n \in \mathbf{Z}^+\}$ containing all these sets. Since $A_1, A_2, A_3, \ldots$ are all denumerable, each set in Φ is nonempty, and since the range of each function in ϕ_n, for each n, is the whole of A_n, no function appears in more than one set in Φ. Hence we can invoke the second formulation of the Axiom of Choice to assert the existence of a set ϕ containing exactly one element from each set in Φ. Now we can define the function f_n, for each positive integer n, as the intersection of ϕ_n and ϕ. These functions can then be legitimately used in the definition of F.

EXERCISE 6. 79: Show that the union of a countable collection of countable sets is countable.

Hint: Proceed as in part (ii) of the proof of Lemma 6. 77, but instead of using one-to-one correspondences between $\mathbf{Z}^+$ and the collection, and between $\mathbf{Z}^+$ and each element of the collection, invoke Lemma 6. 45 (*b*) to get functions with the whole collection, and with the whole of each of its elements, as their ranges. Notice that empty collections are countable, and that the union of a collection one of whose elements is the empty set is identical to the union of the collection that you get by removing the empty set.

In §8 we provided a fairly precise characterization of the behavior of $\aleph_0$ without invoking the Axiom of Choice. We are going to see that the Axiom of Choice will enable us to extend many of the claims about $\aleph_0$ that we established there to every infinite cardinal. With Lemma 6. 45 (*a*) and Exercise 6. 47 we introduced an alternative strategy for showing that a set is dominated by $\mathbf{Z}^+$. Our next result provides a parallel strategy for showing in general that a set is dominated by another set. Unlike the earlier results, the proof of this one requires the Axiom of Choice.

LEMMA 6. 80: For all sets X, Y, if there is a function from Y to X with the whole of X as its range, then $X \preceq Y$.

Proof: Let A, B be sets, and let f be a function from B to A with the whole of A as its range. We have to show that there is a one-to-one function from A to B. For every $a \in A$, let B_a be the set of elements of B having a as their image under f. Let B^* be the collection $\{B_x \mid x \in A\}$. Since f is a function, all the sets in B^* are disjoint, and since the range of f is the whole of A, none of these sets is empty. Hence, by the second formulation of the Axiom of Choice, there is a set C having exactly one element in common with each set in B^*. We now define a function g from A to B as follows: for every $x \in A$, $g(x) = y$ if and only if $f(y) = x$ and $y \in C$. It is easy to verify that g is a one-to-one function from A to B, as desired. ∎

EXERCISE 6. 81: Show that g in the proof of Lemma 6. 80 is a one-to-one function from A to B.

EXERCISE 6. 82: Show that, for every nonempty set X and every set Y, if $X \preceq Y$, then there is a function from Y to X with the whole of X as its range.

Hint: Proceed as in the proof of Lemma 6. 45 (*b*).

We can use these results to prove the following extension of Exercise 6. 79.

EXERCISE 6. 83: Let A be a collection of sets each of which has cardinality κ or less. Show that $Card \bigcup A \leq Card \, A \cdot \kappa$.

Hint: Proceed as in the proof of Exercise 6. 79. Use Lemma 6. 80 and Exercise 6. 82 instead of Lemma 6. 45 and Exercise 6. 47.

All the infinite sets we have encountered so far dominate $\mathbf{Z}^+$, i.e. their cardinality is greater than or equal to $\aleph_0$. We haven't shown, however, that this is always the case—that there are no infinite sets which don't dominate $\mathbf{Z}^+$. The cardinality of such sets would be either less than $\aleph_0$—if $\mathbf{Z}^+$ dominated them—or incommensurable with $\aleph_0$—if $\mathbf{Z}^+$ didn't dominate them either. The following result rules out both possibilities.

LEMMA 6. 84: Every infinite set dominates $\mathbf{Z}^+$.

Proof: Let A be an infinite set. Our goal is to define a one-to-one function from $\mathbf{Z}^+$ to A. Notice that, intuitively, we should be able to do this. We could just pick different elements of A one by one as the images of 1, 2, 3,.... Since A is infinite, we know that we wouldn't run out of elements of A after any finite number of steps in this process. This intuitive reasoning suggests that we should be able to find a one-to-one function from $\mathbf{Z}^+$ to A. Notice, however, that the process that it describes of picking one by one the images in A of the positive integers involves making infinitely many choices—one element of A for each positive integer. To define a one-to-one function from $\mathbf{Z}^+$ to A we need to use the Axiom of Choice.

Let f be a choice function for A. We want to define a one-to-one function h from $\mathbf{Z}^+$ to A. Our strategy will be to use as the image under h of each positive integer the image under f of a certain subset of A. We just need to take care to choose the subsets of A that we are going to use for this purpose in such a way that different positive integers are paired with different elements of A. One way to achieve this is to pair 1 with the image of A under f, and each subsequent positive integer with the image under f of the set that we get by deleting from A the elements that have already been used as images of previous positive integers. Thus, we want to assign elements of A to positive integers in the following way:

$$h(1) = f(A)$$
$$h(2) = f(A - \{h(1)\})$$
$$h(3) = f(A - \{h(1), h(2)\})$$
$$\vdots$$

Notice that this way of proceeding ensures that g is a one-to-one function. For f pairs each subset of A with one of its elements. Hence $f(A - \{h(1)\})$ cannot be $h(1)$, $f(A - \{h(1), h(2)\})$ cannot be $h(1)$ or $h(2)$, etc.

To turn these ideas into an actual definition, we first define the sequence of sets that we need to subtract from A to get the set whose image under f will be paired with each positive integer. We define by recursion on the positive integers the function g, as the unique function satisfying the following conditions:

$g(1) = \varnothing$.

For every positive integer n, $g(n + 1) = g(n) \cup \{f(A - g(n))\}$.

We can now define h in terms of f and g: for every positive integer n, $h(n) = f(A - g(n))$. We just need to verify that h is a one-to-one function from $\mathbf{Z}^+$ to A. Notice that, since f is a function, we can conclude that each positive integer has at most one image under h. Hence to show that h is a function from $\mathbf{Z}^+$ to A, we just need to check that each positive integer has at least one image under h. We know that f pairs each nonempty subset of A with an element of A. Hence we just need to show that for every positive integer n, $A - g(n)$ is not empty. For this purpose, notice that $g(1) = \varnothing$, and that we get $g(n + 1)$ by adding a single element of

A to $g(n)$. Hence, for every positive integer n, $g(n) \sim \{1,..., n-1\}$, i.e. for every n, $g(n)$ is finite. But then it follows that $A - g(n)$ is not empty, since otherwise *A* itself would be finite, against our initial assumption.

It only remains to check that *h* is one-to-one. Let *m*, *n* be two different positive integers. We know that one of them is less than the other, say *m* < *n*. Then we have that $m + 1 \le n$. We need to show that $h(m) \ne h(n)$. Since $h(m) = f(A - g(m))$, and $g(m + 1) = g(m) \cup \{f(A - g(m))\}$, we have that $h(m) \in g(m + 1)$. Also, since $m + 1 \le n$, $g(m + 1) \subseteq g(n)$. Hence $h(m) \in g(n)$. But we have that $h(n) = f(A - g(n))$, and since *f* is a choice function, $f(A - g(n)) \in A - g(n)$. Hence, $h(n) \in A - g(n)$, and $h(n) \notin g(n)$. Since $h(m)$ is in $g(n)$, but $h(n)$ isn't, we can conclude that $h(m) \ne h(n)$, as desired. ∎

The following three exercises express immediate corollaries of Lemma 6. 84.

EXERCISE 6. 85: Show that every infinite set has a denumerable subset.

EXERCISE 6. 86: Show that every countable set is either finite or denumerable.

EXERCISE 6. 87: Show that $\aleph_0$ is less than every other infinite cardinal.

LEMMA 6. 88: If κ is an infinite cardinal and *n* is a finite cardinal, then $\kappa + n = \kappa$.

Proof: Let *K*, *N* be disjoint sets such that *Card K* = κ, and *Card N* = *n*. We need to show that $K \cup N \sim K$. We know from Exercise 6. 85 that *K* has a denumerable subset *S*. By Exercise 6. 51, we have that $S \cup N \sim S$. Let *f* be a one-to-one correspondence between $S \cup N$ and *S*. Now we define a function *g* from $K \cup N$ to *K* as follows:

$$\text{For every } x \in K \cup N, \ g(x) = \begin{cases} f(x) \text{ if } x \in N \text{ or } x \in S, \\ x \text{ otherwise.} \end{cases}$$

We can show that *g* is a one-to-one correspondence between $K \cup N$ and *K*. This is left as an exercise. ∎

EXERCISE 6. 89: Show that *g* in the proof of Lemma 6. 88 is a one-to-one correspondence between $K \cup N$ and *K*.

12. Zorn's Lemma

We saw in Chapter 1 that every collection of sets is partially ordered by
the subset relation, and that some, but not all, of these partial orderings
are linear. Even if a collection is not linearly ordered by $\subseteq$, some of its
subsets might be. When a subset S of a collection of sets X is linearly
ordered by $\subseteq$ we say that S is a *chain* in X (with respect to $\subseteq$). Notice
that every collection will contain chains, since the empty set is a subset
of every collection, and, trivially, the empty set is linearly ordered by $\subseteq$
(it contains no elements which are not connected by the subset relation).
Also, every nonempty collection will contain nonempty chains, since
every one-element set is linearly ordered by the subset relation. A collection may or may not contain chains with more than one element.

A set in a collection may or may not be a subset of other sets in the
collection. When a set A in a collection X is not a subset of any other set
in X, we say that A is a *maximal element* of X. Some collections contain
no maximal elements. Thus, e.g., the collection of all counting sequences contains no maximal element, as every counting sequence is a
subset of other counting sequences.

The existence of maximal elements in certain collections of sets is a
powerful tool for establishing claims concerning cardinality. In order to
use this tool, we need to have procedures for determining that a collection has a maximal element. A proposition known as Zorn's Lemma
provides such a procedure, since it asserts that a certain feature of a collection is a sufficient condition for the collection to have a maximal element. The feature in question has to do with the chains in the collection.

DEFINITION: A collection X is *closed under unions of chains* just in case,
for every chain C in X, the union of C is an element of X.

According to Zorn's Lemma, every collection with this feature will
have a maximal element.

ZORN'S LEMMA: If a collection of sets is closed under unions of chains,
then it contains a maximal element.

The connection between closure under unions of chains and the existence of maximal elements may not be apparent. The following considerations may help establish the connection at the intuitive level. Let's
say that a chain C is *ever-growing* if every set in C is a subset of other
sets in C. Clearly no element of an ever-growing chain in a collection X
can be a maximal element of X. Hence, if every set in X is a member of

an ever-growing chain, X will contain no maximal elements. But if X is closed under unions of chains, for every ever-growing chain C in X, X is guaranteed to contain a set which is not a subset of any member of C, namely $\bigcup C$. $\bigcup C$ may not be a maximal element of X. In fact, it may itself be a member of another ever-growing chain C'. But if X is closed under unions of chains, it will also contain a set, $\bigcup C'$, which is not a subset of any member of C'. Notice, however, that this argument doesn't amount to a proof of Zorn's Lemma, since we haven't ruled out the possibility that the union of each ever-growing chain is a member of another ever-growing chain. To establish that a collection X has a maximal element it's not enough to show that, for every ever-growing chain C in X, X contains a set A which is not a subset of any member of C. We would need to show that X contains a set A such that, for every ever-growing chain C in X, A is not a subset of any member of C.

Zorn's Lemma can be proved with the help of the Axiom of Choice. In fact, Zorn's Lemma is equivalent to the Axiom of Choice. We shall not prove this result here, but we shall use Zorn's Lemma to establish a few further results about cardinality, bearing in mind that in assuming Zorn's Lemma, we are assuming no more, and no less, than in assuming the Axiom of Choice.

The first result that we shall establish with the help of Zorn's Lemma concerns the ordering of cardinals. We know that the cardinals are partially ordered by $\leq$, and that this ordering is linear with respect to the finite cardinals, but we haven't determined whether $\leq$ is a linear ordering of all the cardinals. We haven't ruled out the possibility that there are "incommensurable" cardinals, i.e. cardinals κ, λ, such that neither $\kappa \leq \lambda$, nor $\lambda \leq \kappa$. The claim that the ordering of the cardinals by $\leq$ is linear is a direct consequence of the following lemma.

CARDINAL COMPARABILITY LEMMA: For all sets X, Y, either $X \preceq Y$ or $Y \preceq X$.

Proof: Let A, B be sets. Notice that in order to establish that either $A \preceq B$ or $B \preceq A$, it will suffice to show that there is a one-to-one function either from A to B or from B to A. To show that there is a one-to-one function from A to B, it will suffice to show that there is a one-to-one correspondence between A and a subset of B. And to show that there is a one-to-one function from B to A it will suffice to show that there is a one-to-one correspondence between a subset of A and B, as its inverse will be a one-to-one function from B to A. Hence to establish the desired result, it will suffice to show that there is a one-to-one correspondence between a subset A' of A and a subset B' of B such that either $A = A'$ or $B = B'$. The proof of this result follows the typical pattern of proofs involving Zorn's

Lemma. We begin by forming a collection of functions which satisfies the hypothesis of Zorn's Lemma—being closed under unions of chains. Then we show that a maximal element of this collection will be a function of the kind we are interested in.

Thus our first goal is to define a collection of functions and show that it is closed under unions of chains. Consider the collection $F = \{f \mid f$ is a one-to-one correspondence between a subset of A and a subset of $B\}$. We need to show that F is closed under unions of chains. Let C be a chain in F. We need to show that $\bigcup C \in F$. For this, it will suffice to show that $\bigcup C$ is a one-to-one correspondence between a subset of A and a subset of B. Clearly, in every pair in $\bigcup C$, the first member is an element of A and the second member is an element of B. Hence, we only need to show that different elements of B are not paired with the same element of A (i.e. that $\bigcup C$ is a function) and that different elements of A are not paired with the same element of B (i.e. that $\bigcup C$ is one-to-one). Let $\langle a, b \rangle, \langle a', b' \rangle \in \bigcup C$. We need to show that $a = a'$ if and only if $b = b'$. Since $\langle a, b \rangle, \langle a', b' \rangle \in \bigcup C$, there are functions f, f' in C such that $\langle a, b \rangle \in f, \langle a', b' \rangle \in f'$. Since C is a chain, either $f \subseteq f'$ or $f' \subseteq f$. Hence, either $\langle a, b \rangle, \langle a', b' \rangle \in f$ or $\langle a, b \rangle, \langle a', b' \rangle \in f'$. Since both f and f' are functions, we have that, if $a = a'$, then $b = b'$, and since they are both one-to-one, we have that if $b = b'$, then $a = a'$, as desired.

Now we can apply Zorn's Lemma to assert the existence of a maximal element f^* of F. f^* is a one-to-one correspondence between a subset of A and a subset of B. We need to show that either the domain of f^* is A, or its range is B. Assume, towards a contradiction, that neither is the case. Then there is an element a of A outside the domain of f^*, and an element b of B outside the range of f^*. But then $f^* \cup \{\langle a, b \rangle\}$ is a one-to-one correspondence between a subset of A and a subset of B. Hence $f^* \cup \{\langle a, b \rangle\}$ is in F. But $f^* \neq f^* \cup \{\langle a, b \rangle\}$ and $f^* \subseteq f^* \cup \{\langle a, b \rangle\}$, which contradicts the hypothesis that f^* is a maximal element of F, as desired. ∎

We have shown that the Cardinal Comparability Lemma is a consequence of Zorn's Lemma. In fact the connection goes the other way as well. The Cardinal Comparability Lemma is equivalent to Zorn's Lemma, and hence to the Axiom of Choice. We shall not provide here a proof of this result.

The remaining results in this section concern the addition, multiplication and exponentiation of arbitrary infinite cardinals. The next theorem extends to all infinite cardinals the result about $\aleph_0$ expressed by Lemma 6.53.

THEOREM 6.90: If κ is an infinite cardinal, then $\kappa + \kappa = \kappa$.

Proof: By Exercise 6. 33 (7), it will suffice to show that $\kappa = 2 \cdot \kappa$. Let K be a set of cardinality κ. We need to show that $K \times \{1, 2\} \sim K$. The direct strategy for establishing this claim would be to find a one-to-one correspondence between $K \times \{1, 2\}$ and K. We shall follow a less direct procedure. We shall find a one-to-one correspondence between $K_0 \times \{1, 2\}$ and K_0, for a subset K_0 of K which is similar to K. To find this function we follow the same procedure as in the proof of the Cardinal Comparability Lemma. The function we are looking for will be a maximal element of a collection of functions which satisfies the hypothesis of Zorn's Lemma.

Thus our first goal is to define the collection of functions that we are going to use for this purpose and to show that it is closed under unions of chains. We shall use the collection F, defined as follows: $F = \{f \mid$ for some subset A of K, f is a one-to-one correspondence between $A \times \{1, 2\}$ and $A\}$. We need to show that F is closed under unions of chains. Let C be a chain in F. We need to show that $\bigcup C \in F$. Let R_C be the union of the collection containing the ranges of the functions in C. We are going to show that $\bigcup C$ is a one-to-one correspondence between $R_C \times \{1, 2\}$ and R_C. Since $R_C \subseteq K$, it will follow that $\bigcup C \in F$. Thus we need to verify (i) that every element of $R_C \times \{1, 2\}$ has at least one image in R_C under $\bigcup C$, (ii) that every element of $R_C \times \{1, 2\}$ has at most one image in R_C under $\bigcup C$, (iii) that every element of R_C is the image under $\bigcup C$ of at least one element of $R_C \times \{1, 2\}$, and (iv) that every element of R_C is the image under $\bigcup C$ of at most one element of $R_C \times \{1, 2\}$.

For (i), let $\langle a, n \rangle \in R_C \times \{1, 2\}$. Then $a \in R_C$, and for some function f in C, a is in the range of f. But then $\langle a, n \rangle$ is in the domain of f. Hence, for some $b \in R_C$, $\langle\langle a, n \rangle, b \rangle \in \bigcup C$, as desired.

For (ii), let $\langle\langle a, n \rangle, b \rangle, \langle\langle a, n \rangle, c \rangle \in \bigcup C$. Then there are functions f, f' in C such that $\langle\langle a, n \rangle, b \rangle \in f, \langle\langle a, n \rangle, c \rangle \in f'$. But since C is a chain, either $f \subseteq f'$ or $f' \subseteq f$. Hence either $\langle\langle a, n \rangle, b \rangle, \langle\langle a, n \rangle, c \rangle \in f$ or $\langle\langle a, n \rangle, b \rangle, \langle\langle a, n \rangle, c \rangle \in f'$, and, since f and f' are functions, $b = c$, as desired.

For (iii) let $a \in R_C$. Then a is in the range of a function f in C. Hence a is the image under f of some pair $\langle b, n \rangle$ in $R_C \times \{1, 2\}$, and $\langle\langle b, n \rangle, a \rangle \in \bigcup C$, as desired.

For (iv), let $\langle\langle a, n \rangle, c \rangle, \langle\langle b, n \rangle, c \rangle \in \bigcup C$. Then there are functions f, f' in C such that $\langle\langle a, n \rangle, c \rangle \in f, \langle\langle b, n \rangle, c \rangle \in f'$. But since C is a chain, either $f \subseteq f'$ or $f' \subseteq f$. Hence either $\langle\langle a, n \rangle, c \rangle, \langle\langle b, n \rangle, c \rangle \in f$ or $\langle\langle a, n \rangle, c \rangle, \langle\langle b, n \rangle, c \rangle \in f'$, but since both f and f' are one-to-one, $a = b$, as desired.

Now we know that F is closed under unions of chains. Hence we can apply Zorn's Lemma to conclude that F has a maximal element. Let f^* be a maximal element of F. Then, for some subset K_0 of K, f^* is a one-to-one correspondence between $K_0 \times \{1, 2\}$ and K_0. We need to show that $K \sim K_0$, i.e. *Card* K = *Card* K_0. Notice that we would be able to conclude this if we could establish that there are only finitely many elements of K not in K_0. For we have that $K = K_0 \cup (K - K_0)$, and hence $K \sim K_0 \cup (K - K_0)$. And since K_0 and $K - K_0$ are disjoint, it follows that *Card* K = *Card* K_0 + *Card* $K - K_0$. We know from Lemma 6. 88 that if λ is an infinite cardinal and n is a finite cardinal, $\lambda + n = \lambda$. Hence if $K - K_0$ is a finite set, it follows that *Card* K = *Card* K_0.

Thus our final task is to establish that $K - K_0$ is a finite set. Assume, towards a contradiction, that $K - K_0$ is infinite. Then, by Exercise 6. 85, $K - K_0$ has a denumerable subset S, and, by Exercise 6. 51, $S \times \{1, 2\} \sim S$. Hence there is a one-to-one correspondence g between $S \times \{1, 2\}$ and S. But then, since K_0 and S are disjoint, $f^* \cup g$ is a one-to-one correspondence between $(K_0 \cup S) \times \{1, 2\}$ and $K_0 \cup S$ (see Exercises 1. 46 and 1. 27 (1)). Hence $f^* \cup g$ is in F, but obviously $f^* \neq f^* \cup g$ and $f^* \subseteq f^* \cup g$, which contradicts the hypothesis that f^* is a maximal element of F, as desired. ∎

THEOREM 6. 91: If κ is an infinite cardinal and $\lambda \leq \kappa$, then $\kappa + \lambda = \kappa$.

Proof: Let K, L be disjoint sets such that *Card* K = κ, *Card* L = λ. We need to show that $K \cup L \sim K$. By the Schröder-Bernstein Theorem, it will suffice to show (i) that $K \preceq K \cup L$ and (ii) that $K \cup L \preceq K$. (i) is straightforward (see Exercise 6. 11).

For (ii), notice that it follows from Exercise 6. 16, Exercise 6. 17 and Theorem 6. 90 that $K \times \{1\} \cup K \times \{2\} \sim K$. Hence it will suffice to show that $K \cup L \preceq K \times \{1\} \cup K \times \{2\}$. We have that $L \preceq K$. Let f be a one-to-one function from L to K. We use f to define a function g from $K \cup L$ to $K \times \{1\} \cup K \times \{2\}$ as follows:

$$\text{For every } x \in K \cup L, \ g(x) = \begin{cases} \langle f(x), 1 \rangle \text{ if } x \in L, \\ \langle x, 2 \rangle \text{ otherwise.} \end{cases}$$

It can be easily verified that g is a one-to-one function from $K \cup L$ to $K \times \{1\} \cup K \times \{2\}$. This is left as an exercise. ∎

EXERCISE 6. 92: Show that g in the proof of Theorem 6. 91 is a one-to-one function from $K \cup L$ to $K \times \{1\} \cup K \times \{2\}$.

THEOREM 6. 93: If κ is an infinite cardinal, then $\kappa \cdot \kappa = \kappa$.

Proof: Let K be a set of cardinality κ. We need to show that, *Card* $K \cdot$ *Card* K = *Card* K. As in the proof of Theorem 6. 90, instead of finding a one-to-one correspondence between $K \times K$ and K, we shall find a one-to-one correspondence between $K_0 \times K_0$ and K_0, where K_0 is a subset of K

which is similar to K. And once again as in the proof of Theorem 6. 90, we shall use Zorn's Lemma to find this function. The function we are looking for will be a maximal element of a collection of functions which satisfies the hypothesis of Zorn's Lemma.

Thus our first goal is to define the collection of functions that we are going to use for this purpose and to show that it is closed under unions of chains. The collection that we are going to use in this case exploits the same idea as the one we used in the proof of Theorem 6. 90. Thus let $F = \{f \mid f = \emptyset$ or for some infinite subset A of K, f is a one-to-one correspondence between $A \times A$ and $A\}$. (Notice that, since $\emptyset$ is a chain in every collection, and $\bigcup\emptyset$ is $\emptyset$, a collection cannot be closed under unions of chains unless it has $\emptyset$ as an element.) We need to show that F is closed under unions of chains. This is left as an exercise.

Now we can apply Zorn's Lemma to assert the existence of a maximal element f^* of F. We can easily verify that f^* is not $\emptyset$ (this is left as an exercise) and hence that f^* is a one-to-one correspondence between $K_0 \times K_0$ and K_0, where K_0 is an infinite subset of K. Now we only need to show that K_0 is similar to K. Notice that to establish this it will suffice to show that there are at least as many elements of K in K_0 as outside of it, i.e. that $Card\ K - K_0 \leq Card\ K_0$. For Theorem 6. 91 tells us that if this is so, then $Card\ K_0 + Card\ K - K_0 = Card\ K_0$. But we have (see the proof of Theorem 6. 90) that $Card\ K_0 + Card\ K - K_0 = Card\ K$, which yields $Card\ K = Card\ K_0$.

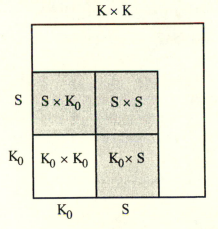

$$K \times K$$

Figure 17

To prove that $Card\ K - K_0 \leq Card\ K_0$, assume, towards a contradiction, that $Card\ K - K_0 \nleq Card\ K_0$. Then, by the Cardinal Comparability

Lemma, we have that $Card\ K_0 \le Card\ K - K_0$. Then, by Exercise 6. 14, there is a subset S of $K - K_0$ of the same cardinality as K_0. Notice that $(K_0 \cup S) \times (K_0 \cup S)$ is the union of $S \times S$, $S \times K_0$, $K_0 \times S$ and $K_0 \times K_0$ (see Figure 17). Consider the set $(S \times S) \cup (S \times K_0) \cup (K_0 \times S)$ (the shaded area in the picture). Since $S \times S$, $S \times K_0$ and $K_0 \times S$ are disjoint, we have that

$$Card\ (S \times S) \cup (S \times K_0) \cup (K_0 \times S) =$$
$$Card\ S \times S + Card\ S \times K_0 + Card\ K_0 \times S$$

Notice also that, since $Card\ K_0 = Card\ S$, each of $S \times S$, $S \times K_0$ and $K_0 \times S$ is of the same cardinality as $K_0 \times K_0$. And since $Card\ K_0 \times K_0 = Card\ K_0 = Card\ S$, each of $S \times K_0$, $S \times S$ and $K_0 \times S$ is of the same cardinality as S. Hence we have that

$$Card\ (S \times S) \cup (S \times K_0) \cup (K_0 \times S) = Card\ S + Card\ S + Card\ S$$

And since S is infinite, from Theorem 6. 90 we get

$$Card\ (S \times S) \cup (S \times K_0) \cup (K_0 \times S) = Card\ S$$

Let g be a one-to-one correspondence between $(S \times S) \cup (S \times K_0) \cup (K_0 \times S)$ and S. We know that $(S \times S) \cup (S \times K_0) \cup (K_0 \times S)$ and $K_0 \times K_0$ are disjoint, and the same goes for S and K_0. Hence $f^* \cup g$ is a one-to-one correspondence between $(S \times S) \cup (S \times K_0) \cup (K_0 \times S) \cup (K_0 \times K_0)$ and $S \cup K_0$, i.e. between $K_0 \cup S \times K_0 \cup S$ and $K_0 \cup S$. Since $K_0 \cup S$ is an infinite subset of K, we have that $f^* \cup g$ is in F. But clearly $f^* \ne f^* \cup g$ and $f^* \subseteq f^* \cup g$, which contradicts the hypothesis that f^* is a maximal element of F, as desired. ∎

EXERCISE 6. 94: Show that F in the proof of Theorem 6. 93 is closed under unions of chains.

Hint: Follow the procedure that we used in the proof of Theorem 6. 90. Notice that $\emptyset$ and $\{\emptyset\}$ are chains in F. They will have to be considered separately.

EXERCISE 6. 95: Show that $\emptyset$ is not a maximal element of F (in the proof of Theorem 6. 93).

THEOREM 6. 96: If κ is an infinite cardinal, λ is a cardinal other than 0, and $\lambda \le \kappa$, then $\kappa \cdot \lambda = \kappa$.

Proof: Let K, L be sets such that $Card\ K = \kappa$, $Card\ L = \lambda$. We have to show that $K \times L \sim K$. By the Schröder-Bernstein Theorem, it will suffice to show (i) that $K \preceq K \times L$, and (ii) that $K \times L \preceq K$. (i) is straightforward, since, if l is an element of L, $f(x) = \langle x, l \rangle$ is a one-to-one function from K to $K \times L$.

For (ii), we know from Theorem 6. 93 that $K \times K \sim K$. Hence it will suffice to show that $K \times L \preceq K \times K$. We know that $L \preceq K$. Let g be a one-to-one function from L to K. Now let h be the function from $K \times L$ to $K \times K$ defined as follows: For every $\langle x, y \rangle \in K \times L$, $h(\langle x, y \rangle) = \langle x, g(y) \rangle$. We can easily show (this is left as an exercise) that h is a one-to-one function from $K \times L$ to $K \times K$, as desired. ∎

EXERCISE 6. 97: Show that h (in the proof of Theorem 6. 96) is a one-to-one function from $K \times L$ to $K \times K$.

Theorem 6. 91 and Theorem 6. 96 give us a complete picture of how cardinal addition and multiplication behave when infinite cardinals are involved. If we add an infinite cardinal κ and any cardinal no greater than κ, or if we multiply κ by any cardinal greater than 0 but no greater than κ, what we get is κ itself. These results are expressed by the following principle (if κ and λ are different cardinals, $Max(\kappa, \lambda)$ is the greater of the two, and if they are identical, $Max(\kappa, \lambda)$ is that cardinal.)

ABSORPTION LAW OF CARDINAL ARITHMETIC: Let κ, λ, be cardinals such that neither of them is 0 and at least one of them is infinite. Then $\kappa + \lambda = \kappa \cdot \lambda = Max(\kappa, \lambda)$.

In proving the Absorption Law, we have made repeated use of Zorn's Lemma. In fact, the Absorption Law of Cardinal Arithmetic is equivalent to the Axiom of Choice (and hence to Zorn's Lemma), although we shall not prove this fact. We can use the Absorption Law to establish results about the cardinalities of sets which will be invoked in subsequent chapters.

EXERCISE 6. 98: Show that if A is an infinite set, and $B \preceq A$, then $Card\ A \cup B = Card\ A$.

Hint: Use the Schröder-Bernstein Theorem. For $A \cup B \preceq A$, use the fact that $A \times \{1\} \cup B \times \{2\}$ is similar to A.

COROLLARY 6. 99: Let A be a collection of sets each of which has cardinality κ or less. If either $Card\ A$ or κ is infinite, then $Card\ \bigcup A \leq Max(Card\ A, \kappa)$.

Proof: This is a direct consequence of Exercise 6. 83 and the Absorption Law. ∎

We know that the behavior of exponentiation with respect to infinite cardinals is different from that of addition and multiplication. Corollary

6. 63 tells us that raising 2 to the power of an infinite cardinal κ yields a cardinal greater than κ. We now round off our presentation of the arithmetic of infinite cardinals with a few further results concerning exponentiation.

We first show that raising an infinite cardinal κ to the power of a finite cardinal (other than 0) yields κ itself. For this purpose, we need to establish first the following result.

LEMMA 6. 100: For every cardinal κ and every finite cardinal n, $\kappa^{n+1} = \kappa^n \cdot \kappa$.

Proof: Let K be a set of cardinality κ. We need to show that the set $^{\{1,\ldots,\,n+1\}}K$ is similar to the set $^{\{1,\ldots,\,n\}}K \times K$. For this purpose we define a function F from $^{\{1,\ldots,\,n+1\}}K$ to $^{\{1,\ldots,\,n\}}K \times K$ as follows: For every $f \in {}^{\{1,\ldots,\,n+1\}}K$, $F(f) = \langle f \restriction \{1,\ldots,n\}, f(n+1) \rangle$. We can easily verify (this is left as an exercise) that F is a one-to-one correspondence between $^{\{1,\ldots,\,n+1\}}K$ and $^{\{1,\ldots,\,n\}}K \times K$, as desired. ∎

EXERCISE 6. 101: Show that F (in the proof of Lemma 6. 100) is a one-to-one correspondence between $^{\{1,\ldots,\,n+1\}}K$ and $^{\{1,\ldots,\,n\}}K \times K$.

EXERCISE 6. 102: Let κ be an infinite cardinal. Show that for every finite cardinal n greater than 0, $\kappa^n = \kappa$.

Hint: Prove by induction on n, starting with 1, that if K is an infinite set, $^{\{1,\ldots,\,n\}}K \sim K$. For the inductive clause invoke Lemma 6. 100 and the Absorption Law.

Exercise 6. 102 tells us what happens when we raise an infinite cardinal to the power of a finite cardinal. We know already what happens when we raise 2 to the power an infinite cardinal. Let's consider now the situation when we raise a cardinal greater than 2 to the power of an infinite cardinal. We start with the following result, according to which when we raise an infinite cardinal κ to the power of κ, we get no more, and no less, than when we raise 2 to the power of κ.

LEMMA 6. 103: For every infinite cardinal κ, $\kappa^\kappa = 2^\kappa$.

Proof: By the antisymmetry of $\leq$, it will suffice to show (i) that $2^\kappa \leq \kappa^\kappa$ and (ii) that $\kappa^\kappa \leq 2^\kappa$. (i) is a direct consequence of Exercise 6. 34 (4). For (ii), we have, from Corollary 6. 63, that $\kappa \leq 2^\kappa$. Hence, again by Exercise 6. 34 (4), we get $\kappa^\kappa \leq (2^\kappa)^\kappa$. But by Exercise 6. 34 (3), we have that $(2^\kappa)^\kappa = 2^{\kappa \cdot \kappa}$. By the Absorption Law, we have that $2^{\kappa \cdot \kappa} = 2^\kappa$. Hence $\kappa^\kappa \leq 2^\kappa$, as desired. ∎

It follows directly from Lemma 6. 103 and Exercise 6. 34 (4) that, if κ is an infinite cardinal, for every cardinal λ between 2 and κ, $\lambda^\kappa = 2^\kappa$. The following result enables us to extend this claim to every cardinal between 2 and 2^κ.

EXERCISE 6. 104: Show that for every infinite cardinal κ, $(2^\kappa)^\kappa = 2^\kappa$.

Hint: Invoke Exercise 6. 34 (3) and the Absorption Law.

When we raise cardinals greater than 2^κ to the power of κ the situation is more complicated, but in some cases we can still give a precise value, as expressed by the following exercise.

EXERCISE 6. 105: Show that if κ is an infinite cardinal, and λ is a cardinal greater than or equal to κ, then $(2^\lambda)^\kappa = 2^\lambda$.

Hint: Proceed as with Exercise 6. 104.

13. Completeness for Uncountable Languages

The results and techniques presented in this chapter provide invaluable tools for the study of first-order logic. We have been dealing all along with infinite sets. The sets which result from the main syntactic definitions of a first-order language L (the set of L-terms, the set of L-formulas, etc.) are infinite, and most interesting structures have infinite sets of objects as their universes. Hence it shouldn't come as a surprise that many important results about the relationship between first-order languages and their structures depend on assumptions about cardinality. In the next two chapters we shall present several important results which exhibit this dependence, but we close this chapter by looking at how facts about cardinality affect the main result about first-order logic that we have established so far, namely the Completeness Theorem.

We showed in Chapter 5 that the Model Existence Theorem holds for small languages, i.e. for every language L such that the sentences of $\bigcup L^+$, as defined in §7 of that chapter, can be enumerated. In this section we are going to do two things. First, we are going to characterize the class of small languages in terms of the cardinality of their extralogical vocabulary. Second, we are going to modify the proof of the Model Existence Theorem provided in Chapter 5 in such a way that the restriction to small languages can be lifted. We shall refer to the cardinality of the extralogical vocabulary of a language as the cardinality of the language.

Notice that we can formulate the claim that the sentences of $\bigcup L^+$ can be enumerated as concerning the cardinality of the set of $\bigcup L^+$-sentences.

Since an enumeration of the $\bigcup L^+$-sentences was defined as a one-to-one correspondence between $\mathbf{Z}^+$ and the set of $\bigcup L^+$-sentences, the claim that they can be enumerated is the claim that the set of $\bigcup L^+$-sentences is denumerable—that its cardinality is $\aleph_0$. We are going to show that the set of $\bigcup L^+$-sentences is denumerable, i.e. that L is small, just in case L is countable. Our first step towards this goal will be to show that if a language is countable, the set of formulas and the set of sentences of the language will be denumerable.

To establish connections between the cardinality of the set of formulas and the set of sentences of a first-order language, and the cardinality of its extralogical vocabulary, we need to take into account the cardinality of the logical vocabulary of first-order languages. We said in Chapter 3 that the logical vocabulary of a first-order language contains infinitely many variables. Now we can be more precise and stipulate that the cardinality of the set of variables of a first-order language is $\aleph_0$. Since the logical vocabulary of a first-order language only contains the variables and ten other symbols, we can conclude, by Exercise 6. 51, that the cardinality of the logical vocabulary of a first-order language is $\aleph_0$.

THEOREM 6. 106: If L is a countable first-order language, then the set of L-formulas and the set of L-sentences are denumerable.

Proof: Let L be a countable first-order language. We want to show that the cardinality of the set of L-formulas and of the set of L-sentences is $\aleph_0$. By the antisymmetry of $\leq$, it will suffice to show (i) that the cardinality of the set of L-formulas and of the set of L-sentences is at least $\aleph_0$, and (ii) that the cardinality of the set of L-formulas and of the set of L-sentences is at most $\aleph_0$.

For (i), consider, e.g., the set $\{\neg \forall x\, x \approx x, \neg\neg \forall x\, x \approx x, \neg\neg\neg \forall x\, x \approx x, \ldots\}$, which is a subset of the set of formulas and the set of sentences of every first-order language. The function pairing each positive integer n with the sentence in this set containing n negations is a one-to-one function from $\mathbf{Z}^+$ to the set of L-formulas and to the set of L-sentences. Hence the cardinality of both sets is at least $\aleph_0$.

For (ii) it will suffice to consider L-formulas, since the set of L-sentences is a subset of the set of L-formulas. Let FL be the set of L-formulas, and, for every positive integer n, let FLn be the set of L-formulas with n symbol occurrences. Since L-formulas are finite tuples of symbols, every L-formula will be in FLn, for some n. Hence FL is the union of the collection containing the set FLn for every positive integer n. Since there are denumerably many sets in this collection, to show that the cardinality of its union is at most $\aleph_0$, it will suffice, by Exercise 6.

79, to establish that, for every positive integer n, the cardinality of FLn is at most $\aleph_0$.

Let n be a positive integer, and let ϕ be an n-symbol L-formula. We can represent ϕ by specifying, for every positive integer m less than or equal to n, which symbol occupies the m-th position in ϕ. We can think of this representation of ϕ as the function from $\{1,\ldots, n\}$ to the set SL of symbols of L pairing each positive integer m in $\{1,\ldots, n\}$ with the m-th symbol in ϕ. Let's refer to this function as the *positional representation* of ϕ.

Now, the set of positional representations of n-symbol L-formulas is a subset of the set $^{\{1,\ldots, n\}}SL$ of functions from $\{1,\ldots, n\}$ to SL. We have that every n-symbol L-formula has a unique positional representation, and that different n-symbol L-formulas have different positional representations. It follows that the function pairing each n-symbol L-formula with its positional representation is a one-to-one function from FLn to $^{\{1,\ldots, n\}}SL$. Hence we have that $FLn \preceq {}^{\{1,\ldots, n\}}SL$. Therefore, to show that FLn is countable, it will suffice to show that $^{\{1,\ldots, n\}}SL$ is denumerable.

We have that $Card\ {}^{\{1,\ldots, n\}}SL = Card\ SL^{Card\ \{1,\ldots, n\}}$. We know that the set of extralogical symbols of L is countable, and that the set of logical symbols of L is denumerable. Hence we have that $Card\ SL = \aleph_0$. We also have that $Card\ \{1,\ldots, n\} = n$. Hence we can conclude that $Card\ {}^{\{1,\ldots, n\}}SL = \aleph_0{}^n$, and by Exercise 6. 102, we get $Card\ {}^{\{1,\ldots, n\}}SL = \aleph_0$, as desired. ∎

Theorem 6. 106 specifies the cardinality of the set of formulas and the set of sentences of a countable first-order language. The following exercise does the same for any infinite language.

EXERCISE 6. 107: Show that if L is a first-order language of cardinality κ, where κ is an infinite cardinal, then the cardinality of the set of L-formulas and the set of L-sentences is also κ.

Hint: Adapt the proof of Theorem 6. 106. To show that the cardinality of the set of L-sentences is at least κ, use the fact that you can form a different sentence with each extralogical symbol. To show that the cardinality of the set of L-formulas is at most κ, invoke the Absorption Law of Cardinal Arithmetic.

It follows from Theorem 6. 106 and Exercise 6. 107 that a first order language is small just in case $\bigcup L^+$ is countable. The next two results connect the cardinality of $\bigcup L^+$ with the cardinality of L itself.

LEMMA 6. 108: If L is a countable language, then $\bigcup L^+$ is also countable.

Proof: Let L be a countable language. The extralogical vocabulary of $\bigcup L^+$ is the union of the collection containing the extralogical vocabularies of the languages in L^+. There are denumerably many of these. Hence, to show that $\bigcup L^+$ is countable, it will suffice, by Exercise 6. 79, to show that each language in L^+ is countable. Since the elements of L^+ are the languages in the sequence $L_1, L_2, L_3,...$, it will suffice to establish that, for every positive integer n, L_n is countable. We show this by induction on n. The base is trivial, since L_1 is L, which we are assuming to be countable. For the inductive step, we assume (IH) that L_n is countable, and try to show that it follows from this that L_{n+1} is also countable. The extralogical vocabulary of L_{n+1} contains all the extralogical symbols of L_n plus one individual constant for each L_n-sentence of the form $\exists x$ α—i.e. it is the union of the extralogical vocabulary of L_n and the set of new individual constants. By IH, the extralogical vocabulary of L_n is countable. By Theorem 6. 106, the set of L_n-sentences of the form $\exists x$ α is also countable, and hence the same goes for the set of new individual constants of L_{n+1}. Hence the extralogical vocabulary of L_{n+1} is the union of two countable sets. Therefore, by Exercise 6. 58, it is also countable, as desired. ∎

EXERCISE 6. 109: Show that if L is a first-order language of cardinality κ, where κ is an infinite cardinal, the cardinality of $\bigcup L^+$ is also κ.

Lemma 6. 108 and Exercise 6. 109 tell us that $\bigcup L^+$ is countable if and only if L itself is countable. Given the connection between the cardinality of $\bigcup L^+$ and the cardinality of the set of $\bigcup L^+$-formulas and the set of $\bigcup L^+$-sentences that we established earlier, we can now conclude, as announced, that the set of $\bigcup L^+$-formulas and the set of $\bigcup L^+$-sentences are denumerable just in case L is countable. Hence we can say that what we established in Chapter 5 was that the Model Existence Theorem holds for countable languages. Our next goal is to show how the proof in Chapter 5 would have to be modified in order to take account of uncountable languages as well.

Lemma 5. 12 is the only step in the proof of Model Existence in Chapter 5 resting on the assumption that we are dealing with countable languages. Hence to remove the restriction to countable languages, it will suffice to extend the result of Lemma 5. 12 to languages of any cardinality. This is achieved by the following result, with which we close this chapter.

LEMMA 6. 110: Let L be a first-order language (of any cardinality). Every consistent set of L-sentences is extended by a consistent, negation-complete set of L-sentences.

Proof: Let Γ be a consistent set of sentences of a first-order language L. We need to show that Γ has a consistent, negation-complete extension. The proof will be based on the fact that, as we shall see presently, any maximal element of the collection containing all the consistent extensions of Γ would be negation-complete. But to make use of this fact we need to ascertain that this collection has indeed a maximal element. We achieve this with Zorn's Lemma, once we have shown that the collection of consistent extensions of Γ is (almost) closed under unions of chains.

Let S be the collection containing $\emptyset$ and every consistent extension of Γ. Our first goal is to show that S is closed under unions of chains. We know that S contains the union of the empty chain and of the chain $\{\emptyset\}$. Hence it only remains to be shown that S contains the union of any chain in S containing at least one consistent extension of Γ. Let C be such a chain. We need to establish that $\bigcup C$ is in S. For this it will suffice to show (i) that $\Gamma \subseteq \bigcup C$ and (ii) that $\bigcup C$ is consistent. (i) is immediate, since Γ is a subset of at least one set in C.

For (ii), assume, towards a contradiction, that there is an L-formula ϕ and finite subsets Γ_1, Γ_2 of $\bigcup C$ such that $\Gamma_1 \vdash \phi, \Gamma_2 \vdash \neg\phi$. Since $\Gamma_1, \Gamma_2 \subseteq \bigcup C$, each sentence in Γ_1 and each sentence in Γ_2 will be contained in at least one set in C. And since Γ_1 and Γ_2 are both finite, and C is linearly ordered by $\subseteq$, C contains a set A such that $\Gamma_1, \Gamma_2 \subseteq A$. But then A is inconsistent. Since $A \in S$, this contradicts the assumption that every nonempty set in S is a consistent extension of Γ, as desired.

Thus we have shown that S satisfies the hypothesis of Zorn's Lemma. Hence we can apply the lemma to assert the existence of a maximal element Γ^* of S. Notice that $\emptyset$ is not maximal, as S contains Γ, and $\emptyset \subseteq \Gamma$. Hence Γ^* is a consistent extension of Γ. It only remains to be shown that Γ^* is negation-complete.

Assume, towards a contradiction, that there is an L-sentence ψ such that $\psi \notin \Gamma^*$, $\neg\psi \notin \Gamma^*$. Since Γ^* is a maximal element of S, and $\Gamma^* \subseteq \Gamma^* \cup \{\psi\}$, $\Gamma^* \subseteq \Gamma^* \cup \{\neg\psi\}$, it follows that $\Gamma^* \cup \{\psi\}$, Γ^* and $\Gamma^* \cup \{\neg\psi\}$ are not in S. Since both sets extend Γ, we can conclude that they are inconsistent. Since $\Gamma^* \cup \{\psi\}$ is inconsistent, there is an L-formula α and finite subsets Δ_1, Δ_2 of $\Gamma^* \cup \{\psi\}$ such that $\Delta_1 \vdash \alpha, \Delta_2 \vdash \neg\alpha$. Hence, by Exercise 4. 4 (1), we have that $\Delta_1 \cup \{\psi\} \vdash \alpha, \Delta_2 \cup \{\psi\} \vdash \neg\alpha$, and, by Lemma 1. 13, $(\Delta_1 - \{\psi\}) \cup \{\psi\} \vdash \alpha, (\Delta_2 - \{\psi\}) \cup \{\psi\} \vdash \neg\alpha$. From this, using $\neg I$, we derive $(\Delta_1 - \{\psi\}) \cup (\Delta_2 - \{\psi\}) \vdash \neg\psi$. $(\Delta_1 - \{\psi\}) \cup (\Delta_2 - \{\psi\})$ is a finite subset of Γ^*. Hence $\neg\psi$ is deducible from a finite subset of Γ^*. We can reason in the same way to show that the inconsistency of $\Gamma^* \cup \{\neg\psi\}$ entails that $\neg\neg\psi$ is also deducible from a finite subset of Γ^*, which contradicts the hypothesis that Γ^* is consistent, as desired. ∎

Chapter 7

Expressive Limitations

1. Representation and Indiscernibility

In Chapter 3, §6, we considered several classes of structures, and set ourselves the task of finding for each of them a set of sentences of the language whose models are precisely the structures in that class. Thus, e.g.,
we found a set of sentences of the first-order language with a two-place
predicate, R, as its only extralogical symbol whose models are the structures in which R is interpreted with an equivalence relation in the universe. We can formulate this kind of result with the help of the following notions.

DEFINITION: A set Γ of sentences of a first-order language L *represents*
a class of L-structures C just in case the models of Γ are precisely the L-
structures in C.

DEFINITION: A class C of structures for a first-order language L is *representable* just in case there is a set of L-sentences which represents C.

What we did in Chapter 3, §6 was to find sets of L-sentences which
represent specific classes of structures. This chapter is devoted to
exploring the limits of representability. We are going to present a series
of results to the effect that many classes of structures are not
representable (representable classes of structures are often known as
elementary classes).

Let C be a class of structures of a first-order language L. In order for a set Γ of L-sentences to represent C, every structure in C will have to make all the sentences in Γ true, and every L-structure outside C will have to make at least one sentence in Γ false. Hence, if $\mathcal{B}$ is an L-structure outside C, Γ will have to contain an L-sentence which is false in $\mathcal{B}$, but if $\mathcal{A}$ is a structure in C, this sentence will have to be true in $\mathcal{A}$. This means that C will only be representable if, for every L-structure in C and every L-structure outside C, there is at least one L-sentence which is true in the former but false in the latter.

This may sound like a very innocuous requirement. For if $\mathcal{A}$ and $\mathcal{B}$ are different L-structures, then we might expect the differences between them to be reflected in the truth value that they assign to some L-sentence. But things don't look so simple on closer inspection. There are lots of cases in which the differences between structures are not reflected by the truth value that they assign to any sentence—different structures which assign the same truth value to every sentence. This situation will have direct repercussions for the representability of classes of structures. For if two structures of a first-order language L assign the same truth value to every L-sentence, every set of L-sentences having one as a model will also have the other as a model. Hence no set of L-sentences will represent any class of L-structures containing one but not the other. When two structures are related in this way we shall say that they are indiscernible.

DEFINITION: Two structures $\mathcal{A}$, $\mathcal{B}$ of a first-order language L are *indiscernible* just in case, for every L-sentence ϕ, $v_{\mathcal{A}}(\phi) = v_{\mathcal{B}}(\phi)$.

We are going to learn in this chapter that indiscernibility is a pervasive phenomenon (indiscernible structures are often known as *elementarily equivalent*).

For the next four exercises, let Γ, Δ be arbitrary sets of sentences of a first-order language.

EXERCISE 7. 1: Show that if $\Gamma \subseteq \Delta$, then every model of Δ is a model of Γ.

EXERCISE 7. 2: Show that a structure is a model of $\Gamma \cup \Delta$ if and only if it is a model of both Γ and Δ.

EXERCISE 7. 3: Show that every model of Γ and every model of Δ is a model of $\Gamma \cap \Delta$.

EXERCISE 7. 4: Show that it doesn't hold in general that every model of $\Gamma \cap \Delta$ is a model of Γ or of Δ.

2. Isomorphic Structures

We can introduce the most basic source of indiscernibility with an illustration. Let L be the first-order language whose extralogical symbols are an individual constant, c, a one-place predicate, P, and a one-place function-symbol, f. Let $\mathcal{A}$ be the L-structure whose universe is the set $A = \{\alpha, \beta, \gamma\}$, and such that $c_{\mathcal{A}} = \alpha$, $P_{\mathcal{A}} = \{\alpha, \beta\}$ and $f_{\mathcal{A}} = \{\langle\alpha, \gamma\rangle, \langle\gamma, \gamma\rangle, \langle\beta, \alpha\rangle\}$. We can represent $\mathcal{A}$ with the diagram in Figure 18.

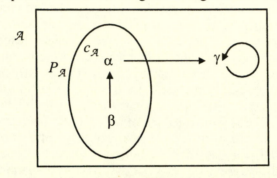

Figure 18

One can easily get the impression that $\mathcal{A}$ is not indiscernible from any other L-structure, since modifying $\mathcal{A}$ in any way would seem to alter the truth value of some L-sentence. Thus, e.g., if we added an object to the universe of $\mathcal{A}$, the truth value that it yields for the L-sentence $\forall x\forall y\forall w\forall z$ $(x \approx y \vee x \approx w \vee x \approx z \vee y \approx w \vee y \approx z \vee w \approx z)$ would change from T to F. Similarly, if we deleted one element from the universe of $\mathcal{A}$, the truth value of the L-sentence $\exists x\exists y\exists z$ ($\neg x \approx y \wedge \neg x \approx z \wedge \neg y \approx z$) would change from T to F. As the following exercise illustrates, we seem to encounter the same situation if we modify the way in which $\mathcal{A}$ interprets the extralogical symbols of L.

EXERCISE 7. 5: For each of the following ways in which $\mathcal{A}$ might be modified, find an L-sentence whose truth value in $\mathcal{A}$ would be affected by the change:
(1) Change the denotation of c from α to γ.
(2) Add γ to $P_{\mathcal{A}}$.
(3) Delete β from $P_{\mathcal{A}}$.
(4) Change the image of γ under $f_{\mathcal{A}}$ from γ to β.
(5) Change the image of β under $f_{\mathcal{A}}$ from α to β.

But in spite of what these cases might suggest, it would be wrong to conclude that no other L-structure is indiscernible from $\mathcal{A}$. Isolated changes to the way in which $\mathcal{A}$ interprets the extralogical symbols of L will normally affect the truth value of some L-sentence. Nevertheless, $\mathcal{A}$ can be changed in any of the respects contemplated in Exercise 7.5 without affecting the truth value of any L-sentence, provided that we are prepared to make "compensating" changes elsewhere in the structure. In fact, if we change $\mathcal{A}$ in *all* these respects, the resulting structure will be indiscernible from $\mathcal{A}$. Thus let $\mathcal{B}$ be the L-structure with the same universe as $\mathcal{A}$ in which the extralogical symbols of L are interpreted in the following way: $c_{\mathcal{B}} = \gamma$, $P_{\mathcal{B}} = \{\gamma, \alpha\}$, and $f_{\mathcal{B}} = \{\langle \gamma, \beta \rangle, \langle \beta, \beta \rangle, \langle \alpha, \gamma \rangle\}$. $\mathcal{B}$ is the structure that would result from making all these changes to $\mathcal{A}$. It is represented by the diagram in Figure 19. As we are about to see, $\mathcal{B}$ is indiscernible from $\mathcal{A}$.

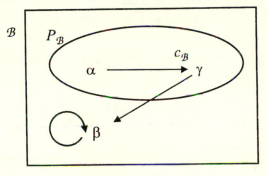

Figure 19

EXERCISE 7.6: Show that all the sentences that you used in Exercise 7.5 have the same truth value in $\mathcal{B}$ as in $\mathcal{A}$.

The indiscernibility of $\mathcal{A}$ and $\mathcal{B}$ arises from the possibility of pairing off the elements of their universes in such a way that every element of each universe is paired with an element of the other universe which plays the same role in the interpretation of the extralogical symbols of L. Thus the role that α plays in the interpretation of the extralogical symbols of L by $\mathcal{A}$ is identical to the role that γ plays in $\mathcal{B}$. Similarly, the role that γ plays in $\mathcal{A}$ is the role that β plays in $\mathcal{B}$, and the role that β plays in $\mathcal{A}$ is the role that α plays in $\mathcal{B}$. We are going to see that this situation will always make two structures indiscernible.

First we need to have a more precise characterization of the relationship between $\mathcal{A}$ and $\mathcal{B}$ that we are blaming for their indiscernibility. We introduce for this purpose the notion of an isomorphism.

DEFINITION: If $\mathcal{A}$ and $\mathcal{B}$ are structures of a first-order language L, an *isomorphism* between $\mathcal{A}$ and $\mathcal{B}$ is a function h from the universe A of $\mathcal{A}$ to the universe B of $\mathcal{B}$ which satisfies the following conditions:

(a) h is a one-to-one correspondence between A and B.

(b) For every individual constant c of L, $h(c_{\mathcal{A}}) = c_{\mathcal{B}}$.

(c) For every m-place function symbol f of L, and all $a_1,\ldots, a_m \in A$, $h(f_{\mathcal{A}}(a_1,\ldots, a_m)) = f_{\mathcal{B}}(h(a_1),\ldots, h(a_m))$.

(d) For every n-place predicate P of L, and all $a_1,\ldots, a_n \in A$, $\langle a_1,\ldots, a_n \rangle \in P_{\mathcal{A}}$ if and only if $\langle h(a_1),\ldots, h(a_n) \rangle \in P_{\mathcal{B}}$.

We shall say that $\mathcal{A}$ is *isomorphic* to $\mathcal{B}$ just in case there is an isomorphism between $\mathcal{A}$ and $\mathcal{B}$. Notice that if h is an isomorphism between $\mathcal{A}$ and $\mathcal{B}$, and a is an element of A, a and $h(a)$ will play the same role in the interpretation of the extralogical symbols of L in their respective structures.

EXERCISE 7. 7: Show that, for all structures $\mathcal{A}$, $\mathcal{B}$, C of a first-order language,

(1) $\mathcal{A}$ is isomorphic to $\mathcal{A}$.
(2) If $\mathcal{A}$ is isomorphic to $\mathcal{B}$, then $\mathcal{B}$ is isomorphic to $\mathcal{A}$.
(3) If $\mathcal{A}$ is isomorphic to $\mathcal{B}$ and $\mathcal{B}$ is isomorphic to C, then $\mathcal{A}$ is isomorphic to C.

We can now formulate the result that we have announced as the claim that isomorphic structures are indiscernible. Notice that this is the claim that if two L-structures are isomorphic, then every L-sentence has the same truth value in each of them. This is a claim about all L-sentences, and to establish it we follow the standard procedure of proving a result about all L-formulas from which the claim about L-sentences follows as a special case. Let $\mathcal{A}$ and $\mathcal{B}$ be two isomorphic structures of a first-order language L, and let h be an isomorphism between $\mathcal{A}$ and $\mathcal{B}$. Notice that the image under h of every element of the universe of $\mathcal{A}$ is an element of the universe of $\mathcal{B}$. Hence, if s is a variable interpretation in $\mathcal{A}$, the composition of h and s, $h \circ s$, will be a variable interpretation in $\mathcal{B}$, since it will pair each variable x with an element of the universe of $\mathcal{B}$, namely $h(s(x))$. We can show, by induction on L-formulas, that, for every variable interpretation s in $\mathcal{A}$, the truth value of every L-formula in $\mathcal{A}$ relative to s will coincide with its truth value in $\mathcal{B}$ relative to $h \circ s$. Since the truth value of an L-sentence in an L-structure is the same for every variable interpretation, we will be able to conclude from this that every L-sentence has the same truth value in $\mathcal{A}$ and in $\mathcal{B}$. But before we establish this result about L-formulas, we need to prove, as usual, a parallel result about L-terms.

ISOMORPHISM THEOREM FOR TERMS: If A and B are two isomorphic structures of a first-order language L, h an isomorphism between A and B, s a variable interpretation in A, and t an L-term, then $h(den_A(t, s)) = den_B(t, h \circ s)$.

Proof: Let A and B be two isomorphic structures of a first-order language L, h an isomorphism between A and B, and s a variable interpretation in A. We prove, by induction on L-terms, that, for every L-term t, $h(den_A(t, s)) = den_B(t, h \circ s)$.

  Base:

  (i) Let x be a variable. We need to show that $den_B(x, h \circ s) = h(den_A(x, s))$. We argue as follows:

$den_B(x, h \circ s)$

    $=$ (definition of denotation)

$h \circ s(x)$

    $=$ (definition of composition)

$h(s(x))$

    $=$ (since, by the definition of denotation, $den_A(x, s) = s(x)$)

$h(den_A(x, s))$

  (ii) Let c be an individual constant of L. We need to show that $den_B(c, h \circ s) = h(den_A(c, s))$. We argue as follows:

$den_B(c, h \circ s)$

    $=$ (definition of denotation)

c_B

    $=$ (definition of isomorphism)

$h(c_A)$

    $=$ (since, by the definition of denotation, $den_A(c, s) = c_A$)

$h(den_A(c, s))$

  Inductive Step: Let $t_1, \ldots, t_n$ be L-terms, and let f be an n-place function symbol of L. Assume (IH) that $den_B(t_1, h \circ s) = h(den_A(t_1, s)), \ldots, den_B(t_n, h \circ s) = h(den_A(t_n, s))$. We need to show that it follows from this that $den_B(f(t_1, \ldots, t_n), h \circ s) = h(den_A(f(t_1, \ldots, t_n), s))$.

$den_{\mathcal{B}}(f(t_1,\ldots, t_n), h \circ s)$

    =   (definition of denotation)

$f_{\mathcal{B}}(den_{\mathcal{B}}(t_1, h \circ s),\ldots, den_{\mathcal{B}}(t_n, h \circ s))$

    =   (IH)

$f_{\mathcal{B}}(h(den_{\mathcal{A}}(t_1, s)),\ldots, h(den_{\mathcal{A}}(t_n, s)))$

    =   (definition of isomorphism)

$h(f_{\mathcal{A}}(den_{\mathcal{A}}(t_1, s),\ldots, den_{\mathcal{A}}(t_n, s)))$

    =   (since, by the definition of denotation, $den_{\mathcal{A}}(f(t_1,\ldots, t_n), s) = f_{\mathcal{A}}(den_{\mathcal{A}}(t_1, s),\ldots, den_{\mathcal{A}}(t_n, s))$

$h(den_{\mathcal{A}}(f(t_1,\ldots, t_n), s))$ ■

ISOMORPHISM THEOREM FOR FORMULAS: If $\mathcal{A}$ and $\mathcal{B}$ are two isomorphic structures of a first-order language L, h an isomorphism between $\mathcal{A}$ and $\mathcal{B}$, s a variable interpretation in $\mathcal{A}$, and ϕ an L-formula, then $v_{\mathcal{A}}(\phi, s) = v_{\mathcal{B}}(\phi, h \circ s)$.

Proof: Let $\mathcal{A}$ and $\mathcal{B}$ be two isomorphic structures of a first-order language L, and let h be an isomorphism between $\mathcal{A}$ and $\mathcal{B}$. We prove by induction on L-formulas that, for every L-formula ϕ and every variable interpretation s in $\mathcal{A}$, $v_{\mathcal{A}}(\phi, s) = v_{\mathcal{B}}(\phi, h \circ s)$. Some of the clauses are left as an exercise.

Base: Let P be an n-place L-predicate, $t_1,\ldots, t_n$ L-terms, and s a variable interpretation in $\mathcal{A}$. We have to show that $v_{\mathcal{B}}(Pt_1\ldots t_n, h \circ s) = v_{\mathcal{A}}(Pt_1\ldots t_n, s)$. We argue as follows:

$v_{\mathcal{B}}(Pt_1\ldots t_n, h \circ s) = T$

    $\updownarrow$ (definition of truth)

$\langle den_{\mathcal{B}}(t_1, h \circ s),\ldots, den_{\mathcal{B}}(t_n, h \circ s)\rangle \in P_{\mathcal{B}}$

    $\updownarrow$ (Isomorphism Theorem for Terms)

$\langle h(den_{\mathcal{A}}(t_1, s)),\ldots, h(den_{\mathcal{A}}(t_n, s))\rangle \in P_{\mathcal{B}}$

    $\updownarrow$ (definition of isomorphism)

$\langle den_{\mathcal{A}}(t_1, s),\ldots, den_{\mathcal{A}}(t_n, s)\rangle \in P_{\mathcal{A}}$

    $\updownarrow$ (definition of truth)

$v_{\mathcal{A}}(Pt_1\ldots t_n, s) = T$

Inductive Step:

∧. Let α, β be two L-formulas. We assume (IH) that for every variable interpretation s in $\mathcal{A}$, $v_{\mathcal{A}}(\alpha, s) = v_{\mathcal{B}}(\alpha, h \circ s)$ and $v_{\mathcal{A}}(\beta, s) = v_{\mathcal{B}}(\beta, h \circ s)$. We have to show that it follows from this that for every variable interpretation s in $\mathcal{A}$, $v_{\mathcal{A}}(\alpha \wedge \beta, s) = v_{\mathcal{B}}(\alpha \wedge \beta, h \circ s)$. Let s be a variable interpretation in $\mathcal{A}$. We argue as follows:

$v_{\mathcal{B}}(\alpha \wedge \beta, h \circ s) = T$

$\Updownarrow$ (definition of truth)

$v_{\mathcal{B}}(\alpha, h \circ s) = v_{\mathcal{B}}(\beta, h \circ s) = T$

$\Updownarrow$ (IH)

$v_{\mathcal{A}}(\alpha, s) = v_{\mathcal{A}}(\beta, s) = T$

$\Updownarrow$ (definition of truth)

$v_{\mathcal{A}}(\alpha \wedge \beta, s) = T$

∃. Let α be an L-formula. We assume (IH) that for every variable interpretation s in $\mathcal{A}$, $v_{\mathcal{A}}(\alpha, s) = v_{\mathcal{B}}(\alpha, h \circ s)$. We have to prove that it follows from this that for every variable interpretation s in $\mathcal{A}$, $v_{\mathcal{A}}(\exists x\, \alpha, s) = v_{\mathcal{B}}(\exists x\, \alpha, h \circ s)$. Let s be a variable interpretation in $\mathcal{A}$. We argue as follows:

$v_{\mathcal{B}}(\exists x\, \alpha, h \circ s) = T$

$\Updownarrow$ (definition of truth)

For at least one $b \in B$, $v_{\mathcal{B}}(\alpha, (h \circ s)_{(x/b)}) = T$

$\Updownarrow$ (from the fact that h is a function from the universe of $\mathcal{A}$ to the universe of $\mathcal{B}$, with the whole universe of $\mathcal{B}$ as its range)

For at least one $a \in A$, $v_{\mathcal{B}}(\alpha, (h \circ s)_{(x/h(a))}) = T$

$\Updownarrow$ (from Exercise 7. 9, below)

For at least one $a \in A$, $v_{\mathcal{B}}(\alpha, h \circ s_{(x/a)}) = T$

$\Updownarrow$ (IH)

For at least one $a \in A$, $v_{\mathcal{A}}(\alpha, s_{(x/a)}) = T$

$\Updownarrow$ (definition of truth)

$v_{\mathcal{A}}(\exists x\, \alpha, s) = T$ ∎

EXERCISE 7. 8: Complete the base clause for $\approx$, and the inductive clauses for $\neg$, $\vee$, $\rightarrow$, and $\forall$ in the proof of the Isomorphism Theorem.

EXERCISE 7. 9: Prove that $(h \circ s)_{(x/h(a))}$ is the same variable interpretation as $h \circ s_{(x/a)}$.

The following two results are immediate consequences of the Isomorphism Theorem.

COROLLARY 7. 10: Isomorphic structures are indiscernible.

COROLLARY 7. 11: Let $\mathcal{A}$, $\mathcal{B}$ be two isomorphic structures of a first-order language L. For every set of L-sentences Γ, if $\mathcal{A}$ is a model of Γ, then $\mathcal{B}$ is a model of Γ.

EXERCISE 7. 12: Let $\mathcal{A}$ be a structure of a first-order language L. Show that if B is a set of the same cardinality as the universe of $\mathcal{A}$, there is an L-structure $\mathcal{B}$ with B as its universe such that $\mathcal{B}$ is isomorphic to $\mathcal{A}$.

EXERCISE 7. 13: Let $\mathcal{A}$ be a structure of a first-order language L, and let h be a one-to-one correspondence between the universe of $\mathcal{A}$ and itself. Show that there is an L-structure $\mathcal{B}$ with the same universe as $\mathcal{A}$ such that h is an isomorphism between $\mathcal{A}$ and $\mathcal{B}$.

The indiscernibility of isomorphic structures imposes clear limits on which classes of structures are representable. Let's say that a class C of structures of a first-order language is *closed under isomorphism* just in case every structure isomorphic to a structure in C is also in C. The indiscernibility of isomorphic structures entails that a class of structures will be representable only if it is closed under isomorphism. Notice that since for every structure $\mathcal{A}$ there will be other structures which are isomorphic to $\mathcal{A}$, it follows from this that no set of sentences can have only one model. The closest we can come to representing a structure $\mathcal{A}$ of a first-order language L with L-sentences is to find a set of L-sentences all of whose models are isomorphic to $\mathcal{A}$.

DEFINITION: A set of sentences Γ of a first-order language L *represents* an L-structure $\mathcal{A}$ *up to isomorphism* just in case Γ represents the class of L-structures which are isomorphic to $\mathcal{A}$.

The indiscernibility of isomorphic structures entails that representation up to isomorphism is the closest we can get to representing a single structure. But we shall soon see that, for most structures, even representation up to isomorphism is an unattainable goal.

3. Isomorphic Structures and Contextual Definitions

In Chapter 6, §10, we suggested that the way in which a set of sentences of a first-order language represents a class of structures can be seen as modeling the process of contextual definition. Thus, e.g., in the language L with a two-place predicate R as its only extralogical symbol, a set of L-sentences whose models are precisely the L-structures in which R is interpreted with a partial ordering of the universe can be seen as modeling a contextual definition of partial ordering. In light of this connection, we can take the fact that a structure can only be represented up to isomorphism as setting limits on what a contextual definition can achieve.

Let L be the language of (first-order) arithmetic, whose extralogical vocabulary contains an individual constant, 0, a one-place function symbol, s, and two two-place function symbols, + and $\cdot$. If we treat the natural numbers as an independently given domain, they generate, as we saw in Chapter 3, §6v, a structure $\mathcal{N}$ for this language, whose universe is ω, and in which 0 denotes number zero, and s, + and $\cdot$ are interpreted with the successor, addition and multiplication functions in ω.

A contextual definition which singled out the domain of the natural numbers and the arithmetical operations would be modeled by a set of L-sentences having $\mathcal{N}$ as its only model. But it follows from the Isomorphism Theorem that such a set of L-sentences is not to be had. If Γ is a set of L-sentences having $\mathcal{N}$ as a model, every other L-structure which is isomorphic to $\mathcal{N}$ will also be a model of Γ. Hence, if we think of the natural numbers as a specific domain of objects, a contextual definition which can be modeled with a set of L-sentences won't single them out from other isomorphic domains (although, as we are about to see, this is by no means the only limitation on a contextual definition of the natural numbers).

Frege rejected conceptual definitions on these grounds. He argued that a contextual definition of the geometrical concept of direction would not be acceptable because it wouldn't rule out the possibility that England is a direction. Most mathematicians, however, do not share Frege's concerns, and seem perfectly happy with singling out the identity of the objects that they deal with only up to isomorphism. So long as it is isomorphic to $\mathcal{N}$, any structure of the language of arithmetic is as good as any other for the purposes of discovering arithmetical truths. Arithmetic is only concerned with what these structures have in common. Which of them should be regarded as the natural numbers is not considered a mathematically interesting question.

This attitude is much more problematic when we try to apply the method of contextual definition outside the realm of abstract objects. Let S be a set of first-order propositions purporting to describe the physical world, and let Γ be a set of sentences of a first-order language L modeling the propositions in S. Assume, for the sake of the argument, that all the propositions in S are true, and that Γ is a negation-complete set of L-sentences, i.e., for every L-sentence ϕ, either ϕ or $\neg\phi$ is in Γ.

We can define an L-structure using as its universe the domain of objects that the propositions in S represent, and interpreting the extralogical symbols of L in this universe with (the extensional surrogates of) the properties, relations, functions and individuals that they model. Let's refer to this structure as the *intended L-structure*. Thus, e.g., if S is a theory about the subatomic particles, and the property of being an electron and the property of having charge figure in it, the vocabulary of L will contain two one-place predicates, E and C, modeling these properties. In the intended L-structure, E will be interpreted with the set of electrons, and C with the set of subatomic particles with charge.

We might have expected that Γ, treated as a contextual definition, could be used to single out the intended L-structure, without invoking our intentions as to how to interpret the extralogical symbols of L. The intended structure would be singled out, on this proposal, as the model of Γ. Nevertheless, it follows from the results of the preceding section that this proposal is incorrect. Since we are assuming that all the propositions in S are true, the intended L-structure will certainly be a model of Γ. But, by Corollary 7. 11, every other L-structure isomorphic with the intended L-structure will also be a model of Γ. In fact, by Exercise 7. 12, for every set A of the same cardinality as the universe of the intended L-structure, Γ will have a model with A as its universe. Thus, e.g., if the set of subatomic particles is denumerable, Γ will have a model whose universe is not this set, but the set of natural numbers. And even if we fix the universe, Γ will have many models, since, by Exercise 7. 13, any permutation of the subatomic particles will generate an L-structure isomorphic to the intended L-structure, and hence a model of Γ. In some of these models, E might be interpreted, for example, with a set containing nothing but protons.

These considerations suggest that a theory which purports to represent the physical world cannot be treated as a contextual definition of the terms which figure in it. One could try to avoid this conclusion by thinking of empirical theories as having as their subject matter what their models have in common. But given that any (consistent) empirical theory will have models which don't even have physical entities in their universe, this route seems rather unpromising (even if we assume that the theory is true and complete). These remarks apply, in the first instance, to the conception of empirical theories as contextual definitions of *all* the terms which figure in them. The situation is more complicated if we think of an empirical theory as contextually defining only some of the terms which figure in it, treating the interpretation of the others as given. We shall not pursue this question here. Nevertheless, it can be argued that any nontrivial proposal of this kind would be undermined by the indiscernibility of isomorphic structures.

4. Representing Finite Structures

We saw in §2 that representation up to isomorphism is the closest we can hope to get to representing a single structure. We are about to see that, for infinite structures (i.e. structures with infinite universes), even this is too ambitious a goal. Nevertheless, for finite structures (those with finite universes), representation up to isomorphism is always a possibility. Our goal in this section is to establish this result, in the case of finite first-order languages.

THEOREM 7. 14: If L is a finite first-order language and $\mathcal{A}$ is a finite L-structure, then there is an L-sentence ϕ which represents $\mathcal{A}$ up to isomorphism.

Proof: Let L be a first-order language with a finite extralogical vocabulary, and let $\mathcal{A}$ be a finite L-structure. Let $a_1,\ldots, a_n$ be the elements of the universe of $\mathcal{A}$, and let f be a one-to-one function from the universe of $\mathcal{A}$ to the set of variables. For every positive integer i less than or equal to n, we represent the variable with which f pairs a_i as x_i. We describe an L-sentence ϕ of which we claim that it has $\mathcal{A}$ as a model and all its models are isomorphic to $\mathcal{A}$. ϕ will be of the form $\exists x_1\ldots \exists x_n \psi$, where ψ is a string of conjunctions containing the following conjuncts:

First we have, for all positive integers i, j less than or equal to n such that i is less than j, the conjunct $\neg x_i \approx x_j$. Notice that these conjuncts will guarantee that the universe of any model of ϕ will have at least n elements.

Next we have the conjunct $\forall y (y \approx x_1 \vee \ldots \vee y \approx x_n)$, where y is different from each of $x_1,\ldots, x_n$. This conjunct will ensure that the universe of any model of ϕ contains at most n elements.

Next we have, for each individual constant c of L, a conjunct of the form $c \approx x_i$, where x_i is the image under f of the denotation of c in $\mathcal{A}$.

Then, for every m-place predicate P, we will have a conjunct for each m-tuple of elements of the universe of $\mathcal{A}$. We will represent these conjuncts with the help of the following notation: If t is a tuple of elements of the universe of $\mathcal{A}$, $\bar{x}_t$ will represent the sequence of variables formed by the variables with which the members of t are paired by f. This, e.g., $\bar{x}_{\langle a_i, a_j \rangle}$ will be $\langle x_i, x_j \rangle$. We can now describe the conjuncts in ψ corresponding to P. For every m-tuple t in $P_{\mathcal{A}}$, ψ will contain the conjunct $P\bar{x}_t$, and for every m-tuple u of elements of the universe of $\mathcal{A}$ outside $P_{\mathcal{A}}$, ψ will contain the conjunct $\neg P\bar{x}_u$. Thus, e.g., if R is a two-place predicate of L, and $\langle a_i, a_j \rangle \in R_{\mathcal{A}}$, ψ will contain as a conjunct the formula $Rx_i x_j$. If $\langle a_k, a_l \rangle \notin R_{\mathcal{A}}$, ψ will contain as a conjunct the formula $\neg Rx_k x_l$.

Finally, for every p-place function symbol g of L, and every p-tuple t of elements of the universe of $\mathcal{A}$, ψ will contain the conjunct $g(\bar{x}_t) \approx x_i$, where x_i is the variable with which f pairs the image of t under $g_{\mathcal{A}}$. Thus, e.g., if h is a two-place function symbol of L, and $h_{\mathcal{A}}(a_i, a_j)$ is a_k, ψ will contain the conjunct $h(x_i, x_j) \approx x_k$.

Clearly, $\mathcal{A}$ is a model of ϕ, since for every variable interpretation s in $\mathcal{A}$, $v_{\mathcal{A}}(\psi, s_{(x_1/a_1)\ldots(x_n/a_n)}) = T$. We now need to prove that every model of ϕ is isomorphic to $\mathcal{A}$. Let $\mathcal{B}$ be a model of ϕ. To show that $\mathcal{B}$ is isomorphic to $\mathcal{A}$, we define an isomorphism h between $\mathcal{B}$ and $\mathcal{A}$. Let s be a variable interpretation in $\mathcal{B}$. Since $\mathcal{B}$ is a model of ϕ, it follows that for at least one sequence $b_1, \ldots, b_n$ of elements of the universe of $\mathcal{B}$, $v_{\mathcal{B}}(\psi, s_{(x_1/b_1)\ldots(x_n/b_n)}) = T$. Notice that the first string of conjuncts of ψ ensure that all of $b_1, \ldots, b_n$ are distinct from each other, and the next conjunct guarantees that they are the only elements of the universe of $\mathcal{B}$. Hence we can define a function from the universe of $\mathcal{B}$ to the universe of $\mathcal{A}$ as follows: For every positive integer i less than or equal to n, $h(b_i) = a_i$. To complete the proof, we only need to show that h is an isomorphism between $\mathcal{B}$ and $\mathcal{A}$. This requires showing that it satisfies all the clauses of the definition of isomorphism. We shall deal with clause (d) here and leave the rest as an exercise.

Let P be an m-place L-predicate. Let t be an m-tuple of elements of the universe of $\mathcal{B}$. Let t_h be the tuple of elements of the universe of $\mathcal{A}$ formed by the images under h of the members of t. Thus, e.g., if t is the pair $\langle b_i$,

$b_j \rangle$, t_h is the pair $\langle a_i, a_j \rangle$. We need to show that $t \in P_{\mathcal{B}}$ if and only if $t_h \in P_{\mathcal{A}}$.

Assume first that $t \in P_{\mathcal{B}}$. We know that either $P\bar{x}_t$ or $\neg P\bar{x}_t$ is a conjunct in ψ, and that every conjunct in ψ is true in $\mathcal{B}$ relative to $s_{(x_1/b_1)...(x_n/b_n)}$. But $\neg P\bar{x}_t$ is false in $\mathcal{B}$ relative to $s_{(x_1/b_1)...(x_n/b_n)}$. Hence $P\bar{x}_t$ is a conjunct in ψ. But since $\bar{x}_t$ is $\bar{x}_{t_h}$, it follows that $t_h \in P_{\mathcal{A}}$, as desired. A similar reasoning establishes that, if $t \notin P_{\mathcal{B}}$, then $t_h \notin P_{\mathcal{A}}$. ∎

EXERCISE 7. 15: Complete the proof of Theorem 7. 14 by showing that h satisfies the remaining clauses of the definition of isomorphism.

EXERCISE 7. 16: Let L be a finite first-order language, and C a finite class of finite L-structures. Let C^* be the class of L-structures consisting of the elements of C and every L-structure that is isomorphic to one of them. Show that there is an L-sentence ϕ which represents C^*. Explain why your argument wouldn't work if C weren't finite.

5. The Downward Löwenheim-Skolem Theorem

The outcome of the preceding section is that the indiscernibility of isomorphic structures is the only obstacle to the representation of a finite structure. In the remainder of this chapter we are going to see that with respect to infinite structures the situation is much more problematic. We are going to see that any set of sentences of a first-order language with an infinite model $\mathcal{A}$ will also have other models which are not isomorphic to $\mathcal{A}$. With infinite structures, representation up to isomorphism is not a possibility.

The first few results of this kind that we are going to consider belong to what is known as the Löwenheim-Skolem family of theorems, after Leopold Löwenheim and Thoralf Skolem, who established the first results in this area in the second decade of the 20th century. They are concerned with the cardinality of the models of a set of sentences. Each of them entails that if a set of sentences has a model $\mathcal{A}$ of a certain infinite cardinality, it will also have models of other infinite cardinalities. Notice that this kind of result renders the representation of $\mathcal{A}$ up to isomorphism impossible, since, given that an isomorphism between two structures is a one-to-one correspondence between their universes, structures of different cardinalities cannot be isomorphic. We start with the following result.

DOWNWARD LÖWENHEIM-SKOLEM THEOREM (countable languages): Every set of sentences of a countable first-order language which has a model has a countable model.

Proof: We know from Exercise 5. 5 that every set of sentences which has a model is consistent. Hence, to prove the theorem it will suffice to show that every consistent set of sentences of a countable first-order language has a countable model. We shall establish this result by taking a closer look at the argument that we used in the proof of the Model Existence Theorem in Chapter 5. The proof that we presented proceeds by describing a model of an arbitrary consistent set of sentences of a countable first-order language. We are going to see that the model that we described is a countable model.

Let L be a countable language, and let Γ be a consistent set of L-sentences. From Lemma 5. 17, we know that Γ is extended by a consistent Henkin set Γ^+ of sentences of the language $\bigcup L^+$, as defined in Chapter 5, §7. We also know, from Lemma 6. 108, that $\bigcup L^+$ is countable, and hence, by Theorem 6. 106, that the set of $\bigcup L^+$-sentences is denumerable. Hence, by Lemma 5. 12, we know that Γ^+ is extended by a consistent, negation-complete set Γ^* of $\bigcup L^+$-sentences which is also a Henkin set. By Lemma 5. 18, Γ^* is a well-rounded set, and, by Lemma 5. 10, the canonical structure of Γ^* is a model of Γ^*, and hence of Γ. Let $\mathcal{A}$ be the reduct to L of the canonical structure of Γ^*. $\mathcal{A}$ is an L-structure which is a model of Γ. We are going to show that $\mathcal{A}$ is a countable structure.

Notice that $\mathcal{A}$ has the same universe as the canonical structure of Γ^*, i.e. the set of equivalence classes generated with the relation $\sim_{\Gamma^*}$ by the closed terms of $\bigcup L^+$. Hence, it follows from Exercise 7. 18, below, that the cardinality of the universe of $\mathcal{A}$ is at most the cardinality of the set of closed terms of $\bigcup L^+$. But we can easily show that the set of closed terms of $\bigcup L^+$ is countable (this is left as an exercise). Hence $\mathcal{A}$ has a countable universe, and since $\mathcal{A}$ is a model of Γ, Γ has a countable model, as desired.   ∎

EXERCISE 7. 17: Show that if L is a countable language, then the set of closed terms of L is denumerable.

Hint: Invoke the results of Chapter 6, §12.

EXERCISE 7. 18: Let R be an equivalence relation in a set A, and let A_R be the set of equivalence classes generated with R by the elements of A. Show that the cardinality of A_R is at most the cardinality of A.

The following exercise generalizes this result to languages of any cardinality.

EXERCISE 7. 19 (*Downward Löwenheim-Skolem Theorem* (general case)): Let L be a first-order language of cardinality κ, where κ is an infinite cardinal. Show that every set of L-sentences which has a model has a model of cardinality at most κ.

Hint: Proceed as with the countable case, invoking the generalization of the proof of the Model Existence Theorem provided in Chapter 6, §12.

The Downward Löwenheim-Skolem Theorem imposes serious limitations on the representation of infinite structures. If $\mathcal{A}$ is an uncountable structure of a countable first-order language L, it follows from the Downward Löwenheim-Skolem Theorem that $\mathcal{A}$ cannot be represented up to isomorphism by any set of L-sentences, since any set of L-sentences having $\mathcal{A}$ as a model will also have countable models—which cannot be isomorphic to $\mathcal{A}$. The same situation ensues from the general version of the theorem for any infinite structure whose cardinality is higher than that of the language.

More generally, the Downward Löwenheim-Skolem Theorem entails that, if L is a countable language, any class C of exclusively uncountable structures will not be represented by any set of L-sentences. For any set of L-sentences having a model will have a model outside C. Similarly, if L is a language of cardinality κ, where κ is an infinite cardinal, any class C of L-structures containing only structures of cardinalities higher than κ will not be represented by any set of L-sentences.

6. Skolem's Paradox

We know from Chapter 6 that there are uncountable sets. The methods that we used to establish this result can be easily adapted to show that there are uncountable pure sets (see Chapter 6, §10). We could argue as follows. For every pure set A, $A \cup \{A\}$ is also a pure set. Let's refer to this set as the *successor* of A, written A^+. The elements of the successor of A are the elements of A and A itself. Since $\varnothing$ is a pure set, every set in the sequence $\varnothing, \varnothing^+, \varnothing^{++}, \varnothing^{+++}, \dots$ is also a pure set. We shall refer to the sets in this sequence (including $\varnothing$) as the *descendants* of $\varnothing$. We have that the set whose elements are the descendants of $\varnothing$ is also a pure set. We shall represent it as $D\varnothing$. We can easily show that the set of descendants of $\varnothing$ is denumerable, since we can define by recursion a one-to-one correspondence f between the set of natural numbers and $D\varnothing$, as the unique function satisfying the following conditions:

$f(0) = \varnothing.$

For every natural number n, $f(n + 1) = f(n)^+$.

This is, in fact, the function standardly used to "define" the natural numbers in set-theoretic terms (see Chapter 6, §6).

EXERCISE 7. 20: Show that f is a one-to-one correspondence between the set of natural numbers and $D\emptyset$.

Now, since every subset of $D\emptyset$ is a pure set, the power set of $D\emptyset$, $\wp D\emptyset$, is also a pure set. Since $D\emptyset$ is denumerable, it follows from Theorem 6. 60 that $\wp D\emptyset$ is uncountable. And since every element of $\wp D\emptyset$ is a pure set, we can conclude that there are uncountably many pure sets.

If we think of the set-theoretic universe as contextually defined by the axioms of ZF (see Chapter 6, §10), we will be able to draw the same conclusion, since the existence and uncountability of $\wp D\emptyset$ are logical consequences of ZF. We find a formal correlate of this situation in the language $L_\in$—whose only extralogical symbol is a two-place predicate, $\in$ (see Chapter 6, §10). The propositions asserting the existence and uncountability of $\wp D\emptyset$ are modeled by $L_\in$-sentences, and these $L_\in$-sentences are logical consequences of Θ_{ZF}—true in every model of Θ_{ZF} (if it has any). Hence the universe of every model of Θ_{ZF} will contain an uncountable set. Since all the elements of this set will also be in the universe of the model, it seems to follow that Θ_{ZF} has only uncountable models. But the Downward Löwenheim-Skolem Theorem tells us that, if Θ_{ZF} has models, then it has a countable model. Hence, if Θ_{ZF} has models, it has a model which is both countable and uncountable. This apparent contradiction is known as *Skolem's Paradox*.

In order to see that the contradiction is only apparent we need to take a closer look at how it is supposed to arise. Let $\mathcal{A}$ be a countable model of Θ_{ZF}. Let's refer to the elements of the universe of $\mathcal{A}$ as $\mathcal{A}$-*sets*. If an $\mathcal{A}$-set A bears to an $\mathcal{A}$-set B the relation $\in_\mathcal{A}$ with which $\in$ is interpreted in $\mathcal{A}$, we shall say that A is an $\mathcal{A}$-*element* of B. The axioms of Θ_{ZF} include the $L_\in$-sentence $\exists x \forall y \; \neg y \in x$, known as the *Empty Set Axiom*, and the $L_\in$-sentence $\forall x \forall y \, (\forall z \, ((z \in x \to z \in y) \land (z \in y \to z \in x)) \to x \approx y)$ already considered in Chapter 6, known as the *Axiom of Extensionality*. Since the Empty Set Axiom is true in $\mathcal{A}$, there has to be an $\mathcal{A}$-set with no $\mathcal{A}$-elements. And since the Axiom of Extensionality is true in $\mathcal{A}$, this $\mathcal{A}$-set will be unique. We shall refer to it as $\emptyset^\mathcal{A}$. We can use the axioms of Θ_{ZF} in the same way to show that, for every $\mathcal{A}$-set S, there is an $\mathcal{A}$-set whose only $\mathcal{A}$-elements are S and the $\mathcal{A}$-elements of S. We shall refer to this $\mathcal{A}$-set as the $\mathcal{A}$-*successor* of S, written $S^{+\mathcal{A}}$. Hence the universe of $\mathcal{A}$ will contain all the $\mathcal{A}$-sets in the sequence $\emptyset^\mathcal{A}$, $\emptyset^{\mathcal{A}+\mathcal{A}}$, $\emptyset^{\mathcal{A}+\mathcal{A}+\mathcal{A}}$,

$\emptyset^{\mathcal{A}+\mathcal{A}+\mathcal{A}+\mathcal{A}},\ldots$. We can refer to the $\mathcal{A}$-sets in this sequence as the $\mathcal{A}$-*descendants* of $\emptyset^{\mathcal{A}}$. We can also use the axioms of Θ_{ZF} to show that there is a (unique) $\mathcal{A}$-set whose $\mathcal{A}$-elements are the $\mathcal{A}$-descendants of $\emptyset^{\mathcal{A}}$, which we shall represent as $D^{\mathcal{A}}\emptyset^{\mathcal{A}}$, and an $\mathcal{A}$-set, $\wp^{\mathcal{A}}D^{\mathcal{A}}\emptyset^{\mathcal{A}}$, whose $\mathcal{A}$-elements are the $\mathcal{A}$-*subsets* of $D^{\mathcal{A}}\emptyset^{\mathcal{A}}$, i.e. those $\mathcal{A}$-sets all of whose $\mathcal{A}$-elements are $\mathcal{A}$-elements of $D^{\mathcal{A}}\emptyset^{\mathcal{A}}$.

The contradiction is supposed to be generated by the relationship between $D^{\mathcal{A}}\emptyset^{\mathcal{A}}$ and $\wp^{\mathcal{A}}D^{\mathcal{A}}\emptyset^{\mathcal{A}}$. We can show that $D^{\mathcal{A}}\emptyset^{\mathcal{A}}$ (or rather, the set of $\mathcal{A}$-descendants of $\emptyset^{\mathcal{A}}$) is denumerable with the same procedure that we used for $D\emptyset$. We can also show that $\wp^{\mathcal{A}}D^{\mathcal{A}}\emptyset^{\mathcal{A}}$ (or rather, the set of $\mathcal{A}$-subsets of $D^{\mathcal{A}}\emptyset^{\mathcal{A}}$) is denumerable. It is at least denumerable because there is a one-to-one function from $D^{\mathcal{A}}\emptyset^{\mathcal{A}}$ to $\wp^{\mathcal{A}}D^{\mathcal{A}}\emptyset^{\mathcal{A}}$ (if d is an $\mathcal{A}$-descendant of $\emptyset^{\mathcal{A}}$, the $\mathcal{A}$-set whose only $\mathcal{A}$-element is d is an $\mathcal{A}$-subset of $D^{\mathcal{A}}\emptyset^{\mathcal{A}}$). And it is at most denumerable because every $\mathcal{A}$-element of $\wp^{\mathcal{A}}D^{\mathcal{A}}\emptyset^{\mathcal{A}}$ is an $\mathcal{A}$-set, and we are assuming that there are only countably many of them. Hence, since $D^{\mathcal{A}}\emptyset^{\mathcal{A}}$ and $\wp^{\mathcal{A}}D^{\mathcal{A}}\emptyset^{\mathcal{A}}$ are both denumerable, there is a one-to-one correspondence between them.

We would have a contradiction if it followed from the fact that $\mathcal{A}$ is a model of Θ_{ZF} that there isn't a one-to-one correspondence between $D^{\mathcal{A}}\emptyset^{\mathcal{A}}$ and $\wp^{\mathcal{A}}D^{\mathcal{A}}\emptyset^{\mathcal{A}}$. But the fact that $\mathcal{A}$ is a model of Θ_{ZF} doesn't entail quite this. What it entails is that there isn't a one-to-one correspondence between these $\mathcal{A}$-sets *in the universe of $\mathcal{A}$*—that no $\mathcal{A}$-set is a one-to-one correspondence between $D^{\mathcal{A}}\emptyset^{\mathcal{A}}$ and $\wp^{\mathcal{A}}D^{\mathcal{A}}\emptyset^{\mathcal{A}}$. And this is perfectly compatible with the existence, outside the universe of $\mathcal{A}$, of a one-to-one correspondence between these $\mathcal{A}$-sets.

Thus, no contradiction results from the fact that Θ_{ZF} has countable models (if it has any). Nevertheless, one could still try to draw from these considerations some unsettling conclusions. Let $\mathcal{A}$ be now an arbitrary model of Θ_{ZF} (whose universe may or may not be countable), and let's say that an $\mathcal{A}$-set S is $\mathcal{A}$-*uncountable* just in case there is an $\mathcal{A}$-set which is a one-to-one function from $D^{\mathcal{A}}\emptyset^{\mathcal{A}}$ to S, but no $\mathcal{A}$-set which is a one-to-one correspondence between $D^{\mathcal{A}}\emptyset^{\mathcal{A}}$ and S. We have seen that, after establishing that $\wp^{\mathcal{A}}D^{\mathcal{A}}\emptyset^{\mathcal{A}}$ is $\mathcal{A}$-uncountable, we are still completely in the dark as to whether $\wp^{\mathcal{A}}D^{\mathcal{A}}\emptyset^{\mathcal{A}}$ (or rather, the set of $\mathcal{A}$-subsets of $D^{\mathcal{A}}\emptyset^{\mathcal{A}}$) is really uncountable.

Compare this with the situation in which we find ourselves with respect to $\wp D\emptyset$, i.e. the "real" power set of the "real" set of the "real" descendants of the "real" empty set. We have established that $\wp D\emptyset$ is uncountable—that there is a set which is a one-to-one function from $D\emptyset$ to $\wp D\emptyset$ but no set which is a one-to-one correspondence between $D\emptyset$ and $\wp D\emptyset$. We feel that this tells us more about $\wp D\emptyset$ than we know about $\wp^{\mathcal{A}}D^{\mathcal{A}}\emptyset^{\mathcal{A}}$. The latter, for all we know, might be really countable, whereas for the former this is not a possibility—our proof of the uncountability of $\wp D\emptyset$ establishes that it is really uncountable.

There is a sense, however, in which we don't seem to know more about $\wp D\emptyset$ than about $\wp^{\mathcal{A}}D^{\mathcal{A}}\emptyset^{\mathcal{A}}$. When we establish that $\wp^{\mathcal{A}}D^{\mathcal{A}}\emptyset^{\mathcal{A}}$ is $\mathcal{A}$-uncountable, we establish that a certain domain (the universe of $\mathcal{A}$) does not contain a one-to-one correspondence between $D^{\mathcal{A}}\emptyset^{\mathcal{A}}$ and $\wp^{\mathcal{A}}D^{\mathcal{A}}\emptyset^{\mathcal{A}}$. Similarly, when we establish that $\wp D\emptyset$ is uncountable, we establish that a certain domain (what we think of as the domain of real sets) does not contain a one-to-one correspondence between $D\emptyset$ and $\wp D\emptyset$. Nevertheless, whereas we accept that we don't know whether there might be a one-to-one correspondence between $D^{\mathcal{A}}\emptyset^{\mathcal{A}}$ and $\wp^{\mathcal{A}}D^{\mathcal{A}}\emptyset^{\mathcal{A}}$ outside the universe of $\mathcal{A}$, we are confident that there isn't a one-to-one correspondence *anywhere* between $D\emptyset$ and $\wp D\emptyset$.

But how, we might ask, can this confidence be justified? Certainly we haven't *ascertained* that what we think of as the real sets are the only sets there are. That would require somehow stepping outside that domain and verifying that there aren't any other sets "out there," but we can't even begin to make sense of what this exercise would involve. Hence, with respect to $\wp D\emptyset$, we seem to find ourselves in the same situation as with respect to $\wp^{\mathcal{A}}D^{\mathcal{A}}\emptyset^{\mathcal{A}}$ before we have determined whether there are any one-to-one correspondences between $D^{\mathcal{A}}\emptyset^{\mathcal{A}}$ and $\wp^{\mathcal{A}}D^{\mathcal{A}}\emptyset^{\mathcal{A}}$ outside the universe of $\mathcal{A}$—we have no idea whether $\wp D\emptyset$ is really uncountable.

Of course this is not right. We do know that $\wp D\emptyset$ is really uncountable. But the reason is not that we can somehow establish a match between two separate concepts—what we call uncountability and real uncountability, or what we call the domain of sets and the real domain of sets. The reason is, rather, that there is no meaningful distinction between these two pairs of concepts. To be a set, a real set, is to be what we call a set, and to be uncountable, really uncountable, is to be what we call uncountable. The question whether what we call uncountability is real uncountability is not analogous to the question whether $\mathcal{A}$-uncountability is what we call uncountability. It is analogous, rather, to the question whether $\mathcal{A}$-uncountability is real $\mathcal{A}$-uncountability. The correct attitude towards this kind of skeptical doubt concerning our set-theoretic concepts is not to try to refute it by appeal to some piece of substantive knowledge about what we call the domain of sets or what we call uncountability. The right attitude is to show that the skeptic has no vantage point from which to challenge our set-theoretic concepts. These are the only concepts with which his challenge can be formulated, and, thus formulated, skepticism is trivially false.

7. The Upward Löwenheim-Skolem Theorem

If L is a countable language, the Downward Löwenheim-Skolem Theorem rules out the possibility of representing an uncountable L-structure up to isomorphism. Similarly, if L is a language of cardinality κ, for any infinite cardinal κ, the general version of the theorem rules out the possibility of representing up to isomorphism any L-structure of any cardinality higher than κ. Nevertheless, the Downward Löwenheim-Skolem Theorem has no bearing on the possibility of representing up to isomorphism a denumerable structure of a countable language, or, in general, an infinite structure of the same cardinality as the language. These possibilities are ruled out by our next result. Let's say that a set of sentences Γ has *arbitrarily large models* just in case, for every cardinal κ, Γ has a model of cardinality at least κ.

UPWARD LÖWENHEIM-SKOLEM THEOREM: If a set of sentences of a first-order language has an infinite model, then it has arbitrarily large models.

Proof: Let L be a first-order language, let Γ be a set of L-sentences with an infinite model, and let κ be an infinite cardinal. We want to show that Γ has models of cardinality at least κ. To establish the result we are going to invoke the Compactness Theorem.

Let L^+ be the language whose extralogical vocabulary is the union of the extralogical vocabulary of L and a disjoint set C of individual constants of cardinality κ. Let Γ^+ be $\Gamma \cup \{\neg c \approx c' \mid c, c' \in C \text{ and } c \neq c'\}$. We have that the reduct to L of a model of Γ^+ will be a model of Γ with the same universe. Also, every model of Γ^+ will have cardinality at least κ, since in order to be a model of Γ^+, an L^+-structure has to interpret the individual constants in C with different elements of the universe, and there are κ many of them. Hence, to show that Γ has a model of cardinality at least κ, it will suffice to show that Γ^+ has a model.

By the Compactness Theorem (second formulation), to show that Γ^+ has a model, it will suffice to show that each of its finite subsets has a model. Hence to complete the proof of the theorem we only need to show that every finite subset of Γ^+ has a model. Let Γ^+_0 be a finite subset of Γ^+, and let $c_1, \ldots, c_n$ be the individual constants from C occurring in Γ^+_0. Let $\mathcal{A}$ be an infinite model of Γ. Let $\mathcal{A}^+$ be an L^+-structure with the following features: (i) The universe of $\mathcal{A}^+$ is the universe of $\mathcal{A}$. (ii) The interpretations of the extralogical symbols of L are the same in $\mathcal{A}$ and in $\mathcal{A}^+$. (iii) $c_1, \ldots, c_n$ are interpreted in $\mathcal{A}^+$ as denoting arbitrary *different* elements of the universe. Since the universe of $\mathcal{A}^+$ is infinite, we know that it will contain enough elements for this.

We can show that $\mathcal{A}^+$ is a model of Γ^+_0. All the elements of Γ in Γ^+_0 are true in $\mathcal{A}^+$, since $\mathcal{A}$ is a model of Γ, and the extralogical symbols of L are interpreted in the same way in $\mathcal{A}$ and $\mathcal{A}^+$. And all the sentences in Γ^+_0 of the form $\neg c \approx c'$, where c, c' are individual constants from C, are also true in $\mathcal{A}^+$, since c and c' denote different elements of the universe. Therefore $\mathcal{A}^+$ is a model of Γ^+_0, as desired.   ∎

The Upward Löwenheim-Skolem Theorem dashes any hopes we might still have of representing an infinite structure up to isomorphism. If $\mathcal{A}$ is an infinite structure of a first-order language L, any set of L-sentences having $\mathcal{A}$ as a model will also have models of greater cardinalities, and hence not isomorphic to $\mathcal{A}$. The theorem also imposes drastic limitations on which classes of structures can be represented. A class C of structures containing an infinite structure will only be representable if it contains arbitrarily large structures. In other words, if there is an upper limit to the cardinalities of the structures in C, C will not be representable. If we combine the arguments that we used to prove the Downward and Upward Löwenheim-Skolem Theorems, we can obtain an even stronger result.

LÖWENHEIM-SKOLEM-TARSKI THEOREM (countable languages): If a set of sentences of a countable language has an infinite model, then it has a model of every infinite cardinality.

Proof: Let L be a countable first-order language, let Γ be a set of L-sentences with an infinite model, and let κ be an infinite cardinal. We want to show that Γ has a model of cardinality κ. Let L^+ be the language whose extralogical vocabulary is the union of the extralogical vocabulary of L and a disjoint set C of individual constants of cardinality κ. Let Γ^+ be $\Gamma \cup \{\neg c \approx c' \mid c, c' \in C \text{ and } c \neq c'\}$. The cardinality of L^+ is the sum of κ and the cardinality of L. Hence, by Lemma 6. 84 and the Absorption Law, the cardinality of L^+ is κ.

Now we can apply the Downward Löwenheim-Skolem Theorem (general case) to assert that if Γ^+ has a model, then it has a model of cardinality at most κ. But by the reasoning presented in the proof of the Upward Löwenheim-Skolem Theorem, the cardinality of any model of Γ^+ will be at least κ. Hence, by the antisymmetry of $\leq$, if Γ^+ has a model, it has a model of cardinality κ. But if Γ^+ has a model of cardinality κ, the same goes for Γ, as the reduct to L of any model of Γ^+ is an L-structure with the same universe which is a model of Γ. Therefore, to show that Γ has a model of cardinality κ, it will suffice to show that Γ^+ has a model. To show this we apply the Compactness Theorem with the argument presented in the proof of the Upward Löwenheim-Skolem Theorem. ∎

EXERCISE 7. 21 (*Löwenheim-Skolem-Tarski Theorem* (general case)): Show that if a set of sentences of a first-order language L has an infinite model, then it has a model of every infinite cardinality greater than or equal to the cardinality of L.

Hint: Adapt the proof of the countable case.

Thus if $\mathcal{A}$ is an infinite structure of a first-order language L, and Γ is a set of L-sentences with $\mathcal{A}$ as a model, it followed from our earlier results that Γ would also have arbitrarily large and arbitrarily small models (down to the greater of $\aleph_0$ and the cardinality of L). What the Löwenheim-Skolem-Tarski Theorem tells us is that Γ will have models of *every* infinite cardinality (from the cardinality of L up). With respect to the representation of classes of structures, the Löwenheim-Skolem-Tarski Theorem has the following consequence. If L is a countable first-order language, any class of L-structures containing structures of some but not all infinite cardinalities will not be represented by any set of L-sentences. In other words, a class of L-structures containing an infinite structure will only be representable if it contains structures of every infinite cardinality. A similar situation obtains for the general case. If L is a first-order language of cardinality κ, where κ is an infinite cardinal, a class of L-structures containing an infinite structure will only be representable if it contains structures of every cardinality greater than or equal to κ.

EXERCISE 7. 22: Let L be a language of cardinality κ, where κ is an infinite cardinal, and let $\mathcal{A}$ be an infinite L-structure. Show that for every cardinal λ greater than or equal to κ, there is an L-structure of cardinality λ indiscernible form $\mathcal{A}$.

8. Finite Structures Again

One immediate consequence of the situation that we have depicted in the preceding section is that sets of first-order sentences cannot set infinite upper limits on the cardinality of their models. This is in sharp contrast with the situation that obtains for finite structures. For a set of first-order sentences can set any specific finite upper limit on the size of its models. Here is one way of doing it. For any positive integer n, consider the sentence $\forall x_1 \ldots \forall x_{n+1}\ \phi$, where $x_1, \ldots, x_{n+1}$ are different variables, and ϕ is a string of disjuncts of the form $x_i \approx x_j$, one for each pair of distinct variables taken from $x_1, \ldots, x_{n+1}$. We have that, for any set of sentences containing the sentence $\forall x_1 \ldots \forall x_{n+1} \ \phi$, the universe of any of its models will have at most n elements.

But can a set of sentences restrict its models to those with finite universes without setting any specific upper limit on their size? Let's say that a set of sentences Γ has *arbitrarily large* finite models just in case for every positive integer n, Γ has a model whose universe has more than n elements. We can formulate the question in terms of this notion, by asking whether a set of sentences can have arbitrarily large finite models, but no infinite models. The following exercise answers this question in the negative.

EXERCISE 7. 23: Show that if a set of sentences has arbitrarily large finite models, then it has an infinite model.

Hint: Follow the procedure that we employed in the proof of the Upward Löwenheim-Skolem Theorem.

This result has repercussions for the question of the representation of classes of finite structures. The only limitation that we had imposed so far on the classes of finite structures that can be represented was that a class of structures is representable only if it is closed under isomorphism. But it follows from Exercise 7. 23 that there are further limitations to the expressive power of first-order logic with respect to finite structures. There are classes of finite structures which are closed under isomorphism but are not represented by any set of sentences. For a class of finite structures (closed under isomorphism) will not be representable unless there is an upper limit to the size of their universes. In particular, the class of *all* finite structures of a first-order language L cannot be represented by any set of L-sentences.

9. Nonstandard Models of Arithmetic

We have established that an infinite structure $\mathcal{A}$ cannot be represented up to isomorphism, since any set of sentences having $\mathcal{A}$ as a model will also have models of every other infinite cardinality. This result leaves room for a much more modest sense in which an infinite structure could be represented. Even if any set of sentences having $\mathcal{A}$ as a model will have models which are not isomorphic to $\mathcal{A}$ because of the cardinality of their universes, we might still expect to find a set of sentences having $\mathcal{A}$ as a model all of whose models *of the cardinality of $\mathcal{A}$* are isomorphic to $\mathcal{A}$.

DEFINITION: A set of sentences Γ *represents* a structure $\mathcal{A}$ *up to isomorphism in its power* just in case $\mathcal{A}$ is a model of Γ and every model of Γ of the same cardinality as $\mathcal{A}$ is isomorphic to $\mathcal{A}$.

Notice that the Löwenheim-Skolem theorems do not rule out the possibility that infinite structures are represented up to isomorphism in their power, and we might expect that every infinite structure is representable in this very weak sense. But even this goal is too ambitious. Some infinite structures are not representable up to isomorphism in their power. In this section we are going to consider a notorious example of this situation.

Let L_A be the language which results from adding a two-place predicate, <, to the extralogical vocabulary of the language of arithmetic considered in §3. Then, the extralogical symbols of L_A will be an individual constant, 0, a one-place function symbol, s, two two-place function symbols, + and · , and a two-place predicate, <. Let $\mathcal{N}$ be the L_A-structure with the set of natural numbers as its universe in which the extralogical symbols of L_A receive the obvious interpretations, given the way we are representing them. Thus 0 will denote number zero, s, + and · will be interpreted with the successor, addition and multiplication functions in ω, and < with the *less than* relation in ω. We shall write $t + u$ and $t \cdot u$ instead of $+(t, u)$ and · (t, u), and $t < u$ instead of $<tu$. We shall refer to the L_A-terms which can be built with s and 0 as *numerals*. Hence the numerals are 0, $s(0)$, $s(s(0))$, $s(s(s(0)))$,.... Notice that, for every natural number n and every numeral t, t denotes n in $\mathcal{N}$ just in case t contains n occurrences of s. Hence every natural number is denoted by exactly one numeral, and every numeral denotes exactly one natural number.

Using the terminology that we introduced in Chapter 5, we can refer to the set of L_A-sentences which are true in $\mathcal{N}$ as *the theory of* $\mathcal{N}$, written *Th* $\mathcal{N}$. Clearly, if any set of L_A-sentences characterizes $\mathcal{N}$ up to isomorphism in its power, then the theory of $\mathcal{N}$ does, since any set of L_A-sentences Δ having $\mathcal{N}$ as a model is a subset of *Th* $\mathcal{N}$, and hence, if every denumerable model of Δ is isomorphic to $\mathcal{N}$, the same goes for *Th* $\mathcal{N}$ (see Exercise 7. 1). Hence to show that $\mathcal{N}$ can't be represented up to isomorphism in its power, it will suffice to show that *Th* $\mathcal{N}$ has a denumerable model which is not isomorphic to $\mathcal{N}$.

THEOREM 7. 24: The theory of $\mathcal{N}$ has a denumerable model which is not isomorphic to $\mathcal{N}$.

Proof: Let $L_A{}^+$ be the language which results from adding to the extralogical vocabulary of L_A a new individual constant, c. Let Δ be the set of $L_A{}^+$-sentences containing, for each numeral t, the sentence $t < c$. Thus Δ

contains the sentences $0 < c$, $s(0) < c$, $s(s(0)) < c$, $s(s(s(0))) < c$,.... Consider the set *Th* $\mathcal{N} \cup \Delta$. Since *Th* $\mathcal{N}$ is a subset of *Th* $\mathcal{N} \cup \Delta$, every model of *Th* $\mathcal{N} \cup \Delta$ is a model of *Th* $\mathcal{N}$, and the reduct to L_A of every model of *Th* $\mathcal{N} \cup \Delta$ is an L_A-structure which is a model of *Th* $\mathcal{N}$. Hence, to prove the theorem, it will suffice to show that *Th* $\mathcal{N} \cup \Delta$ has a denumerable model whose reduct to L_A is not isomorphic to $\mathcal{N}$. We establish this result by showing (A) that *Th* $\mathcal{N} \cup \Delta$ has a denumerable model, and (B) that the reduct to L_A of any model of *Th* $\mathcal{N} \cup \Delta$ is not isomorphic to $\mathcal{N}$.

For (A), notice that, for all different numerals, t, u, the sentence $\neg t \approx u$ is in *Th* $\mathcal{N}$. It follows that each of the (infinitely many) numerals has to denote a different element of the universe in any model of *Th* $\mathcal{N}$, and hence that *Th* $\mathcal{N}$ has no finite models. It follows that *Th* $\mathcal{N} \cup \Delta$ has no finite models either. Hence, to show that *Th* $\mathcal{N} \cup \Delta$ has a denumerable model, it will suffice to show that it has a countable model. For this, by the Downward Löwenheim-Skolem Theorem, it will suffice to show that *Th* $\mathcal{N} \cup \Delta$ has a model. And, by the Compactness Theorem, to establish that *Th* $\mathcal{N} \cup \Delta$ has a model, it will suffice to show that each of its finite subsets has a model (see the proof of the Upward Löwenheim-Skolem Theorem).

Let Γ_0 be a finite subset of *Th* $\mathcal{N} \cup \Delta$, and let $\mathcal{A}_0$ be the $L_A{}^+$-structure with the following features: (i) the universe of $\mathcal{A}_0$ is ω; (ii) all the extra-logical symbols of L_A have the same interpretation in $\mathcal{A}_0$ as in $\mathcal{N}$; (iii) c denotes the successor of the greatest of the natural numbers denoted by the numerals which occur in the elements of Δ in Γ_0. Notice that, in intuitive terms, what $\mathcal{A}_0$ does is to supplement $\mathcal{N}$ by interpreting c with a natural number which is big enough to make all the sentences from Δ in Γ_0 true. We can easily show that $\mathcal{A}_0$ is a model of Γ_0. Every L_A-sentence in Γ_0 is true in $\mathcal{N}$, and hence in $\mathcal{A}_0$, and every sentence from Δ in Γ_0 will also be true in $\mathcal{A}_0$, since, for every sentence of the form $t < c$ in Γ_0, the natural number denoted by c is greater than the natural number denoted by t.

For (B), let $\mathcal{A}^+$ be a model of *Th* $\mathcal{N} \cup \Delta$, and let $\mathcal{A}$ be the reduct of $\mathcal{A}^+$ to L_A. To show that $\mathcal{A}$ is not isomorphic to $\mathcal{N}$, we use the fact that, whereas each natural number is greater than only finitely many natural numbers (for every element of the universe of $\mathcal{N}$ there are only finitely many elements bearing $<_{\mathcal{N}}$ to it), there is an object in the universe of $\mathcal{A}$ which is greater that infinitely many elements of the universe (an object to which infinitely many elements of the universe bear the relation $<_{\mathcal{A}}$)—namely the object with which c is interpreted in $\mathcal{A}^+$ (notice that, although c is not in L_A, its denotation in $\mathcal{A}^+$ is in the universe of $\mathcal{A}$).

We assume, towards a contradiction that $\mathcal{A}$ and $\mathcal{N}$ are isomorphic. Let h be an isomorphism between $\mathcal{N}$ and $\mathcal{A}$, and let n be the natural number whose image under h is $c_{\mathcal{A}^+}$. Since all the sentences in Δ are true in $\mathcal{A}^+$, and since $\mathcal{A}$ and $\mathcal{A}^+$ interpret $<$, s and 0 in the same way, the denotation of each numeral will bear $<_{\mathcal{A}}$ to $c_{\mathcal{A}^+}$. And since $\mathcal{A}$ is a model of $Th\,\mathcal{N}$, each of the infinitely many numerals will denote a different element of the universe. Hence infinitely many elements of the universe of $\mathcal{A}$ will bear $<_{\mathcal{A}}$ to $c_{\mathcal{A}^+}$. But exactly n natural numbers bear $<_{\mathcal{N}}$ to n. Hence there will be (infinitely many) cases in which a natural number m doesn't bear $<_{\mathcal{N}}$ to n, but $h(m)$ bears $<_{\mathcal{A}}$ to $c_{\mathcal{A}^+}$. This contradicts the hypothesis that h is an isomorphism, since $c_{\mathcal{A}^+}$ is $h(n)$ and, by the definition of isomorphism, for all natural numbers x, y, if $\langle x, y \rangle \notin <_{\mathcal{N}}$ then $\langle h(x), h(y) \rangle \notin <_{\mathcal{A}}$. ∎

Notice that Theorem 7.24 could still be established if we hadn't introduced $<$ in the vocabulary. Instead of Δ, we could have used to the same effect the set containing the sentences $\exists x\; 0 + x \approx c$, $\exists x\; s(0) + x \approx c$, $\exists x\; s(s(0)) + x \approx c,\dots$.

The models of the theory of $\mathcal{N}$ which are not isomorphic to $\mathcal{N}$ are normally known as *nonstandard models of arithmetic*. Since the models of the theory of $\mathcal{N}$ are indiscernible from each other, $\mathcal{N}$ is indiscernible from the nonstandard models of arithmetic. In the remainder of this section we are going to consider what the nonstandard models of arithmetic look like. What we want to know is what features an L_A-structure has to exhibit in order to be a model of $Th\,\mathcal{N}$ which is not isomorphic to $\mathcal{N}$. In our search for these features, we shall make use of the fact that, since nonstandard models of arithmetic are indiscernible from $\mathcal{N}$, they will have to exhibit every feature of $\mathcal{N}$ that is expressible with L_A-sentences.

We start by showing that all the models of $Th\,\mathcal{N}$ are similar to $\mathcal{N}$ in one important respect. They all contain, for all intents and purposes (i.e. up to isomorphism), the natural numbers. To formulate this result, we introduce the notion of embedding.

DEFINITION: If $\mathcal{A}$ and $\mathcal{B}$ are structures of a first-order language, an *embedding* of $\mathcal{A}$ in $\mathcal{B}$ is a function from the universe of $\mathcal{A}$ to the universe of $\mathcal{B}$ which satisfies the following conditions:

(a) h is a one-to-one function from the universe of $\mathcal{A}$ to the universe of $\mathcal{B}$.

(b)–(d) As in the definition of isomorphism.

Hence every isomorphism is an embedding, but an embedding of $\mathcal{A}$ in $\mathcal{B}$ could fail to be an isomorphism—by not having the whole universe of $\mathcal{B}$ as its range. The claim that every model of the theory of $\mathcal{N}$ contains the natural numbers, up to isomorphism, is expressed by the following lemma.

LEMMA 7. 25: For every model $\mathcal{A}$ of the theory of $\mathcal{N}$, there is an embedding of $\mathcal{N}$ in $\mathcal{A}$.

Proof: Let $\mathcal{A}$ be a model of the theory of $\mathcal{N}$, and let h be the function from ω to the universe of $\mathcal{A}$ defined as follows: for every natural number n and every element a of the universe of $\mathcal{A}$, $\langle n, a \rangle \in h$ if and only if there is a numeral t such that $den_{\mathcal{N}}(t) = n$ and $den_{\mathcal{A}}(t) = a$. We establish the lemma by showing that h is an embedding of $\mathcal{N}$ in $\mathcal{A}$. We need to establish the following claims: (i) h is a function from ω to the universe of $\mathcal{A}$, (ii) h is one-to-one, (iii) for all natural numbers, m, n, $m <_{\mathcal{N}} n$ if and only if $h(m) <_{\mathcal{A}} h(n)$, (iv) $0_{\mathcal{A}} = h(0_{\mathcal{N}})$, (v) for every natural number n, $h(s_{\mathcal{N}}(n)) = s_{\mathcal{A}}(h(n))$, (vi) for all natural numbers, m, n, $h(m +_{\mathcal{N}} n) = h(m) +_{\mathcal{A}} h(n)$, and (vii) for all natural numbers, m, n, $h(m \cdot_{\mathcal{N}} n) = h(m) \cdot_{\mathcal{A}} h(n)$. (i) and (ii) concern clause (a) of the definition of embedding, (iii) concerns clause (d), (iv) clause (b), and (v)–(vii) clause (c). We deal with (i), (ii), (v) and (vi), leaving the rest as an exercise.

(i) follows directly from the fact that every natural number is the denotation in $\mathcal{N}$ of exactly one numeral, and every numeral has exactly one denotation in $\mathcal{A}$. For (ii), let m, n be two different natural numbers, and let t_m, t_n be the numerals denoting them. Then the sentence $\neg t_m \approx t_n$ is true in $\mathcal{N}$ and hence in $\mathcal{A}$. Hence, by the definition of truth, we have that $den_{\mathcal{A}}(t_m) \neq den_{\mathcal{A}}(t_n)$. But $h(m) = den_{\mathcal{A}}(t_m)$, and $h(n) = den_{\mathcal{A}}(t_n)$. Therefore $h(m) \neq h(n)$, as desired.

For (v), let n be a natural number. We need to show that $h(s_{\mathcal{N}}(n)) = s_{\mathcal{A}}(h(n))$. Let t be the numeral denoting n. We argue as follows:

$h(s_{\mathcal{N}}(n))$

=   (since $den_{\mathcal{N}}(t) = n$)

$h(s_{\mathcal{N}}(den_{\mathcal{N}}(t)))$

=   (definition of denotation)

$h(den_{\mathcal{N}}(s(t)))$

=   (definition of h)

$den_{\mathcal{A}}(s(t))$

=   (definition of denotation)

$s_{\mathcal{A}}(den_{\mathcal{A}}(t))$

=   (definition of h)

$s_{\mathcal{A}}(h(n))$

For (vi), let m, n be two natural numbers. We need to show that $h(m +_{\mathcal{N}} n) = h(m) +_{\mathcal{A}} h(n)$. Let t_m, t_n be the numerals denoting m and n, and let t_{m+n} be the numeral denoting the sum of m and n. We argue as follows:

$h(m +_{\mathcal{N}} n)$

$\quad = \quad$ (definition of h)

$den_{\mathcal{A}}(t_{m+n})$

$\quad = \quad$ (since the sentence $t_m + t_n \approx t_{m+n}$ is true in $\mathcal{N}$ and hence in $\mathcal{A}$)

$den_{\mathcal{A}}(t_m + t_n)$

$\quad = \quad$ (definition of denotation)

$den_{\mathcal{A}}(t_m) +_{\mathcal{A}} den_{\mathcal{A}}(t_n)$

$\quad = \quad$ (definition of h)

$h(m) +_{\mathcal{A}} h(n)$ ∎

EXERCISE 7. 26: Establish (iii), (iv) and (vii) in the proof of Lemma 7. 25.

Lemma 7. 25 tells us that, in any model of $Th\ \mathcal{N}$, the denotations of the numerals behave in every respect like the natural numbers. Hence, without any significant loss of generality, we can assume that, for every model $\mathcal{A}$ of $Th\ \mathcal{N}$, the universe of $\mathcal{A}$ contains the natural numbers, that 0 denotes number zero in $\mathcal{A}$, and that $s_{\mathcal{A}}$, $+_{\mathcal{A}}$, $\cdot_{\mathcal{A}}$ and $<_{\mathcal{A}}$ have $s_{\mathcal{N}}$, $+_{\mathcal{N}}$, $\cdot_{\mathcal{N}}$ and $<_{\mathcal{N}}$ as subsets. It follows from this that, for every natural number n, n will be denoted in $\mathcal{A}$ by the numeral with n occurrences of s. If $\mathcal{A}$ is a nonstandard model of arithmetic, in addition to the natural numbers, its universe will contain other objects. We shall refer to these as *nonstandard elements*.

If $\mathcal{A}$ is a nonstandard model of arithmetic, what can we say about the nonstandard elements of the universe of $\mathcal{A}$? We can show first that every nonstandard element of the universe of $\mathcal{A}$ will have to be greater than every natural number. Notice that no natural number is less than zero, no natural number other than zero is less than one, no natural number other than zero and one is less than two, etc. These features of $\mathcal{N}$ are expressible with L_A-sentences, as, for example, $\forall x \neg x < 0$, $\forall x\ (x < s(0) \rightarrow x \approx 0))$, $\forall x\ (x < s(s(0)) \rightarrow (x \approx 0 \lor x \approx s(0)))$,…. These sentences will be in $Th\ \mathcal{N}$, and hence true in $\mathcal{A}$. Hence, since each numeral denotes a natural number in $\mathcal{A}$, no nonstandard element of the universe of $\mathcal{A}$ will be less than any natural number. But the sentence $\forall x \forall y\ ((\neg x < y \land \neg x \approx y) \rightarrow y$

$< x$) is true in $\mathcal{N}$, and hence in $\mathcal{A}$. Hence every nonstandard element of the universe of $\mathcal{A}$ will be greater than every natural number.

Notice also that no nonstandard element of the universe of $\mathcal{A}$ will be the successor of a natural number, or the sum or product of two natural numbers, since every natural number has another natural number (and nothing else) as its image under $s_{\mathcal{A}}$, and any two natural numbers have a natural number (and nothing else) as their image under $+_{\mathcal{A}}$ or $\cdot_{\mathcal{A}}$. We can also show that no natural number will be the successor of a nonstandard element, or the sum or product of a nonstandard element with any element of the universe.

LEMMA 7. 27: No natural number is the successor of a nonstandard element of the universe of a model of the theory of $\mathcal{N}$.

Proof: Let $\mathcal{A}$ be a nonstandard model of arithmetic, let n be a natural number, and let a be an element of the universe of $\mathcal{A}$ such that $s_{\mathcal{A}}(a) = n$. We need to show that a is not a nonstandard element. We have that every natural number is less than its successor. Hence the L_A-sentence $\forall x \, x < s(x)$ is in the theory of $\mathcal{N}$, and hence true in $\mathcal{A}$. It follows that $a <_{\mathcal{A}} n$. But since, as we saw above, no nonstandard element of the universe of a model of arithmetic is less than any natural number, we can conclude that a is not a nonstandard element, as desired. ∎

EXERCISE 7. 28: Show that no natural number is the sum or product of a nonstandard element of the universe of a model of the theory of $\mathcal{N}$ with any element of the universe.

Let's say that two elements a, b, of the universe of $\mathcal{A}$ are at a *finite distance* from each other just in case there is a natural number n such that either $a +_{\mathcal{A}} n = b$ or $b +_{\mathcal{A}} n = a$. Notice that no nonstandard element of the universe of $\mathcal{A}$ is at a finite distance from any natural number.

EXERCISE 7. 29: Show that the relation ...*is at a finite distance from...* is an equivalence relation in the universe of a model of *Th* $\mathcal{N}$.

Since $s_{\mathcal{A}}$ is a function in the universe of $\mathcal{A}$, nonstandard elements, as well as natural numbers, will have to have successors. Hence, if a is a nonstandard element of the universe of $\mathcal{A}$, the universe will also have to contain $s_{\mathcal{A}}(a)$, $s_{\mathcal{A}}(s_{\mathcal{A}}(a))$, $s_{\mathcal{A}}(s_{\mathcal{A}}(s_{\mathcal{A}}(a)))$,.... All these objects will have to be different from each other, since each of the sentences $\forall x \, \neg x \approx s(x)$, $\forall x \, \neg x \approx s(s(x))$, $\forall x \, \neg x \approx s(s(s(x)))$,... is true in $\mathcal{N}$, and hence in $\mathcal{A}$. Also, by Lemma 7. 27, they will all have to be nonstandard. Furthermore, this chain cannot begin with a, since the L_A-sentence $\forall x \, (\neg x \approx 0 \rightarrow \exists y \, x \approx s(y))$ is true in $\mathcal{N}$, and hence in $\mathcal{A}$. It follows that the universe of $\mathcal{A}$ will have to contain an element having a as its successor, an element having this element as its successor, etc. All these objects will be different from each other and nonstandard. Hence a will be in an infinite chain of nonstandard elements, with no minimal or maximal element, in which each element is followed by its successor. We shall refer to this subset of the universe of $\mathcal{A}$ as the *galaxy* of a. We can define galaxies as the equivalence classes generated by the elements of the universe of $\mathcal{A}$ with the relation *...is at a finite distance from....* Then the natural numbers form a galaxy, to which we shall refer as the *standard galaxy*.

EXERCISE 7. 30: Let a, b be elements of the universe of $\mathcal{A}$. Show that if a and b are in different galaxies and a is less than b, then every element of the galaxy of a is less than every element of the galaxy of b.

Notice that Exercise 7. 30 enables us to speak of a galaxy being less than another.

EXERCISE 7. 31: Show that for any two galaxies A and B, either A is less than B or B is less than A.

EXERCISE 7. 32: Show that the standard galaxy is the least galaxy.

It follows from these considerations that the universe of $\mathcal{A}$ includes the standard galaxy and at least one nonstandard galaxy. We show now that it has to contain a lot more.

LEMMA 7. 33: There is no greatest galaxy.

Proof: Let a be a nonstandard element of the universe of $\mathcal{A}$. The universe of $\mathcal{A}$ will also contain the result of adding a to itself, i.e. $a +_{\mathcal{A}} a$. It will suffice to show (i) that $a +_{\mathcal{A}} a$ is greater than a and (ii) that $a +_{\mathcal{A}} a$ is not in the galaxy of a. (i) follows from the fact that the sentence $\forall x\, (\neg x \approx 0 \rightarrow x < x + x)$ is true in $\mathcal{N}$, and hence in $\mathcal{A}$. For (ii) assume, towards a contradiction that a and $a +_{\mathcal{A}} a$ are in the same galaxy. Then, by the definition of galaxy, there is a natural number n such that $a +_{\mathcal{A}} n = a +_{\mathcal{A}} a$. But, since the L_A-sentence $\forall x \forall y \forall z\, (x + y \approx x + z \rightarrow y \approx z)$ is true in $\mathcal{N}$, and hence in $\mathcal{A}$, it follows from this that $n = a$, which contradicts the assumption that a is nonstandard. ∎

LEMMA 7. 34: There is no least nonstandard galaxy.

Proof: For every natural number n other than zero and one, there is a natural number m smaller than n such that the result of adding m to itself is either n or the successor of n. We can think of m as n divided by two, rounding up when necessary. This property of $\mathcal{N}$ is expressed by the L_A-sentence $\forall x\, ((\neg x \approx 0 \wedge \neg x \approx s(0)) \rightarrow \exists y\, (y < x \wedge (y + y \approx x \vee y + y \approx s(x))))$, which will, therefore, be true in $\mathcal{A}$. Let a be a nonstandard element of the universe of $\mathcal{A}$. It follows that the universe of $\mathcal{A}$ contains an element b such that b is smaller than a and the result of adding b to itself is either a or its successor. It will suffice to show (i) that b is nonstandard and (ii) that b is not in the galaxy of a. This is left as an exercise. ∎

EXERCISE 7. 35: Establish (i) and (ii) in the proof of Lemma 7. 34.

LEMMA 7. 36: Between any two galaxies there is a third.

Proof: If m, n, are two natural numbers, there is a natural number p such that the result of adding p to itself is either the sum of m and n or its successor. We can think of p as the average of m and n, rounding up if necessary. This feature of $\mathcal{N}$ is expressed by the L_A-sentence $\forall x \forall y \exists z\, (z + z \approx x + y \vee z + z \approx s(x + y))$, which will be true in $\mathcal{A}$. Let a, b be two nonstandard elements of the universe of $\mathcal{A}$ in different galaxies, such that a is less than b. It follows that there is an element c of the universe of $\mathcal{A}$ such that the result of adding c to itself is either the sum of a and b or its successor. It will suffice to show (i) that c is greater than a but less than b and (ii) that c is neither in the galaxy of a nor in the galaxy of b.

For (i), notice that the average of two different, nonconsecutive natural numbers will always be between them and different from both. This feature of $\mathcal{N}$ is expressed by the sentence $\forall x \forall y \forall z\, (((z + z \approx x + y \vee z + z \approx s(x + y)) \wedge x < y \wedge \neg s(x) \approx y) \rightarrow (x < z \wedge z < y))$, which will, therefore, be true in $\mathcal{A}$. We know that either $c +_{\mathcal{A}} c = a +_{\mathcal{A}} b$ or $c +_{\mathcal{A}} c = s_{\mathcal{A}}(a +_{\mathcal{A}} b)$, and $a <_{\mathcal{A}} b$. Furthermore, since a and b are in different galaxies, b is not the successor of a. Hence we can conclude that $a <_{\mathcal{A}} c$ and $c <_{\mathcal{A}} b$, as desired.

For (ii) we have that either $c +_{\mathcal{A}} c = a +_{\mathcal{A}} b$ or $c +_{\mathcal{A}} c = s_{\mathcal{A}}(a +_{\mathcal{A}} b)$. Assume that $c +_{\mathcal{A}} c = a +_{\mathcal{A}} b$ (the other case is left as an exercise). To show that c is not in the galaxy of a, we assume, towards a contradiction, that it is. Then there is a natural number n such that either $a +_{\mathcal{A}} n = c$ or $c +_{\mathcal{A}} n = a$. The second case can be ruled out, since the sentence $\forall x \forall y\, (x < y \rightarrow \neg \exists z\, y + z \approx x)$ is true in $\mathcal{N}$, and hence in $\mathcal{A}$, but we have established that $a <_{\mathcal{A}} c$. Now we argue as follows:

$a +_{\mathcal{A}} n = c$

$\Downarrow$ (substituting in $a +_{\mathcal{A}} b = c +_{\mathcal{A}} c$)

$a +_{\mathcal{A}} b = (a +_{\mathcal{A}} n) +_{\mathcal{A}} (a +_{\mathcal{A}} n)$

$\Downarrow$ (since the sentence $\forall x \forall y\, (x + y) + (x + y) \approx x + (x + (y + y))$ is true in $\mathcal{N}$, and hence in $\mathcal{A}$)

$a +_{\mathcal{A}} b = a +_{\mathcal{A}} (a +_{\mathcal{A}} (n +_{\mathcal{A}} n))$

⇓ (since the sentence $\forall x \forall y \forall z \, (x + y \approx x + z \to y \approx z)$ is true in $\mathcal{N}$ and hence in $\mathcal{A}$)

$$b = a +_{\mathcal{A}} (n +_{\mathcal{A}} n)$$

But $n +_{\mathcal{A}} n$ is a natural number. Hence b is at a finite distance from a, which contradicts the hypothesis that they are in different galaxies.

To show that c is not in the galaxy of b, we assume, towards a contradiction, that it is. Then there is a natural number n such that either $c +_{\mathcal{A}} n = b$ or $b +_{\mathcal{A}} n = c$. By the reasoning we presented earlier, we can rule out the second case. Now we argue as follows:

$$c +_{\mathcal{A}} n = b$$

⇓ (substituting in $c +_{\mathcal{A}} c = a +_{\mathcal{A}} b$)

$$c +_{\mathcal{A}} c = a +_{\mathcal{A}} (c +_{\mathcal{A}} n)$$

⇓ (since the sentence $\forall x \forall y \forall z \, x + (y + z) \approx y + (x + z)$ is true in $\mathcal{N}$ and hence in $\mathcal{A}$)

$$c +_{\mathcal{A}} c = c +_{\mathcal{A}} (a +_{\mathcal{A}} n)$$

⇓ (since the sentence $\forall x \forall y \forall z \, (x + y \approx x + z \to y \approx z)$ is true in $\mathcal{N}$ and hence in $\mathcal{A}$)

$$c = a +_{\mathcal{A}} n$$

But this contradicts the result that c is not in the same galaxy as a, as desired. ∎

EXERCISE 7. 37: Complete the reasoning for (ii) in the proof of Lemma 7. 36 by dealing with the case $c +_{\mathcal{A}} c = s_{\mathcal{A}}(a +_{\mathcal{A}} b)$.

Let's sum up all the features that we have ascribed to $\mathcal{A}$. We have seen that the universe of $\mathcal{A}$ is partitioned into galaxies by the relation ...*is at a finite distance from*.... Each galaxy is a chain in which each element is followed by its successor. No galaxy has a maximal element. The standard galaxy has a minimal element (zero), but nonstandard galaxies have no minimal element either. The galaxies are linearly ordered by the ordering of their elements with respect to $<_{\mathcal{A}}$. They form a dense linear ordering with a minimal element (the standard galaxy) but no maximal element.

It may seem hard to reconcile in intuitive terms the exuberance of nonstandard models of arithmetic with the fact, expressed by Theorem 7. 24, that some of them are denumerable, but a simple calculation will show that this is perfectly possible.

EXERCISE 7. 38: Show that every galaxy of a model of the theory of $\mathcal{N}$ is denumerable.

Hint: Apply the procedure that we used for **Z** (see Lemma 6. 44).

We know that a dense, linearly ordered set with a minimal element but no maximal element can be denumerable, as witnessed by the set containing the positive rational numbers and 0. Hence an L_A-structure can satisfy our characterization of nonstandard models of arithmetic even if it has denumerably many galaxies. Exercise 7. 38 tells us that every galaxy is denumerable. Hence, since the union of a denumerable collection of denumerable sets is denumerable (see Lemma 6. 77), a nonstandard model of arithmetic can have a denumerable universe.

EXERCISE 7. 39: Show that the universe of a nonstandard model of arithmetic has the same cardinality as the set of galaxies it contains.

Hint: Use Corollary 6. 99.

10. Strict Dense Linear Orderings with No Minimal or Maximal Elements

The existence of denumerable nonstandard models of arithmetic shows that $\mathcal{N}$ can't be represented up to isomorphism in its power—any set of sentences having $\mathcal{N}$ as a model will also have other denumerable models which are not isomorphic to $\mathcal{N}$. After the barrage of bad news presented in this chapter concerning the expressive power of first-order languages, it might come as no surprise if this were the general situation, i.e. if no infinite structure could be represented up to isomorphism in its power. But things, for once, are not that bad. Some infinite structures, unlike $\mathcal{N}$, can be represented up to isomorphism in their power. In this section, we are going to look at an interesting example of this situation.

Let $L_<$ be the first-order language whose only extralogical symbol is a two-place predicate, $<$. Let $\Theta_<$ be the set containing the following $L_<$-sentences:

$$\forall x \, \neg x < x$$
$$\forall x \forall y \forall z \, ((x < y \wedge y < z) \rightarrow x < z)$$
$$\forall x \forall y \, (\neg x \approx y \rightarrow (x < y \vee y < x))$$
$$\forall x \forall y \, (x < y \rightarrow \exists z \, (x < z \wedge z < y))$$
$$\forall x \exists y \, y < x$$
$$\forall x \exists y \, x < y$$

We can show that an $L_<$-structure is a model of $\Theta_<$ just in case it interprets < with a strict dense linear ordering of the universe with no minimal or maximal elements. This is left as an exercise.

EXERCISE 7. 40: Show that an $L_<$-structure is a model of $\Theta_<$ just in case it interprets < with a strict dense linear ordering of the universe with no minimal or maximal elements.

Let Q be the $L_<$-structure with the set of rational numbers as its universe, in which < is interpreted by the *less than* relation in the rational numbers. The *less than* relation is a strict dense linear ordering of the set of rational numbers with no minimal or maximal elements. Hence Q is a model of $\Theta_<$. We know that $\Theta_<$ will also have models which are not isomorphic to Q, because their universes are not denumerable. Thus, e.g., the $L_<$-structure R, with the set of real numbers as its universe, in which < is interpreted with the *less than* relation in the reals, will also be a model of $\Theta_<$. But R is not isomorphic to Q, since there is no one-to-one correspondence between the set of rational numbers and the set of real numbers. We are going to show that this is the only way in which a model of $\Theta_<$ can fail to be isomorphic to Q, since all the denumerable models of $\Theta_<$ are isomorphic to each other, and hence to Q. It will follow that Q is represented by $\Theta_<$ up to isomorphism in its power.

THEOREM 7. 41: All the denumerable models of $\Theta_<$ are isomorphic.

Proof: Let A, B, be two denumerable models of $\Theta_<$. Then $<_A$ and $<_B$ are strict dense linear orderings of the universes of these structures, with no minimal or maximal elements. Let A be the universe of A, and B the universe of B. Since A and B are both denumerable, there is a one-to-one correspondence f_A between $\mathbf{Z}^+$ and A, and a one-to-one correspondence f_B between $\mathbf{Z}^+$ and B. For every positive integer n, we shall refer to the image of n under f_A as a_n, and to its image under f_B as b_n. Hence the elements of A can be represented as $a_1, a_2, a_3,\ldots$, and the elements of B as $b_1, b_2, b_3,\ldots$.

Our goal is to define an isomorphism between A and B, i.e. a one-to-one correspondence h between A and B such that, for all $a, a' \in A$, $a <_A a'$ if and only if $h(a) <_B h(a')$. A one-to-one correspondence f between A and B can be easily defined as follows: For every positive integer n, $f(a_n) = b_n$. But f would only be an isomorphism between A and B if, for all positive integers i, j, $a_i <_A a_j$ if and only if $b_i <_B b_j$, and we have no reason to think that our enumerations of the elements of A and B satisfy this condition. We need to adopt a more sophisticated approach.

To introduce the intuitive idea behind the strategy that we are going to use, imagine that we define a function g from A to B specifying one by one the element of each set which is paired by g with each element of the other, following as much as possible our enumerations of their elements. Thus, we would start by stipulating that $g(a_1) = b_1$. Next we would specify the image under g of a_2, making sure that, in so doing, the ordering of a_1 and a_2 by $<_{\mathcal{A}}$ is matched by the ordering of $g(a_1)$ and $g(a_2)$ by $<_{\mathcal{B}}$; i.e., if $a_1 <_{\mathcal{A}} a_2$, we would choose as $g(a_2)$ an element of B such that $g(a_1) <_{\mathcal{B}} g(a_2)$, and if $a_2 <_{\mathcal{A}} a_1$, an element of B such that $g(a_2) <_{\mathcal{B}} g(a_1)$. We would choose as $g(a_2)$ the first element of B in the enumeration which satisfies this condition. Notice that, since B has no minimal or maximal element with respect to $<_{\mathcal{B}}$, there will be elements of B satisfying this description.

Next, we would concentrate on the next element of B in the enumeration—b_2 if it hasn't been picked as the image of a_2, and b_3 otherwise. Suppose, for the purposes of the illustration, that b_2 is not $g(a_2)$. Then we would have to specify the element of A which is going to have b_2 as its image under g, making sure that the ordering of $g(a_1)$, $g(a_2)$ and b_2 by $<_{\mathcal{B}}$ is matched by the ordering by $<_{\mathcal{A}}$ of a_1, a_2 and the element we pick. Thus, if b_2 is greater (with respect to $<_{\mathcal{B}}$) than both $g(a_1)$ and $g(a_2)$, we would pick an element of A which is greater (with respect to $<_{\mathcal{A}}$) than both a_1 and a_2; if b_2 is less than both $g(a_1)$ and $g(a_2)$, we would pick an element of A which is less than both a_1 and a_2, and if b_2 is between $g(a_1)$ and $g(a_2)$, we would pick an element of A between a_1 and a_2. We would pick the first element of A in the enumeration which satisfies this description. Since $<_{\mathcal{A}}$ is a dense ordering of A with no minimal or maximal element, it will contain the element that we would need in each case—elements which are greater than both a_1 and a_2, elements which are less than both a_1 and a_2, and elements between a_1 and a_2. The proof of the theorem is based on the idea that if we continued this process, specifying the element of each set which is paired by g with each element of the other, switching back and forth between A and B, the result, after infinitely many steps, would be an isomorphism between $\mathcal{A}$ and $\mathcal{B}$.

Let's say that a one-to-one correspondence f between a subset A_0 of A and a subset B_0 of B is *order-preserving* just in case, for all $a, a' \in A_0$, $a <_{\mathcal{A}} a'$ if and only if $f(a) <_{\mathcal{B}} f(a')$. We reproduce the procedure for defining an isomorphism between A and B that we have just described with a sequence of order-preserving one-to-one correspondences between subsets of A and subsets of B. For every positive integer n, we define by recursion the set f_n as the image of n under the unique function satisfying the following conditions:

$f_1 = \{\langle a_1, b_1 \rangle\}$.

For every positive integer n,

$$f_{n+1} = \begin{cases} f_n \cup \{\langle a_i, b_j \rangle\}, \text{ if } n \text{ is odd, where } a_i \text{ is the first element of } A \\ \text{in the enumeration which is not the first member of any pair} \\ \text{in } f_n, \text{ and } b_j \text{ is the first element of } B \text{ in the enumeration such} \\ \text{that } f_n \cup \{\langle a_i, b_j \rangle\} \text{ is an order-preserving one-to-one} \\ \text{correspondence between a subset of } A \text{ and a subset of } B, \\ \\ f_n \cup \{\langle a_k, b_l \rangle\}, \text{ if } n \text{ is even, where } b_l \text{ is the first element of } B \\ \text{in the enumeration which is not the second member of any pair} \\ \text{in } f_n, \text{ and } a_k \text{ is the first element of } A \text{ in the enumeration such} \\ \text{that } f_n \cup \{\langle a_k, b_l \rangle\} \text{ is an order-preserving one-to-one} \\ \text{correspondence between a subset of } A \text{ and a subset of } B. \end{cases}$$

Notice that it follows from the considerations adduced above that, since both A and B are dense linear orderings with no minimal or maximal elements, the pair that we need to add to f_n in order to form f_{n+1} is guaranteed to exist in each case (see Exercise 7. 42, below).

Let F be the collection containing, for every positive integer n, the set f_n. It follows directly from the definition of f_n that each set in F is an order-preserving one-to-one correspondence between a subset of A and a subset of B, and that the same goes for $\cup F$ (see Exercise 7. 43, below). Clearly, an order-preserving one-to-one correspondence between A and B is an isomorphism between A and B. Hence, to show that A and B are isomorphic, it will suffice to show (i) that the domain of $\cup F$ is the whole of A, and (ii) that the range of $\cup F$ is the whole of B. We deal with (i) and leave (ii) as an exercise.

We establish (i) by showing that, for every positive integer n, each element of A in the enumeration up to and including a_{n+1} is the first member of a pair in f_{2n}. We show this by induction on n. For the base, we need to show that $f_{2 \cdot 1}$, i.e. f_2, contains pairs with a_1 and a_2 as their first members. This follows directly from the definition of f_n, since f_2 is $f_1 \cup \{\langle a_2, b \rangle\}$, for some $b \in B$, i.e. $\{\langle a_1, b_1 \rangle, \langle a_2, b \rangle\}$. For the inductive step, we assume (IH) that every element of A in the enumeration up to and including a_{n+1} is the first member of a pair in f_{2n}, and try to show that it follows from this that every element of A in the enumeration up to and including a_{n+2} is the first member of a pair in $f_{2(n+1)}$. Since $2n < 2(n + 1) - 1$, we have, by the definition of f_n, that $f_{2n} \subseteq f_{2(n+1)-1}$. Hence (IH), every element of A in the enumeration up to and including a_{n+1} is the first member of a pair in $f_{2(n+1)-1}$, and, a fortiori, in $f_{2(n+1)}$. Hence it only remains to show that $f_{2(n+1)}$ contains a pair with a_{n+2} as its first member. If $f_{2(n+1)-1}$ contains such a pair, then so does $f_{2(n+1)}$. Suppose, then that $f_{2(n+1)-1}$ contains no pair with a_{n+2} as its first member. Then, since a_{n+2} is the first element of A in the enumeration which doesn't occur in any pair in $f_{2(n+1)-1}$, and since $2(n + 1) - 1$ is odd, we have that $f_{2(n+1)}$ is $f_{2(n+1)-1} \cup \{\langle a_{n+2}, b \rangle\}$ for some $b \in B$, as desired. ∎

EXERCISE 7. 42: Let f be an order-preserving one-to-one correspondence between a finite subset A_0 of A and a finite subset B_0 of B. Show (1) that, for every $a \in A - A_0$, there is a $b \in B$ such that $f \cup \{\langle a, b \rangle\}$ is an order-preserving one-to-one correspondence between $A_0 \cup \{a\}$ and $B_0 \cup \{b\}$, and (2) that, for every $b' \in B - B_0$, there is an $a' \in A$ such that $f \cup \{\langle a', b' \rangle\}$ is an order-preserving one-to-one correspondence between $A_0 \cup \{a'\}$ and $B_0 \cup \{b'\}$.

EXERCISE 7. 43: Show (1) that every set in F is an order-preserving one-to-one correspondence between a subset of A and a subset of B and (2) that $\bigcup F$ is an order-preserving one-to-one correspondence between a subset of A and a subset of B (see the proof of Theorem 7. 41).

EXERCISE 7. 44: Show that the range of $\bigcup F$, in the proof of Theorem 7. 41, is the whole of B.

Hint: Proceed as we did for the domain of $\bigcup F$. Show first that, for every positive integer n, each element of B in the enumeration up to and including b_n is the second member of a pair in f_{2n-1}.

11. Categoricity in Power

In the last two sections we have approached the question whether a set of sentences represents a structure up to isomorphism in its power from the point of view of structures. We have seen that some structures, e.g. Q, are represented up to isomorphism in their power, while others, e.g. $\mathcal{N}$, are not. We can also consider the situation from the point of view of sets of sentences, asking whether a given set of sentences represents its models of a certain cardinality up to isomorphism in their power.

DEFINITION: If κ is a cardinal, a set of sentences Γ is *categorical in power* κ, or κ-*categorical*, just in case Γ has a model of cardinality κ and all the models of Γ of cardinality κ are isomorphic.

Clearly, if a structure of cardinality κ is represented up to isomorphism in its power by a set of sentences Γ, Γ is κ-categorical. Hence, it follows from Theorem 7. 24 that the theory of $\mathcal{N}$ is not $\aleph_0$-categorical, while Theorem 7. 41 entails that $\Theta_<$ is $\aleph_0$-categorical. In this section we provide an overview of the phenomenon of categoricity in power.

Sets of sentences which are categorical in every power are easy to find.

EXERCISE 7. 45: Let L be the first-order language with a one-place predicate, P, as its only extralogical symbol. Show that the set $\{\forall x\, Px\}$ is categorical in every power.

There are also many sets of sentences which are not categorical in any power.

EXERCISE 7. 46: Let L be the language whose only extralogical symbol is a one-place function symbol f. Show that the set $\{\exists x\, \neg f(x) \approx x\}$ is not categorical in any power.

The theory of $\mathcal{N}$ is another example of a set of sentences which is not categorical in any power. Nevertheless, categoricity in power is not, in general, an all or nothing affair. Some sets of sentences are categorical in some powers but not in others.

Consider again $\Theta_<$. We know that $\Theta_<$ is $\aleph_0$-categorical. We show now that $\Theta_<$ is not $2^{\aleph_0}$-categorical. Let $\mathcal{R}$ be the $L_<$-structure whose universe is the set $\mathfrak{R}$ of the real numbers, in which $<$ is interpreted with the *less than* relation in the reals, and let $\mathcal{R}^*$ be the $L_<$-structure which differs from $\mathcal{R}$ only in that 0 is not an element of its universe. Both $<_{\mathcal{R}}$ and $<_{\mathcal{R}^*}$ are strict, dense linear ordering of the universe of their structures with no minimal or maximal elements. Hence they are both models of $\Theta_<$. The cardinality of both structures is $2^{\aleph_0}$. Hence, to show that $\Theta_<$ is not $2^{\aleph_0}$-categorical, it will suffice to show that $\mathcal{R}$ and $\mathcal{R}^*$ are not isomorphic. To establish this result, we invoke the fact that every cut in the reals is continuous (see Chapter 1, §8).

LEMMA 7. 47: $\mathcal{R}$ and $\mathcal{R}^*$ are not isomorphic.

Proof: We assume, towards a contradiction, that $\mathcal{R}$ and $\mathcal{R}^*$ are isomorphic. Let h be an isomorphism between $\mathcal{R}^*$ and $\mathcal{R}$. Let N be the set containing the images under h of the negative real numbers, and let P be the set containing the images under h of the positive real numbers. The negative and positive real numbers are all the elements of $\mathfrak{R} - \{0\}$ (the universe of $\mathcal{R}^*$). Hence, since h is a one-to-one correspondence between $\mathfrak{R} - \{0\}$ and $\mathfrak{R}$, we have that $N \cup P = \mathfrak{R}$. Obviously, neither N nor P is empty. Also, since every negative real number is less than every positive real number, and h is an isomorphism, it follows that every element of N is less than every element of P. Therefore the division of $\mathfrak{R}$ into N and P is a cut. Every cut in $\mathfrak{R}$ is continuous. Hence, either N has a last element or P has a first element.

Assume that P has a first element, and let a be the positive real number whose image under h is the first element of P. For every positive real number there is another positive real number which is less than it. Let b be a positive real number such that $b < a$. Then, since h is an isomorphism, $h(b) < h(a)$. But since b is positive, $h(b) \in P$, which contradicts the hypothesis that $h(a)$ is the first element of P. We can derive a contradiction in exactly the same way from the hypothesis that N has a last element. ∎

Hence we can conclude that Δ is $\aleph_0$-categorical, but not $2^{\aleph_0}$-categorical. But what about other cardinalities? The answer to this question follows from a result established by M. Morley in 1965, which we state without proof.

MORLEY CATEGORICITY THEOREM: Let Γ be a set of sentences of a countable language. If Γ is categorical in some uncountable power, then Γ is categorical in every uncountable power.

Morley's theorem and Lemma 7. 47 entail that $\Theta_<$ is not categorical in any uncountable power. Thus, we have sets of sentences which are categorical in every power, sets of sentences which are not categorical in any power, and sets of sentences which are $\aleph_0$-categorical, but not categorical in any uncountable power. It follows from Morley's theorem that, with respect to infinite cardinalities, there is only one other possibility— sets of sentences which are categorical in every uncountable power, but not $\aleph_0$-categorical. We close the chapter with an example of this situation.

Let L_{As} be the first-order language whose extralogical vocabulary contains one individual constant, 0, and one one-place function symbol, s. Let $\mathcal{N}_s$ be the L_{As}-structure with the set of natural numbers as its universe, in which 0 denotes number zero and s is interpreted with the successor function in ω.

EXERCISE 7. 48: Show that all the models of the theory of $\mathcal{N}_s$ are infinite.

EXERCISE 7. 49: Show that the theory of $\mathcal{N}_s$ has a denumerable model which is not isomorphic to $\mathcal{N}_s$.

Hint: Follow the procedure of the proof of Theorem 7. 24, bearing in mind that the language of $\mathcal{N}_s$ doesn't contain some of the symbols that figured in that proof.

Notice that it follows directly from Exercise 7. 49 that the theory of $\mathcal{N}_s$ is not $\aleph_0$-categorical.

EXERCISE 7. 50: Show that if $\mathcal{A}$ is a model of the theory of $\mathcal{N}_s$, there is an embedding of $\mathcal{N}_s$ in $\mathcal{A}$.

Hint: Follow the procedure of the proof of Lemma 7. 25.

If $\mathcal{A}$ is a model of the theory of $\mathcal{N}_s$, for every element a of the universe of $\mathcal{A}$, we can define by induction the set D_a of *descendants* of a:

  Base: $a \in D_a$.

  Inductive Clause: For every $x \in D_a$, $s_{\mathcal{A}}(x) \in D_a$.

  Nothing else is in D_a.

EXERCISE 7. 51: Show that, for every element a of the universe of a model of the theory of $\mathcal{N}_s$, (1) a is not the successor of any of its descendants, and (2) no descendant of a is the successor of more than one descendant of a.

Using this notion we can define the *standard galaxy* of $\mathcal{A}$ as the set of descendants of $0_{\mathcal{A}}$. We shall refer to the elements of the standard galaxy of $\mathcal{A}$ as the *standard elements* of its universe. Let's refer to models of the theory of $\mathcal{N}_s$ which are not isomorphic to $\mathcal{N}_s$ as *nonstandard models of successor arithmetic*. The universe of a nonstandard model of successor arithmetic will contain elements which are not standard. We shall refer to them as *nonstandard elements*.

If $\mathcal{A}$ is a nonstandard model of successor arithmetic, the nonstandard elements of its universe will be arranged in galaxies similar to the nonstandard galaxies of nonstandard models of arithmetic—infinite chains of nonstandard elements of the universe, with no minimal or maximal element, in which each element is followed by its successor. We can also use the notion of the set of descendants of an element of the universe of $\mathcal{A}$ to define nonstandard galaxies. For all elements a, b of the universe of $\mathcal{A}$, we say that a is at a *finite distance* from b just in case either a is in the set of descendants of b or b is in the set of descendants of a.

EXERCISE 7. 52: Show that the relation *...is at a finite distance from...* is an equivalence relation in the universe of a model of the theory of $\mathcal{N}_s$.

Now we can define the galaxies of $\mathcal{A}$ as the equivalence classes generated by the elements of its universe with the relation *...is at a finite distance from...* We can show as we did for the theory of $\mathcal{N}$ that every galaxy of a model of the theory of $\mathcal{N}_s$ is denumerable.

EXERCISE 7. 53: Show that the universe of an uncountable model of successor arithmetic has the same cardinality as the set of galaxies it contains.

Hint: Use Corollary 6. 99.

Now we are in a position to establish the result that we have announced.

LEMMA 7. 54: The theory of $\mathcal{N}_s$ is categorical in every uncountable power.

Proof: Let κ be an uncountable cardinal. We need to show (i) that the theory of $\mathcal{N}_s$ has a model of cardinality κ, and (ii) that all the models of the theory of $\mathcal{N}_s$ of cardinality κ are isomorphic. We know that the theory of $\mathcal{N}_s$ has an infinite model, namely $\mathcal{N}_s$. Hence (i) follows directly from the Löwenheim-Skolem-Tarski Theorem.

For (ii), let $\mathcal{A}$, $\mathcal{B}$, be two models of the theory of $\mathcal{N}_s$ of cardinality κ. Let A be the universe of $\mathcal{A}$ and B the universe of $\mathcal{B}$. We need to show that $\mathcal{A}$ and $\mathcal{B}$ are isomorphic. We know that each galaxy in $\mathcal{A}$ and in $\mathcal{B}$ is denumerable. By Exercise 7. 53, we have that both $\mathcal{A}$ and $\mathcal{B}$ have κ many galaxies. Let g be a one-to-one correspondence between the set of nonstandard galaxies of $\mathcal{A}$ and the set of nonstandard galaxies of $\mathcal{B}$.

Let's say that a one-to-one correspondence f between a subset A_0 of A and a subset B_0 of B *preserves succession* just in case, for every $a \in A_0$, $f(s_\mathcal{A}(a)) = s_\mathcal{B}(f(a))$. Thus, if f is succession-preserving and it pairs a with b, it will also pair $s_\mathcal{A}(a)$ with $s_\mathcal{B}(b)$. Clearly, a succession-preserving one-to-one correspondence between the whole of A and the whole of B will be an isomorphism between $\mathcal{A}$ and $\mathcal{B}$. Suppose that we could define a succession-preserving one-to-one correspondence between the standard galaxy of $\mathcal{A}$ and the standard galaxy of $\mathcal{B}$, and for every nonstandard galaxy A^* of $\mathcal{A}$, a succession-preserving one-to-one correspondence between A^* and $g(A^*)$. We could easily show that the union of the collection containing all these functions is a succession-preserving one-to-one correspondence between A and B, i.e. an isomorphism between $\mathcal{A}$ and $\mathcal{B}$. We show how to define a succession-preserving one-to-one correspondence between a nonstandard galaxy of $\mathcal{A}$ and its image under g, leaving the rest of the proof as an exercise.

Let A^* be a nonstandard galaxy of $\mathcal{A}$, and let $a \in A^*$. We define by induction the set N_a of *ancestors* of a:

Base: $a \in N_a$.

Inductive Clause: For every $x \in N_a$, $s_\mathcal{A}^{-1}(x) \in N_a$.

Nothing else is in N_a.

Notice that A^* is the union of the set of descendants and the set of ancestors of a. Let $b \in g(A^*)$. We define by recursion a function f_D from the set of descendants of a to $g(A^*)$ as the unique function satisfying the following conditions:

$f_D(a) = b.$

For every $x \in D_a, f_D(s_{\mathcal{A}}(x)) = s_{\mathcal{B}}(f_D(x)).$

Now we define, also by recursion, a function f_N from the set of ancestors of a to $g(A^*)$ as the unique function satisfying the following conditions:

$f_N(a) = b.$

For every $x \in N_a, f_N(s_{\mathcal{A}}^{-1}(x)) = s_{\mathcal{B}}^{-1}(f_N(x)).$

We can easily show that the union of f_D and f_N is a succession-preserving one-to-one correspondence between A^* and $g(A^*)$. This is left as an exercise. ∎

EXERCISE 7. 55: Show that there is a succession-preserving one-to-one correspondence between the standard galaxy of $\mathcal{A}$ and the standard galaxy $\mathcal{B}$ (in the proof of Lemma 7. 54).

EXERCISE 7. 56: Show that $f_D \cup f_N$, in the proof of Lemma 7. 54, is a succession-preserving one-to-one correspondence between A^* and $g(A^*)$.

EXERCISE 7. 57: Show that if C is a collection containing a succession-preserving one-to-one correspondence between the standard galaxy of $\mathcal{A}$ and the standard galaxy of $\mathcal{B}$ (in the proof of Lemma 7. 54) and, for every nonstandard galaxy A^* of $\mathcal{A}$, a succession-preserving one-to-one correspondence between A^* and $g(A^*)$, then $\bigcup C$ is an isomorphism between $\mathcal{A}$ and $\mathcal{B}$.

Chapter 8

Decidability

1. Decidable Sets of Sentences and Indiscernible Structures

Consider the set of disjunctive formulas of a first-order language, L. To determine whether a given L-formula ϕ is an element of this set, we would just need to check whether the first symbol in ϕ is a left-hand bracket, and whether ϕ contains an occurrence of $\vee$ with the number of left-hand brackets to its left exceeding by one the number of right-hand brackets. Devising this procedure may require some ingenuity, but none is required for applying it. Performing these checks on an L-formula is a purely mechanical task.

DEFINITION: A *decision procedure* for a set of formulas Γ of a first-order language L is a mechanically applicable procedure that would enable us to determine, for any given L-formula ϕ, whether ϕ is an element of Γ.

DEFINITION: A set Γ of formulas is *decidable* just in case there is a decision procedure for Γ. Otherwise Γ is *undecidable*.

We are not going to provide a definition of mechanically applicable procedure. We shall rely instead on our intuitive ability to recognize specific procedures as falling in this category. To support the claim that a set of formulas is decidable, we shall describe a decision procedure for it in terms of basic operations whose mechanical applicability is intuitively unquestionable, such as, for example, obtaining the following items of information about a given finite tuple ϕ of symbols of a formal language: how long ϕ is, which symbol occupies the last position in ϕ, whether ϕ contains more occurrences of a symbol than of another symbol, which tuple results from concatenating ϕ with another tuple, or which tuple results from replacing every occurrence of a symbol in ϕ with an occurrence of another symbol.

DEFINITION: A set of sentences Γ *represents* a structure $\mathcal{A}$ *up to indiscernibility* just in case the models of Γ are the structures which are indiscernible from $\mathcal{A}$.

We know that every set of sentences having $\mathcal{A}$ as a model will also have among its models every other structure which is indiscernible from $\mathcal{A}$. Hence, representing $\mathcal{A}$ up to indiscernibility is the closest we can get to representing $\mathcal{A}$. How close this is will vary from structure to structure. A set of sentences which represents a finite structure up to indiscernibility will represent it up to isomorphism (see Chapter 7, §4), whereas a set of $L_<$-sentences which represents $\mathcal{Q}$ up to indiscernibility will represent it only up to isomorphism in its power (see Chapter 7, §10), and a set of $L_<$-sentences which represents $\mathcal{R}$ up to indiscernibility won't even reach this standard (see Chapter 7, §11).

Every structure is representable up to indiscernibility, and, for any given structure $\mathcal{A}$, we can easily define a set of sentences which does the job. Every structure which is not indiscernible from $\mathcal{A}$ will assign the value false to some sentence which is true in $\mathcal{A}$. Therefore every model of the theory of $\mathcal{A}$ will be indiscernible from $\mathcal{A}$—the theory of $\mathcal{A}$ represents $\mathcal{A}$ up to indiscernibility.

A more substantial question we can raise with respect to a structure is whether it is represented up to indiscernibility by a *decidable* set of sentences of the language. This issue will be our main focus in this chapter. We are going to concentrate mainly on positive results—asserting the existence of a decidable set of sentences which represents a given structure up to indiscernibility. The task of establishing a result of this kind can in principle be approached in two different ways. On the one hand, we can try to show that the structure is represented up to indiscernibility by a set of sentences which is known to be decidable. On the other hand, we can try to find a decision procedure for the theory of the structure, which, as we have seen, represents the structure up to indiscernibility. In §§2 and 3 we are going to explore the first approach. We will present techniques which will enable us to show that a decidable set of sentences represents a structure up to indiscernibility, and use these techniques to establish a few specific results of this kind. Then, in §§4 and 5, we will show that both approaches come to the same. Trivially, if the theory of a structure $\mathcal{A}$ is decidable, then $\mathcal{A}$ is represented up to indiscernibility by a decidable set of sentences. We are going to show that the converse also holds. If $\mathcal{A}$ is representable up to indiscernibility by a decidable set of sentences, then the theory of $\mathcal{A}$ is decidable. Finally, in §§6 and 7, we shall briefly consider some important structures which are not represented up to indiscernibility by a decidable set of sentences.

DEFINITION: A set of sentences Γ of a first-order language L is a *complete theory* just in case, for every L-sentence ϕ, either ϕ or $\neg\phi$ is a logical consequence of Γ.

The following lemma uses this notion to specify which sets of sentences represent a structure up to indiscernibility.

LEMMA 8. 1: For every set of sentences Γ of a first-order language L, and every L-structure $\mathcal{A}$, Γ represents $\mathcal{A}$ up to indiscernibility if and only if $\mathcal{A}$ is a model of Γ and Γ is a complete theory.

Proof: We show first that if Γ is a complete theory with $\mathcal{A}$ as a model, then every model of Γ is indiscernible from $\mathcal{A}$. Assume that Γ is a complete theory with $\mathcal{A}$ as a model. Let $\mathcal{B}$ be an L-structure which is not indiscernible from $\mathcal{A}$. We need to show that $\mathcal{B}$ is not a model of Γ. Since $\mathcal{B}$ is not indiscernible from $\mathcal{A}$, there is an L-sentence ϕ such that $v_{\mathcal{A}}(\phi) \neq v_{\mathcal{B}}(\phi)$. Assume first that $v_{\mathcal{A}}(\phi) = T$. Then $v_{\mathcal{A}}(\neg\phi) = F$, and, since $\mathcal{A}$ is a model of Γ, $\Gamma \nvDash \neg\phi$. Then, since Γ is a complete theory, $\Gamma \vDash \phi$. Since $v_{\mathcal{A}}(\phi) \neq v_{\mathcal{B}}(\phi)$, $v_{\mathcal{B}}(\phi) = F$, and, since ϕ is true in every model of Γ, $\mathcal{B}$ is not a model of Γ, as desired. Assume now that $v_{\mathcal{A}}(\phi) = F$. Then, since $\mathcal{A}$ is a model of Γ, $\Gamma \nvDash \phi$, and since Γ is a complete theory, $\Gamma \vDash \neg\phi$. Now, since $v_{\mathcal{A}}(\phi) \neq v_{\mathcal{B}}(\phi)$, $v_{\mathcal{B}}(\phi) = T$, and $v_{\mathcal{B}}(\neg\phi) = F$. But since $\neg\phi$ is true in every model of Γ, we can conclude, once again, that $\mathcal{B}$ is not among them, as desired.

We show now that if Γ represents $\mathcal{A}$ up to indiscernibility, then $\mathcal{A}$ is a model of Γ and Γ is a complete theory. Assume that Γ represents $\mathcal{A}$ up to indiscernibility. Clearly, $\mathcal{A}$ is a model of Γ. To show that Γ is a complete theory, assume, towards a contradiction, that it isn't. Then there is an L-sentence ϕ such that $\Gamma \nvDash \phi$, $\Gamma \nvDash \neg\phi$. Then both $\Gamma \cup \{\neg\phi\}$ and $\Gamma \cup \{\phi\}$ have models. $\mathcal{A}$ will be a model of one of these sets, and then every model of the other will be a model of Γ which is not indiscernible from $\mathcal{A}$, since it assigns a different truth value to ϕ. This contradicts the assumption that every model of Γ is indiscernible from $\mathcal{A}$, as desired. ∎

The strategies that we are going to present for showing that a structure is represented up to indiscernibility by a decidable set of sentences exploit the connection established by this result. If Γ is a decidable set of sentences of a first-order language L, and $\mathcal{A}$ is a model of Γ, then, according to Lemma 8. 1, to show that Γ represents $\mathcal{A}$ up to indiscernibility, it will suffice to establish that Γ is a complete theory. In the next two sections we are going to present two techniques for showing that a set of sentences is a complete theory. Using these techniques, we shall establish that a few important structures are represented up to indiscernibility by decidable sets of sentences.

2. Vaught's Test

Our first technique for showing that a set of sentences is a complete theory arises from the following result:

VAUGHT'S THEOREM: For every set of sentences Γ of a countable language L, if Γ is κ-categorical for some infinite cardinal κ, and Γ has no finite models, then Γ is a complete theory.

Proof: Let L be a countable language and Γ a set of L-sentences with no finite models, and let κ be an infinite cardinal such that Γ is κ-categorical. Assume, towards a contradiction, that Γ is not a complete theory. Then there is an L-sentence ϕ such that $\Gamma \nVdash \phi$, $\Gamma \nVdash \neg\phi$. Hence Γ has a model, $\mathcal{A}$, such that $v_{\mathcal{A}}(\phi) = F$ and $v_{\mathcal{A}}(\neg\phi) = T$ and a model, $\mathcal{B}$, such that $v_{\mathcal{B}}(\neg\phi) = F$ and $v_{\mathcal{B}}(\phi) = T$; i.e. $\mathcal{A}$ is a model of $\Gamma \cup \{\neg\phi\}$ and $\mathcal{B}$ is a model of $\Gamma \cup \{\phi\}$. $\mathcal{A}$ and $\mathcal{B}$ have to be infinite. Hence, by the Löwenheim-Skolem-Tarski Theorem, $\Gamma \cup \{\neg\phi\}$ has a model, $\mathcal{A}'$, of cardinality κ, and $\Gamma \cup \{\phi\}$ has a model, $\mathcal{B}'$, of cardinality κ. $\mathcal{A}'$ and $\mathcal{B}'$ are models of Γ of cardinality κ, and $v_{\mathcal{A}'}(\phi) \neq v_{\mathcal{B}'}(\phi)$. Since Γ is κ-categorical, $\mathcal{A}'$ and $\mathcal{B}'$ are isomorphic. Then, by Corollary 7. 10 of the Isomorphism Theorem, $\mathcal{A}'$ and $\mathcal{B}'$ are indiscernible. But this contradicts the result that $v_{\mathcal{A}'}(\phi) \neq v_{\mathcal{B}'}(\phi)$. ∎

We can invoke Vaught's Theorem to show that a set of sentences is a complete theory, and hence, by Lemma 8. 1, that it represents its models up to indiscernibility. This procedure is known as *Vaught's test*. In the remainder of this section we use Vaught's test to show that two of the structures that we considered in Chapter 7 are represented up to indiscernibility by decidable sets of sentences.

i.   *Strict Dense Linear Orderings with No Minimal or Maximal Elements*

Consider the first-order language $L_<$, with a two-place predicate, $<$, as its only extralogical symbol, and the $L_<$-structure Q, presented in Chapter 7, §10, with the set of rational numbers as its universe, in which $<$ is interpreted with the *less than* relation. We saw that, since the *less than* relation is a strict dense linear ordering of the rational numbers with no minimal or maximal element, Q is a model of the set of sentences $\Theta_<$ (see Chapter 7, §10). A decision procedure for $\Theta_<$ can be easily obtained from our definition of this set. In order to determine whether any given $L_<$-formula ϕ is an element of $\Theta_<$, we would just need to check whether it matches symbol by symbol any of the elements of $\Theta_<$, using for this purpose the list in terms of which the set has been defined. Hence, $\Theta_<$ is decidable. In fact, since every finite set of formulas can in principle be defined as a list of tuples of symbols, every finite set of formulas is decidable.

According to Vaught's Theorem, to show that $\Theta_<$ is a complete theory, it will suffice to establish that $\Theta_<$ has no finite models and that $\Theta_<$ is κ-categorical for some infinite cardinal κ. Theorem 7. 41 tells us that $\Theta_<$ is $\aleph_0$-categorical. Hence, to apply Vaught's test, we only need to show that $\Theta_<$ has no finite models. This is a corollary of the following lemma.

LEMMA 8. 2:   Every finite $L_<$-structure in which $<$ is interpreted with a strict ordering has a maximal element.

Proof: Let $\mathcal{A}$ be a finite $L_<$-structure, whose universe is the set $A = \{a_1,\ldots, a_n\}$, and let $<_{\mathcal{A}}$ be a strict ordering of A. For every positive integer m, we define by recursion the set A_m of elements of A, as the image of m under the unique function satisfying the following conditions:

$$A_1 = \{x \mid a_1 <_{\mathcal{A}} x\}.$$

For every positive integer m,

$$A_{m+1} = \begin{cases} \varnothing, \text{if } A_m = \varnothing, \\ \{x \mid a_i <_{\mathcal{A}} x\} \text{ otherwise, where } i \text{ is the least} \\ \text{positive integer such that } a_i \in A_m. \end{cases}$$

Thus A_1 contains the elements of A to which a_1 bears $<_{\mathcal{A}}$, and for every positive integer m, if A_m is not empty, A_{m+1} contains the elements of A to which an element of A_m bears $<_{\mathcal{A}}$.

We can show that, for every positive integer m, if A_m is not empty, then A_{m+1} is a proper subset of A_m. This is left as an exercise. Now, we have that A_1 has at most $n - 1$ elements, and every nonempty set of the sequence has at least one element more than the next one. Hence, by A_n, at the latest, the empty set will appear in the sequence. But we can show that it follows from this that $\mathcal{A}$ has a maximal element. This is left as an exercise. ∎

EXERCISE 8. 3: Show that, for every positive integer m, if A_m is not empty, then A_{m+1} is a proper subset of A_m.

EXERCISE 8. 4: Show that if the empty set appears in the sequence of sets defined in the proof of Lemma 8. 2, then $\mathcal{A}$ has a maximal element.

Thus, we have that $\Theta_<$ is $\aleph_0$-categorical and has no finite models. Hence, by Vaught's Theorem, $\Theta_<$ is a complete theory. And since Q is a model of $\Theta_<$, we have, by Lemma 8. 1, that $\Theta_<$ represents Q up to indiscernibility. Notice that, since the models of $\Theta_<$ are all the $L_<$-structures which interpret $<$ with a strict dense linear ordering of their universes with no minimal or maximal elements, we can conclude that these structures are indiscernible. In particular, Q, $\mathcal{R}$ and $\mathcal{R}^*$ (see Chapter 7, §11) are indiscernible from each other.

ii. Successor Arithmetic

Consider now the first-order language L_{As}, whose extralogical symbols are an individual constant, 0, and a one-place function symbol, s, and the L_{As}-structure $\mathcal{N_s}$ described in Chapter 7, §11, whose universe is the set of natural numbers, in which 0 is interpreted with number zero, and s with the successor function in ω. We shall write $s^n\ t$ as an abbreviation for the L_{As}-term $s(...s(t)...)$, built from an L_{As}-term t with n applications of the inductive clause of the definition of L_{As}-term. Thus every L_{As}-term is of the form $s^n\ 0$ or $s^n\ x$, for some variable x (notice that $s^0\ t$ is t itself). Let Θ_{As} be the set containing the L_{As}-sentences

(1) $\forall x\ \neg s(x) \approx 0$
(2) $\forall x \forall y\ (s(x) \approx s(y) \rightarrow x \approx y)$
(3) $\forall x\ (\neg x \approx 0 \rightarrow \exists y\ x \approx s(y))$,

and, for every positive integer n, the L_{As}-sentence

(4) $\forall x\ \neg s^n\ x \approx x$.

We could easily describe a decision procedure for Θ_{As}. To determine whether a given L_{As}-formula ϕ is an element of Θ_{As}, we just need to check whether ϕ matches symbol by symbol (1), (2) or (3), and whether it is an instance of (4). The latter can be done, e.g., by checking whether ϕ is at least nine symbols long, whether its first three symbols are $\forall$, x

and ¬, and its last two symbols ≈ and x, and whether the remainder contains no symbols other than s, x, (, and). Hence, Θ_{As} is decidable.

Clearly, $\mathcal{N}_s$ is a model of Θ_{As}. (1) is true in $\mathcal{N}_s$ because number zero is not the successor of any natural number. (2) is true in $\mathcal{N}_s$ because different natural numbers have different successors. (3) is true in $\mathcal{N}_s$ because every natural number other than zero is the successor of a natural number. And all the instances of (4) are true in $\mathcal{N}_s$ because the sequence of natural numbers generated by the successor function has no loops—applying the successor function to a natural number any number of times never yields that natural number again.

Since Θ_{As} has $\mathcal{N}_s$ as a model, we have, by Lemma 8. 1, that Θ_{As} represents $\mathcal{N}_s$ up to indiscernibility just in case Θ_{As} is a complete theory. And, according to Vaught's Theorem, to show that Θ_{As} is a complete theory, it will suffice to establish that it has no finite models and that it is κ-categorical for some infinite cardinal κ. We know from Chapter 7, §11 that these claims hold of the theory of $\mathcal{N}_s$. To show that they hold of Θ_{As}, we just need to establish that every model of Θ_{As} has the features of the models of the theory of $\mathcal{N}_s$ from which we concluded that they are all infinite (Exercise 7. 48) and that the theory of $\mathcal{N}_s$ is categorical in every uncountable power (Lemma 7. 54). This is left as an exercise.

EXERCISE 8. 5: Show that every model of Θ_{As} is infinite.

EXERCISE 8. 6: Show that a model $\mathcal{A}$ of Θ_{As} consists of a standard galaxy, containing the descendants of $0_{\mathcal{A}}$, and an arbitrary number of non-standard galaxies—disjoint, infinite chains of nonstandard elements of the universe, with no minimal or maximal element, in which each element is followed by its successor.

Having shown that Θ_{As} has no finite models and that it is categorical in every uncountable power, we can conclude, by Vaught's Theorem, that Θ_{As} is a complete theory. Hence, by Lemma 8. 1, it follows that $\mathcal{N}_s$ is represented up to indiscernibility by a decidable set of sentences.

3. Quantifier Elimination

We turn now to our second technique for showing that a set of sentences is a complete theory.

DEFINITION: Let Δ be a set of sentences of a first-order language L. A set Γ of L-sentences is *complete with respect to* Δ just in case, for every δ ∈ Δ, either Γ ⊨ δ or Γ ⊨ ¬δ.

The strategy that we are going to consider for showing that Γ is a complete theory establishes this result in two stages. We show, first, that Γ is complete with respect to a set of L-sentences Δ. Then we show that it follows from this that what goes for the elements of Δ goes for every sentence of the language—i.e. that if Γ is complete with respect to Δ, then Γ is a complete theory. The following exercise provides a procedure for implementing the second step of this strategy.

DEFINITION: If Γ is a set of sentences of a first-order language L, two L-formulas ϕ, ψ are Γ-*equivalent*, written $\phi \doteq_\Gamma \psi$, just in case, for every model $\mathcal{A}$ of Γ, and every variable interpretation s in $\mathcal{A}$, $v_{\mathcal{A}}(\phi, s) = v_{\mathcal{A}}(\psi, s)$.

EXERCISE 8. 7: Let Γ and Δ be two sets of sentences of a first-order language L. Show that if Γ is complete with respect to Δ, and every L-sentence is Γ-equivalent to an element of Δ, then Γ is a complete theory.

Thus to show that Γ is a complete theory using this strategy, we need to find a set Δ of L-sentences with the following features: On the one hand, it has to be relatively easy to show that Γ is complete with respect to Δ. On the other, every L-sentence has to be Γ-equivalent to some sentence in Δ. The sentences to which this role is normally assigned are the quantifier-free sentences of the language. For this reason, the method is known as *quantifier elimination*. It will be convenient, however, to use a slightly bigger set of sentences.

DEFINITION: The *basic formulas* of a first-order language L are the formulas built from atomic L-formulas and the formula $\forall x\, x \approx x$ exclusively with connectives.

The *basic sentences* of L are the L-sentences which are basic formulas. Hence every quantifier-free sentence is a basic sentence, but the basic sentences include, in addition, formulas in which $\forall x\, x \approx x$ occurs. These are the only occurrences of quantifiers in a basic sentence.

We can now provide a more precise characterization of the quantifier elimination method. To show by quantifier elimination that a set of sentences Γ of a first-order language L is a complete theory we show, first, that Γ is complete with respect to the basic sentences of L, and second, that every L-sentence is Γ-equivalent to some basic sentence of L.

Before we apply this technique to specific cases, we need to make some general remarks about how to show that every L-sentence is Γ-equivalent to some basic sentence of L. As with previous results about every sentence of a language, the best way to establish a claim of this form is as a corollary of a claim about every formula of the language.

DEFINITION: If Γ is a set of sentences of a first-order language L, a *basic* Γ-*surrogate* of an L-formula ϕ is a basic L-formula which is Γ-equivalent to ϕ and all of whose free variables are also free in ϕ.

Clearly, a basic Γ-surrogate of an L-sentence ϕ is a basic L-sentence to which ϕ is Γ-equivalent. Hence, if we could show that every L-formula has a basic Γ-surrogate, the claim that every L-sentence is Γ-equivalent to a basic L-sentence would follow as a special case.

The task of showing that every L-formula has a basic Γ-surrogate is greatly expedited by our next lemma, which tells us that, in order to show that this result holds for every L-formula, it will suffice to establish it for formulas of a very specific kind.

DEFINITION: The *benchmark formulas* of L are the L-formulas of the form $\exists y \, (\alpha_1 \wedge \ldots \wedge \alpha_n)$, where, for every positive integer i less than or equal to n, (i) α_i is an atomic formula or the negation of an atomic formula, (ii) y occurs in α_i, and (iii) α_i is not of the form $y \approx t$ or $t \approx y$, where t is an L-term in which y doesn't occur.

LEMMA 8. 8: For every first-order language L, and every set Γ of L-sentences, if every benchmark formula of L has a basic Γ-surrogate, then every L-formula has a basic Γ-surrogate.

Proof: Let Γ be a set of sentences of a first-order language L. We assume that every benchmark formula of L has a basic Γ-surrogate, and show that it follows from this that every L-formula has a basic Γ-surrogate. We establish this claim by induction on L-formulas.

The base is trivial, since an atomic L-formula is its own basic Γ-surrogate. The inductive clauses for the connectives are also straightforward, since the negation of a basic Γ-surrogate of ϕ is a basic Γ-surrogate of $\neg\phi$, and if ϕ' is a basic Γ-surrogate of ϕ, and ψ' is a basic Γ-surrogate of ψ, then $\phi' \wedge \psi'$ is a basic Γ-surrogate of $\phi \wedge \psi$, $\phi' \vee \psi'$ is a basic Γ-surrogate of $\phi \vee \psi$ and $\phi' \rightarrow \psi'$ is a basic Γ-surrogate of $\phi \rightarrow \psi$. It is only in the clauses for the quantifiers that substantive reasoning is required. We deal with $\exists$, leaving $\forall$ as an exercise.

$\exists$. Let ϕ be an L-formula. We assume (IH) that ϕ has a basic Γ-surrogate. We have to show that it follows from this that $\exists y \, \phi$ has a basic Γ-surrogate. Let ϕ' be a basic Γ-surrogate of ϕ. The reasoning that we used to show that every *PL*-sentence is logically equivalent to a *PL*-sentence in disjunctive normal form (see Chapter 2, §7) can be easily adapted to establish that ϕ' is logically equivalent to an L-formula of the form $\alpha_1 \vee \ldots \vee \alpha_n$, where, for every positive integer i less than or equal to n, α_i is a conjunction each of whose conjuncts is an atomic subformula of ϕ' or the negation of an atomic subformula of ϕ', or, if $\forall x \, x \approx x$ occurs in

ϕ', $\forall x\ x \approx x$ or $\neg\forall x\ x \approx x$ (if $x \approx x$ doesn't occur in ϕ' outside the combination $\forall x\ x \approx x$, the same goes for $\alpha_1 \vee...\vee \alpha_n$). Now, since ϕ is Γ-equivalent to ϕ', and ϕ' is logically equivalent to $\alpha_1 \vee...\vee \alpha_n$, it follows that $\exists y\ \phi$ is Γ-equivalent to $\exists y\ (\alpha_1 \vee...\vee \alpha_n)$ (see Exercise 3. 36). And since, by Exercise 3. 30 (8), $\exists y\ (\alpha_1 \vee...\vee \alpha_n)$ is logically equivalent to $\exists y\ \alpha_1 \vee...\vee \exists y\ \alpha_n$, we can conclude that $\exists y\ \phi =_\Gamma \exists y\ \alpha_1 \vee...\vee \exists y\ \alpha_n$. Also, since each variable which is free in $\alpha_1,..., \alpha_n$ is also free in ϕ', and every free variable of ϕ' is free in ϕ, it follows that every free variable of $\exists y\ \alpha_1 \vee...\vee \exists y\ \alpha_n$ is also free in $\exists y\ \phi$. Hence, to show that $\exists y\ \phi$ has a basic Γ-surrogate, it will suffice to establish that $\exists y\ \alpha_1 \vee...\vee \exists y\ \alpha_n$ has one. And for this it will suffice to show that every disjunct of $\exists y\ \alpha_1 \vee...\vee \exists y\ \alpha_n$ has a basic Γ-surrogate.

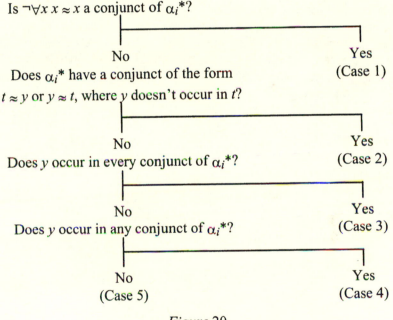

Is $\neg\forall x\ x \approx x$ a conjunct of α_i*?

No

Does α_i* have a conjunct of the form
$t \approx y$ or $y \approx t$, where y doesn't occur in t?

Yes
(Case 1)

No

Does y occur in every conjunct of α_i*?

Yes
(Case 2)

No

Does y occur in any conjunct of α_i*?

Yes
(Case 3)

No
(Case 5)

Yes
(Case 4)

Figure 20

Let i be a positive integer less than or equal to n. Our goal is to show that $\exists y\ \alpha_i$ has a basic Γ-surrogate. Notice, first, that if all the conjuncts of α_i were of the form $\forall x\ x \approx x$, $\exists y\ \alpha_i$ would be logically true, and $\forall x\ x \approx x$ would be a basic Γ-surrogate of $\exists y\ \alpha_i$, as desired. Suppose, then, that α_i has at least one conjunct other than $\forall x\ x \approx x$, and let α_i* be the conjunction which results if we delete from α_i every conjunct of this form. Clearly, α_i is logically equivalent to α_i*, and every free variable of α_i* is also free in α_i. Hence, to show that $\exists y\ \alpha_i$ has a basic Γ-surrogate, it will suffice to establish that $\exists y\ \alpha_i^*$ has one. Notice that the conjuncts of α_i^* can be atomic formulas, negations of atomic formulas, or $\neg \forall x\ x \approx x$. We need to consider five cases, represented in Figure 20.

Case 1: If $\neg \forall x\ x \approx x$ is a conjunct of α_i^*, then $\exists y\ \alpha_i^*$ is false in every L-structure $\mathcal{A}$, relative to every variable interpretation in $\mathcal{A}$, and $\neg \forall x\ x \approx x$ is a basic Γ-surrogate of $\exists y\ \alpha_i^*$, as desired.

Case 2: If α_i^* has a conjunct of the form $t \approx y$ or $y \approx t$, and y doesn't occur in t, then $\exists y\ \alpha_i^*$ is logically equivalent to $(\alpha_i^*)[t/y]$ (see Exercise 8. 10, below), which is a quantifier-free L-formula, and every variable which is free in $(\alpha_i^*)[t/y]$ is also free in $\exists y\ \alpha_i^*$. Hence $(\alpha_i^*)[t/y]$ is a basic Γ-surrogate of $\exists y\ \alpha_i^*$, as desired.

Case 3: In this case, $\exists y\ \alpha_i^*$ is a benchmark formula of L. Hence, by the hypothesis of the lemma, $\exists y\ \alpha_i^*$ has a basic Γ-surrogate, as desired.

Case 4: If y occurs in some but not all of the conjuncts of $\exists y\ \alpha_i^*$, then, by Exercise 3. 31 (4), $\exists y\ \alpha_i^*$ is logically equivalent to $\beta \wedge \exists y\ \gamma$, where β is the conjunction of all the conjuncts of α_i^* in which y doesn't occur, and γ is the conjunction of all the conjuncts of α_i^* in which y does occur. Then $\exists y\ \gamma$ is a benchmark formula, and by the hypothesis of the lemma, it has a basic Γ-surrogate. Let δ be a basic Γ-surrogate of $\exists y\ \gamma$. Then $\beta \wedge \delta$ is a basic Γ-surrogate of $\exists y\ \alpha_i^*$, as desired.

Case 5: If y doesn't occur in any conjunct of α_i^*, then every free variable of α_i^* is also free in $\exists y\ \alpha_i^*$. Also, by Exercise 3. 31 (2), α_i^* is logically equivalent to $\exists y\ \alpha_i^*$. Since α_i^* is a quantifier-free L-formula, α_i^* is a basic Γ-surrogate of $\exists y\ \alpha_i^*$, as desired.   ∎

EXERCISE 8. 9: Complete the proof of Lemma 8. 8 by dealing with the inductive clause for $\forall$.

EXERCISE 8. 10: Show that if x doesn't occur in t, then $\exists x\ (x \approx t \wedge \alpha)\ \Rightarrow\ (\alpha)[t/x]$.

i. Strict Dense Linear Orderings with No Minimal or Maximal Elements

As our first application of the quantifier elimination method, we provide an alternative proof of the fact that $\Theta_<$ is a complete theory. For this, we need to show (i) that, for every basic sentence ϕ of $L_<$, either $\Theta_< \vDash \phi$ or $\Theta_< \vDash \neg\phi$, and (ii) that every $L_<$-sentence is $\Theta_<$-equivalent to some basic $L_<$-sentence. (i) is straightforward. Since $L_<$ has no individual constants, there are no quantifier-free $L_<$-sentences. Hence all the basic $L_<$-sentences are built from $\forall x\ x \approx x$ using the connectives. Therefore, for every basic $L_<$-sentence ϕ, ϕ is either logically true or logically false, and *a fortiori* either $\Theta_< \models \phi$ or $\Theta_< \models \neg\phi$, as desired. According to Lemma 8. 8, to establish (ii) it will suffice to establish the following result:

LEMMA 8. 11: Every benchmark formula of $L_<$ has a basic $\Theta_<$-surrogate.

Proof: Let $\exists y\ \phi$ be a benchmark formula of $L_<$. Then ϕ is a conjunction each of whose conjuncts is either an atomic formula or the negation of an atomic formula. y occurs in every conjunct, and there are no conjuncts of the form $y \approx z$ or $z \approx y$. Hence, every conjunct of ϕ is of one of the following forms:

$$
\begin{array}{ll}
y < y & \neg y < y \\
y < z & \neg y < z \\
z < y & \neg z < y \\
y \approx y & \neg y \approx y \\
 & \neg y \approx z \\
 & \neg z \approx y
\end{array}
$$

where z is a variable different from y.

Three possibilities can be dealt with immediately. If any conjunct of ϕ is of the form $\neg y \approx y$, then $\exists y\ \phi$ is false in every $L_<$-structure $\mathcal{A}$, relative to every variable interpretation in $\mathcal{A}$, and hence $\neg\forall x\ x \approx x$ is a basic $\Theta_<$-surrogate of $\exists y\ \phi$. If any conjunct of ϕ is of the form $y < y$, then, since $\forall x\ \neg x < x \in \Theta_<$, $\exists y\ \phi$ is false in every model $\mathcal{A}$ of $\Theta_<$, relative to every variable interpretation in $\mathcal{A}$, and, once again, $\neg\forall x\ x \approx x$ is a basic $\Theta_<$-surrogate of $\exists y\ \phi$. If all the conjuncts of ϕ are of the form $y \approx y$ or $\neg y < y$, then $\exists y\ \phi$ is true in every model $\mathcal{A}$ of $\Theta_<$, relative to every variable interpretation in $\mathcal{A}$, and $\forall x\ x \approx x$ is a basic $\Theta_<$-surrogate of $\exists y\ \phi$.

Assume, then, that ϕ contains no conjuncts of the form $\neg y \approx y$ or $y < y$, and that it contains at least one conjunct other than $y \approx y$ or $\neg y < y$. Let ϕ^* be the formula which results if we make the following transformations in ϕ:

1. Delete every conjunct of the form $y \approx y$ or $\neg y < y$.
2. Replace every conjunct of the form $\neg y \approx z$ or $\neg z \approx y$ with $y < z \vee z < y$.
3. Replace every conjunct of the form $\neg y < z$ with $z < y \vee y \approx z$.
4. Replace every conjunct of the form $\neg z < y$ with $y < z \vee y \approx z$.

We can easily show that ϕ^* is $\Theta_<$-equivalent to ϕ. This is left as an exercise. ϕ^* is a conjunction whose conjuncts are atomic formulas of the form $y < z$ or $z < y$ or disjunctions of atomic formulas of the form $y < z$, $z < y$ or $y \approx z$. Using the fact that $(\alpha \vee \beta) \wedge \gamma \rightleftharpoons (\alpha \wedge \gamma) \vee (\beta \wedge \gamma)$ (see Exercise 2. 22 (5)), we could show that ϕ^* is logically equivalent to a formula of the form $\alpha_1 \vee ... \vee \alpha_n$, where, for every positive integer i less than or equal to n, α_i is a conjunction each of whose conjuncts is an atomic subformula of ϕ^*. This gives us $\phi \Rrightarrow_{\Theta_<} \alpha_1 \vee ... \vee \alpha_n$, and hence $\exists y\, \phi \Rrightarrow_{\Theta_<} \exists y\, (\alpha_1 \vee ... \vee \alpha_n)$ (see Exercise 3. 36). And since $\exists y\, (\alpha_1 \vee ... \vee \alpha_n)$ is logically equivalent to $\exists y\, \alpha_1 \vee ... \vee \exists y\, \alpha_n$, we can conclude that $\exists y\, \phi \Rrightarrow_{\Theta_<} \exists y\, \alpha_1 \vee ... \vee \exists y\, \alpha_n$. Clearly, every free variable of $\exists y\, \alpha_1 \vee ... \vee \exists y\, \alpha_n$ is also free in $\exists y\, \phi$. Hence, to show that the latter has a basic $\Theta_<$-surrogate it will suffice to establish that the former has one. And for this it will suffice to show that every disjunct of $\exists y\, \alpha_1 \vee ... \vee \exists y\, \alpha_n$ has a basic $\Theta_<$-surrogate.

Let i be a positive integer less than or equal to n. We need to show that $\exists y\, \alpha_i$ has a basic $\Theta_<$-surrogate. α_i is a conjunction each of whose conjuncts is of the form $y < z$, $z < y$ or $y \approx z$, where z is a variable other than y. We have to consider three cases:

Case 1: Suppose first that α_i contains at least one conjunct of the form $y \approx z$. Then $\exists y\, \alpha_i$ is logically equivalent to $(\alpha_i)[z/y]$ (see Exercise 8. 10), and the latter is a basic $\Theta_<$-surrogate of the former.

Case 2: Suppose now that either every conjunct of α_i is of the form $y < z$ or every conjunct of α_i is of the form $z < y$. Then $\exists y\, \alpha_i$ is of the form $\exists y\, (y < z_1 \wedge ... \wedge y < z_m)$ or $\exists y\, (z_1 < y \wedge ... \wedge z_m < y)$, where $z_1, ..., z_m$ are variables different from y. We can show that, for every model $\mathcal{A}$ of $\Theta_<$, and every variable interpretation s in $\mathcal{A}$, these formulas are true in $\mathcal{A}$ relative to s (this is left as an exercise). Hence $\forall x\, x \approx x$ is a basic $\Theta_<$-surrogate of $\exists y\, \alpha_i$.

Case 3: Finally suppose that α_i contains only conjuncts of the form $y < z$ or $z < y$, and at least one conjunct of each of these forms. Then $\exists y\, \alpha_i$ is logically equivalent to a formula of the form

(1) $\exists y\, ((z_1 < y \wedge ... \wedge z_p < y) \wedge (y < w_1 \wedge ... \wedge y < w_q))$,

for variables $z_1, ..., z_p$, $w_1, ..., w_q$ different from y. We can show that (1) is $\Theta_<$-equivalent to

(2) $(z_1 < w_1 \wedge ... \wedge z_1 < w_q) \wedge ... \wedge (z_p < w_1 \wedge ... \wedge z_p < w_q)$

(this is left as an exercise). Hence, since every free variable of (2) is also free in (1), (2) is a basic $\Theta_<$-surrogate of (1), and of $\exists y\, \alpha_i$, as desired. ∎

EXERCISE 8. 12: Show that ϕ^* is $\Theta_<$-equivalent to ϕ (see the proof of Lemma 8. 11).

EXERCISE 8. 13: Show that, for every model $\mathcal{A}$ of $\Theta_<$, and every variable interpretation s in $\mathcal{A}$, if $z_1, ..., z_m$ are variables different from y, then $v_{\mathcal{A}}(\exists y\, (y < z_1 \wedge ... \wedge y < z_m), s) = v_{\mathcal{A}}(\exists y\, (z_1 < y \wedge ... \wedge z_m < y), s) = T$.

EXERCISE 8. 14: Show that, if $z_1, \ldots, z_p, w_1, \ldots, w_q$ are variables different from y, then $\exists y ((z_1 < y \wedge \ldots \wedge z_p < y) \wedge (y < w_1 \wedge \ldots \wedge y < w_q))$ is $\Theta_<$-equivalent to $(z_1 < w_1 \wedge \ldots \wedge z_1 < w_q) \wedge \ldots \wedge (z_p < w_1 \wedge \ldots \wedge z_p < w_q)$.

ii. Successor Arithmetic

We now use the quantifier elimination method to provide an alternative proof of the fact that Θ_{As} is a complete theory. Once again, we need to show that Θ_{As} is complete with respect to the basic sentences of L_{As}, and that every L_{As}-sentence is Θ_{As}-equivalent to some basic L_{As}-sentence.

Θ_{As} is complete with respect to the basic sentences of L_{As} just in case every basic sentence of L_{As} has the same truth value in each model of Θ_{As}. To show that this holds, it will suffice to establish that every atomic L_{As}-sentence has the same truth value in each model of Θ_{As}. An atomic L_{As}-sentence is of the form $t \approx t$, where t is a numeral, or of the form $t \approx u$, where t and u are different numerals. $t \approx t$ is logically true. Hence, in particular, it is true in every model of Θ_{As}. And we can show that if t and u are different numerals, $t \approx u$ is false in every model of Θ_{As}. This is left as an exercise.

EXERCISE 8. 15: Show that if t and u are different numerals, then $t \approx u$ is false in every model of Θ_{As}.

According to Lemma 8. 8, to show that every L_{As}-sentence is Θ_{As}-equivalent to some basic L_{As}-sentence, it will suffice to establish the following result.

LEMMA 8. 16: Every benchmark formula of L_{As} has a basic Θ_{As}-surrogate.

Proof: Let $\exists y \, \phi$ be a benchmark formula of L_{As}. Then ϕ is a conjunction each of whose conjuncts is an atomic formula of L_{As}, or the negation of an atomic formula of L_{As}, in which y occurs. We need to show that $\exists y \, \phi$ has a basic Θ_{As}-surrogate.

We can easily get some possibilities out of the way. Every formula of the form $s^m \, y \approx s^m \, y$ is true in every L_{As}-structure $\mathcal{A}$, relative to every variable interpretation in $\mathcal{A}$, and every formula of the form $s^m \, y \approx s^n \, y$, where $m \neq n$, is false in every model $\mathcal{A}$ of Θ_{As}, relative to every variable interpretation in $\mathcal{A}$. Hence, if every conjunct of ϕ is of the form $s^m \, y \approx s^m$ y or $\neg s^m \, y \approx s^n \, y$, where $m \neq n$, then $\exists y \, \phi$ is true in every model $\mathcal{A}$ of Θ_{As}, relative to every variable interpretation in $\mathcal{A}$, and $0 \approx 0$ is a basic Θ_{As}-surrogate of $\exists y \, \phi$. By the same token, if at least one conjunct of ϕ is of the form $\neg s^m \, y \approx s^m \, y$ or $s^m \, y \approx s^n \, y$, where $m \neq n$, then $\exists y \, \phi$ is false in every model $\mathcal{A}$ of Θ_{As}, relative to every variable interpretation in $\mathcal{A}$, and $\neg 0 \approx 0$ is a basic Θ_{As}-surrogate of $\exists y \, \phi$.

Assume, then, that ϕ contains no conjuncts of the form $\neg s^m \, y \approx s^m \, y$ or $s^m \, y \approx s^n \, y$, where $m \neq n$, and that it contains at least one conjunct not of the form $s^m \, y \approx s^m \, y$ or $\neg s^m \, y \approx s^n \, y$. Let ϕ^* be the formula which results if we delete from ϕ every conjunct of the form $s^m \, y \approx s^m \, y$ or $\neg s^m \, y \approx s^n$ y. ϕ^* is a conjunction each of whose conjuncts is of the form $s^m \, y \approx t$, $\neg s^m \, y \approx t$, $t \approx s^m \, y$ or $\neg t \approx s^m \, y$, where y doesn't occur in t. Clearly, ϕ^* is Θ_{As}-equivalent to ϕ. Hence, $\exists y \, \phi^*$ is Θ_{As}-equivalent to $\exists y \, \phi$ (see Exercise 3. 36). Also, every free variable of $\exists y \, \phi^*$ is free in $\exists y \, \phi$. Therefore, in order to show that $\exists y \, \phi$ has a basic Θ_{As}-surrogate, it will suffice to show that $\exists y \, \phi^*$ has one. We have to consider two cases.

Case 1: Suppose, first, that every conjunct of ϕ^* is of the form $\neg s^m \, y \approx t$ or $\neg t \approx s^m \, y$. We can show that it follows from this that $\exists y \, \phi^*$ is true in every model $\mathcal{A}$ of Θ_{As}, relative to every variable interpretation in $\mathcal{A}$, and hence that $0 \approx 0$ is a basic Θ_{As}-surrogate of $\exists y \, \phi^*$. This is left as an exercise.

Case 2: Suppose now that ϕ^* has at least one nonnegative conjunct. Let t and $s^k \, y$ be the terms on either side of $\approx$ in a nonnegative conjunct of ϕ^*. Then $\exists y \, \phi^*$ is logically equivalent to a formula of the form

(1) $\exists y \, (s^k \, y \approx t \wedge (\alpha_1 \wedge ... \wedge \alpha_p) \wedge (\beta_1 \wedge ... \wedge \beta_q))$,

where, for every positive integer i less than or equal to p, α_i is the formula $s^{m_i} \, y \approx u_i$, and, for every positive integer j less than or equal to q, β_j is the formula $\neg s^{n_j} \, y \approx v_j$. Notice that k has to be greater than 0, since, by the definition of benchmark formula, ϕ has no conjuncts of the form $y \approx t$ or $t \approx y$, where y doesn't occur in t, and $s^k \, y \approx t$ or $t \approx s^k \, y$ is a conjunct of ϕ (the same goes for $m_1, ..., m_p$).

For every positive integer i less than or equal to p, let $\alpha_i^{(k)}$ be the formula $s^{m_i+k} \, y \approx s^k \, u_i$, and for every positive integer j less than or equal to q, let $\beta_j^{(k)}$ be the formula $\neg s^{n_j+k} \, y \approx s^k \, v_j$. We can easily show that, for all L_{As}-terms t, u, and every natural number n, $t \approx u \rightleftharpoons_{\Theta_{As}} s^n \, t \approx s^n \, u$ (this is left as an exercise). Hence (1) is Θ_{As}-equivalent to

(2) $\exists y \, (s^k \, y \approx t \wedge (\alpha_1^{(k)} \wedge ... \wedge \alpha_p^{(k)}) \wedge (\beta_1^{(k)} \wedge ... \wedge \beta_q^{(k)}))$.

Now, for every positive integer i less than or equal to p, let $\alpha_i^{(k,t)}$ be the formula $s^{m_i} \, t \approx s^k \, u_i$, and for every positive integer j less than or equal to q, let $\beta_j^{(k,t)}$ be the formula $\neg s^{n_j} \, t \approx s^k \, v_j$. We can show that (2) is Θ_{As}-equivalent to

(3) $(\neg 0 \approx t \wedge ... \wedge \neg s^{k-1} \, 0 \approx t) \wedge$
      $(\alpha_1^{(k,t)} \wedge ... \wedge \alpha_p^{(k,t)}) \wedge (\beta_1^{(k,t)} \wedge ... \wedge \beta_q^{(k,t)})$.

This is left as an exercise. Hence (3) is Θ_{As}-equivalent to (1), and to $\exists y$ ϕ^*. Furthermore, every free variable of (3) is free in $\exists y \, \phi^*$. Therefore (3) is a basic Θ_{As}-surrogate of $\exists y \, \phi^*$, as desired. ∎

EXERCISE 8. 17: Show that a formula of the form $\exists y \, (\alpha_1 \wedge ... \wedge \alpha_n)$, where, for every positive integer i less than or equal to n, α_i is of the form $\neg s^m \, y \approx t$ or $\neg t \approx s^m \, y$, with y not occurring in t, is true in every model $\mathcal{A}$ of Θ_{As}, relative to every variable interpretation in $\mathcal{A}$.

EXERCISE 8. 18: Show that, for all L_{As}-terms t, u, and every natural number n, $t \approx u \rightleftharpoons_{\Theta_{As}} s^n \, t \approx s^n \, u$.

EXERCISE 8. 19: Show that (2) and (3) (in the proof of Lemma 8. 16) are Θ_{As}-equivalent.

Hint: Notice that (2) is true in a model $\mathcal{A}$ of Θ_{As}, relative to a variable interpretation σ in $\mathcal{A}$, just in case an element of the universe appearing k positions before $den_{\mathcal{A}}(t, \sigma)$ in the sequence generated by $s_{\mathcal{A}}$ satisfies the conditions expressed by $\alpha_1^{(k)}, ..., \alpha_p^{(k)}, \beta_1^{(k)}, ..., \beta_q^{(k)}$. And (3) is true in $\mathcal{A}$ relative to σ just in case $den_{\mathcal{A}}(t, \sigma)$ does not occupy one of the first k positions in the sequence generated by $s_{\mathcal{A}}$ from $0_{\mathcal{A}}$, and it satisfies the conditions expressed by $\alpha_1^{(k,t)}, ..., \alpha_p^{(k,t)}, \beta_1^{(k,t)}, ..., \beta_q^{(k,t)}$. Notice also that $(\alpha_1^{(k)} \wedge ... \wedge \alpha_p^{(k)}) \wedge (\beta_1^{(k)} \wedge ... \wedge \beta_q^{(k)})$ and $(\alpha_1^{(k,t)} \wedge ... \wedge \alpha_p^{(k,t)}) \wedge (\beta_1^{(k,t)} \wedge ... \wedge \beta_q^{(k,t)})$ have the same truth value in $\mathcal{A}$ relative to σ just in case $den_{\mathcal{A}}(t, \sigma)$ appears k positions after $den_{\mathcal{A}}(y, \sigma)$ in the sequence generated by $s_{\mathcal{A}}$.

iii. Ordered Successor Arithmetic

So far we have applied the quantifier elimination method to cases which could also be dealt with using Vaught's test. However, there are other cases in which the quantifier elimination method enables us to show that a set of sentences is a complete theory, but Vaught's test is not applicable. We close this section with an example of this situation.

Let $L_{A<}$ be the first-order language whose extralogical vocabulary consists of an individual constant, 0, a one-place function symbol, s, and a two-place predicate, $<$. Let $\mathcal{N}_<$ be the $L_{A<}$-structure with the set of natural numbers as its universe, in which 0 is interpreted with number zero, s with the successor function in ω, and $<$ with the *less than* relation in ω. Let $\Theta_{A<}$ be the set containing the following $L_{A<}$-sentences:

(1) $\forall x \, \neg x < x$
(2) $\forall x \forall y \forall z \, ((x < y \wedge y < z) \rightarrow x < z)$
(3) $\forall x \forall y \, (\neg x \approx y \rightarrow (x < y \vee y < x))$
(4) $\forall x \, \neg x < 0$
(5) $\forall x \, (\neg x \approx 0 \rightarrow \exists y \, x \approx s(y))$
(6) $\forall x \, x < s(x)$
(7) $\forall x \forall y \, (x < s(y) \rightarrow (x < y \vee x \approx y))$

Clearly, $\mathcal{N}_<$ is a model of $\Theta_{A<}$. (1)–(4) are true in $\mathcal{N}_<$ because the *less than* relation is a strict linear ordering of the natural numbers with number zero as minimal element. (5) is true in $\mathcal{N}_<$ because every natural number other than zero is the successor of some natural number. (6) is true in $\mathcal{N}_<$ because every natural number is less than its successor. And (7) is true in $\mathcal{N}_<$ because there are no natural numbers between a natural number and its successor.

It follows from this, by Lemma 8. 1, that $\Theta_{A<}$ represents $\mathcal{N}_<$ up to indiscernibility just in case $\Theta_{A<}$ is a complete theory. Notice that we cannot use Vaught's test to show that $\Theta_{A<}$ is a complete theory, because $\Theta_{A<}$ doesn't satisfy the hypothesis of Vaught's Theorem. It has no finite models, but it is not categorical in any infinite power.

EXERCISE 8. 20: Show that $\Theta_{A<}$ has no finite models.

EXERCISE 8. 21: Show that $\Theta_{A<}$ is not categorical in any infinite power.

Hint: Notice that $\Theta_{A<}$ has nonstandard models whose galaxies are ordered by the ordering of their elements (see Chapter 7, §9), but this ordering may or may not be dense, and there may or may not be a maximal galaxy or a minimal nonstandard galaxy.

Notice, however, that we cannot conclude from this that $\Theta_{A<}$ is not a complete theory, since the hypothesis of Vaught's Theorem is not a necessary condition for a set of sentences to be a complete theory. $\Theta_{A<}$ is, in fact, a complete theory, and we can use the quantifier elimination method to establish this result.

First we need to show that $\Theta_{A<}$ is complete with respect to the basic sentences of $L_{A<}$. This is left as an exercise.

EXERCISE 8. 22: Show that, for every basic $L_{A<}$-sentence ϕ, either $\Theta_{A<} \vDash \phi$ or $\Theta_{A<} \vDash \neg\phi$.

Then we need to show that every $L_{A<}$-sentence is $\Theta_{A<}$-equivalent to some basic $L_{A<}$-sentence. This is a consequence of the following lemma.

LEMMA 8. 23: Every benchmark formula of $L_{A<}$ has a basic Θ_{As}-surrogate.

Proof: Let $\exists y\ \phi$ be a benchmark formula of $L_{A<}$. We can show that $\exists y\ \phi$ is $\Theta_{A<}$-equivalent to a formula of the form $\exists y\ \psi_1 \vee \ldots \vee \exists y\ \psi_k$, all of whose free variables are free in $\exists y\ \phi$, where, for every positive integer l less than or equal to k, ψ_l is a conjunction, each of whose conjuncts is of the form $s^n\ y \approx t$, $s^n\ y < t$ or $t < s^n\ y$, with y not occurring in t. This is left as an exercise. Hence, to show that $\exists y\ \phi$ has a basic $\Theta_{A<}$-surrogate, it will suffice to show that each disjunct of $\exists y\ \psi_1 \vee \ldots \vee \exists y\ \psi_k$ has one.

Let l be a positive integer less than or equal to k. We need to show that $\exists y\ \psi_l$ has a basic $\Theta_{A<}$-surrogate. We have to consider four cases.

Case 1: Suppose, first, that at least one conjunct of ψ_l is of the form $s^n\ y \approx t$. Then we can show that $\exists y\ \psi_l$ has a basic $\Theta_{A<}$-surrogate using the strategy of Case 2 in the proof of Lemma 8. 16. This is left as an exercise.

Case 2: Suppose now that every conjunct of ψ_l is of the form $t < s^n\ y$. Then we can show that $\exists y\ \psi_l$ is true in every model $\mathcal{A}$ of $\Theta_{A<}$, relative to every variable interpretation in $\mathcal{A}$. This is left as an exercise. It follows that $0 \approx 0$ is a basic $\Theta_{A<}$-surrogate of $\exists y\ \psi_l$.

Case 3: Suppose now that every conjunct of ψ_l is of the form $s^n\ y < t$. Then we can show that $(\psi_l)[0/y]$ is a basic $\Theta_{A<}$-surrogate of $\exists y\ \psi_l$. This is left as an exercise.

Case 4: Finally, suppose that every conjunct of ψ_l is of the form $t < s^n\ y$ or $s^n\ y < t$, with at least one conjunct of each form. Then $\exists y\ \psi_l$ is logically equivalent to a formula of the form

(1) $\exists y\ ((\alpha_1 \wedge \ldots \wedge \alpha_p) \wedge (\beta_1 \wedge \ldots \wedge \beta_q))$,

where, for every positive integer i less than or equal to p, α_i is the formula $t_i < s^{m_i}\ y$, with y not occurring in t_i, and, for every positive integer j less than or equal to q, β_j is the formula $s^{n_j}\ y < u_j$, with y not occurring in u_j.

For every positive integer i less than or equal to p, and every positive integer j less than or equal to q, let $\gamma_{i,j}$ be the formula $t_i < s^{m_i}\ y \wedge s^{n_j}\ y < u_j$. Then, clearly, (1) is logically equivalent to

(2) $\exists y\ ((\gamma_{1,1} \wedge \ldots \wedge \gamma_{1,q}) \wedge \ldots \wedge (\gamma_{p,1} \wedge \ldots \wedge \gamma_{p,q}))$.

Now, for every positive integer i less than or equal to p, and every positive integer j less than or equal to q, let $\gamma_{i,j}^*$ be the formula $s^{n_j}\ t_i < s^{m_i+n_j}\ y \wedge s^{m_i+n_j}\ y < s^{m_i}\ u_j$. We can show that for every natural number n and all $L_{A<}$-terms t, u, $t \approx u =_{\Theta_{A<}} s^n\ t \approx s^n\ u$ (this is left as an exercise). Hence (2) is $\Theta_{A<}$-equivalent to

(3) $\exists y \, ((\gamma_{1,1}{}^* \wedge...\wedge \gamma_{1,q}{}^*) \wedge...\wedge (\gamma_{p,1}{}^* \wedge...\wedge \gamma_{p,q}{}^*))$.

Finally, for every positive integer i less than or equal to p, and every positive integer j less than or equal to q, let $\gamma_{i,j}{}^\circ$ be the formula $s^{nj+1} t_i < s^{mi} u_j$. We can show that (3) is $\Theta_{A<}$-equivalent to

(4) $(\gamma_{1,1}{}^\circ \wedge...\wedge \gamma_{1,q}{}^\circ) \wedge...\wedge (\gamma_{p,1}{}^\circ \wedge...\wedge \gamma_{p,q}{}^\circ) \wedge (\beta_1 \wedge...\wedge \beta_q)[0/y]$.

This is left as an exercise. It follows from this that (4) is $\Theta_{A<}$-equivalent to $\exists y \, \psi_l$. Furthermore, (4) is a basic formula of $L_{A<}$, all of whose free variables are also free in $\exists y \, \psi_l$. Therefore, (4) is a basic $\Theta_{A<}$-surrogate of $\exists y \, \psi_l$, as desired. ∎

EXERCISE 8. 24: Show that if $\exists y \, \phi$ is a benchmark formula of $L_{A<}$, $\exists y \, \phi$ is $\Theta_{A<}$-equivalent to a formula of the form $\exists y \, \psi_1 \vee...\vee \exists y \, \psi_k$, all of whose free variables are free in $\exists y \, \phi$, where, for every positive integer l less than or equal to k, ψ_l is a conjunction, each of whose conjuncts is of the form $s^n y \approx t$, $s^n y < t$ or $t < s^n y$, with y not occurring in t.

Hint: Adapt the argument from the proof of Lemma 8. 11.

EXERCISE 8. 25: Show that if ψ_l (in the proof of Lemma 8. 23) has a conjunct of the form $s^n y \approx t$, then $\exists y \, \psi_l$ has a basic $\Theta_{A<}$-surrogate.

EXERCISE 8. 26: Show that if every conjunct of ψ_l (in the proof of Lemma 8. 23) is of the form $t < s^n y$, then $\exists y \, \psi_l$ is true in every model A of $\Theta_{A<}$, relative to every variable interpretation in A.

EXERCISE 8. 27: Show that if every conjunct of ψ_l (in the proof of Lemma 8. 23) is of the form $s^n y < t$, then $(\psi_l)[0/y]$ is a basic $\Theta_{A<}$-surrogate of $\exists y \, \psi_l$.

EXERCISE 8. 28: Show that for every natural number n and all $L_{A<}$-terms $t, u, t \approx u \Rightarrow_{\Theta_{A<}} s^n t \approx s^n u$.

EXERCISE 8. 29: Show that (3) and (4) (in the proof of Lemma 8. 23) are $\Theta_{A<}$-equivalent.

Hint: Notice that the formula $\exists y \, (s^{nj} t_i < s^{mi+nj} y \wedge s^{mi+nj} y < s^{mi} u_j)$ is true in a model A of $\Theta_{A<}$, relative to a variable interpretation σ in A, just in case (i) $den_A(s^{mi} u_j, \sigma)$ is greater than $den_A(s^{nj} t_i, \sigma)$, but not its successor, and (ii) $den_A(s^{mi} u_j, \sigma)$ doesn't occupy one of the first $m_i + n_j$ positions in the sequence generated by s_A from 0_A. But $\gamma_{i,j}{}^\circ$ is true in A relative to σ just in case (i) holds, and $(\beta_j)[0/y]$ is true in A relative to σ just in case (ii) holds.

We have shown that $\Theta_{A<}$ is a complete theory with $N_<$ as a model. $\Theta_{A<}$ is finite, and hence decidable. Therefore, by Lemma 8. 1, we can conclude that $\mathcal{N}_<$ is represented up to indiscernibility by a decidable set of sentences.

4. The Decision Problem

In Chapter 4, §§3 and 6, we described a technique for establishing deducibility claims. That technique is by no means a mechanically applicable procedure. In order to apply it successfully to a specific deducibility claim, intelligent choices have to be made, concerning which rule to use at each stage, and, with some rules, which formulas or terms to use them with. Notice that this point concerns a specific technique for discharging the task of establishing deducibility claims, not the task itself. In fact, we can describe a mechanically applicable procedure for establishing deducibility claims. This will be our goal in this section.

The procedure that we are going to describe is based on the fact that, subject to some restrictions on L, it is possible to define a sequence, $D_L{}^1$, $D_L{}^2$, $D_L{}^3$... of sets of L-sequents satisfying the following conditions:

1. Every set in the sequence is a subset of D_L (the deducibility relation for L).

2. Every element of D_L is an element of some set in the sequence.

3. Every set in the sequence is finite.

4. There is a mechanically applicable procedure for generating the elements of each set in the sequence.

With this sequence at our disposal, to show that an L-formula ϕ is deducible from a set of L-formulas Γ, we would just need to scan the sets in the sequence in succession until we find one containing $\langle \Gamma, \phi \rangle$. Scanning a set would consist in generating its elements and checking whether $\langle \Gamma, \phi \rangle$ is one of them. The fact that the sequence satisfies conditions (1)–(4) guarantees that this is a mechanically applicable procedure for showing that ϕ is deducible from Γ.

Using the inductive definition of D_L, we could easily define a sequence of sets satisfying conditions (1) and (2). The first set in the sequence would contain the L-sequents in the base of the definition, i.e. the sequents of the form $\langle \Gamma, \phi \rangle$, where $\phi \in \Gamma$, and of the form $\langle \Gamma, t \approx t \rangle$. Then, for every positive integer n, the $n + 1$-th set in the sequence would contain all the elements of the n-th set and every L-sequent which results from one application of a hypothetical rule of the system to L-sequents in the n-th set. Intuitively, the n-th set in the sequence would contain those

L-sequents which can be derived in *n* steps or less. Unfortunately this sequence would not suit our needs, since it doesn't satisfy condition (3). Every set in the sequence is infinite. Hence to scan a set we would need to generate infinitely many sequents—a task that we could never complete.

To overcome this obstacle we need to take a slightly different approach. This will require making a few assumptions about *L*. Let's say that an *enumeration* of a set *S* is a one-to-one correspondence whose domain is either $\mathbf{Z}^+$ or a counting sequence and whose range is *S*. If *S* is a set of finite tuples of symbols of a formal language, let's say that an enumeration *h* of *S* is *effective* just in case there is a mechanically applicable procedure for generating, for any given positive integer *n* in the domain of *h*, the element of *S* with which *n* is paired. We are going to assume that there is an effective enumeration of the set of *L*-formulas (it can be shown, although we shall not do it here, that a sufficient condition for this assumption to hold is that there are effective enumerations of the set of variables, the set of individual constants of *L*, and for every positive integer *n*, the set of *n*-place function symbols of *L* and the set of *n*-place *L*-predicates). Let f_α be an effective enumeration of the set of *L*-formulas. We shall refer to the image under f_α of a positive integer *n* as the *n*-th *L*-formula, written α_n.

Using this enumeration, we can define a sequence of sets which satisfies conditions (1)–(4). In the original proposal, the *n*-th set in the sequence contained those *L*-sequents which can be derived in *n* steps or less. Intuitively, in the modified proposal, the *n*-th set in the sequence will contain those *L*-sequents which can be derived in *n* steps or less, using only the first *n* *L*-formulas. Thus, for every positive integer *n*, we define by recursion the set $D_L{}^n$, as the image of *n* under the unique function satisfying the following conditions:

$$D_L{}^1 = \{\langle \{\alpha_1\}, \alpha_1 \rangle\}$$

For every positive integer *n*, $D_L{}^{n+1}$ contains exactly the following *L*-sequents:

    For every *L*-sequent $\langle \Gamma, \phi \rangle \in D_L{}^n$, $\langle \Gamma, \phi \rangle \in D_L{}^{n+1}$.

(*B*) For every $\Gamma \subseteq \{\alpha_1, ..., \alpha_{n+1}\}$, and every $\phi \in \Gamma$, $\langle \Gamma, \phi \rangle \in D_L{}^{n+1}$.

(≈*I*) For every $\Gamma \subseteq \{\alpha_1, ..., \alpha_{n+1}\}$, and every element of $\{\alpha_1, ..., \alpha_{n+1}\}$ of the form $t \approx t$, $\langle \Gamma, t \approx t \rangle \in D_L{}^{n+1}$.

(∧*I*) For all *L*-sequents $\langle \Gamma, \phi \rangle, \langle \Delta, \psi \rangle \in D_L{}^n$, $\langle \Gamma \cup \Delta, \phi \wedge \psi \rangle \in D_L{}^{n+1}$.

(∧*E*) For every *L*-sequent of the form $\langle \Gamma, \phi \wedge \psi \rangle \in D_L{}^n$, $\langle \Gamma, \phi \rangle, \langle \Gamma, \psi \rangle \in D_L{}^{n+1}$.

(∨*I*) For every *L*-sequent $\langle \Gamma, \phi \rangle \in D_L{}^n$, and every positive integer *i* less than or equal to $n + 1$, $\langle \Gamma, \phi \vee \alpha_i \rangle$, $\langle \Gamma, \alpha_i \vee \phi \rangle \in D_L{}^{n+1}$.

(∨*E*) For all *L*-sequents of the form $\langle \Gamma, \phi \vee \psi \rangle$, $\langle \Delta \cup \{\phi\}, \delta \rangle$, $\langle \Sigma \cup \{\psi\}, \delta \rangle \in D_L{}^n$, $\langle \Gamma \cup \Delta \cup \Sigma, \delta \rangle \in D_L{}^{n+1}$.

(→*I*) For every *L*-sequent $\langle \Gamma, \phi \rangle \in D_L{}^n$, and every $\psi \in \Gamma$, $\langle \Gamma - \{\psi\}, \psi \rightarrow \phi \rangle \in D_L{}^{n+1}$.

(→*E*) For all *L*-sequents of the form $\langle \Gamma, \phi \rangle$, $\langle \Delta, \phi \rightarrow \psi \rangle \in D_L{}^n$, $\langle \Gamma \cup \Delta, \psi \rangle \in D_L{}^{n+1}$.

(¬*I*) For all *L*-sequents of the form $\langle \Gamma, \psi \rangle$, $\langle \Delta, \neg\psi \rangle \in D_L{}^n$, and every $\phi \in \Gamma \cap \Delta$, $\langle ((\Gamma \cup \Delta) - \{\phi\}, \neg\phi \rangle \in D_L{}^{n+1}$.

(¬*E*) For every *L*-sequent of the form $\langle \Gamma, \neg\neg\phi \rangle \in D_L{}^n$, $\langle \Gamma, \phi \rangle \in D_L{}^{n+1}$.

(∀*I*) For every element of $\{\alpha_1, ..., \alpha_{n+1}\}$ of the form $\forall x\ \phi$, and every *L*-sequent of the form $\langle \Gamma, (\phi)[y/x] \rangle \in D_L{}^n$, for some variable *y* which is substitutable for *x* in ϕ and not free in Γ or $\forall x\ \phi$, $\langle \Gamma, \forall x\ \phi \rangle \in D_L{}^{n+1}$.

(∀*E*) For every *L*-sequent of the form $\langle \Gamma, \forall x\ \phi \rangle \in D_L{}^n$, and every element of $\{\alpha_1, ..., \alpha_{n+1}\}$ of the form $(\phi)[t/x]$, for some *L*-term *t* which is substitutable for *x* in ϕ, $\langle \Gamma, (\phi)[t/x] \rangle \in D_L{}^{n+1}$.

(∃*I*) For every element of $\{\alpha_1, ..., \alpha_{n+1}\}$ of the form $\exists x\ \phi$, and every *L*-sequent of the form $\langle \Gamma, (\phi)[t/x] \rangle \in D_L{}^n$, for some *L*-term *t* which is substitutable for *x* in ϕ, $\langle \Gamma, \exists x\ \phi \rangle \in D_L{}^{n+1}$.

(∃*E*) For every *L*-sequent of the form $\langle \Gamma, \exists x\ \phi \rangle \in D_L{}^n$, every *L*-sequent $\langle \Delta, \psi \rangle \in D_L{}^n$, and every $\beta \in \Delta$, such that β is the *y*/*x*-substitution of ϕ for some variable *y* which is substitutable for *x* in ϕ and not free in $\Delta - \{\beta\}$, $\exists x\ \phi$ or ψ, $\langle \Gamma \cup (\Delta - \{\beta\}), \psi \rangle \in D_L{}^{n+1}$.

(≈*E*) For every *L*-sequent of the form $\langle \Delta, t \approx u \rangle \in D_L{}^n$, every *L*-sequent $\langle \Gamma, \psi \rangle \in D_L{}^n$, and every *L*-formula $\gamma \in \{\alpha_1, ..., \alpha_{n+1}\}$, if there is an *L*-formula ϕ and a variable *x* such that ψ is $(\phi)[t/x]$, γ is $(\phi)[u/x]$, and *t* and *u* are substitutable for *x* in ϕ, then $\langle \Gamma \cup \Delta, (\phi)[u/x] \rangle \in D_L{}^{n+1}$.

We can show that this sequence satisfies conditions (1)–(4). (1)–(3) are left as exercises.

EXERCISE 8. 30: Show that, for every positive integer *n*, $D_L{}^n \subseteq D_L$.

Hint: By induction on the positive integers.

EXERCISE 8. 31: Show that for every *L*-sequent $\langle \Gamma, \phi \rangle \in D_L$, $\langle \Gamma, \phi \rangle \in D_L{}^n$, for some positive integer *n*.

Hint: By induction on D_L.

EXERCISE 8. 32: Show that, for every positive integer *n*, $D_L{}^n$ is finite.

Hint: By induction on the positive integers.

For (4), we would need to show that there is a mechanically applicable procedure for generating the elements of each set in the sequence. We could establish this result by induction on the positive integers. The base is straightforward, given that we have mechanically applicable procedure for generating α_1. For the inductive step, on the assumption (IH) that there is a mechanically applicable procedure for generating the L-sequents in $D_L{}^n$, we would need to describe a procedure for generating the L-sequents in $D_L{}^{n+1}$ using basic operations on L-terms, L-formulas, sets of L-formulas and L-sequents, whose mechanical character is intuitively obvious. The details are left to the reader.

The sequence $D_L{}^1, D_L{}^2, D_L{}^3 \ldots$ can also be used to describe a mechanically applicable procedure for showing that an L-formula ϕ is a logical consequence of a decidable set of L-formulas Γ. As with deducibility claims, we would just need to scan the sets in the sequence in succession. In this case we would be looking for an L-sequent with a subset of Γ as its first member and ϕ as its second member. Checking whether a given L-sequent $\langle \Delta, \psi \rangle$ is of this form can be done mechanically, using a decision procedure for Γ to determine, for every L-formula in Δ, whether it is an element of Γ. The Soundness Theorem and Exercise 8.30 ensure that if the procedure yields a positive result for an L-formula ϕ and a set of L-formulas Γ, then ϕ is a logical consequence of Γ. And the Completeness Theorem and Exercise 8.31 ensure that if ϕ is a logical consequence of Γ, and Γ is decidable, then the procedure will yield a positive result for ϕ and Γ. If ϕ is a logical consequence of Γ, the procedure can be used to establish this fact, provided that Γ is decidable.

Let's say that a *decision procedure for logical consequence* in a first-order language L is a mechanically applicable procedure which would enable us to determine, for any L-formula ϕ and any decidable set of L-formulas Γ, whether ϕ is a logical consequence of Γ. The procedure that we have just described for establishing logical consequence claims is *not* a decision procedure for logical consequence. If an L-formula ϕ is a logical consequence of a decidable set of L-formulas Γ, the procedure will enable us to establish this fact. But if ϕ is not a logical consequence of Γ, this fact cannot be established using the procedure. In this case, no set in the sequence will contain an L-sequent with a subset of Γ as its first member and ϕ as its second member. Hence the procedure will not yield a positive result for ϕ and Γ. But it won't yield a negative result either. A negative result could only be obtained if after scanning finitely many sets in the sequence and finding that they don't contain an L-sequent with a subset of Γ as its first member and ϕ as its second member, we could rule out the possibility that an *L*-sequent of this kind will appear in one of the infinitely many sets which remain to be scanned. But this position is never reached. We can't set an upper limit on how far into the sequence an *L*-sequent of this kind will have to appear for the first time if ϕ is a logical consequence of Γ. Hence the scanning process will never put us in a position to conclude that ϕ is not a logical consequence of Γ.

The problem of finding a decision procedure for logical consequence in an arbitrary first-order language is known in the literature as the *decision problem*. We have seen that the procedure that we have described for establishing logical consequence claims doesn't provide a solution to the decision problem. In fact, the decision problem is known to be unsolvable: there can be no decision procedure for logical consequence in an arbitrary first-order language. This result was established by Alonzo Church in 1936. We shall not provide a proof of Church's Theorem, as the techniques that we would need to use lie outside the scope of this book. Notice that the result concerns the decision problem for an arbitrary first-order language. For some specific first-order languages a decision procedure for logical consequence can be provided. They include first-order languages whose only extralogical symbols are individual constants and one-place predicates.

5. Decidable Structures

The theory of a structure $\mathcal{A}$ of a first-order language L can be defined in terms of any set of sentences, Γ, which represents the structure up to indiscernibility—it is the set of *L*-sentences which are logical consequences of Γ. The proof is left as an exercise.

EXERCISE 8. 33: Show that if a set of sentences Γ of a first-order language L represents an *L*-structure $\mathcal{A}$ up to indiscernibility, then for every *L*-sentence ϕ, $\phi \in Th\ \mathcal{A}$ if and only if $\Gamma \vDash \phi$.

It follows from this that if L is a language for which the decision problem is solvable, and $\mathcal{A}$ is an *L*-structure which is represented up to indiscernibility by a decidable set of *L*-sentences Γ, then the theory of $\mathcal{A}$ is also decidable. To determine whether a given *L*-formula ϕ is an element of the theory of $\mathcal{A}$, we would just need to check whether ϕ is a sentence and whether ϕ is a logical consequence of Γ. A decision procedure for the set of *L*-sentences could be easily described, and to determine whether ϕ is a logical consequence of Γ, we would use a decision procedure for logical consequence in L.

Our next goal is to show that even if the decision problem for L is not solvable the same situation obtains: If an L-structure $\mathcal{A}$ is represented up to indiscernibility by a decidable set of sentences Γ, then the theory of $\mathcal{A}$ is also decidable. To support this claim we need to describe a mechanically applicable procedure which would enable us to determine, for any given L-sentence ϕ, whether ϕ is a logical consequence of Γ, without assuming that the decision problem for L is solvable. We can obtain a procedure which does the job with a small modification of the procedure that we described in the preceding section for establishing logical consequence claims. It consists in scanning the sets in the sequence $D_L{}^1, D_L{}^2,$ $D_L{}^3 \ldots$ until we find an L-sequent of the form $\langle \Gamma_0, \phi \rangle$ or $\langle \Gamma_0, \neg\phi \rangle$, where $\Gamma_0 \subseteq \Gamma$. If we find an L-sequent of the form $\langle \Gamma_0, \phi \rangle$, we can conclude that $\Gamma \vDash \phi$. If we find an L-sequent of the form $\langle \Gamma_0, \neg\phi \rangle$, we can conclude that $\Gamma \vDash \neg\phi$, and hence, since Γ has a model, that $\Gamma \nvDash \phi$. And the Completeness Theorem, Exercise 8. 31, and the fact that Γ is a complete theory ensure that an L-sequent of either of these forms will eventually appear in the sequence. Hence the procedure enables us to determine, for any L-sentence ϕ, whether ϕ is a logical consequence of Γ.

In §§2 and 3 we showed that several structures are represented up to indiscernibility by decidable sets of sentences. We can now conclude that the theories of these structures are also decidable. For each of these structures there is a mechanically applicable procedure that would enable us to determine which truth value it assigns to any sentence in the language. We shall refer to structures whose theories are decidable as *decidable structures*.

Notice that a version of the quantifier elimination method could also be used to establish directly the decidability of a structure $\mathcal{A}$ for a first-order language L. This would involve finding mechanically applicable procedures for discharging the following two tasks: (i) generating a basic *Th* $\mathcal{A}$-surrogate of a given L-sentence and (ii) determining the truth value in $\mathcal{A}$ of any given basic sentence of L. Both procedures could be easily described in the case of Q, $\mathcal{N}_s$ and $\mathcal{N}_<$.

6. Gödel's First Incompleteness Theorem

Two of the structures that we considered in §§2 and 3, $\mathcal{N}_s$ and $\mathcal{N}_<$, are reducts of $\mathcal{N}$ to smaller languages. Both have been shown to be representable up to indiscernibility by decidable sets of sentences. A similar result can be obtained for the reduct of $\mathcal{N}$ to the language which results if we delete $\cdot$ from the vocabulary of L_A. We could show with an indirect application of the quantifier elimination method that this structure is representable up to indiscernibility by a decidable set of sentences of the language.

We can raise the same question with respect to $\mathcal{N}$ itself. Notice that, in this case, an affirmative answer would have striking consequences. Infinitely many arithmetical problems can be characterized as concerning the truth value of propositions which can be modeled with L_A-sentences. Many of them have exercised the minds of mathematicians for generations—sometimes to no avail. Take, e.g., the proposition that every even number greater than two is the sum of two primes, known as Goldbach's Conjecture. So far, all attempts to establish the truth value of Goldbach's Conjecture have been unsuccessful. But Goldbach's Conjecture can be modeled with an L_A-sentence. The property of being an even natural number can be modeled with the L_A-formula $0 < x \land \exists y\, x \approx y + y$—i.e. this formula is true in $\mathcal{N}$ relative to a variable interpretation σ in $\mathcal{N}$ just in case $\sigma(x)$ is an even number. Similarly, the property of being a prime natural number can be modeled with the L_A-formula $s(0) < x \land \forall w \forall z\, (w \cdot z \approx x \to (w \approx s(0) \lor z \approx s(0)))$. Hence Goldbach's Conjecture will be true just in case $\mathcal{N}$ yields the value T for the L_A-sentence $\forall x\, ((s(s(0)) < x \land \exists y\, x \approx y + y) \to \exists u \exists v\, (x \approx u + v \land s(0) < u \land s(0) < v \land \forall w \forall z\, ((w \cdot z \approx u \lor w \cdot z \approx v) \to (w \approx s(0) \lor z \approx s(0)))))$.

Suppose now that $\mathcal{N}$ were represented up to indiscernibility by a decidable set of L_A-sentences. Then, as we saw in §5, the theory of $\mathcal{N}$ would be decidable, and the problem of determining the truth value of Goldbach's Conjecture would be reduced to a purely mechanical task: the application of a decision procedure for the theory of $\mathcal{N}$ to an L_A-sentence which models this proposition. And the same would go for any of the infinitely many arithmetical problems which can be modeled with L_A-sentences. If we could show that a decidable set of L_A-sentences represents $\mathcal{N}$ up to indiscernibility, we would, in effect, solve all these problems at once, reducing each of them to a purely mechanical calculation for which no ingenuity would be required.

It is known, however, that $\mathcal{N}$ cannot be represented up to indiscernibility by a decidable set of L_A-sentences, and hence, in particular, that the theory of $\mathcal{N}$ is not decidable. These are direct consequences of a result established by Gödel in 1931:

GÖDEL'S FIRST INCOMPLETENESS THEOREM: For every set of L_A-sentences Γ, if Γ is decidable and $\mathcal{N}$ is a model of Γ, then Γ is not a complete theory.

The claim that $\mathcal{N}$ is not represented up to indiscernibility by a decidable set of L_A-sentences follows directly from this theorem and Lemma 8.1. In fact, Gödel's results concern not only $\mathcal{N}$, but every model of a model of a sufficiently rich set of L_A-sentences having $\mathcal{N}$ as a model, as, for example, Θ_A (see Chapter 3, §6v). A version of Gödel's result along these lines (as strengthened by J. B. Rosser) can be formulated as follows:

STRONG INCOMPLETENESS THEOREM: For every decidable set of L_A-sentences Γ, if $\Gamma \cup \Theta_A$ has a model, then Γ is not a complete theory.

This theorem entails the undecidability, not only of $\mathcal{N}$ but of every model of Θ_A. The proof of this is left as an exercise.

EXERCISE 8. 34: Show that for every L_A-structure $\mathcal{A}$, if $\mathcal{A}$ is a model of Θ_A, then *Th* $\mathcal{A}$ is undecidable.

We are not going to provide here a proof of Gödel's results. This would require techniques from a branch of logic known as *recursion theory* which lies outside the scope of this book. Notice that the limitations that these results impose on the representability of $\mathcal{N}$ are of a different nature from those which we considered in Chapter 7. The existence of nonstandard models of arithmetic entails that every set of L_A-sentences having $\mathcal{N}$ as a model will also have models which are not isomorphic to $\mathcal{N}$, including L_A-structures of the same cardinality as $\mathcal{N}$. The reason is that all these other L_A-structures are indiscernible from $\mathcal{N}$—they agree with $\mathcal{N}$ on the truth value that they yield for each L_A-sentence. What follows from Gödel's First Incompleteness Theorem is that every *decidable* set of L_A-sentences having $\mathcal{N}$ as a model will also have models which are not indiscernible from $\mathcal{N}$—models which disagree with $\mathcal{N}$ on the truth value that they yield for some L_A-sentences.

7. Set Theory Revisited

As we indicated in Chapter 6, §6, it is possible to define arithmetical notions in set-theoretic terms. This involves treating certain sets, namely the descendants of $\emptyset$ (see Chapter 7, §6), as the natural numbers, and defining the successor, addition and multiplication function, and the *less than* relation, in terms of the set-membership relation defined on this domain. Thus, e.g., number zero can be defined as the empty set, the successor function as the function pairing each descendant of $\emptyset$, S, with S^+, i.e. $S \cup \{S\}$, and the *less than* relation as the set-membership relation defined on the set of descendants of $\emptyset$. Similar definitions can be provided for addition and multiplication. Using these definitions, we can interpret each arithmetical proposition with a set-theoretic proposition, in such a way that each arithmetical proposition has the same truth value as the set theoretic proposition with which we interpret it. Thus, e.g., the proposition that zero is less than one will be interpreted with the set-theoretic proposition that $\emptyset \in \emptyset \cup \{\emptyset\}$.

This situation has a formal correlate in the relationship between Θ_{ZF} and Θ_A. Thus, for every model $\mathcal{A}$ of Θ_{ZF}, we can use the universe of $\mathcal{A}$ and the relation with which $\in$ is interpreted in $\mathcal{A}$ to define an L_A-structure $\mathcal{A}^*$ which is a model of Θ_A. The universe A^* of $\mathcal{A}^*$ will be the set of $\mathcal{A}$-descendants of $\emptyset^{\mathcal{A}}$ (see Chapter 7, §6), which can be defined in terms of $\in_{\mathcal{A}}$. The interpretation in $\mathcal{A}^*$ of the extralogical symbols of L_A is also defined in terms of $\in_{\mathcal{A}}$. Thus, e.g., $0_{\mathcal{A}^*} = \emptyset^{\mathcal{A}}$, for every $x \in A^*$, $s_{\mathcal{A}^*}(x) = x^{+\mathcal{A}}$, and for all $x, y \in A^*$, $x <_{\mathcal{A}^*} y$ if and only if $x \in_{\mathcal{A}} y$. Similar definitions can be provided for $+_{\mathcal{A}^*}$ and $\cdot_{\mathcal{A}^*}$. This correlation between each model of Θ_{ZF} and a model of Θ_A enables us to interpret each L_A-sentence ϕ with an $L_\in$-sentence, in such a way that, for every model $\mathcal{A}$ of Θ_{ZF}, the truth value in $\mathcal{A}$ of the interpretation of ϕ coincides with the truth value in $\mathcal{A}^*$ of ϕ itself. We are not going to provide the details of how an interpretation along these lines can be defined. We shall simply assume that we can define a function i pairing each L_A-sentence ϕ with an $L_\in$-sentence, $(\phi)_i$, which satisfies the following conditions:

(1) For every L_A-sentence ϕ, and every model $\mathcal{A}$ of Θ_{ZF}, $v_{\mathcal{A}}((\phi)_i) = v_{\mathcal{A}^*}(\phi)$.

(2) There is a mechanically applicable procedure which enables us to generate the image under i of any given L_A-sentence.

EXERCISE 8. 35: Show that, for every L_A-sentence ϕ, if $\Theta_A \vDash \phi$, then $\Theta_{ZF} \vDash (\phi)_i$.

Using i, we can show that what goes for the models of Θ_A goes for the models of Θ_{ZF}: Every model of Θ_{ZF} is undecidable.

THEOREM 8. 36: For every $L_\in$-structure $\mathcal{A}$, if $\mathcal{A}$ is a model of Θ_{ZF}, then *Th* $\mathcal{A}$ is undecidable.

Proof: Assume, towards a contradiction, that Θ_{ZF} has a decidable model, $\mathcal{A}$. Then, to determine whether a given L_A-sentence ϕ is an element of *Th* $\mathcal{A}^*$, it will suffice to generate $(\phi)_i$ and to check whether it is an element of *Th* $\mathcal{A}$. It follows from our second assumption about i, and from the assumption that *Th* $\mathcal{A}$ is decidable, that there is a mechanically applicable procedure to complete each of these tasks. Hence $\mathcal{A}^*$ is decidable. But since $\mathcal{A}^*$ is a model of Θ_A, this contradicts Exercise 8. 34, as desired. ∎

EXERCISE 8. 37: Show that, for every decidable set of $L_\in$-sentences Γ, if $\Gamma \cup \Theta_{ZF}$ has a model, then Γ is not a complete theory.

Hint: Use Theorem 8. 36 and the results of §5.

We saw in Chapter 6 that the $L_\in$-sentences modeling the Continuum Hypothesis and the Axiom of Choice are true in some models of Θ_{ZF} and false in others (if Θ_{ZF} has models). Hence, used as a criterion of truth in the set-theoretic universe, Θ_{ZF} would yield no verdict on either of these propositions. Needless to say, we could avoid this problem by adopting as a criterion of set-theoretic truth a different set of $L_\in$-sentences, as, for example, the result of adding to Θ_{ZF} either an $L_\in$-sentence modeling the Continuum Hypothesis or its negation, and either an $L_\in$-sentence modeling the Axiom of Choice or its negation. We may wonder, however, whether this or any other decidable set of $L_\in$-sentences could generate a universal criterion of truth in the set-theoretic universe—one yielding a truth value for every proposition which can be modeled with an $L_\in$-sentence. Theorem 8. 36 and Exercise 8. 37 answer this question in the negative, so long as we conceive of sets as making the $L_\in$-sentences in Θ_{ZF} true. For if Γ is a decidable set of $L_\in$-sentences compatible with Θ_{ZF}, there will be $L_\in$-sentences which are true in some models of Γ and false in others. Hence, used as a criterion of set-theoretic truth, Γ will fail to yield a verdict on the propositions modeled by these sentences.

Symbols and Notation

Greek Letters

	α	Alpha
	β	Beta
Γ	γ	Gamma
Δ	δ	Delta
Θ		Theta
	κ	Kappa
	λ	Lambda
	μ	Mu
Π		Pi
	ρ	Rho
Σ	σ	Sigma
Φ	φ	Phi
Ψ	ψ	Psi
	ω	Omega

Index